Staging *Euridice*

Euridice was one of several music-theatrical works commissioned to celebrate the wedding of Maria de' Medici and King Henri IV of France in Florence in October 1600. As the first "opera" to survive complete, it has been viewed as a landmark work, but its libretto by Ottavio Rinuccini and music by Jacopo Peri and Giulio Caccini have tended to be studied in the abstract rather than as something to be performed in a specific time and place. *Staging "Euridice"* explores how newly discovered documents can be used to reconstruct precisely every aspect of its original stage and sets in the room for which it was intended in the Palazzo Pitti. By also taking into account what the singers and instrumentalists did, what the audience saw and heard, and how things changed from creation through rehearsals to performance, this book brings new aspects of *Euridice* to light in startling ways.

TIM CARTER is David G. Frey Distinguished Professor of Music at the University of North Carolina at Chapel Hill. He is author of numerous books on topics ranging from Monteverdi to Rodgers and Hammerstein. He has held fellowships at the Harvard Center for Italian Renaissance Studies in Florence, the Newberry Library in Chicago, and the National Humanities Center.

FRANCESCA FANTAPPIÈ has published widely on Italian theatre from the late sixteenth to the early eighteenth centuries, with a particular emphasis on dramaturgy, music, stagecraft and scenography, architecture, and performers. She is a former fellow of the Harvard Center for Italian Renaissance Studies in Florence and currently holds a Marie Curie Fellowship in the Centre d'Études Supérieures de la Renaissance, Université de Tours.

Staging *Euridice*

Theatre, Sets, and Music in Late Renaissance Florence

TIM CARTER
Chapel Hill, North Carolina

FRANCESCA FANTAPPIÈ
Florence, Italy

Shaftesbury Road, Cambridge CB2 8EA, United Kingdom

One Liberty Plaza, 20th Floor, New York, NY 10006, USA

477 Williamstown Road, Port Melbourne, VIC 3207, Australia

314–321, 3rd Floor, Plot 3, Splendor Forum, Jasola District Centre, New Delhi – 110025, India

103 Penang Road, #05–06/07, Visioncrest Commercial, Singapore 238467

Cambridge University Press is part of Cambridge University Press & Assessment, a department of the University of Cambridge.

We share the University's mission to contribute to society through the pursuit of education, learning and research at the highest international levels of excellence.

www.cambridge.org
Information on this title: www.cambridge.org/9781009005715

DOI: 10.1017/9781009036696

First published 2021
First paperback edition 2023

A catalogue record for this publication is available from the British Library

Library of Congress Cataloging-in-Publication data
Names: Carter, Tim, 1954– author. | Fantappié, Francesca, 1973– author.
Title: Staging Euridice : theatre, sets, and music in late renaissance Florence / Tim Carter, Francesca Fantappié.
Description: [1.] | Cambridge, United Kingdom ; New York, NY : Cambridge University Press, 2021. | Includes index.
Identifiers: LCCN 2021028172 (print) | LCCN 2021028173 (ebook) | ISBN 9781316515402 (hardback) | ISBN 9781009005715 (paperback) | ISBN 9781009036696 (ebook)
Subjects: LCSH: Opera – Stage setting and scenery – Italy – Florence – History – 16th century. | Opera – Stage setting and scenery – Italy – Florence – History – 17th century. | Peri, Jacopo, 1561–1633. Euridice. | Rinuccini, Ottavio, 1562–1621. Euridice. | Cigoli, Ludovico Cardi da, 1559–1613. | Caccini, Giulio, 1551–1618. Rapimento di Cefalo. | Chiabrera, Gabriello, 1552–1638. Rapimento di Cefalo. | Medici, House of. | BISAC: MUSIC / General
Classification: LCC ML1733.8.F6 C37 2021 (print) | LCC ML1733.8.F6 (ebook) | DDC 792.5/42094551–dc23
LC record available at https://lccn.loc.gov/2021028172
LC ebook record available at https://lccn.loc.gov/2021028173

ISBN 978-1-316-51540-2 Hardback
ISBN 978-1-009-00571-5 Paperback

Contents

List of Illustrations [*page* vii]
List of Tables [x]
Preface [xi]
Sources, Transcriptions, and Translations [xxi]
Money, Accounts, Measurements, Dates, and Time [xxiv]
List of Abbreviations [xxix]

1 *Euridice* in Context [1]
The Marriage Negotiations [6]
The 1600 Festivities [15]
Two Invoices and an Inventory [22]
The Performance of "A Comedy by Signor Jacopo Corsi" (Spring 1600) [37]
The Performance of *Euridice* on 6 October 1600 [54]

2 Staging and Sets [64]
Some Theoretical and Other Sources [67]
The Sala delle Statue and Sala delle Commedie [80]
The Framing of the Stage [86]
The Proscenium [88]
The Stage Platform (and Below) [98]
The "Sky" [104]
The Pastoral Set [107]
The Underworld Set [113]
Stage Lighting [123]
The Main Floor [126]

3 *Euridice* in Performance [130]
The Performers [139]
From Page to Stage [145]
"Speaking" and "Singing" [163]
Costumes, Movement, Gesture [176]
Reading *Euridice* [187]

4 Conclusions and Consequences [198]
Later Entertainments in the Sala delle Commedie [198]
Euridice Today [208]

Appendix I:[1] Documents [217]
A Lodovico Cigoli's Invoice for Designing and Painting the Stage and Scenery for *Euridice* [217]
B Gianbattista Cresci's Inventory of Materials for *Euridice* [221]
C Francesco Ricoveri's Invoice for Sewing Canvas, etc. for *Euridice* [227]

Works Cited [229]
Index [242]

[1] Appendix II (a critical edition of Ottavio Rinuccini's libretto for *Euridice*) is located on the Companion Website at www.cambridge.org/9781316515402.

Illustrations

Note: The Companion Website to this book (www.cambridge.org/9781316515402) contains all the images in the printed text (in color, where possible), plus additional ones (cued as *CW*).

1.1 Jacopo Chimenti da Empoli, *The Wedding of Maria de' Medici and Henri IV of France* (1600) [*page* 7]

1.2 The review of expenditure on *Euridice* audited by the Ufficio di Monte e Soprassindaci (28 February 1601/2) [22]

1.3 Lodovico Cigoli's invoice for creating the set for *Euridice* (14 October 1600; complete in *CW*1.3a–b) [26]

1.4 The breakdown of the costs for the banquet and *Euridice* audited by the Ufficio di Monte e Soprassindaci (28 February 1601/2) [34]

1.5 Joseph Furttenbach the Elder, *Architectura civilis* (1628): the *piano nobile* of the Palazzo Pitti [49]

1.6 Ottavio Rinuccini, *L'Euridice . . . rappresentata nello sponsalitio della Christianiss. Regina di Francia, e di Navarra* (1600): annotated cast list [55]

1.7 Giacinto Maria di Francesco Marmi, *Norma per il guardarobba del gran palazzo della città di Fiorenza*: the top floor of the Palazzo Pitti [57]

*CW*1.8 Vincenzo Panciatichi, *L'amicizia costante* (1600), first state

*CW*1.9 Vincenzo Panciatichi, *L'amicizia costante* (1600), second state

*CW*1.10 Michele Caccini's collation of estimates by other artists for the work done by Lodovico Cigoli for *Euridice*

*CW*1.11a–d Gianbattista Cresci's inventory of the stage and sets for *Euridice* as deposited in the Teatro degli Uffizi (18 September 1601)

*CW*1.12a–b Francesco Ricoveri's invoice for sewing canvas, etc. for the 1600 festivities (10 November 1600)

2.1 Lodovico Cigoli, *Prospettiva pratica*, showing planes *in maestà* and *in isfugita* [73]
2.2 Pietro Paolo Floriani, stage design for a pastoral set in the Teatro degli Intrepidi, Ferrara (*c.* 1631) [76]
2.3 The Sala delle Statue, Palazzo Pitti [82]
2.4 Bartolomeo Neroni, stage design for a performance of *Ortensio* (Siena, 1560) [89]
2.5 Reconstruction of Lodovico Cigoli's proscenium for the Sala delle Statue [90]
2.6 Lodovico Cigoli, drawing of a coat of arms (for the proscenium for *Euridice*) [92]
2.7 Reconstruction of Lodovico Cigoli's proscenium in the Sala delle Commedie [95]
2.8 Reconstruction of the stage in the Sala delle Commedie (top-down view) and position of the boards of the stage floor [99]
2.9 A likely layout of the trestles supporting the stage floor [100]
2.10 Reconstruction of the stage in the Sala delle Commedie (side view) [105]
2.11 Reconstructions of the pastoral and Underworld sets [109]
2.12 Lodovico Cigoli, possible sketch for the Underworld set of *Euridice* (GDSU, 59 P) [114]
2.13 Lodovico Cigoli, possible sketch for the Underworld set of *Euridice* (GDSU, 60 P) [115]
2.14 Proposed mechanism for raising and lowering the Underworld flats [118]
2.15 Proposed mechanism for raising and lowering the Underworld backdrop [120]
2.16 Floor plans of the Sala delle Statue and Sala delle Commedie [127]
*CW*2.17 A likely layout of the boards supporting the trestles
*CW*2.18 Perspectival issues
*CW*2.19 Side and top-down views of the "sky"
*CW*2.20 Lodovico Cigoli, possible sketch for the Underworld set of *Euridice* (unknown collection)
*CW*2.21 Pietro Paolo Floriani, mechanism for raising and lowering elements of a set
*CW*2.22 A likely location of the underfloor winches for changing the sets of *Euridice*

3.1 Ottavio Rinuccini, *L'Euridice . . . rappresentata nello sponsalitio della Christianiss. Regina di Francia, e di Navarra* (1600): first and second states [147]
3.2 Ottavio Rinuccini, *L'Euridice . . . rappresentata nello sponsalitio della Christianiss. Regina di Francia, e di Navarra* (1600): copy with added stage directions [156]
3.3 Jacopo Peri, *Le musiche . . . sopra L'Euridice* (1601), 42 [175]
3.4 Jacopo Peri, *Le musiche . . . sopra L'Euridice* (1601), 14, compared with Giulio Caccini, *L'Euridice composta in musica* (1600), 13 [182]
CW3.5 Giovanni Andrea dell'Anguillara, *Le metamorfosi di Ovidio* (1584): representation of Orpheus
CW3.6 Alessandro Allori, costume for Orpheus in *La genealogia degli dei* (1566)
CW3.7 Remigio Cantagallina, engraving (detail) of the ship of Bacchus and Orpheus for *L'Argonautica* (1608)
CW3.8 Alessandro Allori, costume design for a shepherd in *La disperazione di Fileno* (1590)
CW3.9 Alessandro Allori, costume design for a nymph in *La disperazione di Fileno* (1590)
CW3.10 Agostino Carracci, *Aurora and Cephalus* (1598–1600? Rome, Galleria Farnese)
4.1 *Euridice* (directed by Franco Zeffirelli) at the 23rd Maggio Musicale Fiorentino (28–30 June 1960) [212]
CW4.2 Catalog for the exhibition *Firenze e la nascita dell'Opera* (3 April–15 May 2019; Casa Buonarroti, Florence)

Tables

3.1 The casting of Peri's *Euridice* [*page* 142]
3.2 Stage directions in Peri's score of *Euridice* [149]
3.3 The allocation of roles in *Euridice*, Episode 1 [152]
3.4 Stage directions in an annotated copy of the libretto of *Euridice* [157]

Preface

This book has been challenging to write; it also poses a number of challenges to our readers. We say that not just as a conventional means of academic apology. For its two authors, it reflects some five years of work in Florentine archives and libraries, plus a complex process of shared thinking and writing both in person and more recently (by force of pandemic circumstance) at a distance that also required us to negotiate the quite different disciplinary and cultural horizons of an Anglo-American musicologist and an Italian theatre historian. We further needed to draw on the advice of numerous colleagues in our own and other fields, as our acknowledgments, below, reveal. This collaboration led to a multimedia exhibition – *Firenze e la nascita dell'Opera* (*Florence and the Birth of Opera*) – generously hosted by the Casa Buonarroti, Florence, in April–May 2019, which prompted us to revisit issues that we had considered settled. Readers, on the other hand, may be challenged by the wealth of detail we present here – ranging from the purpose of a single nail to the decoration of an entire room – but still more, we hope, by the nature of our work and by the questions we raise concerning the impact endeavors such as ours might (or even should) have on theatrical staging in general in any plausible historical context.

Euridice has long been known as the first "opera" to survive complete. It was performed in Grand Duke Ferdinando I de' Medici's private residence in Florence, the Palazzo Pitti, on the evening of Friday, 6 October 1600 as one of several entertainments presented during the week-long festivities for the marriage of Maria de' Medici and King Henri IV of France. Given its position at the beginnings of so significant a music-theatrical genre, historians have already paid significant attention both to the work in terms of its surviving textual and musical sources, and, if in lesser degree, to its place within the nuptial celebrations. Missing thus far, however, has been any detailed consideration of its actual production in terms of where it was done (often misidentified), the sets, costumes, and other materials prepared for its performance, and the manner in which it was staged – that is, its *mise-en-scène* in the broadest sense of the term. In short, *Euridice* has rarely (if ever) been viewed as a work of and for the theatre, which brings a quite different set of issues into play. However, our trawl of documents in the Florentine archives now offers far more precise details on the production of the opera, including the construction of the stage and the sets, and on what was seen and heard at the time. These discoveries are what prompted us to write this book. Its purpose is twofold: first, to situate the creation of *Euridice* in various contexts above and beyond its role as a wedding entertainment; and second, to set out the evidence that would allow a quite precise reconstruction of the staging of the opera – and therefore new ways of reading its poetic text and musical score – in the space in which it was originally intended to be performed.

Any account of *Euridice* that considers, and integrates, its textual, musical, visual, and performative aspects in this theatrical frame must draw upon, and must appeal to, a number of different historical disciplines (art, architecture, literature, music, and, of course, the theatre itself) extending to political, social, and economic history writ large. We also argue that those who concern themselves with the theatre today – directors, stage designers, performers, and so forth – might benefit from considering the kinds of issues we raise in their own attempts to stage operas from distant times and places. Our basic premises are straightforward: that any theatrical event is a hybrid phenomenon necessarily requiring an interdisciplinary approach to its analysis and interpretation; and that it sits within, and meets the demands of, broader issues of cultural production and consumption.

Therefore it seems useful to start with an obvious question: Whose *Euridice*? This might seem simple enough to answer, but scholars would no doubt respond differently to it depending on their disciplinary orientation. Granting some primacy to the Florentine singer and composer Jacopo Peri (1561–1633), who provided most of the music and published a complete score, is logical enough in music-historical terms, given the canonic status of this *favola in musica*. We might wish to argue over whether it is an "opera" – like most such labels, this one is problematic – but even though *Euridice* must be placed in the broader context of Florentine entertainments of the period, it certainly established a precedent for a genre that eventually came to dominate the European art tradition. However, another Florentine singer and composer beat Peri to the press with a full score of the opera – Giulio Caccini (1551–1618) – and some commentators at the time identified it with yet another prominent musical figure in Medici service, Emilio de' Cavalieri (d. 1602). Moreover, at the performance on 6 October 1600, Caccini had singers from his studio perform his own musical notes rather than Peri's, if for reasons (we shall see) that were probably less malicious than critics have often assumed.

Of course, attributing an opera primarily to its composer could be a troublesome strategy in the first place. Literary scholars would no doubt prefer to give greater recognition to the author of the text of *Euridice*, the poet Ottavio Rinuccini (1563–1621). Historians of stage design would then lament the absence of Lodovico Cardi, called "Il Cigoli" (1559–1613), who created the scenery and designed the costumes. Political and social historians might wish to emphasize and interrogate the motives of the presumed patron of the opera, or of the Medici princess for whom it was written, which would mean crediting *Euridice* to the Florentine patrician Jacopo Corsi (1561–1602) on the one hand, or to Maria de' Medici (1575–1642) on the other, while also taking into account another member of the Medici family, Don Giovanni (1567–1621), who took some supervisory role in the 1600 festivities, as well as, of course, the grand duke and grand duchess, Ferdinando I and Christine of Lorraine. An economic historian would first want to know who paid for what, how much, and why. Add to this the singers involved in the performance of *Euridice* – at least one of whom prompted additions to Peri's score – plus any number of other possible contributors in the actual or metaphorical wings, and it becomes clear that the issue of who "created" the opera is a somewhat complex one. This is not unusual for a music-theatrical genre that has continued, during its long history, to depend on intricate collaborative networks. However, it has posed significant methodological and interpretative challenges for us, as it will, no doubt, for readers willing to follow us down these cross-disciplinary paths.

Partnerships such as ours are relatively rare – despite their obvious advantages for our topic – perhaps because of the fear that individual disciplinary viewpoints (or even scholarly egos) will then get relegated to the margins. But despite our working in different fields, different countries, and different languages, we share a passion for music and theatre in early modern Italy, and a fascination with what can and cannot be achieved by way of tenacious digging in the archives, however laborious it might be. This fascination is certainly time-consuming; it may also appear unfashionable in the current scholarly climate, although analysis and interpretation that lack a secure documentary foundation will always remain problematic at best, so we seek to show. In fact, we started out with the aim of producing a straightforward essay on the theatrical setting and staging of *Euridice* based on what we had each found, separately and together, in the Florentine archives. However, our conversations extended further afield, and in ever more stimulating ways, such as to move well beyond our initial goal. In retrospect, perhaps that was only to be expected. Theatre history and musicology often seem to move along parallel tracks without making contact one with the other, yet they engage with similar sets of problems, particularly when it comes to matters of performance. By combining our approaches, however, we soon realized that our reconstruction of the staging of *Euridice* would lead to some fundamental revisions to numerous assumptions commonly made in our separate fields about opera on the one hand, and the theatre on the other, and about the most useful ways of engaging with them. These revisions also opened up other, new ways of thinking about one specific music-theatrical event, and therefore, perhaps, about such events in general.

This emerged only gradually in our collaboration, given the documentary materials with which we began:

(a) an invoice (14 October 1600) by Lodovico Cigoli to settle payment for his work on the stage and scenery for *Euridice* (Appendix I.A, *Cig1–11*);
(b) an inventory of the sets and stage prepared almost a year later (18 September 1601) on behalf of Gianbattista Cresci, *provveditore* of the Fortezza da Basso in Florence (Appendix I.B, *Cres1–42*);
(c) an invoice by the *materassaio*, Francesco Ricoveri, who sewed the canvas for the stage and sets (Appendix I.C, *Ric1–17*).

The first two of these documents are not entirely new to the field (although the third is): the distinguished theatre historian Anna Maria Testaverde had already published transcriptions of Cigoli's invoice and part of Cresci's inventory. Our task, however, was to try and make some kind of sense of their contents as they relate directly to *Euridice*, and not just in general terms but, rather, according to their very specific and seemingly precise details concerning the number and type of scenic elements extending even to their measurements. We were aided in this undertaking by a large number of other new discoveries in the archives, as well as by placing all these documents in the broader context of what we think we know (though often we do not) about stage design and machinery in Italy during our period.

Such minute details of numbers and measurements might seem a far cry from the grander cross-disciplinary claims we have just made concerning our project, but they reflect very immediate, pragmatic concerns that must have preoccupied the creators of *Euridice* as much as they do us: there was a physical space (in fact, two) of particular size, orientation, and function that needed to be filled in very precise ways. Our point, too, is that engaging with such concerns is an essential first step, rather than a later one, in broaching broader interpretative issues. Comparing Cigoli's and Ricoveri's invoices and Cresci's inventory at this level of specificity seemed set to bear significant fruit. But we needed to find a way to give their contents some kind of visible form, and also to reconcile the evident differences between them – in part a product of their different functions – and also their apparent disagreements. In that light, all our documents became quite difficult to read – not just literally in terms of handwriting but also given their use of technical terms, often with regionally specific meanings – and their interpretation was neither intuitive nor immediate. We decided from the start not to adopt the easy solution of smoothing out the discrepancies by resorting to generalities or the assumption of error; rather, we wrestled over every single item identified by Cigoli, Cresci, and Ricoveri, arguing over its design, purpose, and dimensions – even down to the meter and centimeter (or rather, the *braccio* and parts thereof) – and trying to understand how things that did not seem to fit might in fact do so. Some questions were answered easily enough early on, others only after repeated review and reformulation of their possible answers in the light of ongoing discoveries, and a few others (we are willing to admit) still remain undecided. We also argued point after point from our different disciplinary perspectives. If traces of that process remain in the following text – and likewise any disagreement over its results – we are content to leave the more significant among them exposed as an object lesson in how (or how not) to go about the tasks we set ourselves when beginning our work.

Having dug deep into all these documents, we then had to extricate ourselves from them, moving from an obsession with planks, canvas, pulleys, ropes, and candles to a broader picture of how *Euridice* looked and sounded from the points of view of its performers and its spectators. We did so by way of other textual materials related to the production in the broader context of the preparations for the 1600 wedding and the festivities themselves; by engaging with a broad range of iconographical and similar evidence (some from Cigoli himself); by examining (and measuring!) the specific spaces in the Palazzo Pitti associated with the opera; and, last but not least, by a close reading of the text and the score. Each stage of this inquiry brought the opera increasingly out of the shadows into some kind of light: we were particularly struck by how the text and music – and their representation in the printed editions made of them – took more concrete form in terms of the creative collusions, and at times collisions, forced by any collaborative theatrical endeavor between patrons, artists, poets, composers, performers, and anyone else involved in bringing an opera to the stage. Indeed, *Euridice* becomes an intriguing test case of such matters, and not just because of its function within a Florentine political, social, and even economic context at a particularly charged moment in the city's history. We do not delude ourselves that we have pinned down every single aspect of what was essentially an ephemeral entertainment that only accidentally, as it were, gained its historical status as the earliest opera for which we have the complete text and music. Nevertheless, we certainly expand the notion of what is properly needed to "complete" the work.

Our chapters proceed logically enough, starting with the circumstances of the wedding of Maria de' Medici and Henri IV of France before homing in on the stage and sets constructed for *Euridice*, then issues concerning its performance and reception, and ending with a briefer consideration both of its immediate aftermath and of the possible consequences of our project for how we might best consider, or even present, the work today. Although these chapters might seem freestanding by virtue of their themes and will likely interest diverse readers in diverse ways – as is true of the opera itself, like any other – our argument proceeds across their divides: for example, the broader function of *Euridice* had a significant influence on the choices made by its creators, the location of its performance, and the construction of its stage, while the stage itself inevitably influenced the content of the opera as it went through rehearsal into production.

Thus, our first chapter establishes a frame within which to view *Euridice* in comparison with the other public and private celebrations associated with the 1600 festivities, distinguished by their purpose and design on the one hand, and their funding on the other. We identify and evaluate the various documentary sources available for a reconstruction of the opera, ranging from the official printed description of the 1600 festivities by Michelangelo Buonarroti *il giovane* to the very large amount of manuscript material of greater or lesser formality left by the artists and artisans who worked on the production. We consider the interests of those involved in the work's creation – in particular Jacopo Corsi and Ottavio Rinuccini – thereby treating *Euridice* in more tangible, if perhaps also prosaic, terms than its place within music-history textbooks might suggest, and less as an "academic" attempt to recreate ancient Greek tragedy (so it is commonly viewed) than as something more specific to its time and place. We explore the various physical spaces used for the 1600 entertainments as a way of distinguishing their separate functions and the audiences they were meant to reach, which in turn has a significant impact on how we should read them together and separately in the context of princely celebration. We uncover the various sources of funding for the different elements of the festivities. And we identify the room in the Palazzo Pitti for which the production of *Euridice* was designed (the so-called Sala delle Statue), and one in which it was eventually performed (the Sala delle Commedie).

Chapter 2 is concerned with reconstructing the stage and sets for the opera in terms of their individual elements, item by item, which we then piece together in three-dimensional terms. We start with an overview of the theories and practice of stage design in sixteenth- and early seventeenth-century Italy – also seeking to resolve some of the confusions in modern accounts of them – against which we can measure what was done for, and with, *Euridice*, if on a simpler scale; and we look in more detail at the dimensions and designs of the two spaces in the Palazzo Pitti associated with the work. We then turn to each part of the stage as documented in minute detail in Cigoli's and Ricoveri's invoices and in Cresci's inventory, bringing in other documents that provide additional information, as well as iconographical evidence from a wider range of sources. We seek to be clear on how and why we use these materials as we do, on where speculation has necessarily intervened, and indeed on issues that remain unresolved. In doing so, we push as far as we can in terms of creating a plausible model of the actual stage used for the opera, taking the fullest account of the sources we have to hand. We also establish some premises and principles that should serve, with or without subsequent revision, for future such inquiry on the staging of particular theatrical works based on similar materials rather than on what might now emerge as being untenable generalizations.

Our third chapter moves from the design and construction of the stage and sets for *Euridice* to what was eventually done within them during the opera's performance. Seen in this new light, and on the basis of annotations in two surviving copies of the printed libretto, not just Cigoli's sets but also the work's poetry and music emerge as being theatrically conceived from the outset. Our critical edition of Rinuccini's text in Appendix II (on the Companion Website), documenting the numerous variants in Peri's score (and the far fewer ones in Caccini's), provides further evidence to demonstrate how the work was revised during the production process. In some aspects, at least, these matters required us to engage in greater degrees of speculation than elsewhere. For example, we have little direct information on the costumes created for the opera, although there are parallel examples from Florentine court entertainments in the 1590s on which we were able to draw. In other cases, however, we were surprised – though we probably should not have been – by how many constructive suggestions came from the text and score. A great deal of scholarly ink has been spilled on *Euridice*, but usually treating its theme and its purpose in the abstract, and often with considerable suspicion over its viability in any immediate theatrical context. Starting from the obvious position that the opera was indeed staged – and that a great deal of thought was given to its production by a significant number of people – allowed us to see and understand elements in the work that had previously been overlooked. Putting everything together in this way also enabled us to consider anew how well *Euridice* fulfilled the expectations of its creators, and of the relatively small group of spectators attending its performances to whom its political and other messages were directly addressed.

In Chapter 4, we discuss subsequent uses of the stage and sets for *Euridice* in the Sala delle Commedie, and how the room was a principal location for other entertainments in the first decades of the seventeenth century before other "theatrical" spaces came to supplant it. Although the Medici had a permanent theatre in the Teatro degli Uffizi, it was used only on rare ceremonial occasions; for the most part, they preferred the more "private" setting of their own palace, even if that required adapting its spaces for temporary theatrical use (as was the case for *Euridice*). These issues also help explain the fluctuating fortunes of the *favola in musica* as a genre, which was just one of several types of entertainment adopted by the Medici, and hardly the most predominant one. We then turn to the broader ramifications of our study for modern productions of *Euridice*, and of "early" opera in general. For all the renewed interest in, and even demand for, so-called Historically Informed Performance – that is, in the manner and with the resources similar to those available at the time of a musical work's creation – opera directors and stage designers tend to resist its possibilities, save in certain specialized circumstances and locations. The rigorous philological approaches to sources adopted by musicologists and theatre historians have tended to have only a partial impact on the "real" theatrical world; scholars might provide the materials for a performance but their realization is taken out of their hands. In the case of *Euridice*, this led to an infamous production in the Palazzo Pitti in 2000 (celebrating the work's 400th anniversary in what was wrongly claimed to be the room in which it was first performed) that was certainly historically informed as regards its musical elements, but not at all in terms of its staging, which many considered incomprehensible.

Needless to say, we resist such an approach, and just as we used the 2019 multimedia exhibition in Florence to demonstrate an alternative to it, so would we encourage an actual production of *Euridice* on similar lines not as a mere historical curiosity but, rather, as way of bringing it to new life.

* * * * *

As those prefatory remarks suggest, the nature of our materials and what we have sought to do with them prompted much rewriting and editing to unite our different authorial voices. If separate credit needs to be granted to different portions of this book for bureaucratic reasons, although it hardly reflects the outcome, then it can be assigned as follows: Chapters 1, 3, and Appendix II (Carter), and Chapters 2, 4, and Appendix I (Fantappiè). Those materials also posed challenges in terms of how best to present them, both in print and on the Companion Website (www.cambridge.org/9781316515402). The latter contains all the images presented in the book – but some of them in color, also including complete versions of Cigoli's and Ricoveri's invoices and Cresci's inventory – plus others (cued, for example, as *CW*Fig. 1.8) that further support our arguments. The website also includes our edition of the libretto (Appendix II) given that it could be presented there in a more useful format for those wishing to adopt it for practical purposes. As for the book itself, our reliance on original documents has necessarily required the inclusion of a great deal of Italian within the text and notes; English translations or paraphrases are always provided when needed to follow the broader argument. Readers may also find it useful to read our comments on matters concerning sources, transcriptions, and translations in the next section, and likewise those that follow on money, accounts, measurements, dates, and time, prior to digging into the nitty-gritty of our documents and of our readings of what they contain.

We are grateful to Matteo Ceriana, former director of the Galleria Palatina in the Palazzo Pitti, Florence, and to Simona Mammana, former archivist of the Galleria, for their help in accessing parts of the palace not normally accessible to visitors; and to Francesca Fiori (Archivio di Stato, Florence), Elena Lombardi (Casa Buonarroti, Florence), and Maria Elena De Luca (Gabinetto dei Disegni e delle Stampe degli Uffizi, Florence) for aid in navigating their rich collections. We worked closely with Gian Gabriele Bassanello of MBVision (Peccioli, PI) on the digital reconstructions of the stage and sets for *Euridice*: his multimedia expertise and penetrating questions often forced us to rethink things we might have taken for granted. The Casa Buonarroti (director, Alessandro

Cecchi) and MBVision were also instrumental in creating the exhibition that presented the first fruits of our research, *Firenze e la nascita dell'Opera: fra documenti ritrovati e ricostruzioni virtuali* (*Florence and the Birth of Opera: Documents and Virtual Reconstructions*), held in the Casa Buonarroti, Florence, from 3 April to 15 May 2019. This exhibition was fostered by Pina Ragionieri, president of the Casa Buonarroti Foundation (who died, alas, shortly before it opened), and it served as an excellent training exercise for a remarkable group of students on the Marist College M.A. in Museum Studies program (directed by Maia Wellington Gahtan) at the Istituto Lorenzo de' Medici, Florence (Marissa Acey, Marie-Claire Desjardin, Emily Hurley, Laura McCay, Maryam Neyazi, Phoebe O'Dell, Dailin Portelles). We are also grateful to Serena Botti and Elisa Gradi of the Istituto Lorenzo de' Medici for their significant administrative support for the exhibition and its associated conference, "Florence *circa* 1600: Patrician Families and the Financing of Culture" (11–12 April 2019), plus a concert (based on the "first" version of *Dafne*) presented by Michael Stüve and the ensemble "Musica Ricercata."

We have each, at very different times, had the benefit of a fellowship at the Harvard Center for Italian Renaissance Studies, Villa I Tatti, Florence, and hence access both to its rich intellectual environment and to the abundant resources of the Biblioteca Berenson. The art historian Miles Chappell, economic historian Richard Goldthwaite, literary historian Laura Riccò, and theatre historians Frank Mohler and Anna Maria Testaverde were always ready to answer our questions large and small, prompting significant revisions to our drafts; Maria Alberti of the Fondazione Franco Zeffirelli provided important information on the production of *Euridice* in the 1960 Maggio Musicale Fiorentino; we relied extensively on the generous advice of Nicola Badolato (University of Bologna) for our edition of the libretto; and two anonymous readers for Cambridge University Press enabled us to polish our text in ways we much appreciated. We received significant support from various colleagues and friends, including Kathryn Bosi, Anthony Cummings, Suzanne Cusick, Ilaria Della Monica, Lisa Goldenberg Stoppato, John Nádas, Giovanni Pagliarulo, and Emily Wilbourne. Our respective spouses, Annegret Fauser and Sergio Tognetti, have lived with this project for as long as we have, and have helped sustain it in more ways than we can express.

Sources, Transcriptions, and Translations

The main repositories for the materials used in this study are in Florence, including the Archivio di Stato (ASF), the Biblioteca Nazionale Centrale (BNCF), and the Gabinetto dei Disegni e delle Stampe degli Uffizi (GDSU). In the case of ASF, we draw largely on such *fondi* as the Guardaroba Medicea (*GM*; records of the Medici "wardrobe" and its various subdivisions, which was responsible for all moveable items owned by the grand duke – and for the artisans and artists that created them – as well as for some upkeep of the grand-ducal buildings); Mediceo del Principato (*MdP*; correspondence files for the Medici and their secretaries, etc.); Miscellanea Medicea (*MM*; miscellaneous files culled from various Medici-related sources); Scrittoio delle Fortezze e Fabbriche: Fabbriche Medicee (*SFF*; the office recording actions concerning the construction and maintenance of Medici buildings); and Soprassindaci, Sindaci e Ufficio delle Revisioni e Sindacati (*SS*; the office with oversight of the administration and expenditures of state bodies). Most of these *fondi* were organized as what gradually became ASF took institutional shape – which remains an ongoing process – though save in the obvious case of *MM*, their contents tend to reflect some manner in which they were created and stored by their original offices. Florentine bureaucracies may appear cumbersome, but this is one reason why ASF is so rich a resource, especially as one learns to navigate the administrative systems reflected in its holdings. These bureaucracies were both logical and efficient, with reporting mechanisms and associated checks and balances that, in turn, left trails that one can follow through various administrative levels within and across various offices, insofar as documents survive; many, of course, do not, though traces sometimes remain by way of references made to them (for example, to a numbered entry in some now lost account book). Inevitably, however, as one moves higher up any system, its records take an increasingly summary form.

Most of the files in the *fondi* cited here have their separate items numbered in a later hand usually by folio (consecutive numbers on the *recto*) or – much less frequently – by page (consecutive numbers on *recto* and *verso*). Account books (such as *libri di entrata ed uscita* or *debitori e creditori*) tend to be numbered by opening (hence fol. 12left, often in roman numerals in the original; and fol. 12right, often in arabic ones). Absent such numbering, documents in a file, or entries in a document, can usually be found by date. Save where indicated otherwise, our reference to any given folio is to its *recto*.

Our transcriptions from primary sources adopt the following principles. Original orthographies are retained save *v* for (consonant) *u*, *i* for *j* and vice versa (although we allow both Iacopo and Jacopo, etc., save where the latter makes most sense), *ii* for *ij*, and *s* for *ſ*. Thus, we keep *havere*, *hieri*, *hora*, *humile*, and the like; irregular doubled consonants (*dissegno*; *nell* for *nel*) or single ones (*rapresentato*; *nela* for *nella*) save where there is good reason to make a change; and *et* for *e* or *ed*, although *&* is rendered as *et* or *e*, depending on context. Nor do we rationalize the joining of prepositions and definite articles (so, we allow both *de la* and *della* depending on the original). Accents are added (and sometimes removed) where standard (including the *accento chiuso* on *-é*), as are apostrophes to indicate contractions save in common forms (*sarebbon*, *venir*). Thus, *ne* is transcribed as *ne*, *né*, or *ne'*, depending on sense; and *de* becomes *de'* as a preposition (for *dei*) or as contraction of *deve* (in the typical account-book formula *de' dare*). However, in cases of ambiguity, we have tended to retain the uninflected form: for example, *che* as a relative pronoun is generally clear, but the distinction between the conjunctions *che* and *ché* (the latter a contraction of *perché*, etc.) is not always so. We also keep redundant apostrophes when they are present in the original (*lor'* even though *lor* is an acceptable form of *loro*). Punctuation and the use of uppercase letters are modernized to as minimal an extent as needed to convey the sense, although we have tended to follow the original more strictly in transcriptions from early printed sources. All abbreviations are expanded (including the likes of *8bre* for *ottobre* or a square for [*braccia*] *quadrate*), as are honorifics such as *Sua Altezza Serenissima*, *signore* (*signor* before a name), and the lesser-ranked *messere* (*messer* before a name). For the last, its abbreviation is often indistinguishable from the one adopted for *maestro* (sometimes used for artisans), but we assume, also on the basis of other forms of address, that artists such as Lodovico Cigoli would have merited the higher title. These expansions are done silently save where there is some ambiguity, in which case we use square brackets. Insertions (whether interleaved or in the margins) are placed between > and <; deletions, where it is useful to give them, are bounded by < and >; square brackets are used for editorial additions, though we have preferred to keep these to a minimum.

Almost all the documents transcribed here exhibit legitimate orthographic inconsistencies (*comedia* or *commedia*) and mannerisms (*picholo* and *piccolo*), as well as "errors," that cannot always be reconciled internally or across the board whether or not by way of the principles outlined above. This is particularly in the case of Florentine artisans who often spell words idiomatically, "incorrectly" (*Piti* for *Pitti*), or by transliterating some form of Tuscan pronunciation (*charuhole* for *carrucole*; the name "Caccini" as *Hac(c)ini*). It would be tiresome to an extreme to indicate every such occurrence with an editorial *sic* or other intervention, although we do so judiciously where readers might plausibly suspect error on our part, or where potential ambiguities of meaning need to be resolved. For the rest, however, our transcriptions will have to be taken on faith.

In cases where documents are translated rather than paraphrased, we have tended more toward the literal than the elegant. We have also labored over technical terms (for boards, planks, machinery, types of canvas, etc.), and while we have usually tried to find appropriate English-language equivalents for them, we may not always have succeeded, whether in our translations or in terms of the differences between British and U.S. English. For the Italian, the best places to start for deciphering them are Filippo Baldinucci's *Vocabolario toscano dell'arte del disegno* (1681), which can now be searched online at http://barocchi.sns.it/dizionario/FB_V, and the *Glossario dell'edilizia romana tra Rinascimento e Barocco* at http://wissens-geschichte.biblhertz.it:8080/Glossario. It would be redundant to make repeated references to these two sources in the notes, but we have relied extensively upon them.

Money, Accounts, Measurements, Dates, and Time

Many of the archival sources used for this study involve financial accounts, payment invoices, and the like expressed in the typical monetary units of *lire* (£), *soldi* (*s.*; twenty to the *lira*), and *denari* (*d.*; twelve to the *soldo*). These can be combined in a single formula such as £3.12*s.* (three *lire* and twelve *soldi*) or £3.12*s.*4*d.* (. . . and four *denari*), although the symbols are usually lacking in the documents. Higher-level values are normally expressed as *scudi* (*sc.*; usually indicated in the sources by an inverted triangle) or *ducati* (*du.*; by some florid version of a lower-case "d"); in Florence in our period, each *scudo* or *ducato* had a value of seven *lire*. The *scudo* and *ducato* (and the *fiorino* [*fl.*], also of seven *lire*) are to all intents and purposes the same save in the case of the *scudo d'oro* (7.5 *lire* = £7.10*s.*) or the *fiorino di £4*, neither of which appear in our text. We treat them all as *scudi*, which is the prevalent top-level denomination in the documents anyway. Again, they can be presented in a single formula (*sc.*3 £3.12*s.*4*d.*).

It is important to realize that *scudi* (etc.), *lire*, *soldi*, and *denari*, are all so-called moneys of account rather than actual coins. They are used to record costs, values, credits, and debits. These sums can also be transferred as credits and debits by way of paper transactions – such as from one account to another – and often were, in what operated in part as a cashless economy. However, should anyone require a cost or debt to be paid, or a credit to be liquidated, these moneys of account would usually need to be converted to actual coins such as the silver *piastra* (with a price of £7 or *sc.*1), *testone*, *mezzo testone*, *giulio*, or *crazia* (for further information on the Florentine monetary system to the end of the sixteenth century, see Goldthwaite and Mandich, *Studi sulla moneta fiorentina*). To give a straightforward example, when the poet Battista Guarini wrote to Emilio de' Cavalieri on 14 October 1600 asking that the Giunti press be "paid" *sc.*2 for printing 125 copies of the text he had provided for a short pageant performed during the official banquet in the wedding festivities (the *Dialogo di Giunone e Minerva*) because of an agreement that the pamphlet would be issued at the grand duke's expense, a note was added to the foot of the letter that the Giunti should be given two *piastre* (*GM* 1152, fol. 384). However, payments might also be made in kind by some non-monetary goods or service of the same value that would be recorded, precisely, in moneys of account. Credits or debits could also stay on the books for a long time, and marking an invoice, say, as "paid" does not necessarily mean that any cash or in-kind transaction in fact occurred: rather, such "payment" could involve a paper credit to a different account to be liquidated, or not, at some future date.

The fact that such transactions are recorded in moneys of account requires some understanding of the accounting systems that were second nature to most Florentines, and that underpinned the city's economic life (see the general remarks in Carter and Goldthwaite, *Orpheus in the Marketplace*, 12–14, 129–32). The *quadernucci* and *stracciafogli* (scrap-books, as it were), *giornali* (journals), records of payments in and out (in *libri di entrata ed uscita*), and ledgers listing debits and credits (*libri di debitori e creditori*) each served their separate purposes as well as operating within a hierarchy. They were carefully maintained given that they had status in courts of law; mistakes would be corrected sometimes with laborious explanations; and accounts would be periodically reviewed, or even audited, for accuracy. The system also applied to material items, independent of any monetary value assigned to them, that would be debited to the "account" of a person or office taking temporary charge of them, whether or not in some administrative capacity; they would then be credited to the same account on their return and transferred as a debit to some other account, unless the debit was expunged in some other way (for example, because the item was acknowledged to be damaged or lost). This is one reason, we shall see, why we have Gianbattista Cresci's inventory of the staging and sets for *Euridice*. Likewise, "debits" such as labor costs apparently charged by the officials of the Fortezza da Basso to those of the Palazzo Pitti (for work done in the palace by artisans employed by the Fortezza) need not always have been "costs" at all – in cases where no payment was expected or made – but, rather, were a matter of record in terms of who did what when. Accuracy was important and expected, whether in personal accounts or in official bookkeeping. It is also true, however, that even the most conscientious could make errors (that might or might not be spotted later) or just a slip of the pen.

All this explains the extraordinary level of detail in the main documents used in our study: even high-order accounts could still deal in small sums of *soldi* and *denari*. However, absent the full range of accounting records, it can sometimes be hard to situate a particular record within the system, or to understand properly what it conveys and why. It is also true that even lower-level accounts, which should in principle contain the most detail, do not always contain the information one might wish. As another example from the 1600 wedding, an entry in a *giornale del libro di debitori e creditori della Guardaroba* (*GM* 229, fol. 8left) indicates various payments on 10 November 1600 to the printer Giorgio Marescotti, including two *per libri, leghatur' et altro* (books, binding, and other matters; adding up to *sc.*11 £0.3*s.*8*d.*), plus *sc.*2 £4 allocated to *spese per la Maestà della Regina* (expenses for the queen), and *sc.*8 £3.3*s.*8*d.* to *donativi* (that is, items "given away" as gifts to visitors, etc.). These separate sums are combined in a single entry in *GM* 230 (a *libro di entrata ed uscita* of the Guardaroba, 1600–1601), p. 16, *per conto saldo di robe haùte* (to settle the account for goods received). Marescotti printed a number of items for the festivities, but nothing tells us which were reckoned here.

The same level of detail is true of measurements, especially when they had a direct impact on cost. These are most often expressed by way of the *braccio* (singular, m., *il braccio*; plural, f., *le braccia*) and fractions thereof. A Florentine *braccio* (1 *b.*) is generally reckoned nowadays as equivalent to 58 cm (0.58 m) or close to 23 in. (1 ft. 11 in.; just short of two-thirds of a yard); this equivalence is confirmed so far as we can ascertain from items measured then that can still be measured now, such as the dimensions of certain rooms in the Palazzo Pitti. For ease of reference to the documents, and of calculations arising therefrom, we prefer to retain the expression of measurements in *braccia*, although we provide the modern metric equivalents where it will help the reader; in addition, we infrequently use other units of measurement such as the *piede*, *oncia*, and *palmo* when found in any sources (often non-Florentine ones).

The *braccio* is also adopted in the documents, and by us, to calculate surface area as *braccia quadrate* (sometimes styled in the documents as *braccia quadre*): thus, an area 10 *b.* long by 12 *b.* wide is 120 *b.q.* (40.4 m^2). A further use of the *braccio* (for cloth, wood, wall painting, and similar matters) occurs in measurements expressed as *braccia andante* (*b.a.*), that is, "running" or linear *braccia*, meaning a cumulative total of separate lengths, usually also of unspecified width, though presumably there were notional standards for given materials. (In a similar manner, we might today buy a number of linear feet, yards, or meters of timber or cloth of otherwise standard dimensions.) At widths of 1 *b.*, *braccia andante* will be numerically equivalent to *braccia quadrate*, but for different widths, 1 *b.a.* will represent something more, or less, than 1 *b.q.* Measurements expressed as *braccia andante* can therefore be tricky to reconcile with the actual dimensions of the item(s) being measured.

Our own measurements expressed in *braccia* or meters and portions thereof (rounded up or down to one decimal place) probably appear more precise than they in fact are. One might say the same of measurements in the original documents, which will often have involved some level of approximation even when payment depended on them. Similarly, those that seem suspiciously precise – if still within reason – may be conveniently so in order to impress their recipient, especially if independent verification was no longer possible because an item had been repurposed or lost (the same might be true of some financial accounts). In comparing measurements from one document with those in another, we have tended not to quibble over minor discrepancies, given the need also to allow margins of error. But, in fact, we have regularly been surprised by how close the measurements of the various materials for *Euridice* provided in, or deduced from, our sources came to what we judged necessary for our reconstruction of its stage and sets. Likewise, when they did not seem to match, it was often because we had made some mistake (for example, in the presumed purpose of a given item) that needed to be rectified.

Measurements mattered for those who provided measurable goods (a board or a piece of canvas) or services (painting a wall) at a specified cost per unit. Other items were "measured" by weight (the *libbra*, i.e., pound). Artisans could also charge for services reckoned in terms of the workdays (*giornate*) involved in a particular task, calculated by way of a number of days involving a number of workers (thus, eight workers each working for three days would generate twenty-four *giornate*, as would six workers each working for four days, or ten each working for two days plus one for four). However, even in the case of seemingly standard costs per unit or per workday, Medici administrators tended to reduce them by way of the so-called *tara* (in effect, a review offering some manner of price control) that could prompt a reduction ranging from 10 to 20 percent in the invoiced amount for services, and still more for goods. It is also clear that in the case of higher-value items, these administrators assumed that their prices would be drastically inflated in other ways, and they would find some way to negotiate them down: we shall see how Lodovico Cigoli received only half of the amount he originally requested for creating the scenery for *Euridice* by way of what appears to have been a standard valuation process acknowledged and expected by all parties involved.

Stile fiorentino dating began the year *ab incarnatione*, that is, on 25 March. To avoid confusion, we express all precise dates between 1 January and 24 March by a double formula as 1 January 1600/1 (so, 1 January 1600 *stile fiorentino* and 1 January 1601 in modern style), although we use "early 1601" when the meaning is clear. In principle, Carnival ran from 26 December to the day before the beginning of Lent on Ash Wednesday (which varies according to the date of Easter Sunday), so the Carnival season came toward the end of a single *stile fiorentino* year. For example, in 1600, Easter Sunday fell on 2 April, and what we style as Carnival 1599/1600 ran from 26 December 1599 to Tuesday, 15 February 1599/1600.

Time was reckoned by way of so-called *ore italiane* using a 24-hour clock ending and beginning around sunset (see Talbot, "*Ore italiane*"). Thus, when Salvadore di Piero, *lanternaio*, took charge of the lighting for the performance of *Euridice* on 6 October 1600 "from the 21st hour to the 4th hour of night" (*da le 21 ore insino a le 4 ore di notte*), this would have been roughly from 3:00 p.m. (15:00) to 10:00 p.m. (22:00).

Abbreviations

ASF	Archivio di Stato, Florence
b.	*braccio/braccia*
b.a.	*braccio andante/braccia andante*
b.q.	*braccio quadrato/braccia quadrate*
BNCF	Biblioteca Nazionale Centrale, Florence
d.	*denaro/denari*
doc.	document
du.	*ducato/ducati*
fl.	*fiorino/fiorini*
GDSU	Gabinetto dei Disegni e delle Stampe degli Uffizi, Florence
GM	ASF, Guardaroba Medicea
ins.	insert/*inserto*
KirkCM	Kirkendale, *The Court Musicians of Florence during the Principate of the Medici*
£	*lira/lire*
MdP	ASF, Mediceo del Principato
MM	ASF, Miscellanea Medicea
s.	*soldo/soldi*
sc.	*scudo/scudi*
SFF	ASF, Scrittoio delle Fortezze e Fabbriche: Fabbriche Medicee
SolMBD	Solerti, *Musica, ballo e drammatica alla corte medicea*
SS	ASF, Soprassindaci, Sindaci e Ufficio delle Revisioni e Sindacati

1 *Euridice* in Context

The reign of Grand Duke Ferdinando I de' Medici from 1587 until his death in 1609 was marked by three prominent weddings: his own to Christine of Lorraine in May 1589; that of his niece Maria de' Medici to King Henri IV of France in October 1600; and that of his son Prince Cosimo de' Medici (later Grand Duke Cosimo II) to Archduchess Maria Magdalena of Austria in October 1608. The festivities celebrating the 1589 and 1608 weddings culminated in the performance of a comedy (Girolamo Bargagli's *La pellegrina* and Michelangelo Buonarroti *il giovane*'s *Il giudizio di Paride*) with spectacular *intermedi* before, between, and after the five acts of the play: indeed, the six *intermedi* to *La pellegrina* (1589) are widely regarded as a pinnacle of the genre, and the epitome of Medici court entertainments as political propaganda.

Something quite different occurred in 1600, however. Here the noble guests saw not a play with lavish *intermedi* but, rather, two through-composed "plays in music" – *favole in musica* (what we now call operas): *Euridice*, with words by Ottavio Rinuccini (1563–1621) and music in the main by Jacopo Peri (1561–1633); and *Il rapimento di Cefalo*, to a text by Gabriello Chiabrera (1552–1638) and music by Giulio Caccini (1551–1618) and others. For the Medici to celebrate a wedding of one of their own with a comedy and *intermedi* was to be expected: Duke Cosimo I (he became grand duke only in 1569) established the precedent with his wedding to Eleonora of Toledo in 1539, and the pattern continued through the celebration of the marriages of his son Francesco to Johanna of Austria (1565), and his daughter, Virginia, to Cesare d'Este (1586).[1] Opera, however, was different, and also confusing enough that at least one visitor to Florence in 1600 thought that *Il rapimento di Cefalo* somehow belonged to the older genre – though clearly it did not in terms of its structure and musical setting – perhaps by virtue of its mythological content and spectacular staging.[2] *Euridice*

[1] The literature on the Florentine *intermedi* is large, but one can start with Nagler, *Theatre Festivals of the Medici*; Pirrotta, *Li due Orfei* (translated as *Music and Theatre from Poliziano to Monteverdi*); and M. Fabbri *et al.* (eds.), *Il luogo teatrale a Firenze*.

[2] Carter, "Rediscovering *Il rapimento di Cefalo*," para. 4.3.

drew on Classical myth, too, but here, at least, there could be no doubt: something new was definitely in the air.

Michelangelo Buonarroti *il giovane* (1568–1646) had to tread a fine line in his official description of the 1600 festivities to place them at the apogee of this long tradition of Medici wedding celebrations.[3] But the grand duke and grand duchess (or their advisers) may have cultivated such novelty to mark the great political significance of a marriage (with the King of France, no less) that also marked an important shift in Medici foreign policy. Such novelty also suited the ambitions of the relatively young Florentine patrician, Jacopo Corsi (1561–1602), who was involved in putting *Euridice* on the stage. It was the culmination of a decade of theatrical experimentation in Florence, in which Corsi and others had been actively, and sometimes competitively, involved. They, in turn, built on theoretical investigations into ancient Greek and Roman music and drama going back several decades on the part of Florentine groups such as the "Camerata" sponsored by Giovanni de' Bardi (1534–1612), also involving Vincenzo Galilei (1520–1591), Giulio Caccini, and Piero di Matteo Strozzi (1551–1614).[4] The Accademia degli Alterati in Florence had a role to play here, too: it was founded in 1569 and included a significant number of intellectuals and poets, such as Giovanni de' Bardi, Lorenzo Giacomini, Girolamo Mei, and Giovanni Battista Strozzi *il giovane*, among many others. Although the academy barely met during the 1590s, it was briefly revived under the influence of Don Giovanni de' Medici in late 1599–1600 (and again in 1604): Michelangelo Buonarroti *il giovane*, Jacopo Corsi, Piero di Matteo Strozzi, Alessandro Rinuccini, and Ottavio Rinuccini were among those who attended a session on 24 January 1599/1600.[5] Both Peri and Rinuccini made the connection with such humanist endeavor – as did Buonarroti for *Il rapimento di Cefalo* in his account of the festivities (he associates it with a

[3] Michelangelo Buonarroti (*il giovane*), *Descrizione delle felicissime nozze . . . della Cristianissima Maestà di Madama Maria Medici, Regina di Francia e di Navarra* (Florence: Giorgio Marescotti, 1600); it is also included in Buonarroti, *Opere varie in versi ed in prosa*, ed. Fanfani, 403–54. The 1600 edition lacks page numbers; in subsequent citations we follow the numbering added in pencil to the copy now digitized at www.cinquecentine-crusca.org/scheda2.asp?es=0&radice=000111569_1.

[4] Palisca, *The Florentine Camerata*. Care must be taken not to confuse this Piero Strozzi (baptized as Piero Vincenzo di Matteo Strozzi) with other members of this extended family with the same first name; for the most current information, see Fantappiè, "Strozzi, Piero Vincenzo."

[5] Palisca, "The Alterati of Florence"; Blocker, "The Accademia degli Alterati and the Invention of a New Form of Dramatic Experience." Girolamo Mei (mostly in Rome) was in correspondence with members of the Camerata and also had a significant influence on their thinking. For the January 1600 meeting of the Alterati, see Florence, Biblioteca Medicea Laurenziana, Ashburnham 558.2 (Diary of the Accademia degli Alterati, vol. 2), fol. 105.

revival of the power of ancient music to arouse the emotions of its listeners)[6] – although they also hedged their bets on the fidelity of *Euridice* to any Classical model.

That hedging was inevitable when squaring theoretical investigation with practical exigency. It also reflected a problem of genre. Peri and Rinuccini may have referred to ancient tragedy in their statements on *Euridice*, but they knew full well that they were also working within the more modern context of the pastoral play on the model of Tasso's *Aminta* (1573) and Guarini's *Il pastor fido* (1590), a genre that also gained considerable favor in Florence (and elsewhere) in the 1590s as a suitable medium for princely entertainment.[7] As Guarini discovered to his cost, the pastoral "tragicomedy" was controversial given its lack of Classical precedent and its apparent hybridity. But it had the further advantages of being relatively easy to stage (with fewer demands for complex scenery), and, still more, of offering a more conducive and plausible environment for music by virtue of its location in an idealized Arcadia where songs were naturally in the air. Various theatrical entertainments staged in Florence in the early 1590s inhabited the same mythological–pastoral world, including three (now lost) entertainments with texts by Laura Guidiccioni Lucchesini and music by Emilio de' Cavalieri: *Il satiro* and *La disperazione di Fileno* in 1590 (or early 1591) and *Il giuoco della cieca* (based on an episode in *Il pastor fido*) in 1595. Grand Duchess Christine of Lorraine also seems to have favored pastorals as appropriate for women in her circles, whether as creators (for example, an untitled *tragicommedia* by Leonora Bernardi performed *in villa* in 1591, and Laura Guidiccioni's collaborations with Cavalieri) or in terms of audience.[8] Thus although the first "opera," *Dafne* – to verse by Ottavio Rinuccini and music by Jacopo Corsi and Jacopo Peri – was performed at Corsi's residence in Florence in the presence of Don Giovanni de' Medici in early 1598, it was repeated in the Palazzo Pitti

[6] Buonarroti, *Descrizione delle felicissime nozze*, 22, praises Giulio Caccini for offering a true demonstration of what many might have thought was just unbelievable hyperbole on the part of the ancients in terms of music's ability to arouse the emotions (*Il perché in questa impresa tutto intendendo a sì fatto termine ei la condusse, che in rappresentandosi, quello, che quasi incredibile, et iperbole dell'antica musica da alcuno saria credutosi, tutti gli affetti movente; egli, per la chiara esplicazion degli articoli, e degli accenti, per verissimo ne fè conoscere, svegliandone con efficacia movimenti veraci ne gli uditori*).

[7] Fenlon, "A Golden Age Restored."

[8] Cox, *The Prodigious Muse*, 97 (Bernardi); Riccò, *Dalla zampogna all'aurea cetra*, 55–131 (Guidiccioni and Cavalieri). Both Bernardi and Guidiccioni were singers taken into Medici service in August 1588; Newcomb, *The Madrigal at Ferrara*, 1: 272 (doc. 67). The issue also has a bearing on the projected performance of Tasso's *Aminta* in Florence in Carnival 1589/90 by *le principesse e le dame di palazzo*; see Riccò, *"Ben mille pastorali"*, 264–67.

before the grand duchess and Cardinals Francesco Maria del Monte and Alessandro Damasceni Peretti di Montalto on 21 January 1598/99.[9] That performance followed a revival of Cavalieri's *Il giuoco della cieca* on 5 January (or, more likely, on the 4th).[10] *Dafne* may also have been staged at least once in 1600, if not necessarily with Peri's music (see later in this chapter). Both events in Carnival 1598/99 took place in the Sala delle Statue, which, we shall see, had an impact on the preparations for the production of *Euridice* during the 1600 wedding festivities. The grand duchess and Don Giovanni de' Medici made their influence felt here as well, the latter by being placed in some kind of charge of the celebrations as a whole.

These interconnections between the Medici and Florentine patricians were made particularly apparent in 1600 because of the political and other

[9] For *Dafne*, see most recently Fantappiè, "Una primizia rinucciniana," discussing the newly discovered "original" version of Rinuccini's libretto (with 212 lines of verse rather than 445). In the preface to *Le musiche . . . sopra L'Euridice* (Florence: Giorgio Marescotti, 1600 [= 1601]), Jacopo Peri dates the inception of *Dafne* back to 1594, but some difficulty over the year of the first performance is caused by his subsequent comment that it was performed in three successive carnivals (*E per tre Anni continui, che nel Carnovale si rappresentò* . . .). This is commonly agreed to be Carnivals 1597/98, 1598/99, and 1599/1600, but it is possible that the entire sequence should be shifted back by one year, beginning with Carnival 1596/97. In the dedication to Maria de' Medici of his *L'Euridice . . . rappresentata nello sponsalitio della Christianiss. Regina di Francia, e di Navarra* (Florence: Cosimo Giunti, 1600), Rinuccini refers to the early version of *Dafne*, then notes that it was given a better form and performed at Corsi's residence, and was not only favored by the Florentine nobility but was heard and praised by Grand Duchess Christine and Cardinals del Monte and Montalto (*onde preso animo, e dato miglior forma alla stessa favola, e di nuovo rappresentandola in casa il Sig. Iacopo, fu ella non solo dalla nobiltà di tutta questa Patria favorita, ma dalla Serenissima Gran Duchessa, e gl'illustrissimi Cardinali Dal Monte e Montalto udita, e commendata*). However, he seems to be conflating performances of that "better" version of *Dafne* in two successive years, one in Carnival 1597/98 in Corsi's residence before Don Giovanni de' Medici, as noted later by Marco da Gagliano (*KirkCM*, 195), and one before the grand duchess and the two cardinals in the Sala delle Statue in the Palazzo Pitti on 21 January 1598/99 (*GM*, Diari d'etichetta 2, p. 95: *Adì 21 si fece nella sala delle statue la pastorella in musica del signor Jacopo Corsi*). The evidence of a performance in Carnival 1599/1600 is scant: an entry in Corsi's financial accounts dated 28 January 1599/1600 refers to purchasing *rimesse e ferri per la commedia* (*KirkCM*, 197), although this could refer to anything theatrical. In early April 1600, Emilio de' Cavalieri complained about comparisons being made between *Dafne* and *Il giuoco della cieca*; *KirkCM*, 197–98, uses this in further support of a performance of *Dafne* being held earlier that year, but it need not be so. Only portions of the music for the work survive; see Porter, "Peri and Corsi's *Dafne*."

[10] *GM*, Diari d'etichetta 2, p. 94, notes the performance on 5 January 1598/99, and a comedy by *zanni* the next day (*Adì 5 detto se li fece nel salone delle statue la pastorella in musica dal signor Emilio de' Cavalieri che vi furno 60 gentildonne fiorentine. Adì 6 nella medesima sala e le stesse donne se li fece una commedia di zanni*). However, Belisario Vinta refers to the performance *in palazzo* of *una commedia pastorale molto vaga et piacevole con bellissima musica* that had been given "today" in his letter to Alessandro Beccheria (the Florentine resident in Milan), 4 (*sic*) January 1598/99; *MdP* 3135, fols. 679–80.

circumstances leading up to the wedding. But they also reflect a typical strategy of the Medici as a whole: although their rule as grand dukes of Florence was now undisputed, they were careful to foster patrician involvement in affairs of state, and were eager, of course, to showcase the intellectual and cultural vitality of their extraordinary city. Don Giovanni de' Medici (1567–1621) served a particularly useful function in this light. He was the illegitimate son of Duke Cosimo I and Eleonora degli Albizzi, and was thus in a somewhat similar position to Don Antonio de' Medici (1576–1621), born to Grand Duke Francesco and Bianca Cappello prior to their marriage in 1579. Both Don Giovanni and Don Antonio were subsequently legitimized within limits (and without rights of succession), and Grand Duke Ferdinando I tended to use them in various diplomatic capacities on ambassadorial missions abroad – Don Giovanni was often at the Spanish court – and as intermediaries to act in his interests in Florence and elsewhere. Don Giovanni had a distinguished military career (serving in Flanders, Hungary, and, later, on behalf of Venice), but when not abroad, he was active in Florentine intellectual and social circles such as the Accademia Fiorentina and the Alterati, given his own interests in the arts and sciences, as well as in the theatre. In addition he was an architect who played a leading role in designing military fortifications (for example, in Livorno and for the Fortezza del Belvedere in Florence) and churches (in Livorno, Pisa, and, somewhat controversially, the Cappella dei Principi in S. Lorenzo in Florence). In terms of his Florentine networks of associates and even friends, Don Giovanni was particularly close to, and cultivated by, Jacopo Corsi and Ottavio Rinuccini (they were roughly six and four years older than him, respectively). This created connections that would have a significant impact on the 1600 festivities.[11]

Don Giovanni's role in the celebrations appears to have generated some bad feeling between him and the venerable architect and stage designer, Bernardo Buontalenti, on the one hand, and, on the other, with Emilio de' Cavalieri, who was notionally in charge of the court musicians but felt distinctly sidelined by the whole proceedings. Giulio Caccini also used the festivities to secure his reappointment to Medici service (on 1 October 1600) following his somewhat ignominious dismissal in 1593 (because of a dispute with Antonio Salviati over one of Caccini's female students),[12]

[11] For Don Giovanni de' Medici, see Dooley, *A Mattress Maker's Daughter*. His connections with Rinuccini and Corsi are discussed in Fantappiè, "Una primizia rinucciniana," 211–14.

[12] *KirkCM*, 131–36; Carter and Goldthwaite, *Orpheus in the Marketplace*, 109–10. However, in the interim Caccini had continued to be supported by Florentine patrons, including Jacopo Corsi and Piero di Matteo Strozzi.

chiefly by way of *Il rapimento di Cefalo* but also, if to a lesser degree, by his involvement in *Euridice*. Meanwhile, Emilio de' Cavalieri was becoming increasingly isolated from events in Florence, and the issues surrounding them, despite his supposed authority over the court artists and musicians. Not everything seems to have gone smoothly, but that might well be said of the wedding arrangements as a whole, however much Michelangelo Buonarroti *il giovane* tried to put a positive spin on things in his official *Descrizione* of the festivities, as he was required to do.

The Marriage Negotiations

Don Giovanni de' Medici finds his typical place in the background of the well-known painting by Jacopo Chimenti da Empoli (1551–1640) of Maria de' Medici's wedding, or more properly, the ceremonial giving of the ring (see Fig. 1.1). This has all the hallmarks of such nuptial representations, and the absence of the groom, Henri IV, is not at all surprising: royal etiquette required the bride to meet him first on his terrain rather than hers. Thus Maria's uncle, Grand Duke Ferdinando I (wearing the robe of the *gran maestro* of the Cavalieri di S. Stefano), stood as proxy for the king in the ceremony: Chimenti shows them standing to the left and right of Cardinal Pietro Aldobrandini (nephew of Pope Clement VIII), the papal legate sent from Rome to officiate. They are bounded on either side by other members of the Medici family who, strangely enough, have consistently been misidentified in most scholarly accounts of this image.

Chimenti did the painting before, rather than after, the event: it was prominently displayed in the Salone dei Cinquecento in the Palazzo Vecchio during the banquet on the evening of the ceremony, on the south wall (toward the Uffizi) and to the left of the baldachin over the head table at which was seated Maria de' Medici, her immediate family, and the cardinal.[13] To the right was Chimenti's representation (a mirror image, as it were) of the other royal "French" wedding involving the Medici, that of Caterina de' Medici to Prince Henri, Duke of Orléans (later King Henri II) in 1533. To have yet another Medici as Queen of France was indeed a sign of greatness, so Grand Duke Ferdinando and Grand Duchess Christine must have thought.[14]

13 Compare Buonarroti, *Descrizione delle felicissime nozze*, 13. He situates the painting *à man destra* of the baldachin, i.e., on Maria's right-hand side as she faced the hall.

14 As part of the pro-French Medici policy (and for the improving of relations between the Lorraines and the Bourbons), the grand duchess's brother, Henri II of Lorraine, had married King Henri IV's sister, Catherine de Bourbon, on 31 January 1599.

Fig. 1.1: Jacopo Chimenti da Empoli, *The Wedding of Maria de' Medici and Henri IV of France* (1600). Florence, Galleria degli Uffizi (Inv. 1890/10304). By permission of the Ministero per i beni e le attività culturali e per il turismo della Repubblica Italiana/ Gallerie degli Uffizi.

For that earlier wedding, Chimenti had to draw on his imagination, but in his invoice for the two paintings submitted on 30 September 1600 (the week before the festivities), he made it clear that in the case of the current one he was representing those involved as they would indeed appear in the ceremony itself.[15] Buonarroti likewise wrote that the painting represented the ceremony

[15] *GM* 1152 (*Affari diversi* of the Guardaroba, 1575–1739), fol. 449: *Una Storia dello sposalizio dela regina quando il serenissimo Gran Duca in nome del Re li dà l'anello presente il Cardinale Aldobrandino figure intere di b. 3½ ritratte a natural coli altri ritratti appresso ci[o]è Il Gran Principe, Madama[,] la Duchessa di Mantova e la di* [sic] *Bracciano. Il signor Don Giovanni, il signor Don Virginio e Don Antonio con li abiti ritratti et osservati li proprii che in tal cirimonia avevo da servire.* Chimenti charged *sc.*200 for the two paintings and was paid *sc.*110. This

officiated by Cardinal Aldobrandini "in the presence of those princes who had found themselves there that day."[16] The one person that Chimenti could not paint from life, as it were, was the cardinal himself.

Chimenti listed in his invoice almost all the other persons shown, if not quite in the order they appear. Those he names, save Cardinal Aldobrandini, were Maria's close family members, with women on the left and men on the right (Chimenti switched their positions in his "mirror" representation of the 1533 wedding). The viewer looking leftward from Maria de' Medici sees, in order, the Duchess of Bracciano (Flavia Peretti-Orsini, peeping from behind Maria), Grand Duchess Christine, Prince Cosimo de' Medici (he was ten years old), and the Duchess of Mantua (Eleonora de' Medici, Maria's elder sister). In the rear, between Maria de' Medici and Cardinal Aldobrandini, is what seems to be a young nun, perhaps Passitea Crogi (from Siena), who acted as a spiritual adviser to the Medici women and, so it is sometimes reported, had prophesied Maria's wedding to the King of France.[17] Looking rightward, the sequence is Don Antonio de' Medici (Maria's stepbrother, between the cardinal and the grand duke), Don Giovanni de' Medici (her uncle), and the Duke of Bracciano (Virginio Orsini, her cousin).[18] The apparent prominence given to Virginio Orsini (on the far right) might seem strange, but of the three noblemen shown in this portion of the painting he was the only legitimate son of a Medici: he was Ferdinando I's nephew by way of the grand duke's sister, the ill-fated Isabella, who was murdered (most assume) by her husband, Paolo

document is also transcribed in De Luca, *Le nozze di Maria de' Medici con Enrico IV*, 29, but *Madama la Duchessa di Mantova* is misconstrued as a reference to one person rather than two, prompting surprise at the "omission" of the grand duchess from the list. A prior sketch by Chimenti for the painting (De Luca, ibid., 19) had other figures, including, perhaps, French representatives. His representation of the wedding of Maria became the model for several subsequent ones, including a later version by Chimenti himself (*c.* 1627) in which the Duchess of Bracciano appears more clearly (ibid., 29).

16 Buonarroti, *Descrizione delle felicissime nozze*, 17: *alla presenza di quei principi i quali il giorno vi si erano ritrovati*. However, they stood in somewhat different positions during the actual ceremony, according to Buonarroti's account in ibid., 5–6.

17 De Luca (*Le nozze di Maria de' Medici con Enrico IV*, 21) does not identify the figure but refers to a sketch by Chimenti of an unidentified older nun (perhaps Maria Salviati). Another nun associated with Maria was Francesca Baglioni-Orsini (1538–1626), her governess from 1587 to 1596 (and who professed in 1593 after she was widowed), but her age does not match. For Passitea Crogi (1564–1615), see Formichetti, "Crogi, Passitea," and Tabacchi, *Maria de' Medici*, 25–26, 31–32.

18 For the most part, we follow the identifications in De Luca, *Le nozze di Maria de' Medici con Enrico IV*, 29, 33, based on secure evidence from other portraits. Others have wrongly presumed the male figure on the far right (Virginio Orsini) to be Don Antonio, and the one between the cardinal and the grand duke (Don Antonio) to be Don Giovanni.

Giordano Orsini, Duke of Bracciano.[19] Chimenti's "family" group – plus Eleonora de' Medici's husband, Duke Vincenzo Gonzaga of Mantua – acted as a cohesive unit throughout the wedding festivities, standing close by Maria during the ceremony in the Duomo, taking key positions in the banquet, and lunching together privately in the Sala delle Statue (or its antechamber) in the Palazzo Pitti on Sunday 8 October prior to the entertainment in the gardens of the Palazzo Riccardi in Via Gualfonda.[20]

The typical need to present a unified front at the wedding also helped counter the fact that the negotiations leading up to it had been both long and difficult. Maria de' Medici was born to Grand Duke Francesco and Johanna of Austria on 26 April 1575 and was now moving beyond the typical age for a dynastic wedding:[21] her sister Eleonora (born in 1567) was seventeen when she married Prince Vincenzo Gonzaga on 29 April 1584. Indeed, the first steps toward Maria's union appear to have been taken when she herself was seventeen, as part of Cardinal Piero Gondi's efforts to have Henri IV return to Catholicism; Gondi (the archbishop of Paris) traveled to Italy in 1592 to explore the possibilities with the Pope, stopping in Florence to arrange an incentive to aid the French king's finances by way of the first of several large loans from Grand Duke Ferdinando I (made between 1592 and 1596, and repayable with interest) negotiated via the cardinal's cousin, the Florentine banker Girolamo Gondi. This sowed the seeds of a further alliance, even though Henri was currently married to (if long estranged from) Marguerite de Valois, the daughter of Henri II of France and Caterina de' Medici. Grand Duchess Christine also had her own family reasons for taking an active interest in favoring Henri IV as a means of ending the religious wars in France and neutralizing the increasing influence of the Duke of Savoy and his Spanish allies, a strategy brought

[19] The other "legitimate" Medici son, Grand Duke Ferdinando's younger brother, Don Pietro (1554–1604), was currently in Spain, and out of favor because of his ongoing dispute with Ferdinando over his rightful inheritance from Grand Duke Cosimo I. Also absent from the festivities was Maria's aunt, Virginia, Duchess of Modena.

[20] Buonarroti, *Descrizione delle felicissime nozze*, 5–6 (wedding ceremony), 14 (seating, etc. at the banquet). For 8 October, see the records of Giovanni del Maestro, the *maestro di casa*, in ASF, Carte Strozziane I, 27, fol. 42: *Il dì 8 in domenica desinorno tutti insieme nel salotto delle statue e tutti da un un lato, la Regina in mezo, alla sua man dritta la Duchessa di Mantova, la Gran Duchessa, la Duchessa di Bracciano, da mano sinistra il cardinale legato Aldobrandino, il Duca di Mantova, il Granduca, il Duca di Bracciano, il signor Don Giovanni Medici e il signor Don Antonio Medici.*

[21] For Maria de' Medici's birth (and baptism the following day), see Florence, Archivio dell'Opera del Duomo, Battesimi femmine, Registro 235, fol. 71v (http://archivio.operaduomo.fi.it/battesimi/visualizza_carta.asp?id=235&p=135&ricdir=a&Submit=Visualizza); compare Dubost, *Marie de Médicis*, 48–49; Tabacchi, *Maria de' Medici*, 19. For the persistent error that she was born on 26 April 1573, see Assonitis, "The Birth of Maria de' Medici."

to a head in the successful Florentine efforts to seize the Château d'If (off the coast of Marseilles) for Henri, in which Don Giovanni de' Medici played a leading role. The king (re)converted to Catholicism in 1595, and his marriage to Marguerite de Valois was officially annulled in December 1599 following an agreement reached with her after the death of the king's longtime mistress, Gabrielle d'Estrées, the previous April. Instrumental in that annulment were the pro-Florentine Cardinals del Monte and Montalto (the latter the brother of Flavia Peretti-Orsini, Duchess of Bracciano), bringing yet more Medici supporters into the fray. Meanwhile, for as long as Maria de' Medici remained a pawn in this game of political chess, the grand duke resisted offers for her hand from Archduke Mattias of Austria and even from Emperor Rudolph II, as well as another that he considered derisory from Theodore, Duke of Braganza.[22]

The grand duke and grand duchess clearly had broader political goals in mind by pursuing stronger relationships with France, not least as a counter-balance to Spanish influence on the Italian peninsula. But some significant pressure may also have come from Florentine patricians on more economic grounds, given that the French Wars of Religion, coupled with the death of Caterina de' Medici in 1589, threatened their access to the lucrative financial and commercial markets there: the Gondi family's extensive interests in Lyons were just one of many cases in point.[23] This is probably the reason why Jacopo Corsi, himself a prominent businessman, intervened personally with the grand duke on behalf of his fellow citizens to halt the arguments over the amount of Maria's dowry and to offer their own financial support for it.[24] Henri asked for *sc.*1,000,000 whereas the grand duke was prepared to offer only *sc.*600,000. The negotiations were conducted by the Florentine ambassador to France, Baccio Giovannini (the grand duke feared that Girolamo Gondi was too partial to the French king), and in the end the Florentines paid only *sc.*350,000 in coin, with the remaining *sc.*250,000 deemed as credit for expenses incurred over Château d'If (*sc.*200,000) plus the unpaid remainder of a loan made to the French crown by Grand Duke Cosimo I. That coin was delivered on Maria's arrival in Marseilles on 13 November 1600 by Bardo Corsi, Jacopo's brother.[25]

22 Tabacchi, *Maria de' Medici*, 37.

23 Milstein, *The Gondi*, 58–65; compare Orlando, *Le Grand Parti*, and Tognetti, *I Gondi di Lione*.

24 So the eighteenth-century historian of the Medici, Riguccio Galluzzi, recounted, as cited in Malanima, "Corsi, Iacopo": *informato delle pendenti contestazioni sulla quantità della dote, ebbe il coraggio di supplicare il Gran Duca a nome dei suoi concittadini di desistere dalle opposizioni e offerire le ricchezze di ciascheduno per contribuire alla dote richiesta.*

25 Giovannini's dispatches concerning the negotiations (including his criticisms of Gondi) survive in *MdP* 4615, fols. 5–283 (from 24 November 1599 to 24 April 1600). For the distribution of the

It seems clear that Ottavio Rinuccini was no less motivated by self-interest in securing his involvement in the wedding celebrations. Scholars have tended to associated it with an attempt to gain a position at the French court (Henri IV later named Rinuccini a *gentilhomme du roi*), although the poet had more pressing financial concerns in mind: in 1555, the Rinuccini bank had lent some *sc.*120,000 to Henri II (Caterina de' Medici's husband) – as part of a much larger loan negotiated with a consortium of European bankers – but the capital and much of the interest was never repaid and had more or less been written off. Ottavio Rinuccini made several trips to France between 1600 and 1605 (staying at Girolamo Gondi's residence in Paris) and eventually managed to negotiate restitution to the tune of *sc.*53,000, which was considered more than satisfactory given the general difficulties faced by Florentines when dealing with French debtors.[26]

The marriage negotiations still dragged on. Henri IV's agreement to have Nicolas Brûlart de Sillery, his counselor of state and the French ambassador to Rome, conclude the marriage contract was sealed in Paris on 6 January 1600, but he only arrived in Florence in April, and in the meantime the French and Florentines were still arguing over the amount of the dowry.[27] The contract was signed in the presence of the grand duke, Virginio Orsini, Belisario Vinta (the grand duke's *primo segretario*), and the archbishop of Pisa, Carlo Antonio Dal Pozzo, in the Palazzo Pitti on 25 April, the day before Maria's twenty-fifth birthday. It was announced officially on 30 April, the eleventh anniversary of Grand Duchess Christine's entrance into Florence: the grand duke met with the Florentine senate and leading patricians in his rooms in the Pitti, while cannon fire and bells sounded through the city. Events that day also included a procession to the church of SS. Annunziata to render thanks before the image of the Blessed Virgin, returning via the Corso toward S. Trinita and stopping at the residence of Jacopo Corsi, where "many gentlemen" engaged in tilting at the

*sc.*600,000 between coin and credits, see Belisario Vinta to Alessandro Beccheria (in Milan), Florence, 23 May 1600, in *MdP* 3135, fol. 734. Bardo Corsi was named the grand duke's *tesoriero maggiore* for the transaction; ASF, Guicciardini–Corsi–Salviati (Versamento 1992), 1218, ins. 2 (the patent granting the title given to him in Livorno on 16 October 1600). For the transaction itself, see ASF, Carte Strozziane I, 27 (the *memorie* of Giovanni del Maestro), fol. 56; Carter, "Music and Patronage in Late Sixteenth-Century Florence," 66 (and n. 44).

26 "Relazione di Ottavio di Francesco Rinuccini," in Aiazzi, *Ricordi storici di Filippo di Cino Rinuccini dal 1282 al 1460*, 266–69. Here Rinuccini claims that the sum owed was *sc.*95,000, but his uncle, Tommaso, said in 1564 that it was *sc.*120,000; see Orlando, *Le Grand Parti*, 26–33. Rinuccini also notes the presence in Paris of Don Garzía Montalvo (who was involved in the performance of *Euridice*).

27 Various of these official documents associated with the wedding are in *MM* 18, ins. 5.

ring.[28] There was also a banquet in the Sala delle Statue for the grand duke and grand duchess, Don Giovanni and Don Antonio de' Medici, and the Duke and Duchess of Bracciano, where Maria was granted ceremonial recognition according to her new status as a queen.[29]

That same day (30 April), the grand duke wrote to Eleonora de' Medici, Duchess of Mantua, that his intention was to hold the Florentine festivities, and hence Maria's departure for France, before the season was too hot and bothersome (*stagione troppo calda e noiosa*) – that is, before the summer – and on 10 May the grand duke appointed five *deputati* to oversee the planning in terms of providing lodgings, servants, and stables for the most important visitors and their retinues: the *deputati* were required to meet daily, and to submit regular reports.[30] However, Baccio Giovannini's voluminous correspondence reveals that the grand duke's intentions were misplaced. Between the end of April and mid-May, Giovannini wrote repeatedly to convey Henri IV's different plans in mind: a spring wedding was not possible given the king's efforts to resolve his conflict with Carlo Emanuele I, Duke of Savoy, over the Marquisate of Saluzzo (eventually decided in the duke's favor by the Peace of Lyons in 1601); Grand Duchess Christine was pregnant (with Maria Maddalena, born in late June); Maria could not travel in the hot summer months, and therefore she could not arrive in Marseilles before September, which Henri then started pushing back to October. It also becomes clear that Henri considered the Florentine announcement of Maria's elevation premature on the somewhat dubious grounds that he might die in battle or by some other means in the interim, at which point she could not become Queen of France.[31] The grand duke may have won the battle over the dowry, but the king had the upper hand over the schedule. News of these delays was withheld in Florence until 22

28 ASF, Carte Strozziane I, 27 (the *memorie* of Giovanni del Maestro), fol. 19: *se ne tornorno per il Corso verso Santa Trinita e sbarcorno in casa del signor Jacopo Corsi. Et il Granduca dirimpetto a cavallo, e quivi si corsono le lancie con la niza al anello da molti signori gentilhomini.*

29 Buonarroti, *Descrizione delle felicissime nozze*, 6; ASF, Carte Strozziane I, 27, fol. 14.

30 Ferdinando's letter to Eleonora is in ASF, Capponi 313, fol. 247. For the appointment of the *deputati*, see ASF, Carte Strozziane I, 27, fol. 11v. They were *cavaliere* Raffaello de' Medici, Giulio de' Nobili, Ridolfo Altoviti, Donato dell'Antella, and Vincenzo Medici (*depositario generale*).

31 Giovannini's letter of 24 April 1600 conveys the information about Saluzzo and Henri's understanding that as for Maria's arrival, *che non sia per seguir prima che al settembre et per rispetti della stagione calda et per rispetto ancora della gravidanza di Madama*; *MdP* 4165, fol. 282. Subsequent letters (3, 12, 19 May, in ibid., fols. 284–310) reveal Henri's displeasure at the marriage announcement, and the shift of schedule from September to October. For additional information on this stage of the marriage negotiations and the reports on them made by various ambassadors, see Cormier, "Marie de Médicis vue par les observateurs italiens," 44–94.

May, however, and even then it was suggested that the wedding would likely take place in August, given that the king could not meet Maria in Marseilles before the end of that month: in fact, he never did (the king received her in Lyons in early December).[32] Even in September, the exact date of the Florentine festivities remained unclear, this time because Cardinal Pietro Aldobrandini was delaying his departure from Rome.[33]

Those involved in planning the 1600 wedding entertainments may have been glad of the delay: *Euridice* was probably well in hand by April 1600 and may even have had some kind of performance in the Palazzo Pitti in late May, although some significant questions remain over that (we shall see). Plans for the principal entertainment for the celebrations to be given in the Teatro degli Uffizi appear to have changed. Bernardo Buontalenti designed a set of six *intermedi* for which he built a model of the stage: the sets included a cityscape, an amphitheatre, the burning of Troy, a maritime scene, a garden (for the wedding of Hercules, presumably to Hebe), and as the last *intermedio*, an eagle giving birth to the Virtues.[34] There is no indication of which play was intended to be performed with these *intermedi*,[35] though as we have seen, the format would have fit the typical

[32] According to Giovanni del Maestro (writing on 22 May 1600), *Questo dì si è saputo per Valerio corriere che hiersera arrivò di Francia come il Re Christianissimo non può per degni respetti essere a Marsilia per ricevere la sposa prima che verso la fine d'agosto prossimo a venire*; ASF, Carte Strozziane I, 27, fol. 26. Belisario Vinta noted to Alessandro Beccheria (in Milan) on 9 June 1600 that the wedding celebrations were being postponed until September; *MdP* 3135, fol. 744v.

[33] See the various reports in *MdP* 899, fols. 231, 290, 359.

[34] *GM* 245 (*Filza di conti*, 1599–1609), ins. 4 includes an inventory dated 28 May 1608 of items held by Bernardo Buontalenti that needed to be returned to the Guardaroba and other official bodies; the model is detailed on fol. 436r–v. The document, or collection of documents, in this *inserto* (fols. 425–55) is extremely difficult to read. It seems to have derived from the need for Buontalenti's daughter, Eufemia, to close out her father's accounts just before he died (on 6 June 1608); an equivalent list of items delivered to the Fortezza da Basso is in ASF, Magistrato de' Nove Conservatori del Dominio e della Giurisdizione Fiorentina 3680 (*Quadernaccio . . . per diverse occorrenze per servizio del Castello di Firenze*, beginning in 1598), fol. 58. Eufemia's petition to have these transfers acknowledged is in *SS* 37 (*Atti degli Offitiali di Monte e Soprassindaci*, 1606–9), no. 71 (approved on 5 June 1608). The last *intermedio* described here seems to be the basis for the sketch by Buontalenti in GDSU, 7059 F, that has sometimes been associated with the first *intermedio* for Giovanni de' Bardi's *L'amico fido* (staged for the wedding of Virginia de' Medici and Cesare d'Este in 1586) but more recently with *Il rapimento di Cefalo*; see Garbero Zorzi and Sperenzi (eds.), *Teatro e spettacolo nella Firenze dei Medici*, 188–89. However, the latter association now seems erroneous: while Act V of *Il rapimento* includes the appearance of Giove (Jupiter) on an eagle flying through the air (see Carter, "Rediscovering *Il rapimento di Cefalo*," appendix), Buontalenti's sketch does not match the action here (in contrast to the sketch now in London, Victoria and Albert Museum, E1187/1931, which was previously associated with the second of the 1589 *intermedi* but which more probably relates to the prologue for *Il rapimento* given the presence of Pegasus).

[35] Although a comment made by Cavalieri suggests that it may have been by Guarini; Carter, "Rediscovering *Il rapimento di Cefalo*," para. 2.6.

pattern of Medici wedding entertainments. However, Don Giovanni de' Medici seems to have intervened to force a change to a quite different type of work: Gabriello Chiabrera's *Il rapimento di Cefalo* was not a set of *intermedi* (despite persistent scholarly attempts to read it as such) but, rather, an opera sung to music throughout. Don Giovanni had tussled with Buontalenti in other contexts, too, and he would continue to do so (for example, over the construction of the Cappella dei Principi in S. Lorenzo), although in the case of *Il rapimento*, he eventually forced Michelangelo Buonarroti *il giovane* to remove any reference to himself in connection with the work.[36]

The order to prepare *Il rapimento di Cefalo* appears to have been given only in early July 1600, which meant working to a very tight schedule, even for Florentine artists and artisans accustomed to the format of such festivities.[37] In the case of Girolamo Bargagli's *La pellegrina* and its spectacular *intermedi* staged on 2 May 1589 for the marriage of Grand Duke Ferdinando I and Christine of Lorraine, the detailed notes left by Girolamo Seriacopi (*provveditore delle fortezze*) on the construction of the sets date back eight months, to 31 August 1588.[38] Emilio de' Cavalieri and Giovanni de' Bardi, who had been directly involved in the 1589 festivities but were marginalized in 1600 (Bardi had moved to Rome in 1592) under pressure from younger figures now close to Grand Duke Ferdinando, certainly felt that the 1600 entertainments did not reach their level. In several letters written from Rome in November 1600, a somewhat embittered Cavalieri wrote that the banquet and its decorations were held in high regard: he was biased, given that he had provided the music for the entertainment staged within it, a dialogue between Giunone (Juno) and Minerva, to a text by Battista Guarini. But in the case of *Il rapimento di Cefalo*, he said, few felt that the scenery, machines, and music had made any great effect, and as for *Euridice*, the music had not given satisfaction – though other reports say that it did – and the scenery was "unfinished" (*per non esser terminate*).[39]

[36] Carter, "Rediscovering *Il rapimento di Cefalo*," para. 4.5.

[37] On 13 July 1600, Giovanbattista Cresci requested additional funds given that on the order of the grand duke *si fece dar' principio di lavorar' alla Commedia da farsi nel' salone nuovo del consiglio sopra gli uffizzij*; *SFF* 122 (*Memoriale e ricordanze*, 1598–1604), fol. 65. There are some references in *GM* 1152 from late June that might relate to a production in the Teatro degli Uffizi, but they are unclear.

[38] Testaverde, *L'officina delle nuvole*.

[39] See, for example, Emilio de' Cavalieri's angry letter from Rome, probably sent to Marcello Accolti, in *MdP* 899, fols. 416–17 (extracts in *KirkCM*, 140–41); it is dated 7 October 1600, though this is generally assumed to be a mistake for 7 November on the basis of internal evidence (summarized in Palisca, "Musical Asides in the Diplomatic Correspondence of Emilio de' Cavalieri," 402 n. 53). Among the comments he reports is the claim that *la musica della*

Likewise, Giovanni de' Bardi complained to Cavalieri about the "tragic texts and objectionable subjects" of the 1600 entertainments, and when he was later given the task of arranging the festivities for the marriage of Prince Cosimo de' Medici and Maria Magdalena of Austria in 1608, he reverted to the typical model of a comedy with *intermedi*, and he insisted on the need for adequate rehearsal specifically to avoid things turning out as they had done eight years before.[40] Cavalieri's public response to those negative reports, he said, was to blame the shortage of time. But both he and Bardi clearly felt they would have done better.

The 1600 Festivities

Princely wedding festivities necessarily had certain fixed elements embracing both the sacred and the secular; they also tended to combine "public" events for the general populace with those for a more restricted audience (including distinguished guests) as well as "private" ones for closer family members. But even the family was on public display – Jacopo Chimenti's painting of the wedding makes the point clear – and those entertainments to which the public did not have access were later published, as it were, by way of printed descriptions, librettos, musical scores, and other such sources.[41] Michelangelo Buonarroti *il giovane*'s official *Descrizione delle felicissime nozze . . . della Cristianissima Maestà di Madama Maria Medici, Regina di Francia e di Navarra* appeared some six weeks after the festivities (the dedication to Maria de' Medici is dated 20 November 1600), and only after it had been carefully vetted by court officials and revised accordingly.[42] But it provides a day-by-day account of the celebrations up to Maria de' Medici's

comedia fatta da me che non ha data sodisfatione, come ancho per non esser terminate le prospettive et altre cose; in questo ho risposto che la brevità del tempo lo ha portato. Most scholars agree that this refers to *Euridice* (for which Cavalieri claims ownership), although Kirkendale suggests *Il rapimento di Cefalo.*

40 For Bardi's comment on the 1600 festivities (complaining about *parole tragiche* and *soggetti da potervi opporre*), see Palisca, "Musical Asides in the Diplomatic Correspondence of Emilio de' Cavalieri," 404. His letter to Curzio Picchena, Florence, 31 July 1608, in *MdP* 6068, fol. 386, is given in Carter, "A Florentine Wedding of 1608," 92: *Mi occorre ancora dire che io non posso cominciare à provar le musiche in sul palco, per che vi sono huomini al lagoro nella sala e le macchine sono imperfette et convien provar assai, che non vuole che riesca come alle nozze della Regina.*

41 We use the term "libretto" (meaning a dramatic text intended for music) out of convenience, if remaining aware of its anachronism; see the remarks in Bianconi, "Il libretto d'opera." The same is true of the term "opera."

42 Carter, "*Non occorre nominare tanti musici.*"

embarkation from Livorno (by ship to Marseilles), plus a list of the patricians who played a role in the ceremonies, and the text of the *Dialogo di Giunone e Minerva* performed at the banquet.

Buonarroti begins his account of the festivities themselves with the entry into the city on 4 October (a Wednesday) of Cardinal Pietro Aldobrandini, who conducted the wedding ceremony in the Duomo the next day, then the ceremonial baptisms of Grand Duke Ferdinando and Christine of Lorraine's most recently born sons, Filippo and Lorenzo.[43] That evening there was a banquet in the Salone dei Cinquecento in the Palazzo Vecchio, rich with additional decorations for the occasion. The banquet was preceded by dancing, and also included at its end the dialogue of Giunone and Minerva, who emerged on ceremonial chariots from grottoes built into the room.[44] On the evening of Friday 6 October, Jacopo Corsi's offering for the festivities, *Euridice*, was staged in the Palazzo Pitti; the next day saw a *palio* run through the streets of Florence (and in the evening, an open rehearsal of *Il rapimento di Cefalo*);[45] and on Sunday 8 October, the court paid a visit to the famous gardens in the Palazzo Riccardi (in Via Gualfonda) for another entertainment arranged by a prominent patrician.[46] On Monday

[43] For the baptisms, *SolMBD*, 24, is wrong to say that they concerned Lorenzo (born on 1 August 1599) and Maria Maddalena (late June 1600); Buonarroti's description is clear that it was Lorenzo and Filippo (born on 9 April 1598). Filippo and Lorenzo had already been baptized privately (*in casa*); Florence, Archivio dell'Opera del Duomo, Battesimi maschi, Registro 23, fols. 25v (Filippo, http://archivio.operaduomo.fi.it/battesimi/visualizza_carta.asp?id=23&p=41&ricdir=a&Submit=Visualizza), 53v (Lorenzo, http://archivio.operaduomo.fi.it/battesimi/visualizza_carta.asp?id=23&p=93&ricdir=a&Submit=Visualizza). The same was probably true of Maria Maddalena. It was not at all uncommon for members of the Medici family to hold a ceremonial baptism quite some time after the birth of a child, although the actual baptism always needed to be held immediately for fear of neonatal death.

[44] For the banquet, see Giusti and Spinelli (eds.), *Dolci trionfi e finissime piegature*. Pierre Victor Cayet 's account in *Chronologie septénaire de l'histoire de la paix entre les roys de France et d'Espagne* (Paris: Jean Richer, 1605), based on second-hand reports, says (fol. 179v) that two large clouds arose, one containing a young Florentine girl representing Diana (*sic*, confusing the *festa* in the Riccardi gardens?) and the other, a castrato. The two sang most pleasingly one after the other (*Voicy que d'en haut des deux costez de la sale deux nuées s'esleverent: sur l'une d'elles estoit une fille Florentine, faisant le personnage de Diane, sur l'autre estoit assis un Eunuque, lesquels tous deux, l'un apres l'autre par respons remplissoient la sale d'un doux chant de Musique et d'airs poussez avec un plaisir admirable*).

[45] For the open rehearsal, see *SolMBD*, 26–27 n. 2. According to the Modenese ambassador, this could be attended *per una parte di quelli che desiderano udirla, et un'altro giorno si farà per i principi.*

[46] The texts were by Riccardo Riccardi (1558–1612), Lorenzo Franceschi, and Adamo Bertozzi (even though some sources suggest Gabriello Chiabrera); they were printed as *Rime cantate nel giardino del Signor Riccardo Riccardi con l'occasione d'una festa fatta quivi per la reina* (Florence: Domenico Manzani, 1600), given in *SolMBD*, 239–59. The music (now lost) was by Piero di Matteo Strozzi.

9 October, the court visited the Uffizi Gallery and watched an acrobat walk a tightrope across the Piazza della Signoria from the tower of the Palazzo Vecchio to the statue of Grand Duke Cosimo I.[47] Then at sunset (*le 24 hore*) began the performance in the Teatro degli Uffizi of Gabriello Chiabrera's *Il rapimento di Cefalo*, with music in the main by Giulio Caccini, although some polyphonic choruses were provided by other of the city's musicians, including Stefano Venturi del Nibbio, Piero di Matteo Strozzi, and the *maestro di cappella* of the Duomo and S. Giovanni Battista, Luca Bati.[48]

Buonarroti inevitably devoted most space in his description to the banquet (some ten pages) and *Il rapimento di Cefalo* (nineteen), whereas the entertainments provided by Florentine patricians were given far less (just over one page in the case of *Euridice*). In terms of the banquet, the Salone dei Cinquecento was the principal civic space for such celebrations, while the Teatro degli Uffizi was the typical location for grand theatrical entertainments for Medici celebrations: designed by Bernardo Buontalenti, it was inaugurated in February 1586 with the performance of Giovanni de' Bardi's comedy *L'amico fido* and its spectacular *intermedi* during the festivities for the wedding of Virginia de' Medici and Cesare d'Este, and it was remodeled for *La pellegrina* and its *intermedi* in 1589. Otherwise, however, the theatre was used very infrequently: for more routine entertainments (for example, during Carnival), the Medici tended to prefer more intimate, private spaces, whether in the Palazzo Pitti or, by the early seventeenth century, in the accommodations elsewhere in the city allocated to Medici princes, including the Palazzo del Parione, occupied by Don Giovanni de' Medici, and the Casino di San Marco, the official residence of Don Antonio de' Medici from 1598.[49] This was a matter of function on the one hand, and decorum on the other: the Medici grand dukes were careful to separate the "private" and "public" aspects of their ceremonial lives. It also raises broader, and important, questions about how the Medici configured and used different indoor and outdoor locations available to them for courtly and related functions, as well as matters of financing such pastimes from public or private funds.

[47] *SolMBD*, 26. Buonarroti does not mention this in his description.

[48] The libretto and associated documents are given in Solerti, *Gli albori del melodramma*, 3: 9–58; the music is mostly lost save for some extracts included in Giulio Caccini's *Le nuove musiche* (Florence: I Marescotti, 1601 [= 1602]).

[49] Relatively little is known about theatrical spaces (and performances therein) in the residences of Don Giovanni (who had a significant interest in the *commedia dell'arte*) and Don Antonio. For the former, see Landolfi, "Su un teatrino mediceo e sull'Accademia degli Incostanti a Firenze nel primo Seicento."

Some tricky matters of protocol ensued. It was by no means unusual for Florentine patricians to contribute to Medici celebrations, whether individually or as part of a group such as the Accademia degli Alterati: indeed, it was a smart tactic enabling them to secure, and to demonstrate, grand-ducal favor. Some of them (including Jacopo Corsi) paid a share of the costs of the *sbarra* held in the courtyard of the Palazzo Pitti on 11 May 1589, during the festivities for the wedding of Ferdinando I and Christine of Lorraine, and the practice continued on less formal occasions during the 1590s.[50] Both *Euridice* and the *festa* held in the gardens of the Palazzo Riccardi during the 1600 festivities were par for the course. However, a counter-example reveals some of the issues. The Accademia degli Spensierati (associated at other times with theatrical activity in Florence) wished to stage an entertainment for the wedding, and one of its members, Francesco Vinta (a nephew of Belisario Vinta, the grand duke's powerful *primo segretario*), pursued plans to mount a performance of the *tragicommedia, L'amicizia costante*, by Vincenzo Panciatichi (a *cavaliere di S. Stefano*). The play was printed by Filippo Giunti with a title page saying that it was dedicated to Maria de' Medici on the occasion of her wedding to Henri IV, although there is no actual dedication in the print (see *CW*Fig. 1.8): the license for the printing is dated 26 April 1600.[51] In August 1600, however, Vinta was still searching for a location for a possible performance, and was distinctly unhappy with the offer of the Teatro della Dogana, the "public" theatre in Florence used by the *comici dell'arte*, because the academy considered it undignified.[52] In November 1600, the Giunti press printed a new first signature (A) of Panciatichi's play that replaced the one in the first state of the edition: it had a different title page, this time stating

[50] Carter, "Music and Patronage in Late Sixteenth-Century Florence," 75–76.

[51] Ottavio Rinuccini also used the Giunti press (in this case, Cosimo Giunti) for his edition of the libretto of *Euridice* (although the 1600 edition of *Dafne* was printed by Giorgio Marescotti). It may be significant that in the case of the texts for the 1600 festivities, only Buonarroti's *Descrizione* and Chiabrera's *Il rapimento di Cefalo* were issued by Marescotti, who by then regarded himself as the chief printer for the Medici, although he was never granted any such title; compare Carter, "Music-Printing in Late Sixteenth- and Early Seventeenth-Century Florence," 42–44, 51–52.

[52] For *L'amicizia costante*, see Riccò, *Dalla zampogna all'aurea cetra*, 138 n. 7, 156–68 (which does not recognize the two states of the edition); Giazzon, "Vincenzo Panciatichi da *L'amicizia costante* (1600) a *Gli amorosi affanni* (1605)." Panciatichi published a reworked version of the play as *Gli amorosi affanni* in early 1606. On 31 August 1600, Grand Duke Ferdinando notified Donato dell'Antella of the intention to perform the play *dove habbin recitato istrioni mercenarii* (*MdP* 295, fol. 36), but Francesco Vinta had already complained about the Teatro della Dogana (*facendo eglino scrupolosa difficoltà di recitare in quella stanza, dove dalli publici comici mercenari si recita ogn'anno*); see his letter to Belisario Vinta, 30 August 1600, in *MdP* 898, fol. 493.

that the play was indeed staged during the wedding festivities, plus a dedication from Panciatichi to Vinta (dated 4 November) noting that it was performed in the presence of Maria de' Medici and of other principal guests foreign and domestic (see *CW*Fig. 1.9).[53] However, there is no mention of any such performance in Buonarroti's description of the festivities, nor in any other court record to be found.[54]

The surprising thing about *Euridice*, then, is not so much that Jacopo Corsi was allowed to present it as part of the festivities, but that he could do so within, rather than outside, the Palazzo Pitti. Clearly Corsi had more clout with the Medici (or at least, with the grand duchess and Don Giovanni) than Francesco Vinta, whether because of his contribution to the marriage negotiations or given his previous track record of providing entertainments within the palace (including, of course, his *Dafne* during Carnival 1598/99). Buonarroti tried to keep the record straight, however, in his account of *Euridice*, wording matters quite punctiliously: Jacopo Corsi had it set to music with great learning (*con grande studio*); very rich and beautiful costumes were prepared; the work was offered to, and accepted by, the grand duke and grand duchess; and a noble stage was constructed in the Pitti.[55] Even so, the seemingly unusual circumstances created confusion among court officials who one might expect (perhaps wrongly) to have known better. For example, Cesare Tinghi, the grand duke's *aiutante di*

[53] The dedication to Francesco Vinta also says that the play was staged at his great expense and effort by young noblemen of the city, and with *intermedi* devised by Vinta and staged by Jacopo Pagnini (*havendola voi con tanta spesa, e fatica vostra in queste Serenissime Nozze fatta recitare alla Presenza di Sua Maestà Christianissima, et di tutti gl'altri Principi, e Principesse cosi di Italia come di Francia che in Fiorenza si ritrovavano, e procurato che con l'industria, ingegno, e diligenza di messer Iacopo Pagnini giovane in queste et in altre simili cose esercitatissimo la fosse arricchita d'Intermedij da voi industriosamente inventati*). For Pagnini and a comedy performed in the Casino di S. Marco on 16 May 1602, see *SolMBD*, 28.

[54] Palisca, "The First Performance of *Euridice*," 437 n. 28, notes a French report of the festivities saying that on the Sunday there would be a "superb comedy" and on the Monday, a pastoral (*une Pastorelle*) costing more than *sc.*60,000. Palisca identifies the former as *L'amicizia costante*, but it seems more likely that the visitor was confused in terms both of the dates (so the *Pastorelle* was the entertainment in the Riccardi gardens) and of which entertainment cost what we shall see is in any case an impossible figure. According to the diarist Pierre de L'Estoile (Palisca's source), this report was written on 7 October (Saturday) – although it refers to the wedding ceremony and banquet "yesterday" – and he had received a copy from a "friend." But for the Sunday evening following the Riccardi entertainment, Giovanni del Maestro says that the Medici spent the time dancing in the Pitti; see *SolMBD*, 26 n. 1. And in general, French reports of the Florentine festivities tended to be somewhat vague; see Deutsch, "Jamais il n'y eut Musique si harmonieuse."

[55] Buonarroti, *Descrizione delle felicissime nozze*, 18: *Là onde avendo il Signor Iacopo Corsi fatta mettere in musica con grande studio la Euridice affettuosa, e gentilissima favola del Signor Ottavio Rinuccini, e per li personaggi, ricchissimi, e belli vestimenti apprestati; offertala a loro Altezze; fu ricevuta, e preparatale nobile scena nel Palazzo de' Pitti . . .*

camera, called *Euridice* "a pastoral comedy in music done by Signor Emilio de' Cavalieri" (*una comedia pastorale in musica fatta dal signor Emilio del Cavaliere*).[56] This was an understandable mistake. Cavalieri was a musician who had been brought to Florence from Rome in 1588 to serve as the superintendent of the grand duke's Galleria dei Lavori (Gallery of Works, covering a range of artistic and similar enterprises), and who had overseen almost all the theatrical entertainments held in the Palazzo Pitti and the Medici villas in the 1590s. He certainly had some indirect involvement in *Euridice*, but nowhere near as much as those working in the grand-ducal administration apparently assumed.

Buonarroti's carefully worded account of the genesis of *Euridice* also reflects how it was funded, so far as we can tell. The common assumption that Corsi's provision of the work for the 1600 festivities meant that he also paid for it is not, in fact, borne out by the sporadic references to it in his own account books, such as they survive. Certainly he was responsible for the music (in the sense of commissioning it), and probably also for the singers and instrumentalists (he was one of the latter), although whether he or anyone else actually paid them any money is another matter.[57] He also seems to have covered at least some costs of the costumes, as would have been typical of any patrician involved in Florentine entertainments: an inventory of Corsi's effects prepared after his early death (on 29 December 1602) includes, among items for entertainments and *mascherate*, costumes for Orpheus and for Pluto, as well as ten for nymphs (and three for Furies, who do not appear in *Euridice* unless they are generic characters of the Underworld).[58] As for the stage constructed in the Pitti, however, this fell

[56] For Cavalieri's own claim of ownership of *Euridice*, see note 39. A similar line to Tinghi, with what may or may not be an important difference, was taken in the compiler of the court's *Diari d'etichetta* (vol. 4, in *GM*), where *Euridice* was a "pastoral . . . set to music by Signor Emilio de' Cavalieri" (*pastorale . . . messa in musica dal signor Emilio de' Cavalieri*); see *SolMBD*, 25; *KirkCM*, 204. However, the *Diari d'etichetta* and other such chronicles were later compilations (from Tinghi and other sources), so such shifts of wording may not be significant, and even Tinghi was sometimes prone to relying on reports rather than first-hand experience; compare Fantappiè, "La celebrazione memorabile," 209–10.

[57] Some kind of *mancia* (in coin or in kind) would have been normal: for example, the singers in the performance of *Euridice* directed by Giulio Caccini in December 1602 were given a large boar, presumably to eat; see Enea Vaini's letter to Grand Duchess Christine, 3 January 1602/3, in *MdP* 5885, fol. 299. But performing in the 1600 festivities may have been deemed enough of an honor not to warrant it, or may have gained favors in ways that would not enter any financial accounts.

[58] Pegazzano, *Committenza e collezionismo nel Cinquecento*, 59 (see also Carter and Goldthwaite, *Orpheus in the Marketplace*, 112 n. 170); the inventory was prepared on 28 June 1603. The largest item (£1,685.15*s*.9*d*.) in Jacopo Corsi's accounts relating to *Euridice* does indeed concern costumes; see Carter, "Music and Patronage in Late Sixteenth-Century Florence," 102–3 n. 111.

to the Medici household, which paid for the scenery and covered other costs associated with the sets.[59]

The Medici's financial accounts for *Euridice*, and for the wedding banquet held in the Palazzo Vecchio, were very carefully kept separate from those for the more public celebrations of the 1600 wedding festivities (*Il rapimento di Cefalo*, the triumphal arches for processions through the streets, and so forth), and the grand duke ordered that they be kept secret (*et non si pubblichi questa spesa*, see Fig. 1.2).[60] In part, one assumes, this was because he did not wish to be accused of extravagance. But it was also a question of the source of the funds supporting these various events, whether from the privy purse (the grand duke's *camera*) or the public treasury.[61] As is typical of the grand-ducal administration – and the funding streams that supported it – affairs of state were one thing, and "private" matters another, even when it came to seemingly official entertainments.

Whether the funding was kept so strictly separate in actuality (that is, in terms of disbursements) is a separate matter; accounting is one thing and the real world another. However, the well-known Florentine obsession with keeping proper account books (which had significant legal status in Tuscan law) brings with it several distinct advantages. The surviving *giornali, libri di entrata ed uscita* and *di debitori e creditori*, and the like that now fill the archives offer an unparalleled view of life at all levels of Florentine society. Many more, of course, are lost, or were destroyed once they had fulfilled their purpose: this is particularly true of low-level accounts and supporting documents intended to be subsumed in higher-level ones. Indeed, the survival of the materials presented in this book seems to be more a matter of chance than design. But they enable a close reconstruction of *Euridice* as it was conceived and performed.

59 Likewise, the Medici made some contribution to the cost of the performance of *Dafne* in the Palazzo Pitti on 21 January 1598/99, including *sc.*33 for a carpenter, tailor, materials, and other expenses; see Carter and Goldthwaite, *Orpheus in the Marketplace*, 111. This is a small amount, but the state of the Guardaroba accounts is not always such that one can clearly identify expenses charged to it (as would be true also for *Euridice* if we did not have the low-level accounts, etc. discussed in this book).

60 *SS* 279 (copies of reports, 1574–1608), fol. 144v. This is a note added to the top-level review of the accounts of the 1600 festivities, completed on 28 February 1601/2.

61 There is a great deal of work still to be done to unpick the various operations of the grand-ducal finances during Medici rule. For some broader issues, albeit at higher accounting levels than pertain here, see Litchfield, *The Emergence of a Bureaucracy*, 99–107; Parigino, *Il tesoro del principe*. There are also some useful remarks in Carter and Goldthwaite, *Orpheus in the Marketplace*, 229–30.

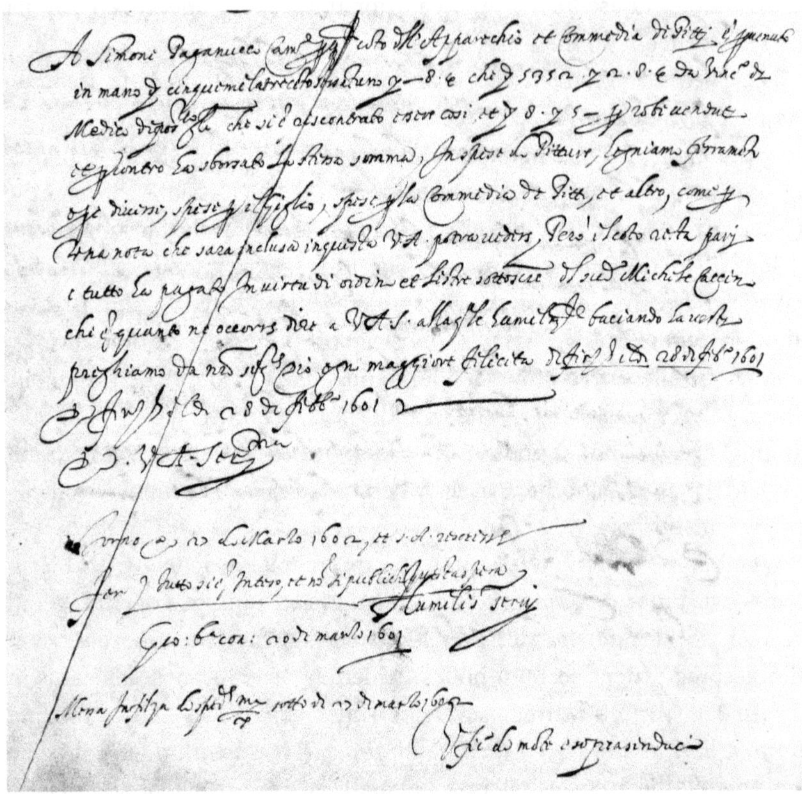

Fig. 1.2: *SS* 279, fol. 144v (bottom half); the review of expenditure on *Euridice* audited by the Ufficio di Monte e Soprassindaci, 28 February 1601/2. The instruction "not to make public" this expense is on the fifth line up from the bottom. By permission of the Ministero per i beni e le attività culturali e per il turismo della Repubblica Italiana/ Archivio di Stato di Firenze.

Two Invoices and an Inventory

Arranging a royal wedding was a massive undertaking, not just in terms of ceremonies and entertainments but also given the need to provide accommodation for the large number of official guests invited to Florence for the occasion. This was a perpetual headache for the five *deputati* appointed on 10 May 1600 to oversee these aspects of the festivities: they also needed to select boys to carry the *baldacchini* in various processions; to find representatives from various Tuscan towns to act as attendants; and eventually to arrange the ten-day holiday declared by the grand duke (on 22 September 1600) so that the populace could give proper signs of devotion, reverence, and joy.[62] Other officials were temporarily appointed to take charge of specific aspects of the festivities. But three others also played leading roles by virtue of their position as permanent heads of particular administrative bodies: Donato dell'Antella, superintendent of the grand-ducal fortresses and buildings (*sopraintendente delle fortezze e fabbriche*); Vincenzo Giugni, keeper of the Guardaroba (he was usually styled the *guardaroba maggiore* or *guardaroba generale*); and Vincenzo Medici, head of the Depositeria Generale (the office in charge of grand-ducal finances). Broadly speaking, dell'Antella's office had charge of all manner of construction and maintenance concerning the grand-ducal buildings, while the Guardaroba (the "wardrobe") was responsible for everything they contained: furniture, utensils, clothing, etc., as well as works of art. Both offices kept detailed accounts from the day-to-day level up – as, of course, did the Depositeria Generale – in addition to making regular inventories of their holdings both for monitoring purposes and as needed for the succession from one head administrator (or grand duke) to another.

Understanding such administrative structures is important given that it enables one to navigate the various archival *fondi* that survive (although some do not) as witness to the operations of these various offices. The strict record-keeping typically required of them in Florence further aids the archival historian, given that particular actions can usually be tracked through the various branches of the system. However, events or actions outside the norm of the regular activities or responsibilities of such offices – or that involved more complex interactions between them – tended to fall between the archival cracks as it would not be clear which office should end up with what in its files. Wedding festivities certainly met that "outside the norm" standard: they were *straordinari* rather than *ordinari*. They also involved more directly the leading members of the Medici family, which could lead to lines of communication becoming crossed or confused: hence the rather shadowy presence of Don Giovanni de' Medici in the 1600 festivities without any clear statement apparent in the archives about his precise role. Thus

[62] For these actions of the *deputati*, see the records of their meetings in *MM* 483 (a bound book of notes), plus the loose items in *MM* 18, ins. 4, and *MM* 695, ins. 4. For the boys for the *baldacchini*, see, e.g., *MM* 18, ins. 4, pp. 1–2, and for the ten-day holiday, see ibid., p. 225. Their total costs for the guests came to *sc.*2,236 £4.12*s.*4*d.*, so the *deputati* informed the grand duke on 30 December 1600, also noting that another *sc.*10 or *sc.*12 of payment requests were still to be received; *MM* 483, fol. 62. Other ceremonial expenses for the festivities (trumpeters, bell ringers, torches, etc.) are in ASF, Camera dell'arme granducale 9 (accounts concerning trumpeters, etc., 1600), fol. 116.

the documents concerning *Euridice* and the banquet discussed here were placed among the records of the Guardaroba once their original purpose had been fulfilled, but the Guardaroba administrators did not quite know what to do with them, which is probably why they ended up (much later) in a somewhat haphazard miscellany of materials from 1575 to 1739 (*GM* 1152) labeled *Affari diversi*. These documents were originally part of a file (*filza*) of 229 receipts (*ricevute*) collated and numbered on 28 November 1601 and connected with the "book of the banquet and royal wedding of the Most Christian Queen of France."[63] This "book" – presumably of accounts – does not survive, so far as we know. Nor do we have the other account books to which cross-references are made here, including a *stracciafoglio de' Pitti*, a *quaderno delle feste* (and a *libro delle feste*, if that is not the same item), a *libro della reale commedia* (*Il rapimento di Cefalo*), and what would probably have been a master ledger covering the whole festivities (identified as "A"):[64] these kinds of documents are typical of Florentine accounting systems, ranging from a low-level waste book (the *stracciafoglio*, recording daily transactions) to higher-level records in more summary form. However, the cross-references in these receipts are sometimes useful to determine which item was allocated to which purpose (the banquet, *Euridice*, or some other heading).

A significant number of the *ricevute* are just slips of paper acknowledging the delivery of construction materials (timber, canvas, hardware, etc.) to carpenters and other artisans working in the Palazzo Pitti. Most of the timber came from the Fortezza da Basso, the principal storehouse of construction materials for military or civil use, and so was under the control of *capitano* Gianbattista Cresci, the chief provisioner of the fortress(es) – he is variously styled *provveditore della fortezza*, *provveditore del castello*, and *provveditore delle fortezze* – who reported to Donato

63 The *filza* is now incorporated as a sequence in *GM* 1152, fols. 96–464; the first page, bearing the title, is now at fol. 433[*bis*] (*Addì 28 di novembre 1601. Filza attenente al libro del banchetto e nozze reale della Cristianissima Regina di Francia fatto adì 5 d'ottobre 1600 numerata da n.° 1 a n.° 229*). Receipt no. 1 refers to a delivery made on 13 May 1600 (fol. 96), and no. 229 is dated 28 November 1601 (fol. 434); their current ordering does not quite reflect the original numbering. For these documents, see Testaverde, "Nuovi documenti sulle scenografie di Ludovico Cigoli per l'*Euridice* di Ottavio Rinuccini"; Spinelli, "Feste e cerimonie tenutesi a Firenze per le 'felicissime nozze'"; Carter and Goldthwaite, *Orpheus in the Marketplace*, 111–18.

64 Cresci's inventory opens with a reference to a *libro della reale comedia fattasi l'anno passato d'ottobre nell Salone sopra gli Ufizi per le feste e nozze della Cristianissima Regina di Francia* which now appears lost. Likewise, documents in *GM* 1152, fols. 96–99, refer to a *quaderno delle feste* and a *stracciafoglio de' Pitti*, which would have been lower-level records of expenses, etc. For the problems, see "Money, Accounts, Measurements, Dates, and Time."

dell'Antella.[65] Cresci further supplied laborers (carpenters, plasterers, etc.) when needed. This made sense: the Fortezza da Basso was the obvious source for such materials and labor, and Cresci's predecessor, Girolamo Seriacopi, had fulfilled the same function for the 1589 wedding festivities, leaving records rich in information on them. Cresci also needed funds to cover his costs. Thus, on 13 May 1600, Donato dell'Antella submitted an order (*mandato*) that the administrators of the Fortezza da Basso be allocated a sum of money for day-to-day expenses in preparing the festivities, to be kept in a separate account: the grand duke approved *sc.*1,000 on 14 May, and the money was assigned from the Michelozzi & Ricci bank on 16 May; additional money was requested on 22 June (another *sc.*1,000 were allocated on 26 June), and further advances were made once the order was given on or about 13 July to prepare *Il rapimento di Cefalo*.[66] All this money was drawn down by Simone Paganucci, Cresci's treasurer (*camerlengo del castello*).

Cresci, in turn, assigned these materials to his subordinate, Michele Caccini (no relation to the singer, Giulio), who had been seconded from his position as *provveditore* of the Fortezza del Belvedere to take charge of the banquet and of what became known as the *commedia de' Pitti*, that is, *Euridice*.[67] Caccini was therefore required to keep detailed accounts both of any financial transactions and of the receipt or disbursement of materials. He was also the direct point of contact for the artists and artisans involved in the construction of whatever was needed for these two events. It was to Caccini that the painter Lodovico Cardi *detto* "Il Cigoli" submitted his invoice for designing and painting the stage and scenery for the opera, on 14 October 1600 (see Fig. 1.3).[68] The invoice is transcribed and translated in Appendix I.A.

Lodovico Cardi was commonly known as "Cigoli" after his birthplace in Tuscany, near San Miniato al Tedesco. His involvement as stage designer for *Euridice* has been known for some time through surviving documents and some sketches by him that appear related to it (discussed in Chapter 2),

65 For the connection between the Fortezza da Basso (also known as the Fortezza – or Castello – di S. Giovanni Battista), the Scrittoio delle Fortezze e Fabbriche, and the Depositeria Generale, see Testaverde, "San Lorenzo 'cantiere teatrale'," 76, 78–79.

66 *SFF* 122 (*Memoriale e ricordanze*, 1598–1604), fols. 58v (16 May), 63 (26 June), 65 (the *Commedia da farsi nel salone nuovo del consiglio sopra gli uffizzii*, i.e., *Il rapimento di Cefalo*).

67 Michele (di Giulio di Biagio) Caccini appears in Florentine documents at least from 1585, and he worked on the wedding festivities for Grand Duke Ferdinando I and Christine of Lorraine in 1589; see Testaverde, *L'officina delle nuvole*, 224. His family was styled the "Caccini di S. Maria Novella"; his testament, dated 3 July 1621, is in ASF, Notarile moderno, Protocolli 11533, fols. 121–26.

68 The complete document is shown in *CW*Fig. 1.3.

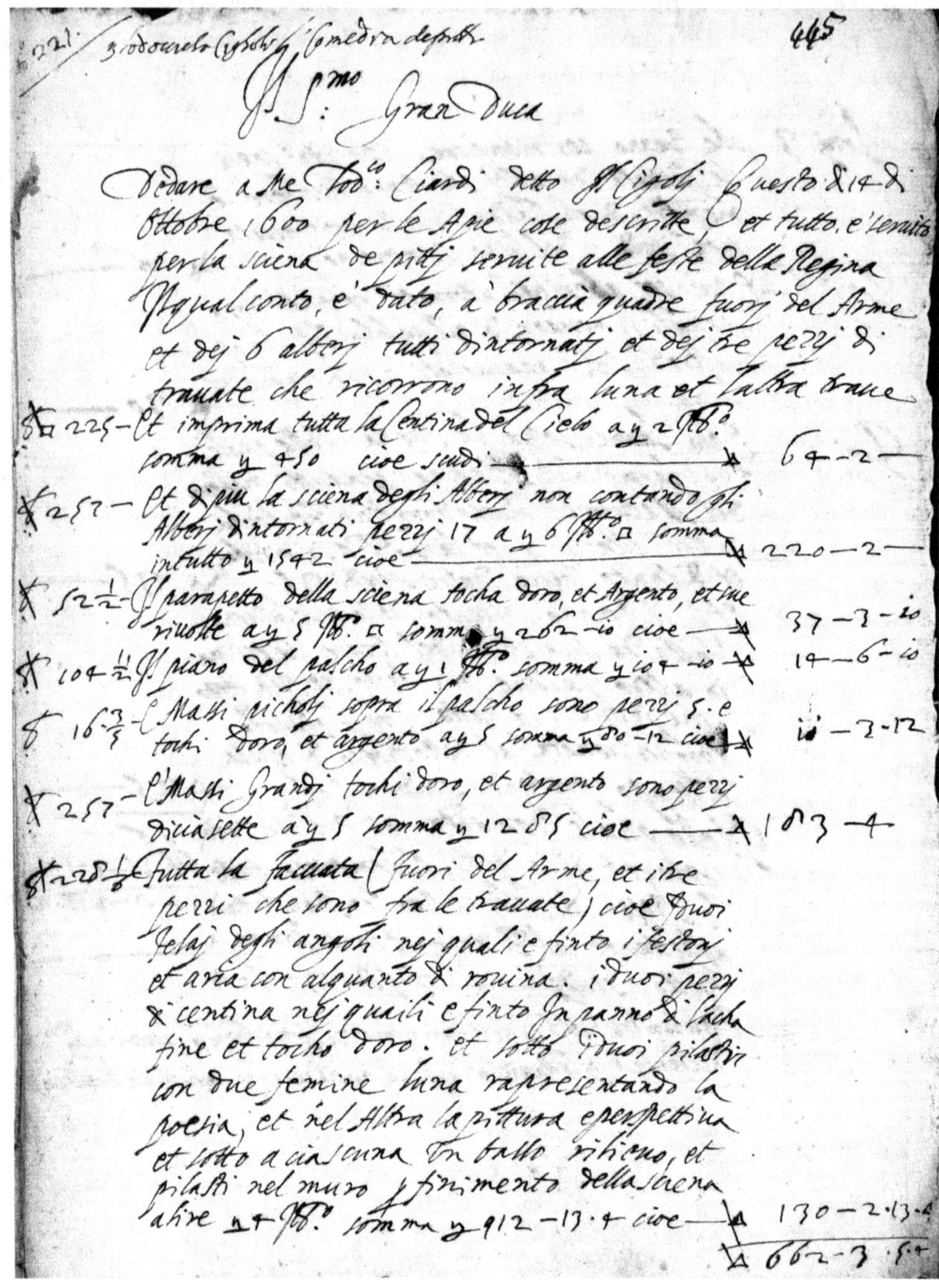
221 / Lodovico Cigoli / Comedia de pitti 445

Ill.mo S.r Gran Duca

Dedare a Me Lod.co Ciardi detto il Cigoli questo dì 14 di Ottobre 1600 per le appie cose descritte, et tutto è servito per la sciena de pitti servite alle feste della Regina il qual conto, è dato, a braccia quadre fuori del Arme et dei 6 alberi tutti dintornati et dei tre pezzi di travate che ricorrono infra l'una et l'altra trave

225 – Et imprima tutta la Centina del Cielo a £ 2 br. somma £ 450 cioè scudi — 64–2–

257 – Et di più la sciena degli Alberi non contando gli Alberi dintornati pezzi 17 a £ 6 br. somma in tutto £ 1542 cioè — 220–2–

52½ – Il parapetto della sciena tocha doro, et Argento, et messo rivolte a £ 5 br. somma £ 262–10 cioè — 37–3–10

104½ – Il piano del palcho a £ 1 br. somma £ 104–10 — 14–6–10

16⅗ – E Massi pichol sopra il palcho sono pezzi 5 e tochi doro, et argento a £ 5 somma £ 80–12 cioè — 11–3–12

257 – E Massi Grandi tochi doro, et argento sono pezzi diciasette a £ 5 somma £ 1285 cioè — 183–4

228⅙ – Tutta la facciata (fuori del Arme, et i tre pezzi che sono fra le travate) cioè i duoi telai degli angoli nei quali è finto i festoni et aria con alquanto di rovina. i duoi pezzi di centina nei quali è finto un panno di tocha fine et tocho doro. et sotto i duoi pilastri con due femine l'una rappresentando la poesia, et nel Altra la pittura e perspettiva et sotto a ciascuna un tallo rilievo, et pilastri nel muro per finimento della sciena a lire 4 br. somma £ 912–13–4 cioè — 130–2–13–4

662–3–5–4

Fig. 1.3: *GM* 1152, fol. 445; Lodovico Cigoli's invoice (first page) for creating the set for *Euridice*, 14 October 1600. By permission of the Ministero per i beni e le attività culturali e per il turismo della Repubblica Italiana/Archivio di Stato di Firenze.

but not to the extent discussed here.[69] He had studied first in Empoli and, from 1574 to 1578, was apprenticed to the artist Alessandro Allori in Florence, with whom he collaborated on decorations for the Galleria degli Uffizi. After a period in the early 1580s back in the provinces, Cigoli returned to Florence to work under the architect (and stage designer) Bernardo Buontalenti; he also studied with Santi di Tito. Typically for his profession he was both an architect and an artist. His subsequent output included architectural designs for the facade of S. Maria del Fiore, decorations for the Uffizi and the Palazzo Pitti, and a large number of works commissioned by the Medici as well as by other private individuals and religious institutions across Tuscany.[70] From 1604 he was based largely in Rome (in part under the patronage of Virginio Orsini, Duke of Bracciano), where he received numerous other commissions, although he returned at times to Florence. He is considered to be one of the more significant painters of the Florentine early Baroque school.

The purpose of Cigoli's invoice is obvious enough: he sought payment for work done, itemized in eleven entries (*Cig1–11*) and amounting to a total of *sc.*758 £3.5*s.*4*d.*, including *sc.*25 because of a change of rooms for the performance (as we shall see). Cigoli submitted it on Saturday 14 October. This appears to have been a typical day of the week for Medici officials to reckon their accounts, so Michele Caccini met with Cigoli there and then to go over the document. He agreed on the extent of the work listed in it, as he wrote in a comment added at its end, but he clearly had concerns over Cigoli's prices. There was a typically Florentine game being played here, where artists and artisans inflated their costs, in part to take account of the reduction in price (as a result of the *tara*) that the Medici conventionally expected for products or materials procured from those who regularly worked for

[69] Cigoli's involvement in the 1600 festivities is noted in general in the biography (1628) by his nephew, Giovan Battista Cardi, in a manuscript now in GDSU, 2660 A, prefacing a copy of Lodovico Cigoli's manuscript treatise *Prospettiva pratica … dimostrata con tre regole, e la descrizione di dua strumenti da tirare in prospettiva e modo di adoperarli, et i cinque ordini di architettura con le loro misure*. The biography is available in Battelli (ed.), *Vita di Lodovico Cardi Cigoli*, but has most recently been transcribed in Camerota, *Linear Perspective in the Age of Galileo*, 99–113. According to the biography, Cigoli also designed all the costumes and masks for the comedy performed in the 1600 festivities (*tutti gli abiti e maschere di personaggi che nella commedia si rappresentavano*), of which many sketches survive; Battelli (ed.), *Vita di Lodovico Cardi Cigoli*, 27; Camerota, *Linear Perspective in the Age of Galileo*, 106. However, the drawings to which Battelli refers in a footnote (as GDSU 8825, 8942, "etc."), while perhaps linked to the 1600 wedding, seem not to relate to *Euridice*.

[70] Chappell, "Lodovico Cigoli"; Gambuti, "Lodovico Cigoli architetto"; Bevilacqua, *I progetti per la facciata di Santa Maria del Fiore*, 25–27, 163–64.

them.[71] Administrators were obliged to query such charges, and, usually, a compromise was reached by some manner of negotiation. The rules were well enough understood on both sides, to the extent that Medici officials could be sympathetic enough to compensate those who somehow neglected to apply them. This seems to have been the case with Jacopo Ligozzi, whose invoice for creating the gigantic lily (*giglio*) as decoration for the banquet was deemed by Gianbattista Cresci and Donato dell'Antella to be too low (*sc.*329 rather than the expected *sc.*370, down by 12.5 percent), prompting payment of the additional *sc.*41 in addition to a one-time "gift" (*donativo*) of *sc.*200 for his services.[72] But in Cigoli's case, Michele Caccini was not going to authorize payment to Cigoli without some further investigation, and he commissioned five other Florentine painters to provide costings for the same work, item by item (see *CW*Fig. 1.10).[73] This was his standard practice in such circumstances: it also raises important questions about how the market worked in terms of the value assigned to artists and their output.[74] From those five estimates, Caccini took an average of the lowest four that enabled him to negotiate downward: on 19 February 1600/1, Cigoli was credited with *sc.*379 £3.9*s.*8*d.*, which is almost exactly half of what he originally requested. The fact that this sum was calculated down to the level of *soldi* and *denari*, however it might have been achieved, is surely a nicety to do more with appearances than with reality. But those appearances mattered, as did the well-tuned system which produced them. The fact that Cigoli accepted the lesser amount, as did other artists in similar situations, suggests that

[71] For the *tara*, see "Money, Accounts, Measurements, Dates, and Time."

[72] As documented in *GM* 1152, fols. 439–44. Dell'Antella said that Ligozzi was perhaps unaccustomed to dealing with officialdom (*huomo forse non pratico con simili ministri*). His lily was certainly one of the great successes of the festivities.

[73] The estimates by Alessandro Allori (*sc.*319 £0.2*s.*8*d.*), Giovanni Maria Butteri (*sc.*587 £4.3*s.*), Bernardino Poccetti (*sc.*290 £6.12*s.*8*d.*), Alessandro Portelli (*sc.*293 £0.17*s.*), and Luca Ranfi (*sc.*514 £6.6*s.*) were itemized by Caccini in a table in *GM* 1152, fols. 446–47; they did not include the *sc.*25 for the change of room. Allori and Poccetti are, of course, well known (and their estimates were significantly lower than Cigoli's). Butteri, Portelli, and Ranfi were lesser artists, but they appear frequently enough in other records. Cigoli would likely have worked with all of them on decorations for the Palazzo Pitti and other Medici buildings.

[74] Caccini did a similar exercise for Gabriello Ughi's claim for painting and similar work done by him and his assistant for the banquet (including the scenery for the *Dialogo di Giunone e Minerva*) and elsewhere, which was thereby reduced from *sc.*1,433 £3.8*s.*8*d.* to *sc.*848 £3.4*s.* (and he was paid on the same day as was Cigoli); *GM* 1152, fols. 451–55. The reduction of Jacopo Chimenti's fee for his paintings of the weddings of Caterina and Maria de' Medici (from *sc.*200 to *sc.*110) was achieved by the same means.

everyone knew how to play the game so as to achieve a (mostly) fair result, satisfactory to all sides.

It is important to remember that all these sums are calculated in terms of moneys of account: how they translated into actual payments in coin, in kind, or by some form of credit, is a separate issue. Nevertheless, such conscientious reckoning was expected of any administrator. It also contradicts the common image of spendthrift rulers engaging willy-nilly in luxury consumption without regard for the consequences: the Medici grand dukes certainly spent money on luxuries befitting their station and duties, but did so with some care on the part of their officials.

Michele Caccini had other obligations as well, given that all the materials he procured for the banquet and *Euridice* were credited to his account. In effect, they became a "debt" that needed to be "repaid" or somehow written off. After the dust had settled on the 1600 festivities, Caccini was therefore required to close his account by transferring the materials he had received – or what had been made of them – to another account not within his present domain (even if it might have stayed under his control under a different heading). This is the reason for the second document concerning *Euridice* presented here (Appendix I.B): an inventory, dated 18 September 1601, of the stage and its sets as placed in storage in space next to Teatro degli Uffizi, and therefore moved both literally, from one place to another, and figuratively within the accounting system. Whereas Cigoli's invoice covers only those elements of the stage and sets for *Euridice* with which he was directly involved, this later inventory of the materials used for the staging is more comprehensive, at least in terms of what remained a year after the production, or that had not already been used for other purposes.

This inventory was prepared on behalf of, and signed by, Gianbattista Cresci, although it was written out by a scribe in his office, Matteo Chelli (see *CW*Fig. 1.11).[75] But its forty-two entries (*Cres1–42*) were compiled on the basis of a (now lost) document completed by Caccini himself on 4 September listing the materials that he had deposited in storage. He identified them in quite precise terms even down to the different types and forms of timber used to construct the stage. The aim was to transfer these materials to the account of the administration of the "royal comedy" of the 1600 festivities (*Il rapimento di Cefalo*). Thus the inventory is, in effect, an annotated copy of Caccini's list, or perhaps even a copy of a copy (that had been entered into the new account). But Cresci needed to arrange

[75] *GM* 1152, fols. 370, 456, are documents signed by Chelli, which allow us to identify his distinctive hand. Cresci's is much less neat.

an audit of those materials to confirm that Caccini's list was correct (or to note discrepancies therein), and to provide Caccini with a version of it that would act as written confirmation of his deposit, canceling his "debt."

Not everything used for *Euridice* was moved to the Uffizi. Items that had been "borrowed" from the Guardaroba (some boards and trestles) were sent back there, while the large coat of arms that Cigoli placed at the center of the proscenium arch had now been mounted above a staircase in the Palazzo Pitti. Cresci noted everything accordingly, both to keep the record straight and as a reminder in case items needed to be retrieved should the grand duke wish to restage the opera (*per ricordo di ritornare dette robe se mai Sua Altezza Serenissima volesse fare rimettere insieme detta prospettiva per recitare detta comedia*). Some of the construction materials suitable for other purposes had already gone elsewhere, as in the case of the wood from the ceiling and other parts of the temporary stage, which had been used to build a *stanzino* in one of the grand duchess's rooms in the Palazzo Pitti (this wood therefore entered a different account relating to the palace). Other items were missing or damaged beyond repair, something which Cresci appears to have accepted as normal, given that he wrote them off rather than pursuing Caccini to remedy matters. As for the rest of the stage and sets, should Caccini or anyone else have needed them again (we shall see in Chapter 4 that someone did), a new account would have had to be opened operating in similar ways.

All this paper-pushing was laborious, but it had the advantage – at least in principle – of knowing not just where everything was at any given moment, but also who was responsible for it. To judge by Cresci's inventory, Caccini's original list had also been fairly methodical in its sequence of different elements of the stage. But how the line-items in any such accounts otherwise squared with reality both before and after the fact is another matter altogether. For example, there was no way for Cresci to ascertain that Caccini's list included absolutely everything he had originally procured for *Euridice*. In other words, there may have been other materials for the production that Caccini chose not to include, or that got diverted elsewhere in ways not otherwise recorded in surviving documents: this has a bearing on whether Cresci's inventory (relying on the list) identifies everything needed to reconstruct the staging. However, the fact that Caccini deposited at least some damaged items suggests that he was extremely conscientious, as would be expected of any good administrator.

The invoice and the inventory needed to be accurate enough to serve their purposes and to meet appropriate standards of verification. Such accuracy was needed for some details more than others, however: a case in point is items listed in bulk, such as Cigoli's claim for painting the stage floor, measuring 104.5 *b.q.*, although he did so by way of painting an unspecified number of separate pieces of canvas (that may or may not then have been stitched together) amounting to that total area (not all of which survived, according to Cresci's inventory). For Cigoli's purposes that level of specificity did not matter (he painted what he painted), just as any eventual loss of the material was not his concern (Cigoli had done the work and needed credit for it). Nor would Cresci necessarily have been aware of the discrepancy unless he were to go back and check an invoice that by then was probably kept in a different place. But it would hardly have mattered if he had: Cigoli was paid in February 1601, whereas Cresci's inventory was made seven months later.

Similar circumstances and caveats apply to the other invoice considered here. Cigoli's charges included the cost of some materials (the colors, gold leaf, and other manufacture pertaining to the painter, so he noted at the end of the invoice), but not all of them. The canvas on which he painted the proscenium and sets was included within a long invoice submitted by Francesco Ricoveri *materassaio* (mattress maker) reflecting his contribution to the festivities since 20 May 1600 (see *CW*Fig. 1.12).[76] Large amounts of canvas were delivered to the Palazzo Pitti, some "old" from the Fortezza da Basso and the Teatro degli Uffizi, and some newly procured from other sources. In both cases this canvas then needed to be sewn (*cucito*), that is, with strips joined together or hemmed (or both). A great deal was needed for the decoration of the Salone dei Cinquecento for the wedding banquet: in addition to new figurative paintings and the scenic elements created for the banquet itself, the walls of that room were almost entirely covered by temporary hangings that concealed the large frescoes by Giorgio Vasari and his assistants done in the third quarter of the sixteenth century, presumably because their subjects – the victories of Florence over Pisa and Siena – were considered indelicate for the occasion. However, Ricoveri also sewed canvas and performed other tasks that can be associated specifically with *Euridice*; the relevant entries (*Ric1–17*) are given in Appendix I.C. The invoice itself is undated (as are its separate items), but it was prepared sometime shortly after the wedding: the account was settled on 10 November 1600.

[76] *GM* 1152, fols. 425–29. This list was clearly prepared in a single sitting late in the course of events – based on (now lost) prior lists – with items grouped by their purpose rather than by the date of delivery.

Not all the canvas used for *Euridice* passed through Ricoveri's firm: for example, on 25 August, Michele Caccini received 110 *b.q. per servitio della comedia de' Pitti* from storage in the Teatro degli Uffizi, possibly intended for the stage floor (measured by Cigoli at 104.5 *b.q.*).[77] Moreover, items in Ricoveri's invoice do not always square precisely with what was delivered: for example, the receipt (dated 11 September 1600) for the 150 *b.a.* of canvas for the "sky" (*tela pagliola ... per il cielo della prospettiva della commedia de' Pitti*) says that it was made up of four pieces, whereas Ricoveri's invoice lists eight.[78] Nor do we know whether that canvas delivered on 11 September had already been painted by Cigoli (it did not matter so far as Ricoveri was concerned), although the relatively late date would suggest that it had. But the relatively close correlation, as regards the canvas, between Ricoveri's invoice and Cigoli's (and what survived according to Cresci's inventory) suggests that Ricoveri was working with materials that had already been fashioned with the measurements of Cigoli's design in mind. Like Cigoli, he, too, needed to accommodate the change of room for the performance of *Euridice*, sewing the additional canvas needed to cover the enlarging of the stage, and the widening of the proscenium. And he was one of two artisans present in the Palazzo Pitti on the day of the performance on 6 October (the other, we shall see in Chapter 2, was the *lanternaio*, responsible for the lighting), probably in case his services were needed for any urgent repairs.

Although Ricoveri's measurements are given in what he calls *braccia*, it seems that his charges for sewing canvas were calculated by the *braccia andante*, that is, a cumulative series of lengths (for example, the four sides of a rectangle added together): he charged a fixed rate of £1 per 10 *b.a.* (2*s.* per *b.a.*), and, for any other labor in his shop, £3.10*s.* per person per workday (though he himself charged £7 for attending the performance of *Euridice*). A single piece of canvas (a *telo*) could be sewn together with other such pieces (to produce a *tela*). If needed (for example, for vertical scenery), the *tela* could then be mounted on a frame (a *telaio*). Thus, when Ricoveri sewed together eight pieces of canvas (eight *teli*) for the "sky" of the stage to produce what Cresci identified as a single *tela* measuring 17 *b.* long and 13.5 *b.* wide "on average" (*ragguagliata*, *Cres8*) – and assuming

[77] *GM* 1152, fol. 247. Similar problems arise with smaller batches of "old" canvas, such as the 8 *b.* of *tela vechia* delivered by Ricoveri's *garzone* for the *commedia de' Pitti* on 20 July (ibid., fol. 185), or the 26 *b.q.* of *tela vecchia* from an unnamed source on 16 September (fol. 305, also *per la comedi[a] de' Pitti*). This could have been for anything to do with the stage, as could other canvas, the purpose of which is unspecified.

[78] The receipt is at *GM* 1152, fol. 283; compare *Ric6*.

that those eight *teli* created the total width (so each *telo* was some 1.7 *b.* wide) – he hemmed two lengths at 17 *b.* each and two at 13.5 *b.* each, and sewed seven joins: this gives a total of 155 *b.a.* The fact that Ricoveri charged for 150 *b.a.* (*Ric6*) is a relatively minor discrepancy on a par with the one between Cresci's measurements (17 × 13.5 = 229.5 *b.q.*) and Cigoli's (he measured the sky at 225 *b.q.*, *Cig1*); indeed, the differences are negligible bearing in mind that Cresci's measurements here were "on average." Other discrepancies in Ricoveri's invoice are probably due to his sometimes sewing more canvas than was needed (in case of wastage) or adding an allowance for construction purposes: for example, *tele* mounted to a *telaio* needed some extra length and width so that their edges could be wrapped around the frame.[79]

The elements of Ricoveri's invoice pertaining to *Euridice* amounted to £294.12*s.*, representing just under 40 percent of his total for the festivities (£755.4*s.*), although the *tara* brought that final total down by over half to £361.16*s.*[80] The sums credited to Cigoli (eventually) and claimed by Ricoveri amount to *sc.*421 £5.1*s.*8*d.* (*sc.*379 £3.9*s.*8*d.* + £294.12*s.*), although Ricoveri would have received less as a result of the *tara*. The final cost of those elements of *Euridice* that fell under the jurisdiction of Michele Caccini (and hence the Fortezza da Basso) was reported by Gianbattista Cresci to be *sc.*678 £0.16*s.*: the difference is presumably due to other costs for materials and labor, although there is scant reckoning of them in the surviving documents.

Cresci submitted a final accounting of his total expenditure for the 1600 festivities in February 1601/2 to the administrators of the Ufficio di Monte e Soprassindaci – the office in charge of auditing all official and public expenditures – which they reported to the grand duke on 28 February (see Fig. 1.4).[81] Cresci's total for the banquet and *Euridice* together was *sc.*5,361 £0.8*s.*4*d.* – he also provided a breakdown, including a separate line *per la commedia et prospettiva fatta nel Pitti* – and for *Il rapimento di*

[79] For example, Ricoveri said that the fourteen pastoral flats at 6 *b.* high (though we shall see that they varied in length) each required 18 *b.* of sewing, i.e., either he sewed two 1.5 *b.* strips of canvas together and hemmed the outer vertical edges, or he hemmed the vertical and horizontal edges of two 1.5 *b.* strips of canvas that had already been stitched together (both scenarios required 18 *b.* of linear sewing).

[80] So it seems from the summary figures provided on a separate sheet interleaved in Ricoveri's invoice; *GM* 1152, fol. 428.

[81] *SS* 279, fols. 144 (*Il rapimento di Cefalo*), 144v (banquet and *Euridice*), 145 (breakdown of the costs for the banquet and *Euridice*). The figures vary slightly in different portions of these documents because of adjustments being made to them depending in part on the accounts to which they were to be charged, and in part on a few items that had been sold and therefore counted as credit, reducing the total sum. Of the total cost for *Il rapimento di Cefalo*, *sc.*5,800 or thereabouts were the responsibility of the Depositeria Generale.

Cefalo, *sc.*5,925 £5.3*s.*4*d.*[82] The grand duke approved this reckoning on 27 March 1602, and that approval was conveyed to Cresci on 16–17 April.[83] The cost to Cresci of *Euridice* (*sc.*678 £0.16*s.*) presumably does not represent the entire amount of the opera: for example, as we have seen, the costumes were probably covered by Jacopo Corsi, and there is no evidence of direct payment to the singers. However, the total somewhat palls in comparison with the *sc.*1,781 £6.9*s.*4*d.* spent on decorating the royal table and its surrounds at the head of the banquet in the Salone dei Cinquecento

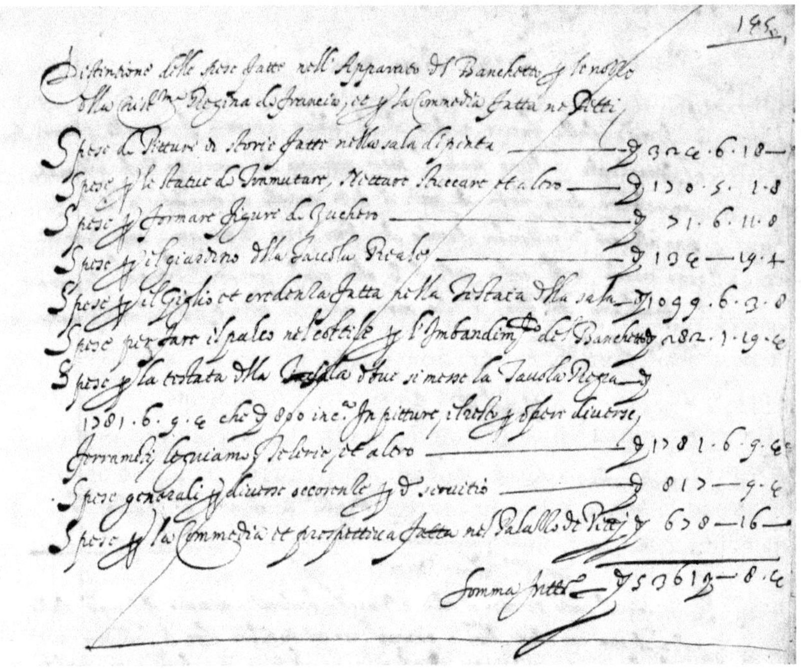

Fig. 1.4: *SS* 279, fol. 145 (top half); the breakdown of the costs for the banquet and *Euridice* audited by the Ufficio di Monte e Soprassindaci, 28 February 1601/2. By permission of the Ministero per i beni e le attività culturali e per il turismo della Repubblica Italiana/Archivio di Stato di Firenze.

82 As with *Euridice*, the expenses for *Il rapimento di Cefalo* devolving to Cresci did not represent the total cost of the production, although here it seems to have included at least some costumes (*abiti* are mentioned on *SS* 279, fol. 144). Some important details of other costumes for *Il rapimento di Cefalo* survive in *GM* 453 (*Affari diversi*, 1577–1685), ins. 6 (*Spese per le commedia rappresentata alle nozze di Maria de' Medici*).

83 Cresci made sure that the matter was recorded in *SFF* 122, fol. 125.

(including around *sc.*800 for paintings), plus *sc.*1,099 £6.3*s*.8*d*. for its *giglio*, *credenza*, and other decorations, and *sc.*134 £0.19*s*.4*d*. for its centerpiece.

This final accounting came quite late in the day, and it took a while to grind through the system. Clearly there was no urgency in closing out the paperwork; nor need there have been, so long as it was done properly in the end. But Cresci was not left waiting until April 1602 for reimbursement of (or credit for) his expenditures. As we have seen, he was given two allocations each of *sc.*1,000, the first in mid-May 1600 and the second in late June. He kept a weekly tally of expenses on the banquet and *Euridice* that would draw down this sum, beginning with the week ending on Saturday 20 May; on 1 September, he reported to one of the court secretaries, Marcello Accolti, that according to this tally up to 26 August (he enclosed a copy broken down by week and heading), the original *sc.*2,000 had been overspent (by just over *sc.*145), meaning that additional money was needed.[84] Cresci also noted that significant payment requests were still to come in because most of the artists and artisans involved would submit invoices only after their work had been completed. The total spent on *Euridice* by 26 August was *sc.*309 £2, which had increased to *sc.*450 by 13 September 1600, so Cresci wrote to Accolti that day. Cresci's principle concern, however, was the cost overrun for the various scenic and other elements of the banquet: he had already transferred *sc.*220 of the total money allocated for *Euridice* to pay some of those bills, although this needed to be reimbursed, given that his juggling of the books contravened the order given by Don Giovanni de' Medici that money budgeted for the opera should not be used for other purposes.[85]

[84] *MdP* 899, fols. 1–2 (Cresci to the grand-ducal secretary, Marcello Accolti, 1 September 1600). The weekly payments for *Euridice* in the attached list were: (week ending Saturday 20 May) *sc.*11 £2.11*s*.; (27 May), *sc.*28 £6.16*s*.; (3 June) *sc.*17 £2.10*s*.; (10 June) *sc.*31 £0.6*s*.; (17 June) *sc.*41 £0.18*s*.; (Thursday 22 June [because of S. Giovanni Battista]), *sc.*25 £6.13*s*.4*d*; (Saturday 1 July), *sc.*19 £4.5*s*.; (8 July), *sc.*19 £2.19*s*.8*d*.; (15 July), *sc.*34 £4.10*s*.4*d*.; (22 July) *sc.*22 £1.3*s*.; (29 July), *sc.*16 £5.15*s*.; (5 August) *sc.*11 £2.16*s*.; (12 August), *sc.*6 £5.15*s*.; (19 August), *sc.*12 £3.2*s*.8*d*.; (26 August) *sc.*10 £0.19*s*. In addition, for the three weeks ending 20 May, 27 May, and 3 June, a total of *sc.*120 £0.11*s*.4*d*. was paid for *Statue e altro ne' Pitti*, which seems to have at least partly involved the performance of Jacopo Corsi's "comedy" on or around 28 May 1600.

[85] *MdP* 899, fol. 159 (13 September 1600): Cresci notes that *il sabato passato bisognò pagare du.220 che li feci pagare al Camarlingo di Castello di quelli della commedia* (i.e., *Euridice*), and therefore that he was faced with having to stop work on the banquet, although *non vor[e]i dare disgusto a levar mano, senza licenzia, et ancora di spendere del assegnatione della commedia il signor Don Giovanni non par lo voglia.* Don Giovanni de' Medici's instruction about not touching the money for *Euridice* was also noted in Cresci's letter to Accolti of 1 September (*MdP* 899, fols. 1–2). The total sum allocated for *Euridice* therefore seems to have been *sc.*670 (*sc.*450 + *sc.*220), which is close enough to its final cost as noted above (*sc.*678 £0.16*s*.).

Francesco Ricoveri was paid only on 10 November 1600, but it seems from Cresci's figures (and from the eventual total cost to him of *Euridice* at *sc.*678 £0.16*s.*) that Cigoli received some payments, or at least credits, in advance for his work. This is also apparent in upper-level accounts held by the Guardaroba: Cigoli was allocated *sc.*18 on 9 June 1600, then near-regular weekly credits (calculated at what seems to have been *sc.*15 per week) from 21 July to 9 September, adding up to *sc.*138.[86] The purpose of these payments is not specified here, although some can be squared with other Guardaroba accounts: the 9 June payment was for *pitture fatte a carrozze* (presumably, for carriages), while the ones on 21 July (*sc.*20) and 25 August (*sc.*15) were for other "pictures."[87] Cigoli was working for the Palazzo Pitti on items other than just for *Euridice*; he also did at least one of the paintings used to decorate the walls of the Salone dei Cinquecento for the wedding banquet.[88] It seems reasonable to assume, however, that at least some of these payments represented advances on the costs of the design and painting of the sets for the opera. Thus, when Cigoli was "paid" *sc.*379 £3.9*s.*8*d.* on 19 February 1600/1, there would have been some reckoning of what he had already received by way of a different account.

Finally, it is important to keep in mind one key difference between the three main documents discussed here. Cigoli's and Ricoveri's invoices reflect work done, or materials delivered, up to the point where that work or those deliveries ceased. Ricoveri's last day on the job was 6 October 1600 (he was present at the performance). Cigoli's, however, was presumably sometime sooner: as the performance approached, it was left to Matteo *imbiancatore* (an artisan who often painted walls, etc. in the Palazzo Pitti) to provide for "the blue part of the sky," which probably means touching it up in places.[89] Cresci's inventory, on the other hand, reflects what was actually used for and in the 6 October performance, in whatever state it survived once the stage had been dismantled, including items not covered

[86] *GM* 179 (records of *mandati*, 1594–1606), by date. The *mandati* were sent (usually on a Friday) to Vincenzo Medici, *depositario generale*, asking him to transfer funds to Matteo Mattei, *cassiere* of the Guardaroba, so that Mattei could allocate payments.

[87] *GM* 204 (*Entrata ed uscita*, 1599–1600), fols. 29 (*a buon conto di pitture*), 30v (*a conto di pitture*). Other payments to Cigoli here are less specific.

[88] *GM* 1152, fol. 460. The painting (8 *b.* high and 12 *b.* wide) represented *quando Il Gran Duca, è creato dalla repubblica*. Cigoli asked for *sc.*170 and was paid *sc.*110. Obviously he was able to raise his charges for a figurative painting: the *sc.*170 represents roughly £12.8*s.* per *b.q.*, compared with his £6 per *b.q.* for painting trees for *Euridice*, or £5 for boulders.

[89] *GM* 1152, fol. 422v: *E per avere datto alla chomedia a Pitti partte lazuro all ciello cioue [sic] nosttra manifattura alla meta dell ciello monta lire tre*. This is the last item in a long list (dated 5 October 1600) of work done by Matteo in the Palazzo Pitti and Palazzo Vecchio since 5 April. It is not clear what the *meta dell ciello* might mean.

by Cigoli and Ricoveri. To recreate the original staging of *Euridice*, the inventory is more useful than those invoices, even if the latter sometimes help explain what the inventory contains.

The Performance of "A Comedy by Signor Jacopo Corsi" (Spring 1600)

The payments for what Cresci tended to call the *commedia de' Pitti*, beginning in the week ending 20 May 1600, are part of a broader pattern as the Medici set plans into action for the forthcoming festivities once the marriage was officially announced on 30 April. Rumors about Corsi's "new pastoral" had in fact been circulating for several weeks: on 7 April, Emilio de' Cavalieri (then in Rome) grumbled to Marcello Accolti about his having heard of many Florentines being told that it would be something "heavenly" (*si è dato conto già a molti fiorentini di una pastorale nuova che fa il signor Jacomo Corsi, che dicono che sarrà cosa celeste*), although Cavalieri, no friend of Corsi and his collaborators, was distinctly unimpressed by the hyperbole, feeling that the heavens and angels were being done a severe injustice (*poveri cieli et angeli*).[90] It was a particularly bitter pill to swallow because just two days earlier Cavalieri had complained to Accolti about the unfavorable comparisons being made between his *Il giuoco della cieca* and Rinuccini's *Dafne* (both performed in the Pitti in January 1598/99), and between the Easter celebrations held in 1600 against those of the previous year (in which Cavalieri had been more directly involved); he was also annoyed by the praise now being given to Giulio Caccini (as "the god of music") and other comments being made in favor of musicians other than those supported by him.[91]

As for Rinuccini, and in the context of what was becoming a heated competition between various Florentine literary and musical figures, the poet was anxious to assert the prominence of *Dafne* as moving beyond

[90] *MdP* 1691, fol. 17; Carter, *Jacopo Peri*, 1: 301; *KirkCM*, 202–3; Carter and Goldthwaite, *Orpheus in the Marketplace*, 112–13. Cavalieri does not name the new pastoral, nor does he mention the wedding.

[91] Cavalieri's letter to Accolti of 5 April 1600 (*MdP* 3622, fol. 177; given in *KirkCM*, 198) complains about *Il sentir dir: che la Portia, et la monacha, canti meglio de Vittoria; la pastorale del Corsi sia piaciuta più della Cieca; che Giulio Romano sia il dio della musica; che siano state megliori le lamentationi questo anno a Pisa dell'anno passato* . . . Cavalieri had provided the music for the Lamentations in 1599; in 1600, Easter Sunday was on 2 April. Both *Il giuoco della cieca* and *Dafne* were performed in the Sala delle Statue in January 1598/99. The singer "Vittoria" was Vittoria Archilei; *KirkCM*, 262–76.

Cavalieri's pastoral experiments toward a more plausible reconstruction of ancient theatrical practice in terms of structure and delivery. A libretto had already been printed, probably in relation to the Carnival 1598/99 performance (the revised prologue refers to the grand duchess, who was present), but with a poorly typeset title page and some errors in the text (and, it seems, without the *licenza* from the religious authorities that would normally be required for anything made "public").[92] The Marescotti press then produced a more elegant edition of *La Dafne d'Ottavio Rinuccini rappresentata alla Serenissima Gran Duchessa di Toscana dal Signor Iacopo Corsi* dated 1600 (after 25 March, given that Marescotti used *stile fiorentino* dating in his prints): it bears the arms of Christine of Lorraine on the title page (but otherwise lacks any prefatory material) and ends with an ode in praise of Corsi ("Qual novo altero canto").[93] Rinuccini associated this edition of *Dafne* with the one of *Euridice* issued by Cosimo Giunti in anticipation of the performance during the 1600 wedding festivities, although the date of its dedication to Maria de' Medici is left incomplete (it specifies the month – October – but the day is left blank) as if the date of the performance itself was still unclear at the time of printing (probably because of the uncertain schedule for the wedding, for reasons already noted).[94] In that dedication, Rinuccini refers to his having published both librettos because of the warm welcome being granted to such musical productions (*Là onde, cominciando io a conoscere quanto simili rappresentazioni in musica siano gradite, ho voluto recare in luce queste due . . .*); this might further suggest that the librettos came out in relatively close proximity. As we shall see, he also made a direct connection between *Dafne* and *Euridice* by way of the latter's final chorus. But by this time, Rinuccini's account in the dedication of *Euridice* to Maria de' Medici of the creation of both operas may also have been intended to counter the claims for priority in

[92] This early edition (*Rappresentazione di Dafne favola pastorale composta dal signor Ottavio Rinuccini. Et fatta recitare in musica dal Signor Iacopo Corsi*), which lacks any indication of the printer or date, is discussed in Sternfeld, "The First Opera Libretto," on the basis of a copy in the New York Public Library (https://digitalcollections.nypl.org/items/9635f75d-ff6e-6929-e040-e00a18061b4b). The font of this edition appears in other prints by both the Giunti press (such as Vincenzo Panciatichi's *L'amicizia costante* of 1600) and the Marescotti one (Giovanni Agnolo Lottini's *Il dannoso piacere* of 1602). The woodblock capital "D" matches the one used in one of Marescotti's two editions of *Il rapimento di Cefalo* (1600), but this is not strong enough evidence to identify Marescotti as the printer of the first *Dafne* edition with any certainty.

[93] A number of copies survive; see, e.g., http://corago.unibo.it/esemplare/BUB0000406/DOE0000379. It was printed *Con Licenza de' Superiori.*

[94] Persistent claims that the dedication of the 1600 edition of Rinuccini's libretto is dated 4 October are not borne out by any surviving copies we have seen, *pace* Palisca, "The First Performance of *Euridice*," 445–46; *KirkCM*, 210.

the "invention" of opera being made (by Alessandro Guidotti) in the dedication to Cardinal Pietro Aldobrandini of Emilio de' Cavalieri's sacred opera, *Rappresentatione di Anima, et di Corpo*, published in Rome by Nicolò Mutii in early September (the dedication is dated the 3rd) following its performance there the previous February. Cavalieri certainly read Rinuccini's comments in that competitive light.[95]

That 1600 edition of *Dafne* acknowledges some performance of the opera before the grand duchess – as occurred during Carnival 1598/99 – but does not say when that was. It also commemorates her role (by virtue of the title page) and gives credit to Jacopo Corsi (the ode) in ways not possible in the printed libretto of *Euridice*, which was perforce dedicated to Maria de' Medici. But the uncertainties surrounding the *Dafne* edition add to a number of problems in interpreting an important document concerning the 1600 festivities in the file of *ricevute* kept by Michele Caccini. On 9 June 1600, one the Palazzo Pitti's carpenters, Camillo di Benedetto Pieroni, issued a request to debit the grand duke a total of £30.10*s*. for work on the construction of a "stage" that the grand duchess had requested be built in the *salone* of the Duchess of Bracciano in the Pitti, and which had served "to perform a comedy by Signor Jacopo Corsi" on 28 May (a Sunday).[96] (It is not clear whether 28 May was the date of the performance, as the wording suggests, or of the grand duchess's order to prepare for it.) Pieroni charged for two days of labor – a Monday and a Tuesday – for him and three *garzoni* (one of whom worked just for a single day) for erecting the stage, and for half a day for him and two *garzoni* to take it down on 6 June (a Tuesday). The wood could have been drawn from the consignment Pieroni had received on Saturday 13 May to adjust the

[95] In his letter to Marcello Accolti, 10 November 1600, *MdP* 3622, fol. 185, given in *KirkCM*, 210. Peri attempted to calm the waters by way of his own remarks in the printed score of *Euridice*; Carter and Goldthwaite, *Orpheus in the Marketplace*, 256–57.

[96] *GM* 1152, fol. 148, dated 9 June 1600: *Serenissimo Gran Ducha de' dare a Camillo legniauiolo a Pitti per un paicho* [sic] *fatto e ne palazo de' Pitti e ne salone della Duchessa di Braciano con comessione di Madama Serenissima serviè per recitare* [a correction of *recitate*] *una comedia del signor Jachopo Corsi sotto dì 28 >di maggio< sopra detto* . . . That *sotto di 28 sopra detto* was incorrect given that the document is dated 9 June, which is why *di maggio* was inserted as a correction; presumably Camillo Pieroni was initially copying some written instruction he had received dated in May. Camillo is not otherwise identified in this document, but his full name is given in other accounts associated with work in the Palazzo Pitti, such as *SFF* 72 (*Quaderno di robe per la fabbrica de' Pitti*, 1600–1603), fols. 15v–16. He was the brother of the painter and architect Alessandro Pieroni, who also worked on the 1600 festivities (and see *KirkCM*, 629). Both Pieronis were involved in different capacities in the 1589 festivities as well; Testaverde, *L'officina delle nuvole*, 201 (Camillo and five *garzoni* for the sixth *intermedio* for *La pellegrina*), 220, 222, 248 (Alessandro). For further information, see Bastogi, "Per una ricostruzione della biografia e dell'attività pittorica di Alessandro Pieroni."

height of various statues in the Pitti and for other purposes (*per servitio di calare figure a Pitti, et altri affari*),[97] or the one obtained on Tuesday 16 May to make a *residenza*, probably in the Sala delle Statue.[98] But if we accept 28 May as the date of the performance, Pieroni's invoice suggests that the stage went up on 22 and 23 May, and was left standing for two weeks.[99]

Adapting spaces in the Palazzo Pitti for multiple purposes, including theatrical ones, was typical of the flexible ways in which many rooms were used in the palace: it made better sense than restricting them to a single function, and labor came cheap. Bernardo Buontalenti also created a model for a temporary theatrical stage that could be installed and dismantled as required within the palace.[100] In the present case, there are two obvious problems to be solved: identifying Corsi's "comedy," and the location of the performance. For the former, the question is whether we are dealing with another performance of *Dafne* or, instead, some manner of preview of *Euridice* that the grand duchess wished to vet for the festivities.[101] For the latter, the issue concerns the rooms in the Palazzo Pitti occupied by the Duchess of Bracciano, and therefore the position of any *salone* that Camillo Pieroni would have associated with her.

The fact that the court diaries and similar documents are silent on any theatrical performances or similar events in late May or early June does not help matters. In fact, this was a fairly quiet time in the Palazzo Pitti. Grand Duke Ferdinando I was away from Florence *in villa*, leaving the grand duchess behind, and as was customary she kept him abreast of things by way of regular letters. She and Maria de' Medici also seem to have reserved that last weekend in May for some manner of planning for the wedding festivities, which Grand Duchess Christine may further have intended as a

97 *GM* 1152, fols. 96–97, dated 24 May 1600.

98 *GM* 1152, fol. 99, detailing large amounts of wood, some of which (fol. 99v) *servirno per Camillo Pieroni per fare la residenza nell Salone*. This was probably a platform for a throne, but the terms are typically confusing: anyone creating such a delivery note might or might not have known the precise purpose of such materials (or cared about it so long as the entries were accurate enough in general terms).

99 If, on the other hand, 28 May was the date of the grand duchess's order, the stage was mounted on 29–30 May, with the performance on some day prior to 6 June (tying up the room for a shorter period of time). It is also worth noting that during Carnival 1598/99 a stage seems to have remained in the Sala delle Statue at least from 4 or 5 January (the performance of *Il giuoco della cieca*) to 21 January (*Dafne*).

100 *GM* 245, ins. 4 (inventory of items held by Buontalenti), fol. 437: *Un modello di una sciena per fare apparire nella sala dove magnia lor Altezze che fa paramento e prospettiva all'improvviso lungo b. 1¼ e largo b. 1¼ e alto ⅔ tutto dipinto d'albero.*

101 Carter and Goldthwaite, *Orpheus in the Marketplace*, 113, assumes *Euridice*; and compare Durante and Martellotti, *Don Angelo Grillo O.S.B. alias Livio Celiano*, 193. But we are more cautious here.

distraction from the stressful circumstances around the marriage negotiations and their repeated delays: indeed, on 28 May the grand duke emphasized that Maria was not to be kept informed of those circumstances precisely because they might cause her too much anxiety.[102] Thus on Saturday 27 May the grand duchess wrote to her husband that the previous evening she had spent some time with Maria discussing the color scheme of the livery for the pages, footmen, guards, and carriages attending her at the wedding, deciding in the end, she says, for what was known in French as *orange, bleu, celeste, et blanc*. The grand duchess included in that letter a sample of Maria's favorite color (presumably in cloth) that Ferdinando was to pass on to the King of France.[103] It then emerges from the grand duchess's next letter, written the following day, that the poet Battista Guarini was in attendance (she writes that he would leave "tomorrow" – Monday), which would have allowed some discussion of the proposed entertainment for the wedding banquet (Guarini wrote the text for the *Dialogo di Giunone e Minerva*).[104] However, there was also a rather tricky diplomatic issue to be resolved. As the grand duchess wrote in her Saturday letter, the papal nuncio had appeared at the Palazzo Pitti earlier on Friday bearing a *breve* from the Pope and letters from Cardinal Pietro Aldobrandini. The nuncio was requesting an audience with Maria de' Medici, but the grand duchess was uncertain about the etiquette for allowing it, given that she was unclear as to what the Pope's *breve* contained: presumably the lack of such knowledge threatened to put the women in a compromising position if some quick response were needed. Ferdinando must have replied immediately, because in her Sunday letter the grand duchess said that she would indeed arrange an audience for the nuncio "today." It is not clear how this might have affected any performance of Corsi's "comedy" taking place that same day, if it did (Christine does not mention it in any letter).

[102] Grand Duke Ferdinando I (in Ambrogiana) to Christine of Lorraine, 28 May 1600, *MdP* 5961, fol. 522: *Alla Regina non me pare che se le possa mostrare nulla, et per respetto di quella cagione, che tanto allegano della gravidanza di Vostra Altezza, et per respetto di Saluzzo che dicono di voler disbrigar prima, acciò che la non facesse mille comenti di pericoli et di perturbatione per questo indugio nel suo animo et tanto più . . .*

[103] The two letters from the grand duchess discussed here are in *MdP* 5962, fols. 521, 522.

[104] Guarini was well enough known to Florence – he received what was in effect an honorarium of *sc.*20 per month as a *segretario*, from 1 April 1599 into the early 1600s (*KirkCM*, 603) – and he was a member of the Accademia della Crusca. His departure on 29 May was to take care of personal matters: on 9 June he was in Venice (letter to Belisario Vinta; *MdP* 897, fol. 655); on 7 July, he was in Mantua (letter to Vinta; *MdP* 898, fol. 18); and on 27 July or thereabouts he was leaving Ferrara for Florence (noted in a letter from Marchesa Bentivoglio; *MdP* 899, fol. 171).

Jacopo Corsi seems to have been even busier at the end of May: his household accounts include an entry for the 30th referring to expenses involved in hosting guests for four days at his villa in Sesto Fiorentino.[105] This may or may not be connected to a visit to Florence made by the Benedictine monk, Angelo Grillo, sometime between late April and early June as he traveled from the *capitolo generale* of his order in Parma, which began on 24 April, back to the Monastero di S. Scolastica in Subiaco, east of Rome (he was its abbot from 1599 to 1602). Grillo was a prolific poet of both spiritual and secular verse (he published the latter under the name Livio Celiano), and his voluminous correspondence reveals extensive connections with a wide range of *literati* and musicians.[106] During what he called his *lungo passaggio* in Florence, Grillo was able to renew acquaintances with the poets Giovanni Battista Strozzi *il giovane* (who also played a leading role in the Accademia degli Alterati) and Ottavio Rinuccini, and with the musician Giulio Caccini, as is clear from letters he wrote to them after his return to Subiaco (where he arrived on 15 June); this sequence further includes a letter to Jacopo Corsi, whom Grillo seems to have met in Florence for the first time.[107] His Florentine encounters appear to have

[105] ASF, Guicciardini–Corsi–Salviati 409 (*giornale* of Jacopo Corsi, 1593–1603), fol. 130right (30 May 1600): *Al nostro signor Jacopo Corsi per le spese di casa £106.9s.4d. contanti resi a Romolo spenditore disse havere spesi a Sesto in 4 giorni per esservi forestieri.*

[106] Various editions of Grillo's letters were published in 1602, 1608, 1612, and 1616; some to Giovanni Battista Strozzi *il giovane* also survive in BNCF, Magl. VIII.1399. The most relevant edition for present purposes is the first: *Lettere . . . raccolte dall'Illust. et Eccellentissimo Signor Ottavio Menini* (Venice: Gio. Battista Ciotti, 1602; the dedication is dated 1 May 1602, and the *licenza*, 20 June). The letters here generally lack dates, but in contrast to the later editions (with letters arranged by theme as epistolary models), these seem to be in rough chronological order (if with some exceptions) from 1594 to Easter 1601, although the sequence apparently from 1596–97 contains one letter to Leonardo Sanudo from 2 January(?) 1602 (at 244), and another to Marino from 13 February that same year (at 246). Precise dates for some of the letters can be confirmed by those to Strozzi in BNCF, and by others given in the first two parts of Bartolomeo Zucchi, *L'idea del segretario* (Venice: Compagnia Minima, 1606; the first part was published in 1600), while other of Grillo's letters can be dated more approximately by way of internal references to events or seasons (and to each other).

[107] Grillo mentions Strozzi and Caccini in a letter to Rinuccini probably dating from mid-1595 (*Lettere* [1602], 166); he met Rinuccini and Caccini in Ferrara in early May 1598 (Durante and Martellotti, *Don Angelo Grillo O.S.B. alias Livio Celiano*, 197). Durante and Martellotti (ibid., 193) briefly discuss his visit to Florence; see also Rossini, "Corrispondenti strozziani," 199–205. Grillo notes his *lungo passaggio* with Strozzi and Rinuccini in his letter to Nicolò Tucci in Lucca; Grillo, *Lettere* (1602), 480. His letter to Corsi is in ibid., 407. Despite the lack of dates in the letters, a significant sequence of them can be identified on the basis of internal evidence as coming from summer 1600 (and the letters to Caccini, Corsi, Rinuccini, and Strozzi may have been sent in the same mail). Another of Grillo's Florentine correspondents around this time, the friar and *literato* Matteo Baccellini, would later (in 1604) become Maria de' Medici's confessor in Paris.

extended to other members of the Alterati – or at least, to their works – and his visit also led to several requests for him to write poetry in honor of Maria de' Medici's wedding, although Grillo gracefully declined, claiming not to be able to set his mind to it.[108]

That letter to Corsi offers a general expression of gratitude and obligation; however, those to Rinuccini and to Caccini are more specific. Grillo asks Rinuccini to write about his latest work and, in particular, about "the outcome [*evento*] of that graceful pastoral which with the music of Signor Giulio Caccini carried our ears to heaven on the very great wings of those angelic voices." Those "angelic voices" seem to be a reference to Caccini's famous *donne*, the female singers under his control, including his second wife, Margherita di Agostino Benevoli della Scala, and two daughters by his first, Francesca (b. 1587) and Settimia (b. 1591).[109] It also seems clear from the continuation of this letter that the *evento* refers to the forthcoming performance of the pastoral in the wedding festivities, although Grillo claims less interest in those future festivities as a whole than in Rinuccini's specific contribution to them.[110] As for Caccini, Grillo praises him as the father of "a new manner of music," a form of sung recitation (*cantar recitativo*) that is noble rather than popular and that does not mangle the words but gives them life and spirit. Moreover, the notion of Caccini being the inventor of this style, or perhaps of his having rediscovered something from the ancients lost in the passage of time, has been confirmed to Grillo following "the performance in this your manner of the beautiful pastoral by Signor Ottavio Rinuccini." That performance also demonstrated how the ancients used choruses and how important to they are to such works, contrary to the opinion of those who think that they are inessential. Finally, Grillo notes that this "new music" (*nuova Musica*) has

[108] For Grillo not writing poetry for the wedding, see his *Lettere* (1602), 408–10 (to Caccini: *Son fatto sterile da un pezzo in quà*), 462–63 (Baccellini), 465 (to Strozzi, datable to 12 August 1600 – not 15 August as given in Rossini, "Corrispondenti strozziani," 202 – from the copy in BNCF, Magl. VIII.1399, fol. 357), 482–83 (Baccellini). In his letter to Nicolò Tucci from summer 1600 (ibid., 480), Grillo refers to reading Raffaello Gualterotti's *poema eroico, L'universo, ovvero Il Polemidoro* (published in January 1600/1), which had been discussed in the Accademia degli Alterati on 24 January 1599/1600 at a meeting in which Rinuccini, Buonarroti, and others were present (as was Corsi as a guest); see the diary of the Alterati in Florence, Biblioteca Medicea Laurenziana, Ashburnham 558.2, fol. 105.

[109] In a later letter (after July 1602), Grillo asks Caccini for news of *quel suo Choro Angelico*; see Durante and Martellotti, *Don Angelo Grillo O.S.B. alias Livio Celiano*, 454.

[110] Grillo, *Lettere* (1602), 407–8: *mi scriva dello stato de' suoi studi, et in particolare dell'evento di quella sua gratiosa pastorale, che sotto la musica del Signor Giulio Caccini portava le nostre orecchie sopra il Cielo con l'ali massime di quelle voci Angeliche. Non passo alla notitia delle pompe reali, degli spettacoli regii, né della Regina medesima. Vo' solamente vedere, et udir Vostra Signoria parlar di se stessa, et delle cose sue.*

been universally embraced by all those with good ears, and has moved beyond the Italian courts to those of Spain, France, and other parts of Europe, so Grillo has been told.[111]

That final claim about the geographical spread of Caccini's "new music" seems an exaggeration for 1600: Caccini's first collection of solo songs, *Le nuove musiche*, was due to be published in February 1601/2 but only appeared in the following July, that is, long after the apparent date of the final letter in Grillo's 1602 collection (which itself was published in June). But the songs it contained had been in circulation for a fair while, and Grillo's other comments about Caccini's style, including the term *cantar recitativo* and the reference to reviving the practice of the ancients, certainly square with hot topics in Florence in spring 1600. Clearly Grillo paid attention to these issues during his visit – there is no other way he could have engaged with them in such detail – and particularly, it seems, in multiple conversations with Caccini.[112] The obvious question, however, is what might have been the unnamed pastoral by Rinuccini in which Grillo took such musical delight, and which he knew, or thought, would be performed during the wedding celebrations.

Peri says in the preface to his score of *Euridice* (published in February 1600/1) that some of Caccini's music was used in the performance of the opera on 6 October 1600 – including the "arias" for Euridice, "some" of the same for a shepherd and nymph, and three of the choruses marking the end of each episode in the action – because it involved singers "dependent" on him.[113] Caccini then published a complete setting of Rinuccini's libretto in

[111] Grillo, *Lettere* (1602), 408–10: *Dico senza fargli torto; perché ella è padre di nuova maniera di Musica, d'un cantar senza canto, ò più tosto d'un cantar recitativo nobile, et non popolare, che non tronca, non mangia, non toglie la vita alle parole, non l'affetto, anzi glielo accresce, raddoppiando in loro spirito, et forza. È dunque invention sua questa bellissima maniera di cantare, ò forse ella è novo ritrovatore di quella forma antica perduta già tanto tempo fà nel vario costume d'infinite genti, et sepolta nell'oscura caligine di tanti secoli. Il che mi si và più confermando doppo l'essersi recitata sotto cotal sua maniera la bella pastorale del Signor Ottavio Rinuccini. Nella quale coloro che stimano nella poesia drammatica, et rappresentativa il choro cosa otiose, possono, per quanto mi hà detto esso Signor Ottavio medesimo, benissimo chiarirsi à che se ne servivano gli antichi, et di quanto rilievo sia in simili componimenti. In somma questa nuova Musica hoggidì viene abbracciata universalmente dalle buone orecchie, et dalle corti de' principi Italiani è passata à quelle di Spagna, et di Francia, et d'altre parti d'Europa come hò da fedel relatione.* In this and other letters to Caccini, Grillo also refers to the composer having set his poetry to music, although there are no known settings of Grillo/Celiano by Caccini.

[112] In this same letter to Caccini, Grillo notes how he had bothered him many times during his visit to Florence (*Non sarò neanco sterile in servirla, se vorrà valersi di me con quella fede, con la quale io l'hò nel mio passar per costà più volte incommodata, et annoiata*).

[113] Peri, *Le musiche . . . sopra L'Euridice* (1600 [= 1601]): *Non dimeno Giulio Caccini (detto Romano) il cui sommo valore è noto al Mondo, fece l'arie d'Euridice, et alcune del Pastore,*

December 1600, although Peri noted that it had been composed and printed "after" his own was performed. However, we shall see (in Chapter 3) that Caccini's score, unlike Peri's, does not take advantage of improvements to the libretto that were made during the preparations for the performance in October. Peri, too, staked his claim for writing "new" music in his dedication to Maria de' Medici of his score (*Poiché Le [*sic*] nuove Musiche fatte da me, nello sponsalizio della Maestà Vostra* . . .), and he would probably have felt that Grillo's claim for the wonders of, and intent behind, Caccini's *cantar recitativo* applied even more to him. If Grillo heard a complete performance of Rinuccini's pastoral in spring 1600 somewhere in Florence, and if that pastoral was *Euridice*, then it cannot have been with Caccini's music alone, at least if we trust Peri's later remark (*composta . . . pur dopo*), even if Grillo was unaware of that fact. However, it is also possible that Grillo heard only portions of *Euridice* – those composed by Caccini for "his" singers – and assumed (when asking Rinuccini to send him news of the performance during the wedding festivities) that the rest would be by Caccini as well. This also fits with Grillo's reference to Caccini's *donne*, and his claim about the new-found efficacy of dramatic choruses (given that Caccini provided the music for three of them in the *Euridice* performed in October 1600).

The fact that the singer Ginevra di Piero *mazziere* was being taught the music of the prologue to *Euridice* by Caccini's son, Pompeo, probably in late April or early May (see Chapter 3) suggests that at least some of the opera was composed by then, whether by Caccini or Peri (or both). However, there is another possibility: that what Grillo heard in Florence in spring 1600 was a complete setting by Caccini of the libretto that had previously been performed to music by Corsi and Peri (at least, so Peri says): Rinuccini's *Dafne*. There is some evidence for Caccini having produced such a setting at some point, although it has tended to be dismissed by scholars. During the visit of Caccini and his *donne* to Paris in 1604–5, Maria de' Medici proposed a performance of *Dafne* given the impending arrival of Rinuccini there.[114] Caccini himself said in the preface to his *Nuove musiche e nuova maniera di scriverle* (1614) that his early

e Ninfa del Coro, e de' Cori, "Al canto, al ballo," "Sospirate," e "Poi che gli eterni imperi." E questo, perché dovevano esser cantate da persone dependenti da lui, le quali Arie si leggono nella sua composta, e stampata pur dopo, che questa mia fu rappresentata a sua Maestà Cristianissima. Caccini published his *L'Euridice composta in musica in stile rappresentativo* (Florence: Giorgio Marescotti, 1600) some three months after the festivities (the dedication to Giovanni de' Bardi is dated 20 December), whereas Peri's came out six weeks later (dedicated to Maria de' Medici on 6 February 1600/1).

[114] *KirkCM*, 149–50. However, Caccini says that the performance did not take place.

achievements included his music for *Dafne*, performed before "their most serene highnesses" of Tuscany and other princes in the residence of Jacopo Corsi.[115] And in Rinuccini's libretto for *Narciso* (never set to music, it seems), Caccini, delivering a biographical prologue addressed to Grand Duchess Christine, notes his music for *Il rapimento di Cefalo*, *Euridice*, and *Dafne* (in that order).[116] Peri's own statement on *Dafne* in his preface to *Euridice* – that his setting was presented in three successive Carnival seasons (including the performance before the grand duchess and Cardinals del Monte and Montalto on 21 January 1598/99) – would seem to exclude any *Dafne* produced by Caccini. But if we accept that Caccini did indeed compose a setting of *Dafne*, and that it was performed in Corsi's residence in the presence of the Medici, then two options follow. First, Peri was not telling the whole story: what happened with *Dafne* was the same as with *Euridice* – Caccini had "his" singers perform his own music and then produced a complete setting. Or second, Corsi had two separate complete settings of *Dafne* in hand, one by Peri (if with some music by Corsi himself) performed in those successive Carnivals, and one by Caccini performed in Corsi's residence (so Caccini says in 1614) on some other occasion. The latter could have been what Angelo Grillo heard on his visit to Florence in spring 1600, although there is no evidence that "their highnesses" were present in Corsi's residence then. If so, Grillo was almost certainly mistaken that this "graceful pastoral" that so delighted his ears was the one that would be attached to the forthcoming wedding celebrations: it seems unlikely that Corsi intended to present at the festivities a work (with or without new music) that had been done so often before, especially given that his *pastorale nuova* was already on the cards in early April 1600. Or perhaps Grillo was just as confused as modern scholars have been (and we still to some degree remain) about what was done when within the highly competitive environment surrounding early opera in Florence.

115 Giulio Caccini, *Nuove musiche e nuova maniera di scriverle* (Florenze: Zanobi Pignoni & Co., 1614): *la musica, che io feci nella favola della Dafne del Sig. Ottavio Rinuccini, rappresentata in casa del Sig. Iacopo Corsi d'onorata memoria à quest'Altezze Serenissime, et altri Prencipi.*

116 Solerti, *Gli albori del melodramma*, 2: 191–92: *Colmo d'alto stupor le scene aurate / de la bell'Alba allor le voci udiro, / allor gli abissi al gran cantor s'apriro / e pianse Apollo su le fronde amate.* This prologue in effect outlines Caccini's biography delivered in retrospect by the singer in old age (*benché dagli anni stanco*). That same quatrain, however, also appears in a prologue written by Rinuccini (delivered by La Musica) for a performance of *Dafne* in the residence of Don Giovanni de' Medici, presumed to be the one given on 9 February 1610/11 (*SolMBD*, 60–61); see Solerti, *Gli albori del melodramma*, 2: 103–4. Another version of this *Dafne* prologue replaces the reference to *Il rapimento di Cefalo* with one to *Arianna*, therefore mentioning all three of Rinuccini's opera librettos to date. Scholars have tended to assume that the 1611 *Dafne* was the setting by Marco da Gagliano, first performed in Mantua in early 1608.

These ambiguities may also have been a result of the shifting timetable of the wedding festivities, which were originally intended to take place before the summer but then were repeatedly postponed to August (so Giovanni del Maestro noted on 22 May) and then September, before being fixed for early October. This further raises questions about the *comedia* presented by Corsi in the Palazzo Pitti on the order of the grand duchess in late May or early June. The label itself does not aid in any identification; Corsi applied it to both *Dafne* and *Euridice* in his own account books. But if we assume that Grillo is unlikely to have had access to the Pitti, then the performance here cannot be the one where he heard Caccini's music, which is not to say that he did not hear the same music in a different location. The fact that Camillo Pieroni erected his stage in the *salone della Duchessa di Bracciano* is somewhat odd, however. Navigating one's way around the Palazzo Pitti as it was at the time is not always an easy task: the palace was still a work in progress in terms of its overall footprint and its separate floor plans for the *piano terreno*, the *piano nobile*, and what was sometimes called the *piano della terza habitazione* (the top floor), also with various mezzanines and attic space in different parts of the roof (the *piano a tetto*).[117] Their layout also changed over time as additions were made and spaces altered, as can clearly be seen in the two plans most relevant to our inquiry: the ones of the *piano terreno* and *piano nobile* included in the appendix to Joseph Furttenbach the Elder's *Architectura civilis* (Ulm: Saur, 1628) – which contains some surprisingly precise measurements – and those of all three floors by Giacinto (Iacinto) Maria di Francesco Marmi, prepared early in the third quarter of the seventeenth century.[118] Furthermore, the names applied to the various spaces in the palace changed according to their use, if with some time lag and depending on the custom (or error) of individual

[117] We seek to label the floors carefully, also given the potential confusion in modern usage in terms of what constitutes the "first" floor of a building. As for the orientation of the Palazzo Pitti, it is positioned longitudinally from southwest to northeast, but for convenience we treat the facade as "north" and the central courtyard (leading to the Boboli Gardens) as "south," bounded by north–south wings on the "west" and "east" sides.

[118] Furttenbach's two volumes, one of text and one of engravings, can be seen at http://digi.ub.uni-heidelberg.de/diglit/furttenbach1628a and http://digi.ub.uni-heidelberg.de/diglit/furttenbach1628; his plans of the two lower floors of the Palazzo Pitti square with Justus Utens's painting of the palace which was included in his series of representations of Medici residences done in 1599–1602 (see www.wga.hu/html_m/u/utens/pitti.html). Marmi's *Norma per il guardarobba del gran palazzo della città di Fiorenza dove habita il Serenissimo Gran Duca di Toscana*, in BNCF, Magliabechiano II.I.284, covers all three main floors; there are reproductions in Bertelli, "Palazzo Pitti dai Medici ai Savoia," 77–92. Furttenbach's and Marmi's plans more or less match, save that the former's do not include the lateral wings added to the Pitti beginning in 1618.

administrators. Likewise, a number of rooms varied in their function (and frequency of occupation) according to the season, and even on a day-to-day basis – or a day-to-night one, as beds were rolled out for all residents save those who had permanent quarters.[119]

Flavia Peretti-Orsini (1574–1606), Duchess of Bracciano, fell into that latter category. The grand duchess does not mention her in those letters to Grand Duke Ferdinando written on 27 and 28 May, but she was a close companion to Maria de' Medici (they were one year apart in age). She had married Virginio Orsini, Grand Duke Ferdinando's nephew, in 1589, and they had separate suites of rooms in the Pitti, Virginio on the west end of the *piano terreno*, on the north side facing the piazza, and Flavia directly above on the *piano nobile* and possibly the next floor up as well (in the latter case, next door to Maria's suite on the top floor of the palace in the middle of its north side), as well as having access to the mezzanine spaces between both floors.[120] Furttenbach's plan of the *piano nobile* makes the location of Flavia's rooms there clear (see Fig. 1.5): they were what he identified as two *camere* at the bottom right (the northwest corner in our orientation of the Pitti), each with one window on the north facade. By the time Giacinto Marmi drew his own plan of the *piano nobile* early in the third quarter of the seventeenth century, those two rooms had been converted into one (two windows on the north facade), in part as a result of additional construction extending the palace on either side. But if we stick to Furttenbach's plan, it is not clear which of Flavia's two rooms on the *piano nobile* were used as a *salone*.

According to Furttenbach, each room was roughly 13 *b.* long on the west–east axis, and 18 *b.* wide (7.5 m by 10.4 m). A stage located across its width (north–south) could have been the same size as the one often mounted for theatrical performances in the much longer room next door, which Furttenbach calls the *Sala maggiore* (that is, the Sala delle Statue). However, there would have been limited room for any audience.

[119] For the broader issues, see Bertelli, "Palazzo Pitti dai Medici ai Savoia"; the roll-out beds are discussed in ibid., 26–29.

[120] For Flavia Peretti-Orsini's rooms (and the allocation of others in the palace, if with some errors), see Facchinetti, "Le vicende costruttive," 35; Facchinetti draws on the two partial inventories of the Palazzo Pitti (1597, 1607) in *GM* 422, which also provide details of the mezzanine rooms between the main floors. The catalog entry in Giusti and Spinelli (eds.), *Dolci trionfi e finissime piegature*, 116, associates Flavia with rooms on the top floor of the palace, behind the *Salone delle commedie* (but they were occupied by Emilio de' Cavalieri instead). It is true that the 1597 inventory in *GM* 422 lists (fol. 16) *stanze della Duchessa di Bracciano al secondo piano* (i.e., the top floor), but if anything, these were probably directly above her rooms on the *piano nobile* (see Marmi's plan in Fig. 1.7), next door to Maria de' Medici's suite.

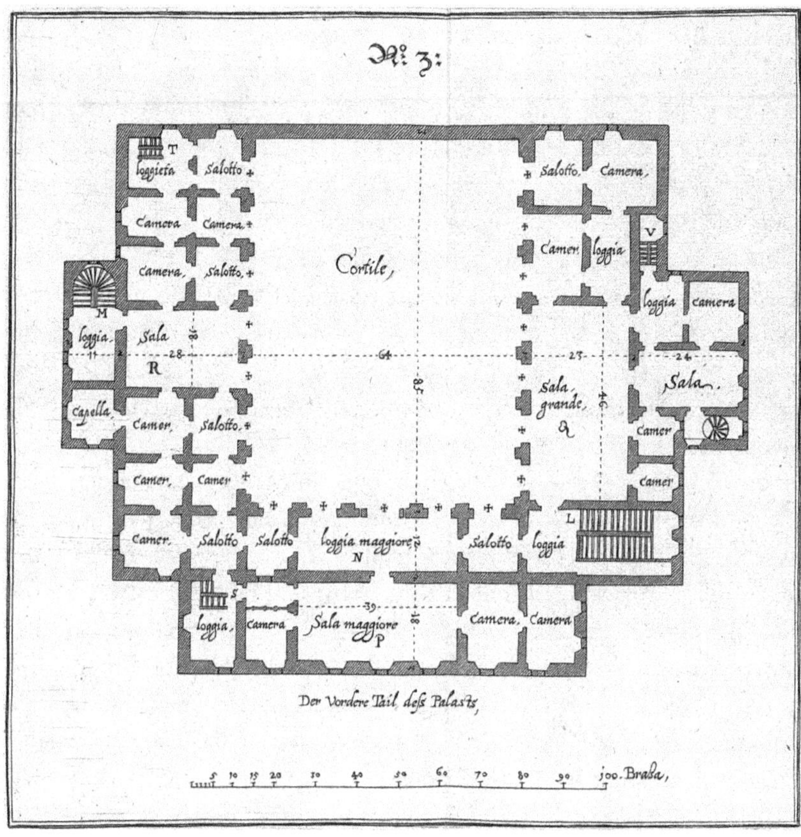

Fig. 1.5: Joseph Furttenbach the Elder, *Architectura civilis* (Ulm: Saur, 1628), fig. 3; the *piano nobile* of the Palazzo Pitti. The "north" facade of the palace (facing the piazza) is at the bottom of the image; the Boboli Gardens are at the top. The "Sala maggiore" on the north side is the Sala delle Statue; the two rooms to its right were occupied by the Duchess of Bracciano. The "Sala grande" to the right (in the west wing) facing the courtyard was also known as the "Sala dei forestieri" and is now the Sala Bianca. Heidelberg University Library, T 2269 RES:Abb.

This may or may not have mattered depending on the grand duchess's intentions behind the order she gave to Camillo Pieroni. We have seen that she and Maria de' Medici spent time in late May discussing arrangements for the wedding, and that Maria was in need of distraction; so, too, may have been the grand duchess, given that her third daughter, Maria Maddalena, would be born within a month. A *comedia* by Corsi within one of the more private spaces in the Pitti would have served both purposes.

A somewhat cryptic, undated note included in a set of documents associated with Bernardo Buontalenti around the time of his death (1608) says that he had spent two days working on *Dafne* for a performance in the Palazzo Pitti, and that he had heard it said that work needed to begin on the "big" comedy (for the 1600 festivities, it seems): this latter comedy cannot have been *Il rapimento di Cefalo* (which was decided upon only in early July), but it may have been the work originally intended to stand in its place for which Buontalenti designed a set of *intermedi* (so we have seen).[121] Buontalenti could have been mistaken, or perhaps misled (if Corsi had not yet made public the subject of his *pastorale nuova*). But if we take his comment at face value, it would seem that Corsi's *comedia* was another performance of *Dafne*. The same might be suggested by an entry dated 25 August 1600 in Corsi's personal accounts, referring to payment for gloves, including ten pairs used "in the comedy of *Dafne*."[122] The construction of a "stage" by Pieroni in the *salone* of the Duchess of Bracciano would also seem strongly to imply the presence of some manner of scenery, which presumably survived for *Dafne* (given the performance in the Pitti in Carnival 1598/99) but was not yet ready for *Euridice* as Cigoli would design it. However, assuming that some form of the *Dafne* set could have been made to fit the Duchess of Bracciano's *salone*, it could also have sufficed as a temporary option for at least the pastoral elements of *Euridice* – the reverse occurred in the later performance of *Dafne* in October 1604 (see Chapter 4).

Of course, it is very tempting to suggest that the grand duchess wanted to see some or all of Corsi's *pastorale nuova* in its present state in order to approve its performance in the wedding festivities. Michele Caccini certainly made a connection between Corsi's *comedia* and the one to be done in October 1600 by virtue of filing Pieroni's document with others pertaining to his work for the wedding (on the banquet and what turned out to be *Euridice*). Nor would this have been the first time that the grand duchess had informally previewed an entertainment planned for subsequent production: she did the same with an (unknown) *commedia pastorale* rehearsed in the Villa Petraia in June 1598, then advising the grand duke that it needed to be done in a different room there, and supporting the

121 *GM* 245, ins. 4, fol. 439: *Io feci lavorare alla commedia due giorni per la commedia di Daffene per a Pitti e si diceva che se havea a conminciar la grande* . . . For the contents of this *inserto*, see note 34. This somewhat illegible paragraph seems to be in the manner of a *copialettera*, i.e., a record of a letter sent to unknown recipient. No date is given.

122 Solerti, *Gli albori del melodramma*, 1: 63: *serviti per la comedia di Dafane* (*sic*). This was clearly a late payment, and it, too, may reflect some misprision.

actors' request that they be given new costumes for its *intermedi*.[123] For the moment, however, the question must remain moot.

As we have seen, Corsi was significantly involved both in the negotiations over the marriage of Maria de' Medici and Henri IV, and in the celebrations in Florence on the day of its official announcement (30 April), gaining much favor from the Medici as a result. He also variously supported Caccini and Peri in their musical and other ventures.[124] Like Rinuccini, he may also have been sympathetic to Caccini's clear (and successful) attempt to use the 1600 festivities to regain his salaried position among the Medici musicians. In spring 1600, it was not yet clear that the main theatrical performance in the festivities would be *Il rapimento di Cefalo*, in which Caccini as composer and his *donne* as performers featured much more prominently. The decision to stage *Il rapimento* – made in July 1600, it seems – may also have cleared the way for Peri to play a bigger role as composer and performer in *Euridice*.

Whatever the case, any *salone* of the Duchess of Bracciano was never going to be the location of a theatrical performance in the Palazzo Pitti during the wedding festivities themselves. The performances of *Il giuoco della cieca* and of *Dafne* in Carnival 1598/99 had taken place in the room that Furttenbach identified as the *Sala maggiore*, next to the rooms on the *piano nobile* occupied by the duchess. This was the so-called Sala delle Statue, named after the fact that during the reign of (Grand) Duke Cosimo I, it had housed a prominent collection of antique statues both in niches in the walls and freestanding, as well as other artworks, and although some of them had now been moved to the corridors of the Uffizi, other statues took their place, at least in the niches.[125] It served as one of the principal reception rooms in the palace: the banquet celebrating the announcement of Maria de' Medici's impending marriage took place here on 30 April

[123] See her letter to the grand duke, 1 June 1598, from Villa Petraia, *MdP* 5962, fol. 485: *Hieri si provò alla mia presenza la commedia pastorale, la quale crede che donerà gusto, ma bisognerà che Vostra Altezza la lasci fare nella sua sala, perché nell'altre non si sentirebbe* . . . This was done at Petraia by the boys of the Compagnia di S. Alberto Bianco, noted in a document from 1602 as having performed four years earlier; *GM* 236 (orders concerning theatrical costumes, 1600–1602), fol. 127.

[124] Corsi's connections with Peri are discussed extensively in Carter and Goldthwaite, *Orpheus in the Marketplace*; for Corsi and Caccini, see ibid., 109.

[125] The label *Sala delle statue* was the one most commonly used in our period, although the 1597 inventory of the Palazzo Pitti in *GM* 422 refers to it (fol. 4) as the *Salone grande detto delle Nicchie* (and nowadays the room is called the Sala delle Nicchie). It is not to be confused with what is currently called the Galleria delle Statue, a room (formerly a loggia) next to, and parallel to, the Sala delle Statue but facing the courtyard (see Fig. 1.5). For all these spaces, see Fantappiè, "Sale per lo spettacolo a Pitti."

1600, and there was a similar gathering for Cesare d'Este, Duke of Modena (husband of Ferdinando I's stepsister, Virginia), with the grand duke, grand duchess, and Maria de' Medici on 21 May.[126] The court diaries are silent on any events immediately thereafter, although there was a significant amount of repair work being done in the Sala delle Statue from late May on, in terms of its wall coverings and fixtures – including rehanging its three sets of doors and adding windows to them – with the costs charged to the account of the wedding festivities.[127] Therefore, the room may not have been available for use, which could also be why the grand duchess turned to the *salone* of the Duchess of Bracciano for Corsi's *comedia*.

The Sala delle Statue would have been a prestigious location for any performance of *Euridice*, and it is clear that so far as Lodovico Cigoli was concerned when starting out on the design and construction of its stage and sets, this was indeed originally intended to be its location during the festivities. The room remains today in something close to its original form, save for a different decorative scheme adopted in the eighteenth century (see Fig. 2.3). According to Furttenbach's plan, it was 39 *b.* long on its west–east axis (along the facade) and 18 *b.* wide, which is very close to the room's current measurements at 22.8 m by 10.4 m (39.3 *b.* by 17.9 *b.*).[128] We shall see (in Chapter 2) that the width matches Cigoli's original design for the stage (the room's height works as well), and his proscenium picked up on other architectural elements within the room. It was the later decision to move the opera to a different location in the palace that caused Cigoli some difficulties in terms of reconfiguring his design and then of adding new elements to it.

How much of the stage for *Euridice* to be used in the Sala delle Statue was actually constructed prior to that move remains unclear. The 229 *ricevute* kept by Michele Caccini and linked to the "book of the banquet and royal wedding of the Most Christian Queen of France" begin on 13 May 1600, and the earliest ones concern planks of wood being consigned

126 *GM*, Diari d'etichetta 2, p. 115.

127 On 2 June 1600, Cosimo Latini, *Ministro della Galleria di Sua Altezza Serenissima*, received 300 *occhi di vetro da finistre* to add to the 276 previouly delivered, *e son serviti a fare 6 sportelli a 3 portoni della sala delle statue, rasente li archi che v[']era impannate di commissione di Sua Altezza Serenissima*; *SFF* 72, fol. 2. Their cost, and that of the metal fixtures (*ferri*) needed to hold them, were charged to the festivities. Camillo Pieroni included rehanging the doors (because they had dropped on their hinges) in his invoice of 31 May 1600 (reflecting work done from 8 to 29 May); *GM* 1152, fol. 139 (and compare *SFF* 72, fol. 15v, a list of work done from 21 March 1599/1600 to 5 January 1600/1).

128 These current measurements were done on site by hand with a laser measuring tool, so one needs to allow a small margin of error.

to Caccini from the Fortezza da Basso and thence to various carpenters, including one batch given to Matteo Nigetti for work in the Palazzo Pitti for the wedding (*per far lavori costì a Pitti per le noze* [sic]); by 9 June, Nigetti was also procuring hardware (nails, etc.) allocated to the account of what was now identified as the *commedia de' Pitti*, and he is the carpenter who seems to have supervised construction of the actual stage.[129] Some of the elements of Cigoli's design were clearly manufactured early on; otherwise they would not have been altered, and additional ones added, following the decision to move *Euridice* to a different room. Moreover, materials relating to the opera received by Michele Caccini in the second week of July still seem intended for (or measured for) the Sala delle Statue.[130] However, we do not know whether they were ever mounted in place.

But the switch of rooms was part of a broader pattern in the Palazzo Pitti of refurbishing or otherwise preparing different spaces as they would be needed for the festivities to accommodate guests and so forth (this is documented extensively in the accounts considered here). The postponement of the ceremonies to early October also affected matters, given that the palace's rooms tended to be occupied differently according to the season: the upper floors were not preferred in the summer (it was cooler on the *piano terreno*), whereas they could be heated more easily when temperatures started to fall.[131] During the festivities themselves, foreign guests were accommodated on the *piano terreno* (Roger de Bellegarde, also known as Monsieur le Grand) and *piano nobile* (Cardinal Aldobrandini; Nicolas Brûlart de Sillery), whereas the Duke and

[129] *GM* 1152, fols. 101 (15 May), 298 (a list of purchases for *Il lavoro dela chomedia de' Pitti* beginning on 9 June). Matteo di Dionigi Nigetti (in this period, generally styled just Matteo di Nigi *legnaiolo*) was also involved in the construction of the Cappella dei Principi in S. Lorenzo, working alongside Bernardo Buontalenti and then Don Giovanni de' Medici; he rose in status to become an important architect (see Rinaldi, "Nigetti, Matteo"). His father was the master carpenter Dionigi di Matteo alla Neghittosa, who had earlier worked with Giorgio Vasari on the Uffizi; see also Fantappiè, "La chiesa di San Lorenzo tra due dinastie," 546, 560 n. 27.

[130] See, for example, Caccini's receipt on 10 July of *una tela dipinta per la comedia de' Pitti* measuring 9.5 *b.* by 4.5 *b.*, which looks suspiciously like one of the backdrops painted by Cigoli with measurements intended for the Sala delle Statue; *GM* 1152, fol. 174. Likewise, the sewn canvas for the "sky" of the stage was delivered surprisingly late (on 11 September; *GM* 1152, fol. 283), perhaps because the new room altered its dimensions.

[131] Marmi's plans for the Palazzo Pitti distinguish the *piano terreno* and *piano nobile* as where the grand duke (etc.) lived in the summer and winter respectively (whereas the top floor was for the princes and princesses). Testaverde, "Nuovi documenti sulle scenografie di Ludovico Cigoli per l'*Euridice* di Ottavio Rinuccini," 314, also uses the season as an argument for shifting the performance of *Euridice*.

Duchess of Mantua were in a suite on the top floor (next to Maria de' Medici).[132] Shifting *Euridice* may have been caused by these arrangements, or just by the need to keep the Sala delle Statue free for other uses (such as the family meal before the *festa* in the Riccardi gardens on 8 October). However, Michele Caccini and his colleagues could have become aware of other issues as well. *Euridice* required a more complex stage than normally used in the Pitti (for example, for *Dafne*) precisely because of its change of scene from a pastoral setting to the Underworld and back. Moreover, the lighting effects needed for the Underworld increased the ever-present risk of fire in any theatrical endeavor. But Cigoli was left with the problem of reconfiguring his stage for a room lower in height and wider than the one originally intended (*Cig11*: *in altro salone più basso et più largo che per dove era fatta*). He charged an additional *sc.*25 for the inconvenience.

The Performance of *Euridice* on 6 October 1600

Switching rooms for the production of *Euridice* during the wedding festivities was just one of a number of changes made to the work in the course of its creation, from the drafting of the libretto and of Peri's score through the rehearsals to the performance. Some of them reflected creative decisions made in light of experience, while others were determined by circumstance. For example, it seems clear that the intended casting of the opera changed in the course of the summer, with a consequent impact on the work itself. One surviving copy of the first printing of Rinuccini's libretto contains handwritten annotations adding the names of performers alongside the printed list of "Interlocutori" (see Fig. 1.6 and Table 3.1). These annotations appear to have been made by Michelangelo Buonarroti *il giovane*.[133] The names do not quite square with those who Peri says (in his preface to the score) played those roles on 6 October 1600, given the presence of local performers instead of the two "outside" singers named by him, the tenor Francesco Rasi (Aminta), employed by Duke Vincenzo Gonzaga of Mantua, and the Roman bass Melchiorre Palantrotti (Plutone). Rasi came to Florence in mid-August and also performed in *Il rapimento di*

[132] ASF, Carte Strozziane I, 27 (the *memorie* of Giovanni del Maestro), fols. 27v–28v, 30v, 38[*bis*], 39v, 41. The Duchess of Mantua (Eleonora de' Medici) had been there since mid-June; the duke arrived on 29 September.

[133] We are grateful to Janie Cole for aid with this identification of the handwriting.

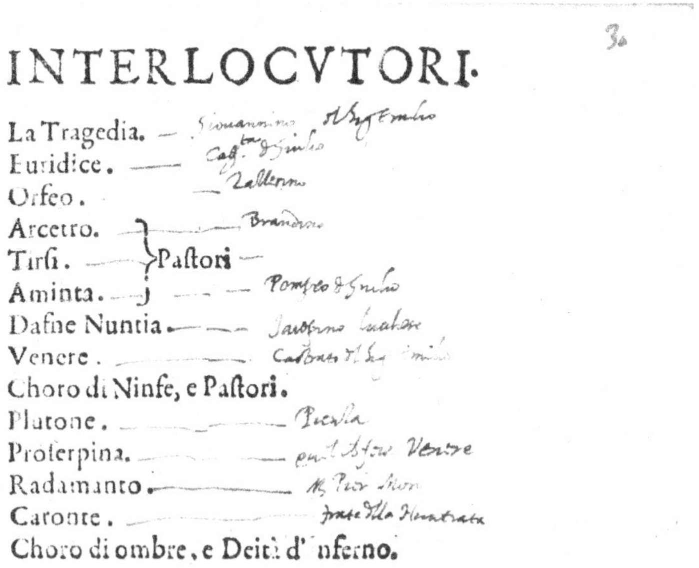

INTERLOCVTORI.

La Tragedia.
Euridice.
Orfeo.
Arcetro.
Tirsi. Paſtori
Aminta.
Dafne Nuntia.
Venere.
Choro di Ninfe, e Paſtori.
Platone.
Proſerpina.
Radamanto.
Caronte.
Choro di ombre, e Deità d'Inferno.

Fig. 1.6: Ottavio Rinuccini, *L'Euridice ... rappresentata nello sponsalitio della Christianiss. Regina di Francia, e di Navarra* (Florence: Cosimo Giunti, 1600), fol. [A4]r; the cast list of *Euridice* annotated (by Michelangelo Buonarroti *il giovane*?) with the names of performers. University of Illinois at Urbana–Champaign, Rare Book and Manuscript Library, Italian Plays 0520.

Cefalo, as did Palantrotti, who may have arrived in July.[134] Thus the annotations do not relate to the performance of *Euridice* during the festivities: scholars have assumed that they were intended for a second one shortly after, though there is no other evidence for it, nor any obvious occasion on which it might have been done.[135] Clearly these annotations were made after the libretto of *Euridice* was first printed (but not in its second state; see Chapter 3). However, one of them is in the past tense, with Proserpina sung by *quel che fece Venere*.[136] It seems at least possible that Buonarroti was seeking information on the cast that would be used in the performance of *Euridice* during the festivities

[134] *KirkCM*, 565 n. 83 (Palantrotti), 566 (Rasi).

[135] We shall see (in Chapter 3) that the other assumption – that this was the cast for the performance of *Euridice* directed by Giulio Caccini in December 1602 – is also implausible.

[136] In other words, the roles in *Euridice* of Venere and Proserpina were doubled, although it is just possible that the reference to Venere is to the character in *Dafne*.

for the purpose of his description, but he had not been made aware of Rasi's and Palantrotti's involvement; if so, that information must have been gained on the basis of some prior plan from earlier in the summer, whether or not related to any possible preview performance in late May or early June.

So far as Lodovico Cigoli was concerned, however, it was the change of venue for *Euridice* to a differently sized space that most affected his work on the opera. Michele Caccini noted that it was moved to a room higher up within the palace, with the result that the stage had to be enlarged and altered (*per havere mutato la sciena dalla sala da basso alla sala da alto de' Pitti che s'ebbe a cresciere e variare*).[137] Precisely which room this was has been a matter of some confusion in the literature. So it was also at the time. For example, Gianbattista Cresci noted in September 1601 that the opera was done in the *salone grande delle stanze de' forestieri*, which most nowadays would take to mean the large room on the *piano nobile* in the west wing facing the central courtyard, known in the period as the Sala (Grande) dei Forestieri, and today called the Sala Bianca (the name changed in the eighteenth century). This room was next to the so-called *stanze dei forestieri*, allocated to guests (*forestieri*) staying in the palace – Cardinal Aldobrandini was accommodated there in October 1600 – and it was used for larger-scale receptions, *balli*, and so forth.[138] However, Cresci made a mistake: in early 1601, a payment was made to Matteo di Domenico *e compagni* (*imbiancatori*) for work that include painting the walls of the room on Maria de' Medici's floor – one higher – "where the comedy was done."[139] Other documents also make it clear that the 6 October performance of *Euridice* was indeed in the so-called *salone di sopra* on the top floor of the west wing of the palace.

[137] *GM* 1152, fol. 448, in the note that Caccini made approving the revised payment to Cigoli (based on the five estimates) while still allowing the *sc.*25 fee that Cigoli added to his invoice because of the change of rooms.

[138] Fantappiè, "Sale per lo spettacolo a Pitti," 150–56.

[139] *SFF* 72, fol.15: *per avere inbiancato su al piano della regina el salone dove se fatto la commedia tutto quello che si vede di brachi [q.] 630*. This is in a list of work done since 17 September 1600, for which payment was made on 5 January 1600/1. Matteo di Domenico and/or his employees painted the walls of the room that were visible (so, minus the stage), and presumably those (upper, it seems) portions not covered by other decoration. His company was often used for such services in the Palazzo Pitti, moving through rooms on a regular cycle, although the work increased as rooms were smartened up for the wedding festivities. Compare the similar entry in *SFF* 72, fol. 28v, noting payment on 2 January 1601/2 *per havere inbiancato su alto il salone quondam Don Antonio quando teneva la commedia insino al palcho*. This is in a set of entries relates to work done since 17 February 1600/1, so if it refers to *Euridice* (as the *quando* suggests), it is some kind of back payment which Matteo di Domenico forgot to put in an earlier invoice.

Giacinto Marmi's later plan of that floor of the Pitti makes the location clear (see Fig. 1.7, rooms "S" and "T" on the right), although the room had been divided into two unequal parts by the time it was made. This *salone di sopra* was in the area of the Pitti that had formerly been occupied by Don Antonio de' Medici; the west wing also contained rooms at the rear, two of which were allocated to Emilio de' Cavalieri. Don Antonio's suite was

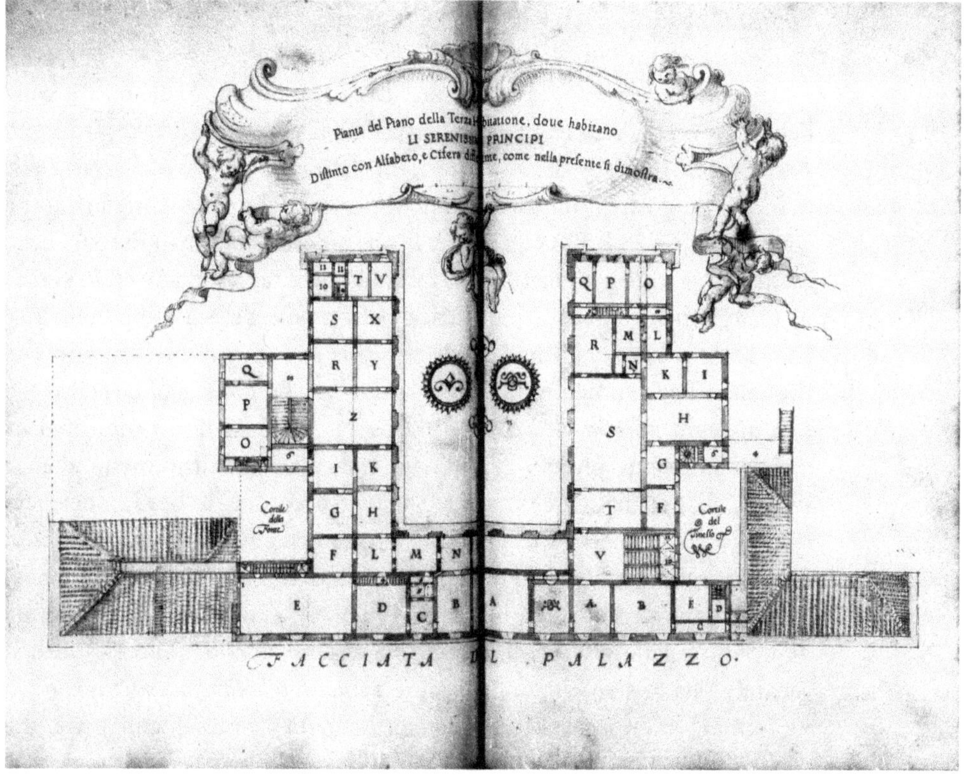

Fig. 1.7: Giacinto Maria di Francesco Marmi, *Norma per il guardarobba del gran palazzo della città di Fiorenza dove habita il Serenissimo Gran Duca di Toscana*, BNCF, Magliabechiano II.I.284, fol. 154; the top floor of the Palazzo Pitti. The orientation is the same as Furttenbach's plan of the *piano nobile* (Fig. 1.5). The wall separating rooms "S" and "T" on the right (the west wing) facing the courtyard subdivided what was variously known as the "Sala di Don Antonio [de' Medici]," the "Salone di sopra," the "Sala della veglia," and the "Sala delle commedie." By permission of the Ministero per i beni e le attività culturali e per il turismo della Repubblica Italiana/Biblioteca Nazionale Centrale, Firenze. No further reproduction permitted.

around the corner from the one allocated to Maria de' Medici, who treated him affectionately as her stepbrother (he was one year younger), and even though he had moved out of the Palazzo Pitti to his own residence, the Casino di S. Marco, in February 1598 – in part because of a fire in the attic above his rooms – that section of the palace remained linked to his name.[140] This helps explain why Cesare Tinghi referred to *Euridice* as "a pastoral comedy in music done by Signor Emilio de' Cavalieri up in the rooms of Signor Don Antonio de' Medici in the Pitti" (*una comedia pastorale in musica fatta dal signor Emilio del Cavaliere su alle stanze del signor Don Antonio Medici a Pitti*).[141]

The *salone di sopra* was of a similar length and width to the one directly beneath it on the *piano nobile* (the Sala dei Forestieri), which according to Furttenbach (see Fig. 1.5, on the right, labeled *Sala grande*), was 46 *b.* (26.7 m) long extending along four windows of the west wing facing the courtyard, and 23 *b.* (13.4 m) wide. It was indeed wider than the Sala delle Statue (23 *b.* rather than 18 *b.*), as Cigoli noted, and longer (46 *b.* versus 39 *b.*). It remained in use for theatrical performances at least into the 1620s: it was briefly known as the Sala della Veglia and then more commonly as the Sala delle Commedie, although even in 1608 it could still be styled the *sala di sopra nominata di Don Antonio.*[142] The fluid terms indicated its variable functions, given that any stage and associated furniture (audience seating, etc.) could be put up or taken down according to need rather than being kept in place. But the Sala delle Commedie was also convenient in other ways: unlike the Sala delle Statue, some rooms behind it were now occupied by court officials, including Emilio de' Cavalieri, rather than the grand-ducal family (so performers had easier "backstage" access); it had separate sets of stairs linking it to the *piano nobile* and *piano terreno* (so performers did not need to encumber the main staircase); and, given the

140 For Don Antonio's residing in the Palazzo Pitti until February 1598, see Covoni, *Don Antonio de' Medici al Casino di San Marco*, 96. Luti, *Don Antonio de' Medici e i suoi tempi*, 126, says that he moved out in 1597, although this may reflect a confusion over Florentine-style dating.

141 For the various contemporary mentions of the location of the 6 October performance of *Euridice*, see the extracts given in *SolMBD*, 25; *KirkCM*, 203–6. Giovanni del Maestro, the *maestro di casa*, referred to *una comedia nel palazzo de' Pitti sul salone di sopra*; the Modenese ambassador also said that *Euridice* was done *in una saletta nella parte di sopra del palazzo a Pitti.* Palisca, "The First Performance of *Euridice*," 433, opts for the Sala dei Forestieri, presumably on the basis of M. Fabbri *et al.* (eds.), *Il luogo teatrale a Firenze*, 144, which wrongly labels the Sala dei Forestieri as "la 'Sala di Don Antonio' detta attualmente Sala Bianca." Baldini Giusti ("Il salone da ballo e la sala della musica," 15–16), and Fantappiè ("Sale per lo spettacolo a Pitti," 136–38) were the first to identify the upstairs room as the proper location.

142 See Cesare Tinghi's comment on Francesco Cini's *veglia*, *Notte d'Amore*, in *SolMBD*, 45. For the shifting terminology, see Fantappiè, "Sale per lo spettacolo a Pitti," 140–50.

risk of fire, a room on an upper floor posed less of a threat to an entire building.

Unlike the Sala delle Statue, the Sala delle Commedie no longer survives intact: by the third quarter of the seventeenth century it had already been divided into two rooms at a quarter of its length (just after the first window) – as seen in Marmi's plan – and it now survives as three, with ceilings of different heights. As a result, it is impossible to verify how the measurements of Cigoli's revised stage conformed exactly to the room. However, the evidence is clear on how Cigoli needed to adjust his overall design to accommodate the new location, reducing the height of the stage to accommodate the lower ceiling, and adding additional elements on either side to extend its width (see Chapter 2).

We have relatively little information on the actual performance of *Euridice* on 6 October. In the preface to his score published in early 1601, Jacopo Peri listed some of the singers and the four instrumentalists who accompanied them (including Jacopo Corsi on the harpsichord). He also noted the presence of music by Giulio Caccini in the performance, which, he said, could be found in Caccini's own score composed and published after Peri's had been performed.[143] Scholars have tended to assume that Caccini's involvement was a later, somewhat malicious, intervention, given the competition surrounding the "invention" of opera in Florence, although our previous discussion of events in spring 1600 suggests that it may have been in effect early on. There is also a more charitable reading of Caccini's actions in terms of how singers were taught their musical roles for theatrical productions (see Chapter 3). By printing his score first, Caccini also ended up letting Peri have the last word, as it were, and Peri took full advantage, making it clear in a note at the end of his score that it was an indeed accurate representation of the performance (*E con questo ordine, che s'è descritta, fu rappresentata*), even though it was not, at least in terms of the music included by Peri in place of Caccini's contributions.

Although the Sala delle Commedie was larger than the Sala delle Statue, the audience for *Euridice* seems to have been very restricted in number: Giulio Thiene, the Modenese ambassador, said that few gained admission other than the *principi*, some noblewomen, and a few guests.[144] The *principi* would have included Maria de' Medici, the grand duke and

[143] See note 113.

[144] Given in *SolMBD*, 26–27 n. 2, and *KirkCM*, 204: *hieri fu fatta una pastorale rappresentata in musica, dove non entrorno se non pochissimi oltre ai principi, alcune gentildonne e qualche forestiere.* The other reports cited here are taken from *KirkCM*, 204–6. Kirkendale errs, however, in reading the Modenese ambassador's report as recording additional performances

grand duchess, the Duke and Duchess of Mantua, and the Duke and Duchess of Bracciano. Among the guests were the ambassadors from Modena, Parma, and Venice (Niccolò Molino), and, one assumes, Cardinal Aldobrandini and the leading French representatives, Nicolas Brûlart de Sillery and Roger de Bellegarde (Monsieur le Grand); the papal nuncio and resident ambassadors also watched from a doorway.[145] Other French visitors were excluded, however.[146] The performance lasted two hours according to Cesare Tinghi, or one and a half according to the Farnese ambassador, who also noted that it was followed by more than two hours of dancing involving the queen, princesses, and noblewomen.[147] It is not clear where the dancing took place, whether in the Sala delle Commedie or one floor down, where there would have been more room in the Sala dei Forestieri, although this might not have been convenient given that Cardinal Aldobrandini was lodging in rooms nearby.

Those ambassadors gave favorable accounts of *Euridice*: it succeeded very well (Modena: *riuscì molto bene*), was performed entirely by musicians with sweetest songs (Venice: *una comedia recitata tutta da musici in suavissimi canti*), and it was most beautiful, albeit simple in terms of its stage machines (Parma: *fu cosa bellissima, seben semplice in quanto alle*

of *Euridice* on 7 and 9 October (i.e., the open rehearsal of *Il rapimento di Cefalo* and the production itself).

[145] *SolMBD*, 25: *dove entrorno tutti questi principi et ambasciatori* (to which Tinghi adds a marginal note: *Nuntio et ambasciatori residenti steteno su in una porta di una camera a vedere*). That doorway was presumably the one leading to room G on Marmi's plan in Fig. 1.7. Something similar happened for the seating arrangements for Cini's *Notte d'Amore* in October 1608, where the grand duke watched from one door (because of the heat) and the Venetian ambassador and the papal nuncio from another; see Cesare Tinghi's *Diario di Ferdinando I e Cosimo II granduca di Toscana* (22 July 1600 to 12 September 1615), BNCF, Capponi 261/1, fol. 230 (*Sua Altezza stava ritirato in s'una porta di una camera per il rispetto del caldo*).

[146] For example, Cayet's second-hand *Chronologie septénaire de l'histoire de la paix entre les roys de France et d'Espagne* (1605) could only note (fol. 179v) that the three days between the banquet and *Il rapimento di Cefalo* were taken up with hunts, jousts, tilting at the ring, and other such princely exercises (*Les trois iours suivants furent employez en chasses et en ioustes, courses de bagues et autres exercices de Rois et Princes en telles solemnitez accoustumees*). The same report was given in the anonymous *Traicté du mariage de Henri IIII, Roy de France e de Navarre avec la Serenissime Princesse de Florence* (Honfleur: Jean Petit, 1606), 17; see Palisca, "The First Performance of *Euridice*," 439 (but citing a 1601 edition that appears not to exist).

[147] Modern performances of *Euridice* tend to come in at around 1h45m. For the Farnese ambassador's comment on the dancing, see *SolMBD*, 25 n. 1: *poi si ballò più di doi ore, mesticate la Regina e l'altre principesse con le private*. Buonarroti does not mention it in his description, just as he does not note the dancing in the Palazzo Pitti on the Sunday evening after the *festa* in the Riccardi gardens (reported by Giovanni del Maestro; see *SolMBD*, 26 n. 1). Nor would one expect him to. However, it was a standard way of framing an entertainment; compare Carter, "New Light on Monteverdi's *Ballo delle ingrate*," 86, 89, and the comments on the genre of the *veglia* in Carter and Goldthwaite, *Orpheus in the Marketplace*, 250–52.

machine). As we have seen, however, Emilio de' Cavalieri offered more negative reports circulating in Rome about the theatrical entertainments as a whole during the festivities, including scenery being incomplete or failing to operate properly, and music not giving satisfaction. The fact that Maria de' Medici seems to have preferred *Dafne* over *Euridice* – to the extent of proposing a performance of it by Caccini and his *donne* in Paris in early 1605 – may also be revealing. But in general most of the criticisms seem to have been directed at *Il rapimento di Cefalo*, which as the main entertainment of the festivities was clearly meant to make more of an impact than it did: its seeming to last some five hours in performance may not have helped.[148] The eighteenth-century diarist Francesco Settimanni repeated the more extravagant claims about that production made at its time: it was done before 3,000 gentlemen and 800 ladies (so Buonarroti also says in his description of the festivities); there were more than a hundred musicians, and more than a thousand stagehands operating the machines; and the whole entertainment cost *sc*.60,000. These numbers are wholly improbable given the likely seating capacity of the Teatro degli Uffizi and, indeed, the money that we have seen was spent by Gianbattista Cresci if just on part of the production costs.[149]

Buonarroti had every reason to exaggerate matters when it came to *Il rapimento di Cefalo*. There was far less need to do so when it came to

[148] Various contemporary comments on *Il rapimento di Cefalo* (some positive) are given in *KirkCM*, 137–42. Emilio de' Cavalieri later said that people felt that *Il rapimento di Cefalo* lasted five hours, although in fact it was just short of three; *KirkCM*, 141. It is clear, however, that the performance was in some sense incomplete. In a letter to Giovanni Battista Concini of 31 October 1600, Buonarroti wondered about removing from his description (of *Il rapimento*) *quelle cose che poi nella commedia non si feciono per mancamento di tempo*, but he was instructed to retain them; see Cole, *Music, Spectacle and Cultural Brokerage in Early Modern Italy*, 1: 189–90. Compare also Cavalieri's letter of 7 October (*recte* November) 1600, given in *KirkCM*, 140, where he says that in the case of *Il rapimento*, if Don Giovanni de' Medici and Bernardo Buontalenti had followed his advice *ogni cosa saria restate terminato, et finito*.

[149] There is no firm documentation for the capacity of the Teatro degli Uffizi, but Anna Maria Testaverde has confirmed to us her view that it must have held fewer than a thousand spectators. Two later Florentine theatres constructed in the seventeenth century, with boxes, held 800 (Teatro della Pergola) and 408 (Teatro del Cocomero); see Garbero Zorzi and Zangheri (eds.), *I teatri storici della Toscana*, 8: *Firenze*, 93, 123. When Florence was the capital of the Kingdom of Italy (1865–71), the senate (numbering 320 senators) met in the former Teatro degli Uffizi; see the image at https://it.wikipedia.org/wiki/Senatori_della_IX_legislatura_del_Regno_d%27Italia; the Camera dei Deputati, which met in the Salone dei Cinquecento, had around 500 members. The *sc*.60,000 figure was certainly in circulation in 1600; see the French report cited in Palisca, "The First Performance of *Euridice*," 437 n. 28. However, such numbers (as with those for the audience given by Buonarroti) tend to be conventional hyperbole, and they are rightly considered suspect in Mamone, *Firenze e Parigi*, 144 n. 26.

Euridice: indeed, as the grand duke's officials reviewed the draft of his description prior to publication he was required to slim down his comments on it, removing a reference to Peri and Caccini.[150] As a result, his one-page account of the opera tends to stick to the facts. As we have seen, he begins by properly – and very carefully – describing the circumstances of Corsi's offering it to the court. He then gives a concise summary of the plot:

While Orfeo and Euridice, married and in love, enjoy a tranquil life, she dies, bitten by a snake hiding in the grass. Orfeo weeps for her, and following the advice of Venere, from the mouth of the Inferno (led there by her) he calls for her, singing lamentingly. Wherefore, moved to pity by the sweetness of his singing, and on the advice of Proserpina, Plutone returns her to him more beautiful than ever. As a result, they rejoice, being in love once more.[151]

He continues:

The magnificent scenery in a worthy room, behind the curtains, between the view of a large arch – with two niches on its sides within which Poetry and Painting, by the good judgment of the inventor, were represented as statues – showed most beautiful woods, both in relief and painted, accommodated there with fine design, and by way of the lamps well placed there, full of light as if it were day. But since there was then to be seen the Inferno, those [woods] having changed, horrendous and frightening boulders revealed themselves which seemed real, upon which appeared leafless trees and ash-colored grass. And there in addition through the gap in a large cliff one saw the city of Dis burning, with tongues of flames licking through openings in its towers, the air around flaring in a color like copper. After this single change, the initial scene returned; nor was any other change seen.[152]

The whole was done with honor by all those involved in whatever capacity (*con onore di chi à condurla in qualunque parte vi intervenne*), and it

[150] Carter, "*Non occorre nominare tanti musici*," 92–93 n. 8.

[151] Buonarroti, *Descrizione delle felicissime nozze*, 18–19: *Mentre che Orfeo, e Euridice sposi, e amanti godono vita tranquilla; muore ella ferita da serpe tra l'erba ascosa. Piangela Orfeo, e per consiglio di Venere dalla bocca dello 'nferno (da lei condottovi) la richiama lamentevolmente cantando. Onde mossosi alla suavità del canto, e per lo consiglio di Proserpina Plutone a pietà, gliele rende più che mai bella. Il perché essi amando di nuovo gioiscono.*

[152] *Il magnifico apparato in degna sala dopo le cortine fra l'aspetto di un grand'arco, e di due nicchie da fianchi suoi, entro le quali la Poesia, e la Pittura con bell'avviso dello inventore vi erano per istatue; mostrava selve vaghissime, e rilevate, e dipinte, accomodatevi con bel disegno, e per i lumi ben dispostivi piene di una luce come di giorno. Ma dovendosi poscia veder lo 'nferno, quelle mutatesi, orridi massi si scorsero, e spaventevoli, che parean veri, sovra de' quali sfrondati li sterpi, e livide l'erbe apparivano. E là più ad entro per la rottura d'una gran rupe la Città di Dite ardere vi si conobbe, vibrando lingue di fiamme per le aperture delle sue torri, l'aere d'intorno avvampandovi di un colore come di rame. Dopo questa mutazion sola la scena di prima tornò, ne più si vide mutare.*

brought varied pleasure to both the mind and the senses of the spectators (*e con piacer vario, e di mente, e di senso in chi vi fù spettatore*).

Buonarroti's account of the staging of *Euridice* matters most for present purposes. It remains unclear whether he was describing the actual performance on 6 October 1600 or some plan for it created beforehand (whether or not for the Sala delle Statue); likewise we do not know to what extent he exaggerated its effects. But in general, he provides a clear impression of what the audience saw, or at least was meant to see, during the performance of the opera. The documents we present here provide much further information on how that was achieved.

2 | Staging and Sets

In the dedication to Maria de' Medici of his libretto for *Euridice*, Ottavio Rinuccini offers a brief account of the origins of opera (by way of *Dafne*) and then turns to practical matters concerning his latest work. He explains that he needed to alter the traditional ending of the myth where Orpheus loses Eurydice after failing the test imposed by Pluto, ruler of the Underworld, given the festive occasion on which his opera is to be performed (*così m'è parso convenevole in tempo di tanta allegrezza*); he also cites the example of (unnamed) Greek poets and of Dante in changing a story to suit their purpose. Rinuccini then goes still more on the defensive over the fact that in *Euridice* he was forced to break the Classical unity of place by requiring a change of scene (*in far rivolger la Scena*) – here the precedent is Sophocles's *Ajax* – because he could not otherwise represent Orpheus's prayers and laments (*non potendosi rappresentar altrimenti le preghiere, et i lamenti d'Orfeo*). Stage directions in the libretto itself also mark where the changes occur, first from the pastoral set to the Underworld one (*Qui il Choro parte, e la Scena si tramuta*) and then back (*Si rivolge la Scena, e torna come prima*).[1] The new documents on *Euridice* presented in this book reveal exactly how the scene shifted from one set to the other, just as they cover numerous other elements of the opera's staging that demand our attention. But they also invoke a much broader set of arguments that remain a matter of significant debate among historians of theatre architecture, scenography, and stagecraft in sixteenth- and early seventeenth-century Italy.[2]

This subject is difficult to navigate: despite recent research on various of its topics, there is no up-to-date overview of the whole. Eugene J. Johnson's 2018 study of theatre architecture in Renaissance and Baroque Italy covers the emergence of permanent theatres in our period and their various

[1] Ottavio Rinuccini, *L'Euridice ... rappresentata nello sponsalitio della Christianiss. Regina di Francia, e di Navarra* (Florence: Cosimo Giunti, 1600). Peri's score uses similar terminology; Jacopo Peri, *Le musiche ... sopra L'Euridice* (Florence: Giorgio Marescotti, 1600 [= 1601]), 28 (*la Scena si muta in Inferno*), 41 (*Qui torna la scena come prima*).

[2] We use "scenography" and "stagecraft" in the senses of the Italian *scenografia* and *scenotecnica*, the former concerning sets, and the latter the machinery, etc., needed to operate them.

designs. However, it says relatively little about sets and machines, for which Elena Povoledo's essay originally included in Nino Pirrotta's *Li due Orfei* (1969) remains essential, even though it stops at the *intermedi* for the wedding of Grand Duke Ferdinando de' Medici and Christine of Lorraine in 1589.[3] As for the period around 1600, our knowledge of Florence might seem to have particularly benefited from more recent research, but this has tended to focus on just one space: the Teatro degli Uffizi.[4] Scholarly studies of seventeenth-century architecture and stage design proceed apace, but taken as a whole they appear somewhat fragmentary, in part because they are limited to specific places and times, and in part given their emergence from disciplines (architecture, art, theatre, and music) that tend to operate on distinct and different terms.[5] The one attempt at a more comprehensive study of the entire century, Ferruccio Marotti's *Lo spazio scenico* (1974), limits itself to treatises of the period more than to their practical consequences, despite the fact that such texts often tend to conceal rather than divulge the secrets of their art. However, we shall see that there are other sources created for more particular use that enable us to penetrate those secrets to a greater degree, including, of course, the ones presented here on *Euridice*.[6]

Despite these differences in approach, most accounts of the evolution of stage design – normally presented alongside that of theatre architecture – tend to proceed in a fairly linear fashion, marked by various defining moments of transition from one element to another. One such "moment" in architectural terms concerns the shift from a "luogo teatrale" (that is, a space adapted temporarily for theatrical use) to the construction of permanent theatres designed specifically for the purpose. This occurred in the course of the sixteenth century, prompted by the renewed interest in the architecture of ancient Greek and Roman theatres. A second typical "moment" in these narratives concerns scenography: the emergence of

[3] Povoledo, "Origini e aspetti della scenografia in Italia." For a useful overview of European trends, see Gonzáles Román, *Spectacula*, while the images in Mazzoni, *Atlante iconografico* are particularly helpful.

[4] Compare Zorzi, *Il teatro e la città*, 109–28; Garbero Zorzi and Sperenzi (eds.), *Teatro e spettacolo nella Firenze dei Medici*, 167–98; Testaverde, "L'avventura del teatro granducale degli Uffizi."

[5] It is impossible to list all the relevant studies here, but the principal ones (in chronological order) include: Murata, *Operas for the Papal Court*; Battistelli, "Scenografia, scenotecnica e teatri"; Tamburini, *Due teatri per il principe*; Milesi (ed.), *Giacomo Torelli*; Adami, *Scenografia e scenotecnica barocca tra Ferrara e Parma*; the essays by Adami, Adorni, Cavicchi, and D'Amia in C. Cavicchi *et al.* (eds.), *Giovan Battista Aleotti e l'architettura*, 197–265; Daolmi, "La drammaturgia al servizio della scenotecnica"; Tamburini, *Gian Lorenzo Bernini e il teatro dell'arte*.

[6] Compare the comments on printed and manuscript treatises in Camerota, "La scena teatrale."

fixed perspective sets (tragic, comic, pastoral) that allowed the dramatic action to be presented on a single stage facing the audience, abandoning the disjunct "mansions" (*luoghi deputati*) of the medieval stage.[7] Again according to the conventional narrative, the desire to prompt marvel and the need to make scene changes then led to moveable sets, done initially by way of *periaktoi* (vertical prisms rotating on their axes, with portions of different scenes represented on each face), and, later, by flats sliding out from the wings.[8] The last fundamental change occurred during the seventeenth century, with the removal of tiered seating for the bulk of the audience and its replacement with theatrical boxes.

While such an account might seem straightforward enough in broad terms, greater or lesser disagreements arise when scholars seek to understand precisely how and why these various developments occurred. The literature is rife with debates on a wide range of issues, often fiercely so in the case of establishing a precise date for the adoption of one or another technical device. When did the proscenium arch first appear? When the curtain, and did it rise or fall? How were the clouds made to move? When were *periaktoi* first used in the Renaissance theatre? And when were they abandoned in favor of sliding flats? That last question perhaps prompts the most debate, alongside the one concerning the replacement of tiered seating by boxes.[9] Both issues in fact concern changes over a lengthy period of time that led to the predominance of the *teatro all'italiana*, with the audience arranged in boxes on several levels in a horseshoe configuration facing a deep stage with perspective sets that could be changed by means of sliding flats to reveal multiple scenes. This became the standard model for the opera houses that soon spread across Europe.[10]

But for all the disagreement among scholars in matters of detail, there is a strong tendency to take an evolutionary view wherein changes in stage design or theatrical architecture are to be read in the context of a teleological approach to innovation. This hardly squares with the realities of theatrical life, where theory and practice must necessarily work in tandem,

7 Attolini, *Teatro e spettacolo nel Rinascimento*; Alonge and Bonino (eds.), *Storia del teatro moderno e contemporaneo 1*, 90–94, 905–25, 1139–62, 1207–34.

8 Nicoll, *The Development of the Theatre*, 69–92, 103–94; Surgers, *Scénographies du théâtre occidental*, 88–112, 148–56.

9 For thoughts on the functions and evolution of the proscenium arch and of the curtain, see Tamburini, *Il quadro della visione*; Hénin, "Le rideau de théâtre." For the debate over the use of *periaktoi* and flats, see later in this chapter; for boxes, see Johnson, *Inventing the Opera House*, 225–76.

10 Bosisio, *Teatro dell'Occidente*, 1: 237–58, 269–81, 357–68; Fagiolo, *La scenografia dalle sacre rappresentazioni al futurismo*, 7–25; Pinelli, *I teatri*, 12–34.

and where practical problems needed to be solved in practical ways. Likewise, new techniques in terms of, say, music, text, staging, and acting do not replace older ones from one day to the next, nor do they spread instantaneously from one place to another. To avoid falling into the trap of the debates that have tended to dominate the literature, it therefore seems necessary to drop any presumption of linear development and to accept that some questions have answers that are different from what one might expect, or indeed as yet have no answers at all.

Some Theoretical and Other Sources

Much hangs on the nature of the sources available to uncover these issues, which can vary enormously according to time and place. In the case of late sixteenth- and early seventeenth-century theatre architecture and stage design, the sources require very careful treatment because they are for the most part only indirect. Despite the large number of theatres (temporary or permanent, courtly or public) known to have been in use, only three survive from this period in some concrete shape or form: the Teatro Olimpico in Vicenza (completed in 1585 and inaugurated with a performance of Sophocles's *Oedipus rex*, translated as *Edipo tiranno*), the Teatro Gonzaga (Teatro all'Antica) in Sabbioneta (1590), and the Teatro Farnese in Parma (1618; remodeled in 1628).[11] Of those three, only the Teatro Olimpico preserves its original stage, although its Roman-style *scaenae frons* (a fixed, immoveable architectural facade) was wholly atypical for its time, and was scarcely functional beyond its original quasi-archeological purpose. In the case of the Gonzaga and Farnese theatres, their stages lack any physical evidence of the original sets or machinery. This highlights the chief difficulty for theatre historians – defining the space in which the dramatic action took place – because any stage, by its very nature, was subject to modification according to need. In effect, the greater the use of particular sets and machinery, the less likely they were to survive. The well-known historical theatres in Český Krumlov and Drottningholm, both from the third quarter of the eighteenth century, are very much the exception than the rule.

As for any documentation concerning theatres of our period, this, too, varies over time. For the bulk of the sixteenth century, we primarily have

[11] Mazzoni and Guaita, *Il teatro di Sabbioneta*; Ferrone, *Attori, mercanti, corsari*, 50–88; Mazzoni, *L'Olimpico di Vicenza*; Johnson, *Inventing the Opera House*, 122–64, 173–204.

treatises on stage design and descriptions of particular entertainments. Toward the end of the century and the beginning of the next, we start to find engravings on the one hand, and, on the other, more detailed lists of scenic elements and drawings of stage machinery, therefore moving from theoretical and descriptive documents to those more practical in orientation. But in either case, interpreting these sources is tricky because each of them emerged for different reasons and from different situations, and their derivation from, or application to, specific theatrical circumstances can be tested only by way of those (rarer) documents related to specific productions.

Even just the treatises change their focus and purpose over the course of these two centuries. The best-known ones from the sixteenth century belong to the broader field of architecture and concern visual matters, principally of perspective design.[12] For example, Sebastiano Serlio's celebrated *Il secondo libro di perspettiva* (1545), the second to be published of his seven "books on architecture," begins with the basic rules for placing solid figures in perspective but then moves on to matters concerning the theatre and then the stage.[13] Here, Serlio draws on his theatrical experience to provide a detailed account of the construction of three types of set, labeled as tragic, comic, and "satyrica" (for satyr plays usually in a rustic setting), that would take on near-canonic status; he also offers important advice on matters of stage lighting.[14] Daniele Barbaro dedicated the fourth part of his *La pratica della perspettiva* (1569) to stage design ("Scenographia, cioè Descrittione delle scene"), largely following Serlio with regard to practical problems, although when dealing with theoretical issues he turns repeatedly to Vitruvius, to whom he refers in providing the correct interpretation of the use of triangular *periaktoi* to effect changes of scene in ancient theatres.[15] On the other hand, Ignazio Danti's

[12] For useful translations, see Hewitt (ed.), *The Renaissance Stage.*

[13] Serlio's *Il secondo libro di perspettiva/Le second livre de perspective* was first published alongside the *Premier livre de géometrie* in a bilingual volume titled *Il primo libro d'architettura/Le premier livre d'architecture* (Paris: Barbé, 1545); for a facsimile, see Serlio, *L'architettura*, ed. Fiore, vol. 1 (the treatise on perspective is on fols. 25–71v of the original edition). In some copies of the 1545 edition (as at http://architectura.cesr.univ-tours.fr/Traite/Images/LES1736Index.asp), the title is styled *Il secondo libro di perspettia.*

[14] Serlio describes a temporary theatre that he had constructed in Vicenza; see *Il secondo libro di perspettiva*, fol. 64v. For his likely involvement in other such ventures, see Johnson, *Inventing the Opera House*, 85–86. The engravings of the three types of sets included in his text (and copied elsewhere) are so widely available as not to need reproduction here.

[15] Barbaro, *La pratica della perspettiva*, 129–58. In terms of the three types of set, Barbaro refers directly to those "already made by others" (*fatte già da altri*; ibid., 155) and reproduces the engravings of the tragic, comic, and *satyrica* sets used in the 1566 edition of Serlio's works

commentary (1583) on *Le due regole della prospettiva pratica* by Giacomo Barozzi da Vignola is the first to offer an explanation of the use of *periaktoi* on the modern stage.[16] Danti also describes two productions involving *periaktoi* that he witnessed during his time in Florence as mathematician and geographer at the court of (Grand) Duke Cosimo I. The first, the staging of Giovan Battista Cini's *La vedova* (Florence, Salone dei Cinquecento, 1569), is covered in detail. The second – a "commedia" done by the Compagnia di S. Giovanni Evangelista in the presence of the grand duke – receives only a brief mention, but one that is important because it confirms the notion that the scenic devices that became celebrated in Medici entertainments were not exclusive to the court but were commonly used in academies and confraternities, where indeed they may have first been developed, insofar as Florence was concerned.[17] Danti's

(Venice: Francesco Franceschi and Johann Krüger; Barbaro was the dedicatee). This edition is in quarto format (the 1545 Paris edition was in folio), so the engravings were redone in smaller size and became the ones most used in subsequent editions of Serlio (and, perhaps surprisingly, in modern reproductions in scholarly treatments of them); see Vène, *Bibliographia serliana*, 66–67, 110–11, 174. As for *periaktoi* (which he calls *macchine triangolari*), Barbaro does not speak of their modern use but only of their being typical of ancient theatres, where "in the niches and in the recesses and openings of the fixed stage there turned some wooden machines, which had three sides on which were painted the scenes appropriate to the plays which were to be performed" (*ne' nicchi e nei fori e apriture della scena stabile, si volgevano alcune machine di legno, che havevano tre faccie, nelle quali erano le perspettive convenienti alle favole, che si dovevano rappresentare*); *La pratica della perspettiva*, 130. For the precedent for such a "rotating machine" (*macchina girevole*) in Vitruvius, see also Alberti, *L'architettura*, ed. Orlandi and Portoghesi, 2: 738.

16 A facsimile of Ignazio Danti 's *Le due regole della prospettiva pratica di Messer Iacomo Barozzi da Vignola con i commentari del Reverendo Padre Messer Egnatio Danti dell'ordine de' predicatori, matematico dello studio di Bologna* (Rome: Francesco Zanetti, 1583) is placed alongside a translation in Danti, *Les Deux Règles de la perspective pratique de Vignole*; *periaktoi* are discussed at 296–301 (90–92 in the original). See also Povoledo, "Origini e aspetti della scenografia in Italia," 412. Danti claims to have heard that the first modern experiments with *periaktoi* were done by Bastiano da Sangallo for a production in Castro commissioned in 1543 by Duke Pier Luigi Farnese. A sketch by Sangallo for a rotating "triangular machine" (*machina tri[a]ngola*) also survives; see Blumenthal, *Giulio Parigi's Stage Designs*, vol. 2, fig. 162. Computer models of some of Danti's options, and later solutions discussed here, can be seen on the website developed by Frank Mohler (Appalachian State University) at https://spectacle.appstate.edu/.

17 Danti may be referring to the production of Giovanni Maria Cecchi's *La coronazione di Re Saul* done by the confraternity in 1569, which certainly had elaborate revolving scenery; see Evangelista, "L'attività spettacolare della Compagnia di San Giovanni Evangelista," 333, 335, 336. For Ignazio Danti and his brother, Valerio (a sculptor and architect), in Florence, see Danti, *Les Deux Règles de la perspective pratique de Vignole*, 25, 27–39. On the involvement of such architects and scenographers as Vasari, Bronzino, Bastiano da Sangallo, and Baldassare Lanci in academies and confraternities, see Testaverde, "L'avventura del teatro granducale degli Uffizi," 45–52. Compare also Anton Francesco Doni 's account in his *I marmi* (Venice: Francesco Marcolini, 1552 [= 1553]), 1: 22–24, of a civic entertainment in Florence in which "in

discussion also disproves the much later claim, made in the early 1630s by the anonymous author of *Il corago*, that the modern use of triangular *periaktoi* in Florence was an invention by Bernardo Buontalenti.[18]

Ignazio Danti further devotes considerable space to illustrate how the "feigned" (*finto*) elements of any painted backdrop at the rear of the stage might be integrated with the three-dimensional elements of the set on either side (*con quello che si dipigne nelle case vere che di rilievo si fanno sopra il palco*), thereby engaging with the fundamental problem of creating a perspective view with volumetric wings.[19] Serlio also engaged with this issue when he writes of the "facades of buildings" (*faccie de' casamenti*) placed "in maiestà" (facing the viewer) in contrast to those that recede diagonally (*i casamenti che scurtiano*), for which he makes the eminently pragmatic suggestion of using two horizons (*dua horizzonti*) and therefore two vanishing points, one for the side elements and the other for the rear. Although this solution, he says, involves a method different from the rules (*diverso modo dalle regole*) established thus far in his treatise, it is the one most widely used in practice.[20] Barbaro, on the other hand, refers only briefly to this problem, mentioning the experience of the painter and scene designer, Pompeo Pedemonte, who had used only a single vanishing point.[21] Danti initially follows Barbaro in claiming that, as a matter of principle, theories of perspective force everything seen to end at a single point (*tutte le cose viste vanno a terminare in un sol punto*). Nevertheless, if one follows Danti's long explanation of the method for indicating perspective lines for the side elements of the stage, it becomes clear that he, too, resorts to the necessity of two vanishing points, even though he does not admit it.[22] For all their

the second act, given that the scenery turned little by little on a pivot, the audience scarcely realized that it was revolving" (*al secondo atto, essendo la scena sopra un perno che si voltava a poco a poco che, appena s'accorsero le brigate che la si volgesse*); for a complete description of the event, see Armellini, "Musica e musicisti nei *Marmi* di Anton Francesco Doni," 334.

18 P. Fabbri and Pompilio (eds.), *Il corago*, 117. This treatise (Modena, Biblioteca Estense, γ.F.6.11) was clearly written by someone moving in Florentine circles; Pierfrancesco Rinuccini (the son of Ottavio) has been identified as one candidate for its authorship, but more recently the argument has shifted in favor of Ferdinando Saracinelli; see Harness, *Echoes of Women's Voices*, 112–13 n. 6; Fantappiè, "Saracinelli, Ferdinando."

19 Danti, *Les Deux Règles de la perspective pratique de Vignole*, 296 (at 90 in the original).

20 Serlio, *Il secondo libro della perspettiva*, fol. 63.

21 Barbaro, *La pratica della perspettiva*, 153.

22 The contradictions become clear in Danti's successive diagrams of the stage presented in the course of his treatise. For the backdrop, he indicates only a single vanishing point (C) saying that it should be used to trace the perspective lines for planes facing the viewer (he draws one: FE). As for the side elements, he says that one should adopt line EB. But if one extends line EB, it reaches a point higher than C and therefore different from it. Danti conveniently neglects to point out the discrepancy.

differences, however, these three treatises remain predominantly theoretical in focus: any references to contemporary stages – if present at all – appear incidental. They also reveal the difficulty of marrying theory and practice.

Other sixteenth-century treatises are more directly concerned with the theatre, dealing in detail with matters of production, text and delivery, lighting, and costumes, but glossing over questions of scenography and stagecraft. Typical examples include Leone de' Sommi's *Quattro dialoghi in materia di rappresentazioni sceniche* (written in Mantua in the late 1560s, if not later) and Angelo Ingegneri's *Della poesia rappresentativa, et del modo di rappresentare le favole sceniche* (Ferrara: Vittorio Baldini, 1598), both of which combine theory with practical explanations that reflect the direct experience of their authors as stage directors.[23] Less well known (and still awaiting a proper critical edition) is Ercole Bottrigari's dialogue, *La mascara, overo Della fabbrica de' teatri et dello apparato delle scene tragisatiricomiche* (1596–98; in autograph manuscript), an erudite, if opinionated, conglomeration of facts and precepts that also makes reference to contemporary theatrical productions. It is divided into two parts: the first is a commentary on Classical texts geared toward the potential reconstruction of ancient theatres, and the second offers a critique of more contemporary theatrical treatises.[24]

Various texts from around 1600 continue the focus on perspective and therefore on the relationship between what Ignazio Danti (and later, many others) called the "feigned" (*finto*) backdrop and the "real" wings (*case vere*). Lorenzo Sirigatti's *La pratica di prospettiva* (1596) has just a very short chapter dedicated to the problem ("Per disegnare il finto della scena talmente che unisca con le case del palco"),[25] but Guidobaldo Bourbon del Monte Santa Maria dedicates to it the entire Sixth Book (*De scenis*) of his

[23] De' Sommi, *Quattro dialoghi in materia di rappresentazioni sceniche*, ed. Marotti (trans. in Blanchard-Rothmuller, "Leone Ebreo de' Sommi's *Four Dialogues on Stage Presentations*"); Ingegneri, *Della poesia rappresentativa*, ed. Doglio. For de' Sommi's dialogues, it is usually assumed on the basis of internal evidence that they were largely written toward the end of the 1560s or even later (he died in the early 1590s), despite the date given in his preface (1556). Ingegneri's treatise contains traces of his experience as the stage designer for *Edipo tiranno* (Vicenza, 1585); see Mazzoni, *L'Olimpico di Vicenza*, 98–103, 113–16, 124–66, and Migliarisi, *Renaissance and Baroque Directors*, 13–117. However, it also offers important advice on more contemporary pastoral plays.

[24] Bologna, Museo Internazionale e Biblioteca della Musica, MS cod. 47 B45 (there is a transcription at http://mimtt.co.uk/files/Bottrigari_La_Mascara_Italian.pdf). Another manuscript version survives in Bologna, Biblioteca Universitaria, MS 326 b. III/5; see Giuliani, "'La Mascara' di Hercole Bottrigari."

[25] Lorenzo Sirigatti, *La pratica di prospettiva* (Venice: Girolamo Franceschi, 1596), fols. 42v–43 (Chap. 23). Sirigatti's treatise is dedicated to Grand Duke Ferdinando I de' Medici.

Perspectivae libri sex (Pesaro: Girolamo Concordia, 1600),[26] and his account is followed in Scipione Chiaramonti's *Delle scene e teatri* (1614),[27] which is in effect a vernacular redaction of *De scenis*. The stage designer for *Euridice*, Lodovico Cigoli, took the same approach in his manuscript treatise *Prospettiva pratica ... dimostrata con tre regole* (see Fig. 2.1).[28] They each distinguish two types of plane, one parallel to the front of the stage (*piani eretti all'orizzonte in maestà*) and one moving from front to back at an oblique angle on each side (*eretti all'orizzonte in isfugita*).[29] Although none of these treatises identifies the precise type of stage for which these approaches are designed, they clearly presume a flat backdrop and volumetric wings. In fact, while both wings and flats can create a plane "in maestà," the oblique plane "in isfugita" as conceived here can be achieved only by way of such wings (whether as *periaktoi* or other three-dimensional structures) and not by flats, save by some manner of painting them (which is suggested in *Il corago*, as we shall see). Pietro Accolti's *Lo inganno de gl'occhi: prospettiva pratica* (1625) follows the thread:[30] like his predecessors, he presumes that the wings are volumetric (with foreshortening), but his focus on theory prevents any explanation of current practices in set design. As for the latter, they appear to have been the intended focus of the Eleventh Book of Teofilo Gallaccini's *Teoriche e pratiche di prospettive scenografiche* (1641) – a treatise yet to be properly explored by theatre historians – although this part was never written, due to the death of the author.[31]

These and other issues gain greater coverage in perhaps the best-known texts on theatrical practice from the second quarter of the seventeenth century, the anonymous manuscript treatise *Il corago* (from Florence, *c.* 1630) and Nicola Sabbatini's (1574–1654) *Pratica di fabricar scene, e machine ne' teatri* (Pesaro: Flaminio Concordia, 1637; with an enlarged second edition issued in

[26] Bourbon del Monte Santa Maria, *I sei libri della prospettiva*, ed. Sinisgalli.

[27] Scipione Chiaramonti, *Delle scene e teatri, opera postuma* (Cesena: Verdoni, 1675). The text was originally written in 1614; see Marotti, *Lo spazio scenico*, 51–56.

[28] GDSU, 2660 A. The most recent edition in Camerota, *Linear Perspective in the Age of Galileo*, 93–339, now supersedes Cigoli, *Trattato pratico di prospettiva*, ed. Profumo. Cigoli's treatise is divided into five parts, the second of which contains a discussion of theatres ("Delle scene"; fols. 61–69).

[29] Chiaramonti, *Delle scene e teatri*, fol. 3.

[30] Pietro Accolti, *Lo inganno de gl'occhi: prospettiva pratica ... trattato in acconcio della pittura* (Florence: Pietro Cecconcelli, 1625), 89–94 (Chap. 17: "Pratica per disegnare apparati prospettivi scenici"). Accolti was a member of the Florentine Accademia del Disegno, and a secretary to Don Giovanni de' Medici from 1606 to 1616; see Parenti, *Pietro Accolti e "Lo inganno de gl'occhi"*, 59–72.

[31] Payne, *The Telescope and the Compass*, 115–21, 202–3. Gallaccini's manuscript (Siena, Biblioteca Comunale degli Intronati, MS L.IV.4) is divided into eight "books" with numerous illustrations; see Morolli (ed.), *Siena 1600 circa*, 12–19, 29, 35–36, 48–53, 58–61, 211–12.

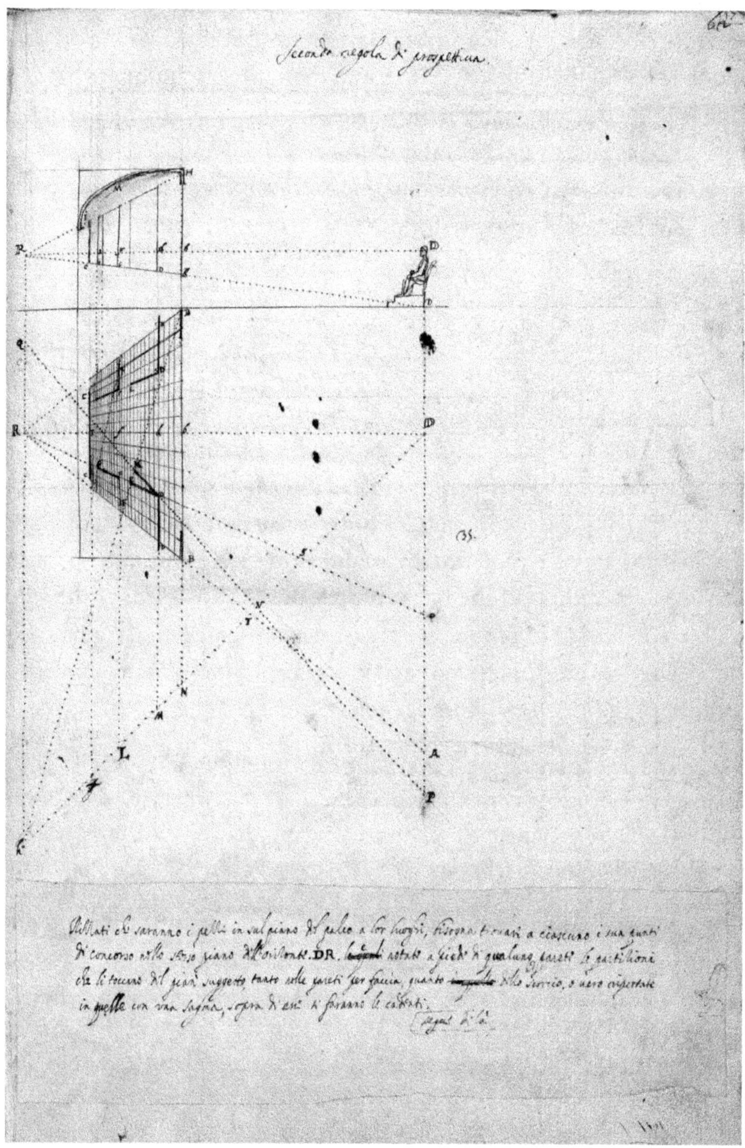

Fig. 2.1: Lodovico Cigoli, *Prospettiva pratica . . . dimostrata con tre regole*, fol. 62, showing planes *in maestà* and *in isfugita*. GDSU, 2660 A. By permission of the Ministero per i beni e le attività culturali e per il turismo della Repubblica Italiana/Gallerie degli Uffizi.

Ravenna by Pietro de' Paoli and Giovanni Battista Giovanelli in 1638). *Il corago* engages with a broad range of matters concerning theatrical production (poetry, music, acting, choreography, scenography, costumes, and the like), while Sabbatini is more concerned in particular with set design and machinery, and includes a rich array of illustrations.[32] Both cover a great deal of ground in terms of the issues discussed and the various solutions proposed for dealing with them, ranging from the movements of clouds to the use of the understage area, as well as lighting and so on.

Il corago identifies six ways of changing sets, although two are clearly preferred. The first of those two (*quello de' triangoli*) seems to involve *periaktoi* – although they could also be L-shaped structures revolving around a pivot – and their modern use is credited (incorrectly, we have seen) to the Florentine architect and stage designer, Bernardo Buontalenti (the *non mai appieno lodato Bernardo delle Girandole*): this is a "very beautiful" (*bellissimo*) method and one that allows an "infinite number of scene changes" (*infinite mutazioni*). The second – which the author says he has never observed in use (*benché non l'abbi mai visto porre in uso*) – involves flats moving sideways parallel to the front and back of the stage (*parallele all'orlo del palco et al foro*) but painted in such a way as to create a perspective view receding to the backdrop by being two-thirds *in isfugita* and one-third *in maestà* (*dipinte come le case del foro, cioè 2/3 a scorcio e 1/3 in faccia*).[33] This has advantages not just in terms of functionality and cost, but still more in that it allows homogeneous scene changes:

> Of no little charm will be seeing the scene change in a wholly uniform manner, that is the backdrop and the houses on either side in the same way, which does not occur in the case of *periaktoi*, because the backdrop changes by having the canvas frames move in and out, whereas the side elements do so by revolving.[34]

Another means of changing sets described in *Il corago* involves raising flat canvases from underneath the stage (*sorgere dal basso*). This has the advantage of being very inexpensive, although it is not particularly desirable because it is not pleasing "to see a scene half of one kind and half of another" (*vedere una scena mezza d'una sorte e mezza d'un'altra*).[35]

[32] *Il corago* also has references to illustrations – more than forty were intended to support Chap. 21 ("Le macchine") – but if they were ever prepared, they are now lost; see P. Fabbri and Pompilio (eds.), *Il corago*, 116–23.

[33] *Periaktoi* constitute the "fourth" method, and moveable flats the "sixth"; P. Fabbri and Pompilio (eds.), *Il corago*, 118–19.

[34] P. Fabbri and Pompilio (eds.), *Il corago*, 119: *Di non poca vaghezza sarà ancora il vedere mutarsi la scena con modo tutto uniforme, cioè nel medesimo modo il foro e le case dalle bande, che non accade ne' triangoli, perché il foro si muta con l'andare i telari innanzi e indreto e quelle dalle parti col girare.*

[35] P. Fabbri and Pompilio (eds.), *Il corago*, 117–18.

Sabbatini, on the other hand, offers fewer methods, and none of his three involves simple flats (whether sliding in and out or moving up or down) save in the case of changes to the backdrop. His first two methods involve two-sided components (L-shaped or its mirror image), in the first case changed (once only) by unrolling (*srotolare*) canvases sideways, and in the second by horizontally sliding similar structures over the original ones. But, once again, the preferred option is to have revolving three-sided *periaktoi*.[36] A similar approach is adopted in the treatises on architecture by Joseph Furttenbach the Elder (1591–1667): the only solution he offers for the movement of the side wings is by way of what seem to be pairs of triangular *periaktoi*, while flats are described only to change the backdrop.[37]

Sabbatini, Furttenbach, and the anonymous author of *Il corago* each demonstrate the increasing inclination of seventeenth-century theorists to explain practical aspects of stagecraft, even if they are not always able or willing to reveal all their secrets. More glimpses into the latter are provided by less formal sources closely tied to specific theatrical productions. We have a manuscript notebook by Furttenbach the Elder (Munich, Bayerische Staatsbibliothek, Codex iconographicus 401) that contains sketches and explanatory notes of stage machinery associated with the entertainments done in Florence in 1608 during the festivities for the wedding of Prince Cosimo de' Medici and Maria Magdalena of Austria (including the *intermedi* designed by Giulio Parigi for Michelangelo Buonarroti *il giovane*'s *Il giudizio di Paride*), as well as for *La liberazione di Tirreno e d'Arnea* staged in the Teatro degli Uffizi in early 1617.[38] An anonymous manuscript now in the Library of Congress, Washington, D.C. (Lessing J. Rosenwald Collection, MS no. 27), dating from after 1624, also contains drawings that can be linked to Giulio Parigi and the Teatro degli Uffizi; the handling of the wings here is similar to Furttenbach's in terms of the rotating elements.[39] However, various

36 These various methods are discussed and illustrated in Sabbatini, *Pratica di fabricar scene, e machine ne' teatri* (1638), Book 2 (starting at page 71); see https://hdl.handle.net/2027/gri.ark:/13960/t2s47ns34.

37 Joseph Furttenbach the Elder, *Architectura recreationis* (Augsburg: Johann Schultes, 1640, https://hdl.handle.net/2027/gri.ark:/13960/t9n35mg6q), 60–70 and figs. 21–23; Joseph Furttenbach the Elder, *Mannhaffter Kunst-Spiegel* (Augsburg: Johann Schultes, 1663, https://digi.ub.uni-heidelberg.de/diglit/furttenbach1663), 111–37 and figs. 11–12. These illustrations, which reflect Furttenbach's experiences in Florence and elsewhere in Italy, are well known; see also Hewitt (ed.), *The Renaissance Stage*, 195, 197, 201, 205, 213.

38 Lazardig and Rößler (eds.), *Technologies of Theatre*.

39 The Rosenwald MS (www.loc.gov/item/50032645/) is a sketchbook (largely unpaginated) also dealing with military fortifications, artillery, mechanics, and pyrotechnics; images 549–57 concern the theatre.

drawings by the military engineer Pietro Paolo Floriani offer a different approach.[40] During his time in Ferrara (1629–34), Floriani collaborated on a number of occasions with the architects and stage designers Giovan Battista Aleotti and Francesco Guitti, and following their example, it seems, he illustrates flats sliding in laterally from the wings, a technique previously reserved just for the backdrop (see Fig. 2.2).[41] All these sources also contain detailed illustrations of a large number of stage machines – both for changing sets and for additional stage machinery (for clouds, carriages, trapdoors), lighting

Fig. 2.2: Pietro Paolo Floriani, stage design for a pastoral set in the Teatro degli Intrepidi, Ferrara (*c.* 1631). Archivio Compagnoni Floriani di Villamagna (Macerata), Cod. β, fol. 2. Associazione Compagnoni Floriani di Villamagna. Tutti i diritti riservati – All rights reserved ©.

40 Adami, *Scenografia e scenotecnica barocca tra Ferrara e Parma*, discussing two manuscripts now held in the Archivio Compagnoni Floriani di Villamagna, Macerata. Floriani's drawings can be linked directly to productions in Ferrara (a set of *intermedi* for the visit to Ferrara of Taddeo Barberini, Teatro S. Lorenzo, 1625; a tournament, *La contesa*, in the Palazzo Bevilacqua, 1630) and in Parma (*Mercurio e Marte*, a tournament staged during the festivities for the wedding of Duke Odoardo Farnese and Margherita de' Medici in 1628).

41 Adami, *Scenografia e scenotecnica barocca tra Ferrara e Parma*, 63; compare also his *Tavola* LVII, which shows the flats each moving by way of an understage frame mounted on wheels. The fan-type mechanism shown in Fig. 2.2 creates a tree-like profile for the onstage edge of the flat, in a manner not dissimilar to one of Sabbatini's devices for the movement of clouds; see *Pratica di fabricar scene, e machine ne' teatri* (1638), 145–46, 152–54.

systems, mechanisms for opening and closing the curtain, winches, pulleys, etc. – most with additional notes explaining their operation. Given that the manuscript ones were largely made for personal use and intended for limited circulation at most, they go into far greater detail than is customary in texts designed for a wider readership, and they tend to be more practical and less prone to rhetorical embellishment. They also reveal the connections between scenography, stagecraft, and general technological developments in the period.

Other surviving materials come even closer to the nuts and bolts of specific productions by deriving directly from the artists, artisans, and administrators involved in them. The documents associated with *Euridice* presented in this book are an obvious case in point, but they are not unique. For example, Gianbattista Cresci's predecessor as the *provveditore* of the Medici fortresses, Girolamo Seriacopi, kept a daily journal of the materials and labor needed for the construction of the scenery and other apparatus for the festivities celebrating the wedding of Grand Duke Ferdinando de' Medici and Christine of Lorraine in 1589, including the remodeling of the Teatro degli Uffizi and the staging of Girolamo Bargagli's comedy, *La pellegrina*, with spectacular *intermedi*.[42] His account also allows us to see the frequent discrepancies between the official descriptions of such entertainments (in the case of the 1589 festivities, Bastiano de' Rossi's is the best known) and what was actually achieved.

Seriacopi's entries clearly demonstrate the enormous amount of work and the frequent changes of direction lying behind any theatrical endeavor. Nevertheless, despite his meticulous record-keeping, key questions remain concerning the stage machinery used in the Teatro degli Uffizi in 1589: witness the heated arguments over whether Bernardo Buontalenti's stage for *La pellegrina* and its *intermedi* used volumetric wings (whether or not *periaktoi*) or sliding flats for its side elements.[43] Those arguments are now

[42] Seriacopi's *Memoriale et ricordi* (ASF, Magistrato de' Nove Conservatori del Dominio e della Giurisdizione Fiorentina 3679) is transcribed and discussed in fine detail in Testaverde, *L'officina delle nuvole*.

[43] Testaverde, *L'officina delle nuvole*, 98–101, outlines the disagreements but favors *periaktoi* for the side elements of the stage, suggesting that they were four-sided (rectangular or trapezoidal). However, given that four sides would not have been sufficient for all the changes of set, she also suggests (following P. Fabbri and Pompilio [eds.], *Il corago*, 118), that the canvas sides of the *periaktoi* not visible to the audience at any given moment were changed. Mohler ("Medici Wings," 59–61) agrees on *periaktoi* and also suggests that they were used in subsequent productions (for 1608, see also Blumenthal, *Giulio Parigi's Stage Designs*, vol. 2, figs. 3–4). Nagler (*Theatre Festivals of the Medici*, 79–80) and Povoledo ("Origini e aspetti della scenografia in Italia," 369–70) favor the use of flats on the basis of their presumed greater efficiency. Saslow (*The Medici Wedding of 1589*, 81–83) posits a combination of fixed wings in the manner of

rendered still more troublesome because of the apparent suggestions in the Rosenwald MS and elsewhere that what have been identified as "periaktoi" and interpreted as solid prisms rotating around their center point might, in fact, be more complex folding structures that could not only revolve (allowing scene changes to be made on their hidden sides) but also somehow open and close. It is clear from Floriani's drawings, however, that despite the advantages of volumetric wings in terms of visual appearance and access points to the stage (including upper-level balconies, etc.),[44] sliding flats were becoming viewed as a more efficient option depending on the construction of any given theatre and the nature of its machinery.

Although it is widely accepted that such flats were in common use in the new Venetian "public" opera houses after 1637, particularly under the influence of Giacomo Torelli, Floriani's notebooks reveal that Torelli reworked and improved upon now-familiar systems.[45] Some scholars argue that flats were adopted in the Teatro S. Lorenzo in Ferrara (1618) and by Giovan Battista Aleotti in his original design for the Teatro Farnese in Parma that same year, while most agree that they were used in the latter theatre when it was remodeled in 1628 for the festivities celebrating the wedding of Duke Odoardo Farnese and Margherita de' Medici.[46] However, Floriani shows not only rectangular canvases on moveable frames (*telari*) sliding in sideways through channels in the stage platform, but also how they could be changed simultaneously by way of a central winch connected to each flat by ropes and pulleys.[47] It is worth noting that Floriani's sets

Serlio for the play, and flats sliding parallel to the stage front for the *intermedi*. However, this creates three significant problems in terms of changing the sets on the oblique; of leaving room in the wings for the entrance and exit of actors, machines, etc.; and, last but not least, of coordinating multiple movements for each change of set. Both Testaverde and Saslow agree, however, that the various rear views of the stage were created by sliding shutters that met in the middle.

44 For accessible wings, see Sabbatini, *Pratica di fabricar scene, e machine ne' teatri* (1638), 80–82; Furttenbach, *Architectura recreationis*, figs. 21–23; Furttenbach, *Mannhaffter Kunst-Spiegel*, figs. 11–11½.

45 For Torelli, see Glixon and Glixon, *Inventing the Business of Opera*, 227–39.

46 Adorni, "Il Teatro Farnese a Parma," 214–15. According to some scholars, Aleotti used flats already in the Teatro della Sala Grande in Ferrara for two tournaments in 1610 and 1612. However, this is not based on any documents but, rather, on the (incorrect) assumption that *periaktoi* were of little use for scene changes and hard to maneuver; see, for example, the statements in Fabretti, "Il teatro della Sala Grande a Ferrara e i tornei aleottiani," 185.

47 Adami, *Scenografia e scenotecnica barocca tra Ferrara e Parma*, 200–201 and *Tavola* LVII. Presumably these were pulled by a central winch as discussed in ibid., 135–36, 139–42, and *Tavole* IX, XI, although this is not associated exclusively with flats but also with a mechanism for L-shaped flats that could turn on a vertical axis. Floriani's sliding flats are scarcely different from the system described toward the end of the seventeenth century by Fabrizio Carini Motta; see Tamburini (ed.), *Scenotecnica barocca*, 25–33 and figs. 3–4.

tended to be woodland ones, meaning that they were intended for pastoral plays. It may well be that this type of scene, which was less rigidly constrained than the city-views typical of tragedy and comedy, was more open to experimentation, and easier to construct.

Cigoli's stage design for *Euridice* was far less complicated. Rinuccini's libretto says that the initial pastoral set "changes" to the Underworld one (*la Scena si tramuta*), which then "turns around" and returns as before (*Si rivolge la Scena, e torna come prima*). However, in common theatrical parlance of the period – requiring something less than theoretical exactitude – verbs such as *voltare* and *volgere* could stand in for *mutare* or *cambiare* (and vice versa) depending on the nature of the source and on who was writing it.[48] We shall see that Cigoli in fact used simple vertical flats, with the Underworld scene being raised, then lowered, in front of the pastoral one. This was one of the set-changing methods that did not meet with the approval of the author of *Il corago* (because the movement was so visible to the audience), but it was almost inevitable in any temporary theatre constructed in a relatively narrow space – as with the Sala delle Statue and Sala delle Commedie in the Palazzo Pitti – because there was scant room in the wings or above the stage for any more complex machinery. Something similar appears to have been adopted for at least some of the changes of set in the performance in Parma of Tasso's *Aminta*, with seemingly elaborate *intermedi*, for the Farnese–Medici wedding in late 1628, done in a temporary theatre constructed in the courtyard of S. Pietro Martire.[49] It is also worth noting that previous entertainments staged in the Palazzo Pitti in Florence (including *Dafne*) appear not to have required any changes of set. To that extent, if not others, *Euridice* was something new: Cigoli was dealing with a set of challenges that he needed to address in the most effective way possible given the constraints.

Cigoli's attention to detail is clear in the documents associated with his involvement in *Euridice*. Indeed, all these materials offer the possibility of a quite precise reconstruction of its staging by virtue of the specific information they provide on the materials used to create it, even extending to measurements that, we shall see, match the room originally planned for it (the Sala delle Statue) and the one in which it was performed on 6 October

48 Compare Testaverde, *L'officina delle nuvole*, 98–101, 159–60. Floriani makes the distinction, however; see Adami, *Scenografia e scenotecnica barocca tra Ferrara e Parma*, 135.

49 See the various comments and instructions in Lavin, "Lettres de Parmes," 120–22, 129–36 (Letters 3, 12, 13, 14); one of the scenes that rose then fell was an Underworld scene (*Città di Dite*) that was needed for the appearance of Plutone in the third *intermedio* and perhaps also the fifth; it was operated by a system of counterweights.

1600 (the Sala delle Commedie). The extent and nature of these materials is quite unusual: our task now is to see what sense can or cannot be made of them.

The Sala delle Statue and Sala delle Commedie

We have seen that *Euridice* was essentially a "private" entertainment within the 1600 wedding festivities, offered (and largely funded) by the grand duke in his primary residence, the Palazzo Pitti, to a limited number of guests. Its first intended location within the palace, the Sala delle Statue on the *piano nobile*, was certainly grand enough, and Cigoli's original design for the stage was clearly intended to mesh with its dimensions and architectural elements (and its "antique" ones), including the statues located in niches along its walls. The Sala delle Statue was not a theatrical space, but those niches and statues gave it some elements typical of Renaissance theatres (compare also the statues painted in niches in the Teatro degli Uffizi).[50] Moving the production upstairs to what later became known as the Sala delle Commedie caused Cigoli some problems, and deprived the stage of much of its intended architectural integrity. However, it inaugurated a new space for theatrical activity in the palace that would become increasingly important in the years to come.

In both cases, we are still dealing with rooms temporarily adapted for theatrical purposes and then returned (sooner or later) to their original state for other day-to-day use. This was a more efficient use of limited space in the Pitti that necessarily served multiple functions: the artisans who worked in the Medici palaces seem to have been well accustomed to putting things up and taking them down on demand; labor and construction materials were not necessarily expensive in this period; and some materials could easily be cycled and recycled for different purposes. The disadvantage of such adaptation was that the stage could not contain the more elaborate scenic elements and associated machinery, or the seating arrangement for the audience, to be found in more permanent theatres. How any consequent expectations on the part of the audience might be met or thwarted would vary, inevitably. From Michelangelo Buonarroti *il giovane*'s official description of the 1600 festivities, it is clear that *Euridice* was done on a

[50] Testaverde, *L'officina delle nuvole*, 83–85 and figs. 7–8. On the tendency in the late sixteenth and early seventeenth centuries to frame temporary and permanent stages with statues (real or painted) as elements harking back to ancient theatres, see Johnson, *Inventing the Opera House*, 77–104, 122–64, 173–200.

small scale, with none of the spectacular stage effects seen in *Il rapimento di Cefalo*. Within those limits, however, Buonarroti offers significant praise for the scenery (of course, he could not do otherwise). Emilio de' Cavalieri, on the other hand, reported on the opinion circulating in Rome that *Euridice* had failed to satisfy the audience not just because of the music but also that the scenery was somehow inadequate (see Chapter 1). Cavalieri's wording is *per non esser terminate le prospettive*, which could mean that the scenery gave the impression of being "unfinished," although in theatrical terms, *terminare* and its cognates tends to be associated with correct perspectival rendering to a vanishing point.[51] Given that Cigoli was not just a painter but also a skilled architect, it is unlikely that he would have made so fundamental a mistake, although it is possible that it was forced upon him when he had to reconfigure the *Euridice* sets for the Sala della Commedie, reducing them by some 1.5 *b.* in height (as we shall see).[52]

The Sala delle Statue survives today in something close to its original proportions such that its present measurements can be reconciled (quite precisely, in fact) with Cigoli's original design and construction of the stage, save for the elements that he added or altered in the move to the Sala delle Commedie. Although the current form of the Sala delle Statue dates largely from the eighteenth century (a more fundamental reconstruction was proposed in the nineteenth century but never carried out), its basic structure has remained the same (including most of the niches), as can be seen by comparing the room in a recent state with a plausible recreation of its original one (see Fig. 2.3). The vaulted ceiling has not been altered significantly, nor its internal arches supported by corbels, although the cornice running just above them was not present in the original room; the entrance door on the south side (from what was originally a loggia) was somewhat differently configured; and the room was not so richly decorated.[53]

[51] See, for example, Serlio, *Il secondo libro di perspettiva*, fol. 26v (*il termino del quadro in scortio*); Danti, *Les Deux Règles de la perspective pratique de Vignole*, 296 (at 90 in the original; *che tutte le cose viste vanno a terminare in un sol punto*); Sabbatini, *Pratica di fabricar scene, e machine ne' teatri* (1638), 28 (*indi si tiraranno dalli segni e dall'imposte linee, che vadano a terminare nell'angolo che fa la facciata retta con la sfuggita*). There are many other possible examples.

[52] However, another negative comment reported by Palisca ("The First Performance of *Euridice*," 434), that the movement of the machines was not always felicitous, refers, rather, to the "principal" comedy in music of the festivities, i.e., *Il rapimento di Cefalo*.

[53] Farneti, "La Sala delle Nicchie"; the virtual reconstruction in Fig. 2.3 is taken from Marinazzo, "La Sala delle Nicchie," 127.

Fig. 2.3: (Upper) The present-day Sala delle Nicchie (formerly Sala delle Statue), Palazzo Pitti, Florence (Scala/Art Resource, NY). (Lower) Reconstruction (by Adriano Marinazzo) of the Sala delle Statue, Palazzo Pitti, Florence, as it was in the late sixteenth century (© Adriano Marinazzo).

Two of the dimensions to take into account are those provided by the plan of the Pitti's *piano nobile* in Joseph Furttenbach the Elder's *Architectura civilis* (1628), which are close enough to the room as it survives today (see Fig. 1.5, Chapter 1): he gives the length of the room (west–east) as 39 *b.* (22.6 m), and the width as 18 *b.* (10.4 m). Our own measurements of the room give the height to the top of the vault as 10.7 m (18.4 *b.*), and to the top of the current cornice (that is, the original corbels) as 6.3 m (10.9 *b.*). The corbels divide the room lengthwise into three equal portions of just under 13 *b.* (7.5 m) each. The north wall (facing the piazza) has three large windows, positioned symmetrically between the corbels. The room originally had ten niches for statues in the walls: three on either side of the central door on the south wall; one each on the west and east walls; and two (aligned with the corbels) between the three windows on the facade.[54] As we shall see, Cigoli appears to have designed his original stage to be 11 *b.* (6.4 m) deep, standing 0.5 *b.* clear of the rear wall. Assuming that it was situated at the east end of the room (adjoining the wing containing the grand duke's apartments), this means that it would have covered the first window moving from east to west, but not the first niche between that window and the next.[55] This left some two-thirds of the room free for the audience. Cigoli's planned width of the stage (17 *b.*) was 1 *b.* less than the width of the room, in order to take account of the depth of the corbels.

Cigoli would likely have wanted to cover as few of the niches in the Sala delle Statue as possible – seven were left visible – because he sought to integrate them into his design for the proscenium arch with the *chiaroscuro* statues of Painting and Poetry.[56] We have various details of the actual statues placed in the room's ten niches in the 1590s, including Michelangelo's *Apollo* (or *Apollo-David*, currently in the Museo Nazionale del Bargello in Florence), a Bacchus by Andrea Sansovino (also now in the Bargello), and other mythological subjects: an Adonis, a Flora (or Pomona), and several of Venus.[57] These figures are, of course, suggestive of their seeming to come to life in entertainments known to have been done in the room, such as *Dafne* in January 1598/99 (it has Apollo and Venus among its characters), although we cannot be sure which statues remained in view during these productions.

It remains unclear precisely when and why the decision was made to move *Euridice* from the Sala delle Statue to the Sala delle Commedie, one

[54] The current room has six niches: two on either side of the central door on the south wall – because that central door was widened in the eighteenth century – and one on each end wall, but no longer any between the windows.

[55] This assumption is a guess, but a plausible one. Putting the stage at the west end would have created problems in terms of access from the rear (through Flavia Peretti-Orsini's rooms); see Fig. 1.5.

[56] The three niches covered by the stage were two on the south wall (from the east wall to the first corbel), and one on the east wall (south of the door).

[57] See the lists in Saladino, "L'arredo statuario della Sala delle Nicchie."

floor higher, unless it was just because the Sala delle Statue was needed for other purposes. It made sense, however, in terms of the fire hazards associated with any theatrical endeavor in this period (a fire on a top floor could cause less vertical damage than one lower down). The Sala delle Commedie was convenient in other ways as well, in terms of its size and its ease of access from the rear (behind the stage); Giacinto Marmi's plan of the top floor (*terzo piano*) of the Pitti makes things clear (see Fig. 1.7). The Sala delle Statue had its main entrance halfway down the south wall (opposite the windows): the shorter east and west walls had just one door each, leading from private rooms (for the grand duke and Flavia Peretti-Orsini respectively). In contrast, the main entrance to the Sala delle Commedie was in the north wall, turning right at the top of the grand staircase, but there were also other entries on the west wall (with separate access from below via a spiral staircase), and two separate doors on the south wall (behind the stage) leading to a suite of rooms (with another staircase), some of which – we have seen – were occupied by Emilio de' Cavalieri. This was far more convenient in terms of granting separate access for the performers.

Unfortunately, the Sala delle Commedie does not survive in anything like its original state: it was severely damaged by a fire in the upper part of the west wing in 1638 (when the Guardaroba was located in the attic), and it was remodeled several times thereafter, being divided into two rooms, and then three.[58] As a result, it is harder to pin down the new dimensions to which Cigoli had to accommodate his design. In width and length, the original Sala delle Commedie was the same size as the Sala dei Forestieri (now the Sala Bianca) immediately below it one floor down, which Furttenbach (Fig. 1.5) measured at 23 *b.* wide and 46 *b.* long (13.3 m × 26.7 m). Unlike the vault of Sala delle Statue (and the Sala dei Forestieri), the ceiling of the Sala delle Commedie was flat, supported by exposed longitudinal and transverse beams. There is also the added complication of the room having had a *palcaccio*, a loft-style storage space lowering the ceiling at one end: we do not know whether this was on the north or south wall, so cannot gauge its impact on the construction of any

[58] Fantappiè, "Sale per lo spettacolo a Pitti," 172–73. For a while, we were strongly tempted to suggest that the room represented in Stefano della Bella's engraving of a banquet held in 1627 by the hunting society named the Signori Piacevoli in honor of Prince Giovan Carlo de' Medici (see www.alamy.com/stefano-della-bella-the-banquet-of-the-piacevoli-1627-the-banquet-of-the-piacevoli-1627-date-image336071118.html) represented the Sala delle Commedie, but a number of features (including the side and rear doors) do not quite match. Nevertheless, this image does give some sense of how the room might have looked without a stage.

temporary stage.[59] But although it is no longer possible to ascertain the original height of the room, the various measurements in Cresci's inventory suggest that in the part where the stage was constructed, it was 17 *b.* (9.9 m) up to the large longitudinal beams (*travate*) supporting the ceiling (or the loft-style *palcaccio*), and 18.5 *b.* (10.7 m) to the ceiling (or *palcaccio*) itself. Thus, the space for the stage was less high than in the Sala delle Statue by just under 1.5 *b.* (the height of the *travate*), but wider by 5.5 *b.* (3.2 m). As a result, Cigoli was forced to rethink his plan from the floor up, particularly with regard to the proscenium and the flats: it was a tricky problem, and he charged *sc.*25 for solving it. Logically enough, however, he sought to minimize the changes to the visible portion of the stage: rather than start again from scratch, he made various compromises.

The move from one room to another also has an impact on how to interpret our principal sources for any reconstruction of the stage in either location: that is, Cigoli's invoice for painting and Ricoveri's for sewing canvas, and Cresci's inventory of the materials put into storage (or sent elsewhere) in September 1601. Clearly Cigoli painted, and charged for, canvases intended for the Sala delle Statue which were then modified as a result of the move; likewise, Ricoveri's invoice refers to additional materials, and work done, for the sets in the Sala delle Commedie, meaning that a significant number of items had already been finished. Cresci's inventory, on the other hand, reflects only the state of the stage and sets after they had been adapted for the Sala delle Commedie. However, it is presented in a systematic fashion that also offers some sense of the Sala delle Statue version of Cigoli's design. The inventory first lists what was put into storage near the Teatro degli Uffizi by Michele Caccini in early September 1601, starting with the pastoral set (*Cres1–2*), then the proscenium (*3–7*), the "sky" (*8*), the moveable trees (*9*), the stage platform (*10–12*), the Underworld set (*13–14*), additional items added to accommodate the Sala delle Commedie (*15–16*), the Underworld backdrop (*17*), and various materials – timber, pulleys, ropes, etc. – needed to construct and operate the stage (*18–31*) and used in the main part of the room (*32*). The rest of the inventory (*Cres33–42*) concerns materials returned or used elsewhere, mostly consisting of additional boards (or panels) for the stage platform

[59] It is called a *palcaccio sopra al Salone della commedia* in the 1607 inventory of the Palazzo Pitti in *GM* 422, fol. 60. But we do not know its precise location in the room, nor how access was gained to it. In the present configuration, the middle room of what was the original Sala delle Commedie has a musicians' gallery (concealed by shutters) on its north wall, i.e., above the ceiling – which is lower – of the first room entering from the main staircase. However, this was constructed later.

and the trestles needed to support it (*33–35*), and timber that was used for the upper part of the stage and beneath it (*36–42*).

The Framing of the Stage

From 13 May 1600 to early October, large amounts of timber (planks, boards or panels, etc., of various sizes and thicknesses, and from different types of wood) and other construction materials were delivered to the Palazzo Pitti for the purposes of the banquet in the Palazzo Vecchio and a separate platform in that building's courtyard; for *Euridice*; and for other work in the Pitti associated with the wedding festivities.[60] These materials came largely from the storehouses of the Fortezza da Basso – where significant stocks were always kept on hand for construction and similar purposes – although some were obtained from the Opera del Duomo (whether or not passing through the Fortezza), and other items had already been credited to the Fabbrica de' Pitti. The notes recording all these deliveries to the palace rarely refer to their intended use, which would not necessarily have been known anyway by the administrators of the Fortezza. Some of the timber was "old," meaning that it had already been used and was intended to be reused: in effect, it was loaned to the festivities and needed to be returned. What seem to have been the planks and boards (etc.) from the Opera del Duomo were also numbered individually in order to keep track of them. Timber not identified as "old" was newly procured, largely through the Fortezza da Basso, and was regarded as specific to its present function, and also to some degree as expendable, even if it needed to be accounted for in the end.

Some of that new timber remained associated with the stage and sets of *Euridice* when they were transferred to the Teatro degli Uffizi. Some of it, however, was diverted to other uses. Cresci's inventory illustrates the distinctions: it lists five boards or panels of fir (each 6 × 2.5 *b.*) from the floor of the stage placed in storage in the Uffizi (*Cres28*); eleven old boards or panels of fir (5 × 2 *b.*) loaned by, and returned to, the Guardaroba

[60] *GM* 1152 contains a large number of scrappy documents recording such deliveries; many are signed by Francesco "Ghorini," who worked in the Fortezza da Basso. It is clear that similar materials would have been sent to the Teatro degli Uffizi for *Il rapimento di Cefalo*: the final audit of accounts for the latter (*SS* 279, fol. 144) refers to *legniame di più sorte, pitture, ferramenti, telerie, abiti et altre occorrenze per detta commedia*. However, we do not have regular receipts for them (they would have been kept in a separate file), and few of those in *GM* 1152 relate to *Il rapimento* (although some do); this is what one would expect given that its contents are largely limited to costs for the banquet and for *Euridice*.

(*Cres33*); and thirty-five pieces of timber of various types and sizes that had served to construct the frame of the "sky" (what Cresci called the *armadura dell cielo*) and other parts of the stage, but which had been transferred to the Fabbrica de' Pitti and used as part of the construction of a *stanzino* within the grand duchess's chambers in the east wing of the palace (*Cres36–42*).[61] This wood for the *stanzino* was therefore no longer available for reuse. But other such elements could always be retrieved if needed: this is the case with the trestles (*Cres34–35*) used to support the stage platform, which had been obtained from, and were returned to, the Guardaroba and the Fabbrica de' Pitti (at least in terms of their records), although Cresci made specific note of them in case the grand duke ever wished to rebuild the stage for another performance of *Euridice* (*Cres35*), or, presumably, any similar work.[62] Thus Cresci's entire inventory comes very close to what was needed for the complete stage as Cigoli designed it for the Sala delle Statue and then modified it for the Sala delle Commedie, even if not everything remained in one place thereafter.

The reference to the *armadura dell cielo* in Cresci's inventory involved an emendation to the text: he first associated this wood with the floor of the stage. The correction was made for the sake of accuracy but it also serves a useful purpose, reminding us that there was more to the stage of *Euridice* than just the scenic and decorative elements created by Cigoli. A "temporary" stage in any given room would have required a three-sided structural frame able to stand on its own – whether or not with additional anchoring to the walls (and/or in the Sala delle Commedie, the ceiling) – to which functional elements (for example, the movable flats and backdrop, and the frontstage curtain) and decorative ones (the proscenium) could be attached. This is precisely what is suggested by the term *armadura* (*armatura*) in the sense of framing or scaffolding. It also explains why at least some of these materials could then be used to construct the new *stanzino*, meaning that any rebuilt stage would require a new *armadura*. But not all the materials used for *Euridice* were so easily replaceable: it makes sense that those sent for storage appear to have been associated with particularly

[61] The transfer of these materials is also noted in *SFF* 72 (*Quaderno di robe per la fabbrica de' Pitti*, 1600–1603), fol. 25v (a credit to Gianbattista Cresci), which specifies that they were used *per fare un tetto e armadura di stuoia a uno stanzino fatto in camera per Madama Serenissima nel Bosco delli Allori*. The purpose of the *stanzino* (a "small room" or anything of that kind) is unclear.

[62] It is worth noting that such transfers to the Guardaroba or the Fabbrica de' Pitti may have been to accounts in those names rather than to any physical location. Thus anything assigned to, say, the Fabbrica de' Pitti could well have been stored in the Fortezza da Basso alongside materials credited to other accounts.

important elements of the stage and sets rather than generic items that could easily be obtained from elsewhere in the future.[63]

The Proscenium

As an architect, Cigoli may have had some say in how the stage's frame was constructed, but this was not something for which he expected to be paid, at least directly. So far as his invoice was concerned, then, Cigoli had no interest in the frame save for the overall dimensions that determined the spaces he needed to fill. However, he did care about what the spectators saw, and his proscenium therefore needed to make an immediate impact: he worked hard at creating it.

We do not have much visual evidence of the design of proscenium arches from this period as surviving engravings, etc., tend to focus on the actual stage and its sets rather than on what framed it. An early example, however, is the design by Bartolomeo Neroni ("Il Riccio") for the performance of *Ortensio* by the Accademia degli Intronati in Siena in 1560 (see Fig. 2.4).[64] A later one is Oliviero Gatti's engraving (1618) of the stage of the Teatro degli Intrepidi in Ferrara.[65] Both consist of columns on either side containing statues, a decorated transverse beam at the top with a large device at the center and decorative drapes hanging down, and a parapet at the bottom covering the height of the stage platform from the floor of the

[63] *Cres28* is a revealing case in point. It refers to boards or panels (*tavole*) for the stage floor with multiple slots that presumably were in specific places to allow for the operation of the scenery. Therefore they went to the Uffizi, whereas other such boards, even if with some slots (*Cres33*), did not.

[64] For *Ortensio* (and the erroneous attribution to a single author, Alessandro Piccolomini), see Riccò, *La "miniera" accademica*, 40 n. 58. For the stage, sources citing this design sometimes appear to confuse the dates: Neroni's original drawing (1560) is at www.themorgan.org/drawings/item/187270; Fig. 2.4 shows the version engraved by Girolamo Bolsi in 1589. An engraving of a similar city set for Lionardo Salviati's *Il granchio* (Florence, 1566) does not indicate the side columns but has a central *stemma* supporting a curtain held up by a *putto* on either side; see Bartoli Bacherini (ed.), *"Per un regale evento"*, 85 (also https://issuu.com/m.cobweb/docs/dramaoftheancients).

[65] Adami, *Scenografia e scenotecnica barocca tra Ferrara e Parma*, 61 (fig. 12). Adami further notes (at 82) the theatre constructed for the performance of *Amor pudico* in the Palazzo della Cancelleria in Rome in 1614 (for the wedding of Michele Peretti and Anna Maria Cesis), where the stage had a painted architrave (and a cornice above) mounted on two pilasters each containing a niche with an allegorical statue, with a divided curtain (in red) and a shield and a motto in the center. A similar treatment of the architrave is apparent in some of the designs by Inigo Jones, albeit without lateral columns (Peacock, *The Stage Designs of Inigo Jones*, figs. 33, 114), while in other cases the architrave is a type of cornice (fig. 51) normally linked by statues on either side (figs. 97, 143, 144).

Fig. 2.4: Bartolomeo Neroni ("Il Riccio"), stage design for a performance of *Ortensio* by the Accademia degli Intronati, Siena, in 1560 (1589 engraving by Girolamo Bolsi). Library of Congress (Washington, D.C.), Prints & Photographs Division, LC-DIG-ppmsca-18716.

room (thereby hiding the understage area). This seems to have become a standard design for early seventeenth-century stages.[66] It is also revealing that Cigoli used a similar framing device in non-theatrical contexts, including a sketch for a tapestry for Cardinal Montalto.[67]

Reconstructing the proscenium for *Euridice* requires reconciling Cigoli's invoice for the painting of it (for the Sala delle Statue) with what survived according to Cresci's inventory (for the Sala delle Commedie). In his design for the Sala delle Statue, Cigoli drew on many of the same architectural elements, including side columns with statues, decorative drapes, and a central coat of arms (see Fig. 2.5). However, instead of a horizontal beam

[66] Compare also the sketches by the Sienese scientist and architect Teofilo Gallaccini in Morolli (ed.), *Siena 1600 circa*, 29.

[67] Mersmann, *Lodovico Cigoli*, 307; the image is also at http://arts-graphiques.louvre.fr/detail/oeuvres/3/1432-Un-pape-ecrivant-sous-linspiration-divine-avec-des-anges-a-ses-cote-max. For the subject, see Chappell, *Disegni di Lodovico Cigoli*, 35–38.

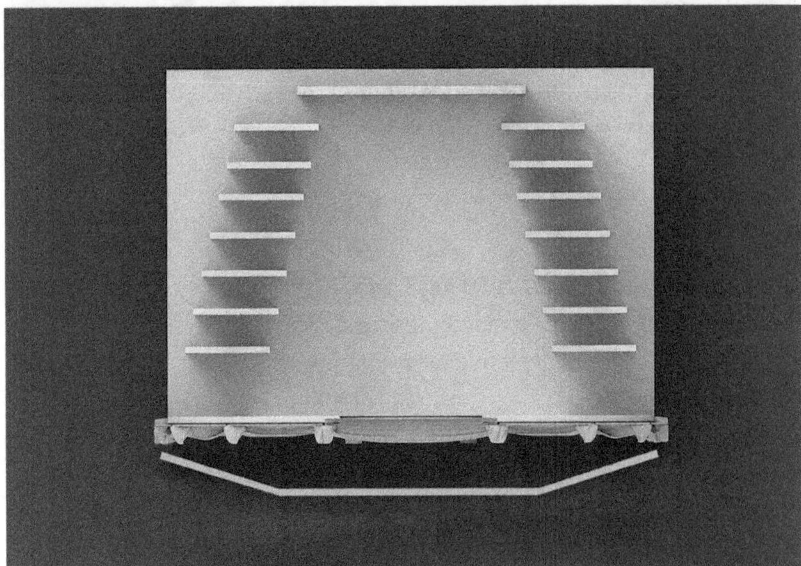

Fig. 2.5: (Upper) Reconstruction of Lodovico Cigoli's proscenium (and pastoral set) for the Sala delle Statue. (Lower) Top-down view of the same. © Gian Gabriele Bassanello.

between the two columns he opted, instead, for what would appear to the viewer to be an arch (although there was probably some kind of structural beam behind it, perhaps supported by the corbels). This may have been for pragmatic reasons because the Sala delle Statue had a high vault, but it also allowed Cigoli to invoke the triumphal arches commonly erected in Florence for ceremonial occasions.[68] By removing the visual impediment of the architrave, he gave the proscenium a greater sense of height, and steered the spectator's gaze onto the stage itself; he probably drew on the lessons learnt here for his later architectural projects that made prominent use of arches, such as his choir for the church of S. Gaggio (or its associated convent, 1603) and the Loggia de' Tornaquinci (1608).[69]

Cigoli's original design for the proscenium and its framing needed to take up almost the full width of the Sala delle Statue (18 *b.*), and more or less its full height (18.4 *b.*). His side columns were originally probably 8.5 *b.* high and 3 *b.* wide (their height was reduced to 8 *b.* for the Sala delle Commedie; *Cres4*). The columns rested on the stage platform that at the front was raised some 3 *b.* above the floor of the room (the height of the parapet calculated from *Cig3*, although its upper edge may have stood slightly above the platform itself). This would place the top of the columns just above the height of the corbels in the Sala delle Statue (10.9 *b.* above the floor by our modern measurements). The upper space created by the vault (18.4 – 11.5 = 6.9 *b.*) was to be filled in the center by the coat of arms of Maria de' Medici, which was around 7 *b.* high and 5 *b.* wide, with *putti* "larger than life" on either side (*Cig10*). Francesco Ricoveri sewed 20 *b.a.* of canvas for it (*Ric9*), which is close enough to the circumference of the ellipse (19 *b.a.*). A drawing for the coat of arms by Cigoli survives (see Fig. 2.6): it also has the *putti* noted in his invoice and appears to be positioned under an arch.[70] On either side of the coat of arms hung a canvas-covered frame (two in all) shaped to create the arch and painted to represent cloth

[68] Compare also Siena, Archivio di Stato, Tavolette di Biccherna 76 (depicting the wedding of Grand Duke Ferdinando I and Christine of Lorraine), at www.archiviodistato.siena.it/museobiccherne/it/107/biccherna-76.

[69] The Loggia de' Tornaquinci seems particularly "theatrical" in design; prior to 1865 it was on the south side of the Palazzo Corsi on Via Tornabuoni offering a perspectival view on the Palazzo Strozzi. For S. Gaggio, see Gambuti, "Lodovico Cigoli architetto," figs. 12–13, 54–56. Gambuti's study also provides other similar examples.

[70] Doubts have sometimes been raised about Cigoli's sketch being linked directly to *Euridice*, although the *putti* and the faint outline of an arch make it clear. Also (and *pace* Chappell, *Disegni di Lodovico Cigoli*, 92–93), the two different coats of arms that formed part of the decoration of the banquet were created by Jacopo Ligozzi, as noted in his list of expenses in *GM* 1152, fol. 442v. Cigoli's device is mentioned in *Cres35* but is not inventoried because rather than being placed in storage it was soon mounted above a staircase in the Palazzo Pitti.

Fig. 2.6: Lodovico Cigoli, drawing of a coat of arms (for the proscenium for *Euridice*). GDSU, 433 O. By permission of the Ministero per i beni e le attività culturali e per il turismo della Repubblica Italiana/Gallerie degli Uffizi.

in fine lacquer with gold flecks (*Cig7*; the *duoi pezzi di centina*); these pieces were made to appear as red brocade, and when they were placed in storage in the Uffizi they were each 10 *b.* long and 7 *b.* high where they met in the middle (*Cres5*), making them somewhere under 140 *b.q.* in size (Ricoveri sewed 150 *b.a.* of canvas; *Ric8*).[71]

[71] It is not clear whether Cresci is measuring the length along the straight edge or the ellipse; if the former, the two pieces (10 + 10 = 20 *b.*) were too long for the width of the Sala delle Statue (so they would need to have overlapped behind the coat of arms), but they may have been modified for the (wider) Sala delle Commedie, which, in turn, is perhaps why they were in disrepair (so Cresci noted).

The side columns were made up of two pilasters of timber and canvas; their architectural function and appearance was emphasized by capitals in relief for which Andrea Ferrucci provided a clay mold and 150 *libbre* (pound weight) of plaster.[72] On them were painted in *chiaroscuro* two figures (*Cres4*), one representing Poetry and the other Painting, with a bas-relief under each one (*Cig7*); Ricoveri sewed 40 *b.a.* of canvas for both of them (*Ric11*). These are the "statues" noted in Buonarroti's description of the set. Given that the "statues" were mounted on the stage, they help determine the maximum height of the visible opening of the proscenium. Their width (3 *b.*) reflects Cigoli's sense of proportion with regard to the width of the Sala delle Statue (18 *b.*): the pilasters each take up one-sixth of it, leaving two-thirds (12 *b.*) for the width of the open stage, although from other measurements it seems that its actual width was 11 *b.*, given that the proscenium was to stand 0.5 *b.* away from each side wall (because of the corbels, we have suggested).

That gap between the side walls and the outer edges of the proscenium is confirmed by the length of the parapet painted by Cigoli with gold and silver flecks to run along the lower edge of the proscenium and therefore hide the understage area (*Cig3*). According to Cresci's inventory (*Cres7*), this was made up of two canvas-covered panels (on a wooden frame), each 8.5 *b.* long and 2 *b.* high, although one of them had been lost: by his and Caccini's measurements, therefore, the total length of the parapet was 17 *b.* (not the 18 *b.* of the width of the Sala delle Statue). According to Cigoli (*Cig3*), the parapet had *rivolte* – that is, each end turned inward at an angle so as to create a narrow well in front of the stage.[73] Thus the total length may have slightly exceeded 17 *b.* (and depending on how the *rivolte* were constructed, Caccini and Cresci may not have counted them in their measurements). Cigoli would have wanted to be more accurate so as to be paid for the work he did: he measures the parapet and its *rivolte* at 52.5 *b. q.*, which seems so precise as to suggest a structure 17.5 *b.* long (so we have shown it in Fig. 2.16) and 3 *b.* high ($17.5 \times 3 = 52.5$). The difference between Cigoli's height and Cresci's (2 *b.*) is a result of the fact that the parapet was cut down in the move to the Sala delle Commedie. In turn, the height of the original parapet in the Sala delle Statue (Cigoli's 3 *b.*) provides a clear sense of the height of the front of the stage platform in that room, although the

[72] *GM* 1152, fol. 196, dated 21 July 1600: *Conto del modello di terra e del cavo di gesso fatto per il capitello che va alla comedia de' Pitti.*

[73] Cigoli uses the term *rivolta* in the sense of a side turning in at an obtuse angle in his *Prospettiva pratica*; see Camerota, *Linear Perspective in the Age of Galileo*, 239.

platform may have been slightly lower so that the upper edge of the parapet would partially conceal any footlights positioned there.[74]

The wooden frames (*telai*, etc.) on which much of the canvas of the proscenium was mounted would have given it some stability. It is also clear that Cigoli intended the proscenium to have an architectural integrity consonant with the room for which he was designing the stage. The arch behind the coat of arms, painted as red brocade, probably matched the color of the walls in the Sala delle Statue (compare the reconstruction in Fig. 2.3).[75] More important, the *chiaroscuro* "statues" of Poetry and Painting in the niches on either side of the proscenium would in some sense have continued the sequence of statues located in the rest of the room, while, as we have seen, the mythological subjects of those statues would have resonated with the action onstage.[76] It was a well-crafted design that raises broader questions about the various themes of *Euridice* to which we shall return in Chapter 3. However, it lost its focus with the subsequent switch of rooms to the top floor of the Palazzo Pitti.

Given the greater width but lesser height of the Sala delle Commedie, as well as its flat ceiling, Cigoli had to modify his proscenium with the move to the new room (see Fig. 2.7). In doing so, he retained elements of his original arch as needed for the vault in the Sala delle Statue, but he brought the whole closer to the more classical proscenium framed with an architrave as discussed above. However, the different dimensions of the Sala delle Commedie also forced some more rough-and-ready adjustments. For example, we have seen that Cigoli charged for painting a parapet 17.5 *b.* long and 3 *b.* high, but by the time it entered Cresci's inventory it was only 2 *b.* high. This was a result of the frontstage platform being lowered from

[74] These measurements seem consistent with Sabbatini, *Pratica di fabricar scene, e machine ne' teatri* (1638), 3–5, which suggests that the parapet should be 4.5 *piedi* high (2.9 *b.*) rising 0.5 *piedi* (0.3 *b.*) above the floor of the stage to conceal the lighting, and should be positioned 1 *piede* (0.7 *b.*) in front of it. These conversions assume that Sabbatini was using Bolognese *piedi* (at 0.38 m).

[75] Farneti, "La Sala delle Nicchie," 133, notes a description (1577) of the wall coverings of the Sala delle Statue (*damasco rosso con fregio tra l'un telo e l'altro di raso turchino, ricamato d'oro e tela d'oro con fregio da capo*). These coverings seem to have remained until the mid seventeenth century.

[76] *GM* 1152 contains a number of documents referring to work done for the statues in the Sala delle Statue, including (fol. 139v) making pedestals to ensure that they all stood at the same height. As for painted "statues" (in niches) as a framing device, compare Bernardino Poccetti's on the two short walls in the current Sala di Bona (next to the Sala Bianca) in the Palazzo Pitti; see Padovani, "Il quartiere dei cardinali e principi forestieri," 51. In the absence of appropriate paintings or drawings by Cigoli, our representation of the statues in Fig. 2.5 (etc.) draws upon Ripa, *Iconologia*, ed. Maffei, 480–82 (Poetry), and Cantelli, *Francesco Furini e i Furiniani*, figs. 2, 13 (Painting).

Fig. 2.7: (Upper) Reconstruction of Lodovico Cigoli's proscenium (and pastoral set minus the moveable trees) in the Sala delle Commedie. (Lower) The elements of that proscenium listed in Cigoli's invoice and Cresci's inventory. © Gian Gabriele Bassanello.

3 *b.* to 2 *b.* (or just below) to accommodate the lower height of the room. Because of the increased width, the parapet also needed to be extended on either side, which was done by adding to each end a framed canvas

depicting boulders measuring 2.5 *b.* long and 2 *b.* high (*Cres15*; they do not appear in Cigoli's invoice but may have been created from elements of the Underworld set that were cut down for the new room). Likewise, Cigoli added additional pilasters to the outside edges of the two columns to join the proscenium to the side walls (*Cig7*; they do not appear in Cresci's inventory); Ricoveri charged £20 (the equivalent of sewing 200 *b.a.* of canvas, far more than was needed) for these two "banners" (*bandinelle*) noting that their size had been increased and then decreased (*Ric5*), which in turn suggests a degree of uncertainty in adjusting to the new location. Cigoli included them in a general entry covering the elements of the proscenium amounting to 228⅙ *b.q.*; deducting the dimensions of the proscenium elements identified by Cresci (*Cres3–5* = 173.6 *b.q.*) leaves 54.5 *b.q.*, sufficient for two extra pilasters each 2.5 *b.* wide and 10.9 *b.* high, which is what was needed for the new room.

The longitudinal beams supporting the ceiling (or the loft-style *palcaccio*) of the Sala delle Commedie created issues for the upper portion of the proscenium. Although Cigoli retained elements of the arch mounted on the two side columns (with their statues), plus its central coat of arms, he needed to square off the top, which he did by way of two right-angled triangles of canvas (*Cig7*, with frames), with the sides bounding the right angle each measuring 7.5 *b.* (*Cres3*): he painted them to represent festoons, sky, and a few ruins (*finto i festoni et aria con alquanto di rovina*), but they must have included a representation of an architrave (otherwise those elements would just appear hanging in midair).[77] These triangles would then have been attached to a (hidden) transverse beam anchoring the proscenium to the longitudinal beams supporting the ceiling of the room.[78] Furthermore, those longitudinal beams created three additional spaces (*Cig8*) that needed to be filled with canvas-covered wooden panels 1.5 *b.* high, which Cigoli painted *a sfondato* (*Cres6*, creating the *trompe l'oeil* illusion of an opening revealing a view beyond). Because the arch no longer stood freely under a vault, the entire height of the room needed to be covered by the new design without giving the impression of merely plugging gaps within a proscenium altered haphazardly for want of something better. Those added ruins, however, brought an additional visual image

[77] The total surface area of these two triangles was 56.25 *b.q.* (compare the 52 *b.a.* of canvas in *Ric10*). For Cigoli's painting of *fregi*, see also Padovani, "Il quartiere dei cardinali e principi forestieri," 48, which provides an example on which any recreation of those for the proscenium of *Euridice* might be based; and compare GDSU, 164 O.

[78] A *puntone* (girder) that may have served this purpose was delivered to the Sala delle Commedie on 6 September 1600; *GM* 1152, fol. 265.

into the frame as a counterpart to the "ancient" form of drama that *Euridice* was now reviving on the modern stage. It was a rather neat solution to what must have seemed to Cigoli to be a frustrating problem.[79]

Presumably the transverse beam also provided anchoring for the "curtain of green canvas used to close the stage in front" (*Cres16*) measuring 22 *b.* wide and 16 *b.* high (so, 352 *b.q.*). The width makes it clear that this was for the Sala delle Commedie; the height also fits, assuming that it did not quite reach the main floor of the room (its bottom edge was mostly behind the parapet). A similar curtain may have been made previously for the proscenium designed for the Sala delle Statue: in early 1607, a green curtain measuring 16 *b.* high and 17 *b.* wide at the top (and 18 *b.* wide at the bottom) and kept in the Guardaroba was sent to the grand duchess in Pisa *per far commedie*, along with lighting equipment.[80] In either case, the curtain matched the dimensions of the entire proscenium, including the coat of arms and the side columns with the statues; although Buonarroti's description refers to "curtains" (plural), it seems clear that there was only one, and that at the beginning of the performance in the Sala delle Commedie it was lowered to remain hidden behind the parapet.[81]

[79] For our representation of the upper portion of the Sala delle Commedie proscenium in Fig. 2.7, we have also drawn on Francesco Guitti's design for a temporary theatre constructed in Ferrara in 1632 reproduced in Adami, *Scenografia e scenotecnica barocca tra Ferrara e Parma*, 124 (fig. 36), and Adami, "Nel segno di Aleotti," 257 (fig. 143). This has *alquanto di rovina*, as it were, plus three friezes above the architrave.

[80] *GM* 780 (*Affari diversi*), fol. 591 (12 February 1606/7): *Una tenda di tela verde con sua corda e campanelle alta braccia 16, larga da capo braccia 17 e da piede braccia 18.* Ferdinando Gonzaga presented a *comedia in musica* in Pisa on 26 February; *SolMBD*, 38–39. The dimensions of this curtain match the Sala delle Statue; the larger one for the Sala delle Commedie (*Cres16*) would presumably have been kept for use there. In 1600, Francesco Ricoveri sewed a *tenda* of 100 *b.a.* (*Ric12*) and a *tenda verde* of 200 *b.a.* (*Ric13*), which seem associated with a frontstage curtain, although the measurements do not match in any obvious way.

[81] Michelangelo Buonarroti (*il giovane*), *Descrizione delle felicissime nozze . . . della Cristianissima Maestà di Madama Maria Medici, Regina di Francia e di Navarra* (Florence: Giorgio Marescotti, 1600), 18, describing *Il magnifico apparato in degna sala dopo le cortine.* Buonarroti's account here, as elsewhere, may reflect some prior plan for the production (even in the Sala delle Statue); his use of the plural *cortine* may also reflect a different intention for how they would frame the stage when open (hence our reconstruction in Fig. 2.5). For another possible treatment of the curtain (raised behind the proscenium and therefore leaving the latter visible even when closed), see the Rosenwald MS, images 551–54 (Francesco Guitti adopted a similar device in Ferrara in 1632; see Adami, "Nel segno di Aleotti," 258 [fig. 144]). While this could have been done in the Sala delle Commedie, the measurements of the curtain in *Cres16* plus a handwritten stage direction in a copy of the printed libretto of *Euridice* (see Table 3.4, *bottata giù la tela*) suggest that the curtain did indeed fall. For the general principle, compare Ariosto, *Orlando furioso* XXXII: 80.1–2: *Quale al cader delle cortine suole / parer fra mille lampade la scena . . .* There are plenty of examples of the curtain being lowered at the start of a

The Stage Platform (and Below)

It is not possible to determine the intended depth of the stage in the Sala delle Statue on the basis of Gianbattista Cresci's inventory, given that the latter reflects what was constructed for the Sala delle Commedie. However, given the dimensions of the room and Cigoli's recommendations in his *Prospettiva pratica*, it would seem to have been around 11 *b.* deep, standing 0.5 *b.* from the east wall (see Fig. 2.16). The move to the Sala delle Commedie enabled Cigoli to extend the depth of the entire stage to around 13 *b.* The total depth of the stage in the Sala delle Statue (11 *b.*) would have meant that the backdrop stood slightly in front of its rear edge (say at 9.5 or 10 *b.* from the front). Cigoli seems to have taken advantage of the extra space in the Sala delle Commedie to shift the backdrop slightly further to the rear (at 11 *b.* from the front of the stage), leaving another 2 *b.* behind the backdrop, and therefore facilitating any backstage movement. Francesco Ricoveri noted that the stage floor was lengthened (*che s'ebbe allungare, Ric4*), and he sewed an extra 80 *b.a.* of canvas for that purpose (although that seems too much).

In terms of the wood for the platform, *Cresc28* lists five boards or panels of fir (*tavole d'abeto*), each 6 *b.* long and 25 *b.* wide (so, 75 *b.q.*) with slots (*traforate*) in various places, which "served for the floor of the stage." In addition, *Cres33* has eleven "old" boards or panels of fir, each 5 *b.* long and 2 *b.* wide (110 *b.q.*); some also *traforate.* We shall see that these slots were necessary to allow for the understage operation of the sets. Combined, these materials produce a total of 185 *b.q.* for the platform, which would be sufficient for one measuring about 17 × 11 *b.* (187 *b.q.*), as was plausibly intended for the Sala delle Statue. Extending the depth of the stage for the Sala delle Commedie was achieved by way of the additional planks of fir (*asse d'abeto da ⅓*) in *Cres39–40*, giving a total surface area of some (17 × 13 =) 221 *b.q.* (see Fig. 2.8).[82] Fir was a favorite source of timber for construction purposes (and was used in various thicknesses) due to its tensile strength.

This surface area matches what could have been supported by the number of trestles (*capre*) noted in Cresci's inventory. There were four trestles each 10 *b.* long and six each 3 *b.* long (*Cresc34*), plus another seven, each 3 *b.* long (*Cresc35*), all of which had been lent by different offices in the

performance; compare Evangelista, "L'attività spettacolare della Compagnia di San Giovanni Evangelista," 330, 332 (*caschi la vela*).

[82] *Cres39* lists just three planks (plus the seven in *Cres40*) although our reconstruction in Fig. 2.8 requires four; we assume that one was lost. This reconstruction does not indicate the slots or channels needed for the movement of the trees for the pastoral set.

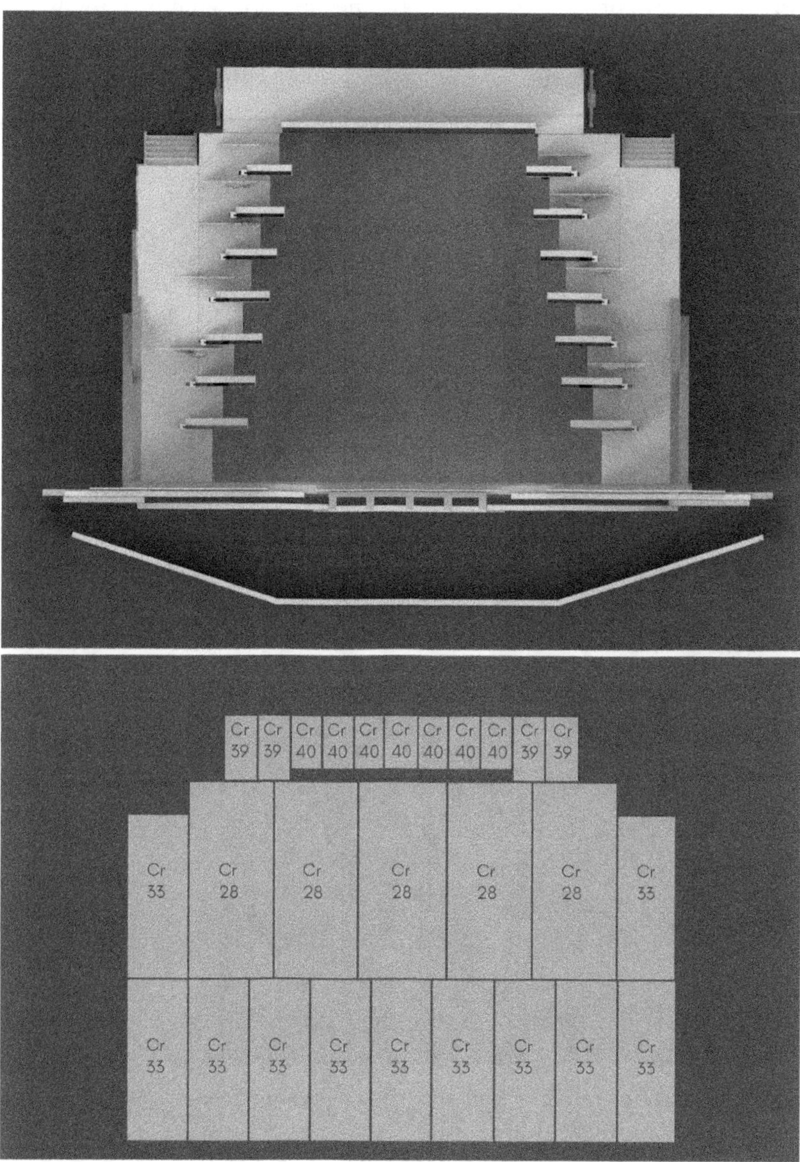

Fig. 2.8: (Upper) Reconstruction of the stage in the Sala delle Commedie (top-down view) showing the position of the flats. (Lower) A likely position of the boards of the stage floor. © Gian Gabriele Bassanello.

Palazzo Pitti (the Guardaroba and the Fabbrica). They would have been sufficient to support a stage made up of two rectangles, one in front measuring 17 × 10 *b.* and one at the rear measuring 13 × 3 *b.*, creating a total stage depth of 13 *b.* (see Fig. 2.9). They did not stand directly on the floor but, rather, were mounted on planks positioned longitudinally, to which they could be attached to provide stability (see *CW*Fig. 2.17).[83] Those planks included the seven long *pianoni* in *Cres42* (7 *b.* long) and

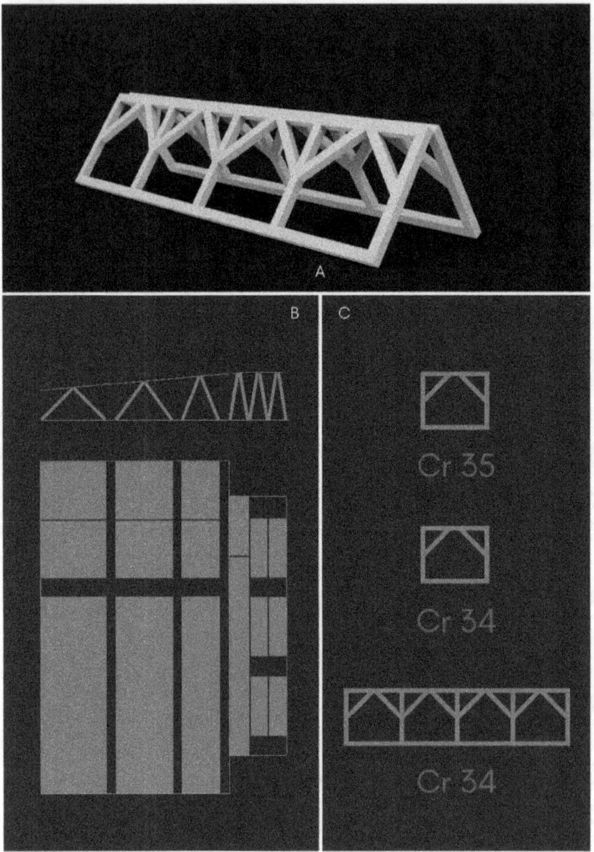

Fig. 2.9: A likely layout of the trestles supporting the stage floor in the Sala delle Commedie. © Gian Gabriele Bassanello.

[83] The architect Francesco Guitti described this part of the construction of the temporary stage in the courtyard of S. Pietro Martire (Parma) for the festivities celebrating the marriage of Odoardo Farnese and Margherita de' Medici in 1628, calling it *il letto della fabbrica*; see Lavin, "Lettres de Parmes," 119–20. Guitti notes the importance of placing the planks longitudinally and an equal distance apart, and provides a sketch (Lavin, "Lettres de Parmes," fig. 1 [following 158]) to emphasize the point. *Piane* and narrower *correnti* were typically used to construct floors, ceilings, roofs, etc. Baldinucci, *Vocabolario toscano dell'arte del disegno* (1681), defines both *correnti* and *piane* as *Legni lunghi quadrangolati, servono a più e diversi usi, ma particolarmente per far palchi, e copertura d'edifizi.*

three *piane* in *Cres36* (3 *b.*), plus the variously sized ones in *Cres38* (three at 3 *b.* in length) and *Cres41* (four at 13 *b.*). In addition, the two battens (*correnti*) at *Cres19* which served to "guide" the set changes would have been mounted to these planks at an oblique angle, further helping to anchor the structure.

This understage support determined the height of the stage floor itself. The trestles were each around 2.5 *b.* high (*Cres34*). Assuming that they were foldable, and that 2.5 *b.* was their height when closed, then opening the legs would have lowered them proportionally to varying degrees (compare Fig. 2.10). The portion of the rear of the stage (behind the backdrop) added for the Sala delle Commedie (2 *b.* in depth) would have been level, probably about 3 *b.* above the floor of the room (taking into account the maximum possible standing height of the trestles plus the thickness of the planks underneath them and the boards or panels on top). However, the visible stage floor from the backdrop to the front needed to be raked for the purpose of the perspectival set, with the standing height of the trestles being progressively reduced by increasing their angle of opening. The front of the stage floor would have been about the height of the parapet in front of it (2 *b.* in the Sala delle Commedie), which over 11 *b.* (the depth of the visible stage) gives a rake somewhere between the 1:12 recommended in *Il corago* and the 1:9 in Cigoli's *Prospettiva pratica*.[84] It is not possible to determine what the rake would have been of any stage constructed in the Sala delle Statue, although given that Cigoli intended a higher front of the stage there (some 3 *b.* to judge by the height of the parapet he originally painted), the rear would have been raised still further.

The stage platform was covered with canvas, presumably to create a uniform surface (also in terms of color). The visible part of the stage floor formed a trapezoid 11 *b.* wide at the front (the width of the stage opening), just under 8 *b.* wide at the rear (the width of the backdrop, as we shall see), and 11 *b.* deep. Here, Cigoli's measurements were very precise: he painted 104.5 *b.q.* of canvas for the floor (*Cig4*), which is exactly the area of a

[84] P. Fabbri and Pompilio (eds.), *Il corago*, 34–37: the stage should be 5 or 6 *palmi* high at the front and 7 or 8 *palmi* at the rear, with 24 *palmi* from the front to the rear perspective, but this concerns a wider stage, forcing a steeper perspective (for present purposes, one can assume that a *palmo* is 0.5 *b.* – although it was slightly less – and therefore dividing the number of *palmi* by two allows for a rough comparison with the stage for *Euridice*). For Cigoli, see Camerota, *Linear Perspective in the Age of Galileo*, 237. Compare Adami, *Scenografia e scenotecnica barocca tra Ferrara e Parma*, 139–40, where Pietro Paolo Floriani recommends 1:9, which is sanctioned (ibid., 196) by Serlio. Sabbatini, *Pratica di fabricar scene, e machine ne' teatri* (1638), 3, recommends a shallower rake of a *mezz'oncia per piede* (1:24) if there is dancing, and otherwise *due terzi d'oncia* (1:18).

trapezoid with those linear dimensions. However, the canvas also extended into the wings. By the time of Cresci's inventory, only a total of 79 *b.q.* of it survived: one strip 12 *b.* long and 2 *b.* wide (24 *b.q.*, *Cres10*), which presumably ran across the stage at the front; one rectangular piece 8 *b.* by 6 *b.* (48 *b.q.*, *Cres11*), which would have been placed center stage; and three smaller pieces totaling 7 *b.q.* (*Cres12*). Clearly other canvas was damaged beyond repair, or may have been made up of old materials that did not merit being kept in storage.[85] But the width of that first strip (*Cres10*) is revealing: it suggests that the first set of flats in the wings was positioned 2 *b.* behind the proscenium arch (the other six sets of flats were therefore closer together). This squares with Cigoli's recommendation in his *Prospettiva pratica* that the space before the first set of flats should be as wide as possible so as to facilitate the entrances and exits of the actors.[86] Having them enter or stand toward the rear of the stage was always discouraged anyway, because they would appear disproportionately tall within the receding perspective view (see *CW*Fig. 2.18), although as we shall see, an exception was made for spirits of the Underworld.

The increased width of the Sala delle Commedie compared with that of the Sala delle Statue (23 *b.* versus 18 *b.*) may have helped solve a further problem. The stage as originally designed by Cigoli had almost no room at the rear – hence the 2 *b.* added behind the backdrop for the Sala delle Commedie – and relatively little on either side. Therefore the question was where to put the instruments needed to provide the accompaniment: Jacopo Peri said in the preface to the score of *Euridice* that four were used – a harpsichord, a chitarrone, a *lira grande*, and a *liuto grosso*. This was a perennial problem in early modern theatres: the instrumentalists needed to be able to see the singers onstage, but ideally should not impede the sight lines for the audience.[87] Cigoli's plan for the Sala delle Statue may have been to put them in front of the stage: hence his parapet 3 *b.* in height (which therefore would have had to stand at least the width of a harpsichord in front of the stage). This was the solution preferred by the Florentine Giulio Parigi, as shown in the Rosenwald MS, and by Joseph

[85] Relatively late in the day, Michele Caccini received various deliveries of *tela vecchia* which presumably provided additional material for the flooring: *GM* 1152, fols. 185 (8 *b.* on 20 July 1600), 305 (26 *b.q.* on 16 September).

[86] Camerota, *Linear Perspective in the Age of Galileo*, 239.

[87] For the contentious arguments over the position of the instruments in the theatrical entertainments for the Farnese–Medici wedding in Parma in 1628 (and the complaint that stage designers never paid attention to the needs of musicians), see Lavin, "Lettres de Parme," 115–16, 126, 143, 146, 147–48. The eventual solution there was in a space on the floor in front of the stage between two sets of steps.

Furttenbach the Elder, who had been in Florence.[88] Cigoli's *rivolte* to his single parapet would also have partially closed it off on either side, conforming in part to the recommendation in *Il corago* that, particularly in the case of string instruments (such as the four mentioned by Peri), the sound needed to be directed upward rather than outward so as not to overpower the singers.[89]

Lowering the stage and the parapet by 1 *b.* for the Sala delle Commedie made this a less attractive option, however, given that the instrumentalists would have been more visible. Furthermore, in the case of the Sala delle Commedie at least, the space behind the parapet was also needed for the curtain in its "open" (lowered) position. Peri in fact said that for the performance of *Euridice* the instrumentalists were placed "within" the stage (*dentro alla Scena*): if the instrumentalists were still to see the singers, this most likely means that they were somewhere in the wings (invisible to the audience), and probably somehow distributed on both sides. Nicola Sabbatini did not recommend this option because the position of the players and their instruments would impede the actors and the stagehands operating any machinery, although he was willing to allow it if the musicians were on platforms significantly higher than the stage on either side so that others could move beneath them.[90] Such high platforms

[88] The Rosenwald MS (images 551–52) identifies the space between the stage and the parapet as the *luogo de' musici, sonatori, e rammentatori* (the last meaning "prompters"). For Furttenbach, see Hewitt (ed.), *The Renaissance Stage*, 185, 195 (behind the parapet is "an excellent position for the musicians"), 199, 201. However, *Il corago* (P. Fabbri and Pompilio [eds.], 88), recommends that the parapet should not be so low as to allow the audience to see the heads of any tall instrumentalists (*i sonatori . . . se saranno più alti, si vedranno i loro capelli e loro teste con enorme difetto*), nor too high as to destroy the perspective view and to prevent sight of the actors' feet (*più alto della fine del palco, rompe i termini della prospettiva, e impedisce che si vedano i piedi e i borsacchini dei recitanti*). Another option offered by both Sabbatini and *Il corago* was to have musicians in front and on either side of the stage, behind separate parapets at an angle between the proscenium arch and the side wall; see Sabbatini, *Pratica di fabricar scene, e machine ne' teatri* (1638), 57 (*due poggiuoli con legnami buoni e murati nelle pareti*); P. Fabbri and Pompilio (eds.), *Il corago*, 88 (*ai fianchi del palco . . . con palchetti d'uguale altezza con la fine del palco . . . per impedire meno che si può il luogo e vista agli spettatori hanno forma di triangolo*). However, this seems to have been intended for theatrical spaces wider than either the Sala delle Statue or the Sala delle Commedie.

[89] P. Fabbri and Pompilio (eds.), *Il corago*, 87: *che adoperandosi l'istrumenti di corde, si procuri che il suono vada all'insù e non ai fianchi prossimi, perché essendo la sala grande e dovendosi sonare alquanto forte, i principali personaggi dell'udienza, che sogliono essere accanto al palco si stordiranno per il sono troppo gagliardo e non intenderanno bene il canto. Per questo gioverà il fare lo steccato [tra] l'instromenti e l'uditore sia di tavole grosse e ben chiuse.*

[90] Sabbatini, *Pratica di fabricar scene, e machine ne' teatri* (1638), 57: *non volendosi che stiano dentro le scene per l'impedimento che sogliono dare alle macchine, sì con le persone loro, come anco con gli organi e altri strumenti.* However, platforms were possible, *tanto alti dal piano del palco, quanto vi si possa passare sotto comodamente.*

would be implausible in the Sala delle Commedie – and *Il corago* advises against them because of sight-line issues for the performers[91] – but with a stage platform 17 *b.* wide, there was just about enough room in the wings for the instruments to be on the edges of the stage toward the rear (although that would have created coordination problems); at floor level closer to front of the stage between the edges of the stage and the walls (better for seeing the singers); or (best) on separate risers, for which no evidence survives.[92] However, *Il corago* also warns against a different problem of balance: if string instruments were placed in the wings, they would not be heard by the audience unless they played very loudly (*a coro pieno*), which was something to be avoided when accompanying a solo voice.[93] This raises a broader question about the role of the instruments in *Euridice* (largely functioning as a *basso continuo* group) in terms of whether they just supported the singers or contributed to its broader musical impact as perceived by the audience.

The "Sky"

Sabbatini offered quite precise instructions for constructing the "sky" (*cielo*) of any stage, which could be either a single unit (*intero*) – the easiest to construct – or could be "split" (*spezzato*) into strips, allowing for the descent of cloud machines and the like mid-stage. In either case the *cielo* needed to curve downward from front to back. It should be mounted on three or four arc-shaped pieces of wood (*centine, o arcali fatti in minor portione di cerchio*) placed longitudinally above the stage, with additional supports nailed latitudinally beneath them; Sabbatini calls those supports *ciavaroni* or, as is the style in Tuscany (he says), *correnti*. The canvas then needed to be stretched under this frame and kept as taut as possible to avoid sagging. The *centine* were also to be attached to the ceiling of the room by way of good, strong *tiranti* (braces, rods, or ropes)

91 P. Fabbri and Pompilio (eds.), *Il corago*, 88: *e quel che è peggio il suonatore di gravicembalo, quale più di tutti si suole adoprare, non vedrà il cantore, et allora se la sua voce sarà debole non lo sentirà, onde o bisognerà far la battuta o mettersi a pericolo di discordare.*

92 Sabbatini, *Pratica di fabricar scene, e machine ne' teatri* (1638), 57, also says that if the instrumentalists are to be in the wings, any platforms on which they are placed should be constructed separately from, and not attached to, the stage as otherwise any onstage dancing would cause them to bounce, creating problems for the instruments (*nel tempo di morescare, sconterebbono gli organi e altri instromenti*).

93 P. Fabbri and Pompilio (eds.), *Il corago*, 87–88: *non saranno sentiti per tutta la sala, se non quando si soneranno a coro pieno, cosa che si deve fuggire quando si canta a solo a solo.*

Fig. 2.10: Reconstruction of the stage in the Sala delle Commedie (side view), also showing the structure of the "sky." © Gian Gabriele Bassanello.

to make them secure.[94] This is precisely what Cigoli did, at least in the Sala delle Commedie (see Fig. 2.10); additional framing would have been necessary for the Sala delle Statue due to its vault.

The curved shape of the *cielo* required more canvas than was needed to cover the equivalent flat area of the stage floor. Cigoli measured "the whole arch of the sky" at 225 *b.q.* (*Cig1*); Cresci noted that this was a single piece of canvas (*tela*) 17 *b.* long and 13.5 *b.* wide "on average" (*Cres8*), which gives 229.5 *b.q.*; Ricoveri sewed together eight strips of canvas totaling

[94] Sabbatini, *Pratica di fabricar scene, e machine ne' teatri* (1638), 5–6: *Stabilito il piano del palco, si doverà dar principio a fare il Cielo, quale doverà essere o intiero, o spezzato; se intiero, vi sarà poca fatica, poiché farassi con tre o quattro centine, o arcali fatti in minor portione di cerchio, dando loro (nel metterli in opera), il suo declivio di due oncie per piedi, raccomandandogli con buoni e forti tiranti alle travi del tetto, o ad altro, acciochè stiano sicuri. // Di poi si stenderanno per lo lungo sotto ad esse centine, legnami lunghi, e sotili in giusta lontanza, bene inchiodati, quali legni da noi volgarmente vengono nominati ciavaroni e in Toscana correnti; compita questa seconda orditura, vi si stenderanno le tele, le quali vogliono essere imbrocate più spesso che sia possibile, acciochè non vengano a fare qualche cattivo effetto e così sarà compito il Cielo intero.* Sabbatini's verb *imbrocare* is the equivalent of the modern *imbrocchettare*, referring to the stretching and nailing of canvas to a frame.

150 *b.a.* for it (*Ric6*).[95] It seems likely that part of the *cielo* was delivered in four strips to Michele Caccini on 11 September, while another part arrived the next day:[96] Caccini refers to *tela pagliola*, a relatively fine form of canvas that was also used for various decorative elements of the banquet in the Salone dei Cinquecento.[97] These records suggest that the materials for the *cielo* were commissioned after the decision had been made to change the room for the performance.

Cresci's "length" of the canvas for the *cielo* matches the total width of the proscenium intended for the Sala delle Statue (17 *b.*), the framing of which was presumably retained in the Sala delle Commedie (even though the actual proscenium was wider in that room by virtue of the extra pieces added on either side). Cresci's "width" (13.5 *b.*) is close to the length of the four arc-shaped *centine* that supported the canvas from front to back of the stage (*Cres21*), with nine lateral *correnti* each 17 *b.* in length (*Cres37*; see *CW*Fig. 2.19).[98] With a *cielo* 13.5 *b.* in depth, its arc would have been relatively shallow, but it would have extended over the backdrop in such a way as to leave space for lighting positioned at that upper level, just as Cigoli recommended in his *Prospettiva pratica.*[99] It is clear that the final version of the *cielo* was treated as a single piece of canvas; there was no need for it to be *spezzato*, anyway, given that *Euridice* did not require any cloud machines or similar devices descending from above.

[95] Eight pieces of canvas producing a single piece measuring 17 *b.* by 13.5 *b.* required seven joins along the shorter sides (13.5 × 7 = 94.5 *b.a.*) plus hemming the two shorter sides (27 *b.a.*) and the two longer ones (34 *b.a.*), giving a total of 155.5 *b.a.* As we have noted elsewhere, it would be implausible to expect Cigoli's, Cresci's, and Ricoveri's measurements to match precisely, but in this case they are close enough.

[96] On 11 September 1600, Michele Caccini received 150 *b.a.* (in four pieces) *di tela pagliola . . . per il cielo della prospettiva della commedia de' Pitti*; *GM* 1152, fol. 283. Another 27 *b.* of the same material was delivered for the comedy (but with no statement as to purpose) the next day; ibid., fol. 291.

[97] GM 1152: *tela pagliola nuova per la tavola* (fol. 238); *tela bianca pagliola per la fonte della tavola* (fol. 254), *tela pagliola pe' carretti delle nughole della tavola* (fol. 296).

[98] Cresci's calculations need some explaining. For *Cres21*, four *centine* each 13 *b.* long and 0.5 *b.* wide produce 26 *b.a.* of wood, 1 *b.* wide. Likewise, for *Cres37*, nine *correnti* producing 84 *b.a.* (at 1 *b.* wide) would suggest that if each *corrente* was 17 *b.* long, then it was slightly more than 0.5 *b.* wide. Cresci seems to have used a similar system reckoning *braccia* by way of standard widths elsewhere in his inventory.

[99] Camerota, *Linear Perspective in the Age of Galileo*, 239: *e sopra la scena si farà il Cielo, con una centina curva e non retta*, separate from *tutti i pezzi della scena*, and raised above the backdrop *quanto vi si possino accomodare e nascondere alcuni piccoli lumi che fanno diventar l'orizzonte naturalissimo et intanto porta gran comodità alla mutazione delle scene.*

The Pastoral Set

All these measurements, and others still to come, establish the dimensions of the visible stage that Cigoli designed for *Euridice* in the Sala delle Statue: 11 *b.* wide at the front (6.4 m), some 8 *b.* wide at the rear (4.64 m), and probably 9.5–10 *b.* deep to the backdrop (5.5–5.8 m) with a total stage depth of some 11 *b.* (6.4 m). The height of the stage at the front (from the stage platform to the lower edge of the proscenium arch) was 8.5 *b.* (4.6 m); this receded (by way of the curved sky and the raked stage) to a height of 4 *b.* at the rear (2.3 m). This is smaller, and also quite different in proportion, from what is proposed in *Il corago* as an "average" stage, with a visible width at the front of 42 *palmi*, and a visible height of 34 *palmi*; a backdrop 20 *palmi* wide and high; and a stage 24 *palmi* deep.[100] Those measurements suggest something about twice the width and height of the visible stage of *Euridice* at the front (the backdrop is significantly higher, too), although the depth is not so different (meaning that the stage recommended in *Il corago* would have produced a perspectival view that receded more sharply).

The visible width of the stage did not change in the move to the Sala delle Commedie, where the extra width of the room was concealed behind the new side elements added to the proscenium. However, we have seen that the stage increased in depth from a total of 11 *b.* to 13 *b.* (7.5 m), with the backdrop in the Sala delle Commedie now 11 *b.* from the front of the stage. The vertical dimensions were also reduced by 1.5 *b.* (0.9 m) as even after positioning the entire stage closer to the main floor of the room (at a height of 2 *b.* rather than 3 *b.* in the Sala delle Statue), the Sala delle Commedie was still not high enough for what Cigoli had originally planned.

These broad dimensions of the visible stage determined what Cigoli was able to fit on it in terms of the pastoral and Underworld sets required for *Euridice*. He needed to be very inventive in terms of both the limited space and the required scenic effects. Daniele Barbaro, in his *La pratica della perspettiva* (1569), had already been clear on the challenges posed by creating a rustic set, which required

> great discernment, both because it is necessary to take the eye into account as in the case of the other [types of set], and because the trees, mountains, villages, huts, and

[100] P. Fabbri and Pompili (eds.), *Il corago*, 34–37; as noted previously, *palmi* can be divided by two to get a rough comparison in *braccia*. The visible height of the stage at the front is indicated by the measurement in *Il corago* for the first set of flats (*l'altezza delle prime due case*).

shelters which are present are by their nature indeterminate in shape and therefore need much understanding of lights, of shadows, of vistas, and of the effects created by these views. Thus, in addition to placing the vanishing point in its proper place and to direct everything toward it, it is necessary to understand natural effects well, and to imitate the real as much as one can with the appropriate colors.[101]

Barbaro was drawing on Sebastiano Serlio's well-known design for a *scena satyrica*, as did Leone de' Sommi when prescribing a stage high and full of greenery representing woods in the summer with leaves and flowers; fruit-bearing trees with birds in their branches; and rabbits, hares, and the like capering around; also with mountains, valleys, huts, springs, caves, surrounding a flowering meadow to serve as the performance space.[102] But as pastoral plays came into fashion in the last quarter of the sixteenth century, the possibilities of Serlio's *scena satyrica* became expanded still further: in 1598, Angelo Ingegneri added temples to the standard list of woods, mountains, valleys, rivers, springs, and huts, all of which, in his case, were to be seen up close and in the distance.[103]

The dramatic action within the pastoral episodes of *Euridice* takes place entirely in the open air within a landscape to which the characters make regular reference (so Rinuccini is careful to ensure), although, as we shall see in Chapter 3, mention is made of an offstage temple (so as to facilitate the exit of the chorus prior to the action in the Underworld). Michelangelo Buonarroti *il giovane*'s account of the pastoral set for *Euridice*, with its "most beautiful woods both in relief and painted" (*selve vaghissime, e rilevate, e dipinte*), also suggests something more limited in scope than Leone de' Sommi and Angelo Ingegneri would have preferred. However, by mixing two- and three-dimensional elements – the latter including six

101 Barbaro, *La pratica della perspettiva* (1569), 158: *La scena satirica richiede gran discretione, sì perché bisogna havere a consideratione all'occhio come nelle altre sì perché gli alberi, le montagne, i paesi e le capanne, e coperti che vi vanno sono cose per natura loro indeterminate e hanno bisogno di molta intelligentia dei lumi, delle ombre, dei lontani e degli effetti che fanno le vedute però, oltra a ponere il punto al luogo suo, e a quello riferire ogni cosa è necessario intendersi bene degli effetti naturali e imitare il vero quanto si può con i debiti colori.*

102 De' Sommi, *Quattro dialoghi . . .*, ed. Marotti, 66–67 (trans. in Blanchard-Rothmuller, "Leone Ebreo de' Sommi's *Four Dialogues on Stage Presentations*," 178–79).

103 Ingegneri, *Della poesia rappresentativa*, ed. Doglio, 26: *Ma se si trattasse di pastorale, quanto il tutto sia rustico, ogni cosa servirà, avegna che anco quivi sia bene l'accostarsi il meglio che si possa alla similitudine del sito di quella regione, sia Arcadia od altra, dove si presuppone che il fatto succeda. E in ogni caso le selve, i monti, le valli, i fiumi, le fontane, i tempi, le capanne e soprattutto le prospettive, eziandio di tai cose lontane, daranno grazia maravigliosa.* Compare P. Fabbri and Pompilio (eds.), *Il corago*, 40, which distinguishes between sets for the *pastorale* (*boschi, scogli, giardini e foresta con antri et anche tempii tondi tra cipressi e simili alberi*) and for the *satira* (*selve, capanne e più salvatiche foreste*).

freestanding trees with fruits and leaves – Cigoli got close enough to the convention given the constraints under which he was working (see Fig. 2.11).

Fig. 2.11: Reconstructions of the (upper) pastoral and (lower) Underworld sets in the Sala delle Commedie (with the moveable trees and boulders). © Gian Gabriele Bassanello.

Despite Barbaro's warning about the vanishing point, a pastoral set was likely easier to handle than a tragic or comic one with buildings receding in perspective (the same is true, on the whole, for the rocky landscape needed for the Underworld set). Cigoli painted seventeen pieces of canvas for "the scene of the trees" (*la sciena degli alberi*) measuring a total of 257 *b.q.* (*Cig2*).[104] Fourteen of them, representing woods (*a boscaglie*), were simple straight-edged flats mounted on frames to make what Cresci called "the streets of the stage" (*Cres1*, *le strade della sciena*), using a standard term going back at least to Serlio. There were seven each on the left and right, parallel to the front of the stage and receding along its oblique sides, with heights ranging from 7 *b.* to 5 *b.* and each about 2 *b.* wide (*Cres1*).[105] The remaining three canvases were used to create the rear backdrop, 8 *b.* wide and 4 *b.* high (*Cresc2*). Cigoli's and Cresci's figures do not quite match – the total area suggested by Cresci's measurements (for the flats and the backdrop), some 200 *b.q.*, is less than Cigoli's 257 *b.q.* – but this reflects the fact that Cigoli's invoice reflects work done for the Sala delle Statue whereas Cresci's inventory itemizes what was left of the cut-down scenery from the Sala delle Commedie.[106] Francesco Ricoveri measured the (original) pastoral and Underworld backdrops at 8.5 × 5 *b.* (*Ric3*); and these plus the total amount of sewing he did for the fourteen pastoral flats (252 *b.a.*) and the Underworld ones brings us close to Cigoli's figure.[107] This, in turn, suggests that the flats that Cigoli painted for the Sala delle Statue ranged from 8.6 *b.* to 6.6 *b.* in height, and that they therefore each lost 1.6 *b.* in the move to the Sala delle Commedie); the backdrop was reduced in size as well.

[104] In the separate list that Michele Caccini created for the purpose of assessing Cigoli's prices (by gaining estimates from other artists, see CWFig. 1.10), he called them *17 tele a' boschaglie* (*GM* 1152, fol. 446).

[105] Our reconstruction presumes that the seven flats on each side had the following heights from front to back: 7 *b.*, 6.7 *b.*, 6.3 *b.*, 6 *b.*, 5.7 *b.*, 5.3 *b.*, 5 *b.*

[106] For example, on 10 July 1600, Michele Caccini received *una tela dipinta per la comedia de' Pitti* measuring 9.5 × 4.5 *b.* (the delivery note is issued by Matteo Chelli, *scrivano*), which looks suspiciously like one of the backdrops painted by Cigoli with measurements intended for the Sala delle Statue; *GM* 1152, fol. 174.

[107] Ricoveri's measurements can seem confusing because he is sewing linear *braccia andante*, i.e., around edges and at joins. In the case of *Ric3* (the two backdrops), a backdrop measuring 8.5 × 5 *b.* would require 27 *b.a.* of sewing around the edges, but Cigoli provided three pieces of canvas, adding two 5 *b.* joins (so, 37 *b.a.* in total). Ricoveri then seems to have rounded this up to 40 *b.a.* for each backdrop, and hence 80 *b.a.* in total. He used approximations in other ways, too, when he noted (*Ric1–2*) that the flats were each 6 *b.* high (and by implication, 3 *b.* wide, producing 18 *b.a.* for each flat), even though they were of different heights (and narrower, though the difference may be due to Ricoveri adding an allowance to mount the canvas on its frames).

As noted earlier (on the basis of the canvas for the stage floor), the first flats on either side stood 2 *b.* behind the proscenium arch, leaving enough room for the actors to make their entrances and exits; the other flats would therefore have had about 1.3 *b.* between them (about the width of a narrow doorway), which would have been tight (though not impossible) for any significant movement on and off the stage, although save in special circumstances, this would not have taken place toward the rear anyway for reasons of perspective. Having seven flats on either side seems a large number for what was a fairly shallow stage, although they would have prevented any audience members viewing at an angle from seeing into the wings. Cigoli's design for the Sala delle Statue had the front flats (8.6 *b.*) higher than the visible height of the stage (8.5 *b.*), although given their position 2 *b.* behind the proscenium their tops would still have been visible (hence the need for the *cielo* to extend into the wings). But because of the adjustments needed for the Sala delle Commedie, those front flats, at 7 *b.* (*Cres1*), were now too low. This may be one of the reasons for the negative comments on the scenery for *Euridice* conveyed by Emilio de' Cavalieri.

Scaling the flats from 7 *b.* at the front to 5 *b.* at the back (*Cres1*) created the receding perspective on the raked stage leading to the backdrop. Although Cresci measured the backdrop at 8 *b.* wide (*Cres2*), less of it may in fact have been visible: the rear flats would typically have covered its edges to some degree. Cresci gives the height of the backdrop as 4 *b.*, which squares with the structure that supported it (*Cres20*) comprising three "guides" made up of two battens each and a transverse beam: the *guide* were necessary for the pulley mechanism to allow for the scene change to the Underworld.

In addition to the flats, Cigoli made six separate trees in the round and moveable on stage, 5.5 *b.* in height on average (*raguagliati*, *Cig9*), which would therefore have appeared more realistic than anything painted on the straight-edged flats. These were made of *papier-mâché*, with fruits and leaves (flecked with gold), and each mounted on its base (*il pedale*, *Cres9*); Cresci measured them at 7 *b.* each, adding their *pedali*, with branches 2 *b.* wide.[108] Both Cigoli's and Cresci's measurements would appear to suggest that the trees were made with the new dimensions of the stage for the Sala delle Commedie in mind, that is, after the move from the Sala delle Statue. It seems logical to presume that they were positioned

108 The *pedale* of a tree can be its entire trunk or its base (from which the roots emerge). Cresci seems to be using the term in the latter sense, i.e., as what supported the upper structure of the tree itself.

with three on either side of the stage, emerging from the *strade* between the flats (with other *strade* left free for the rocks used for the Underworld scene, as we shall see).[109] They must also have been scaled so that their visible height was reduced from the front to the rear of the stage according to the perspective (hence Cigoli's measurement "on average"). We also assume that the *pedali* on which the trees were mounted were positioned on the flat floor underneath the stage – given the rake, it seems most unlikely that they stood free on the stage itself, given their height and weight and the danger of them tipping over – and therefore that they moved on and off through slots or channels in the stage floor (our layout of the trestles supporting it allows for this; see Figs. 2.9, 2.10). Thus, while each tree with its *pedale* may indeed have been 7 *b.* high in total (so Cresci says), the proportion between what was visible on the stage and what rested beneath it will have varied according to the rake of the stage (in the Sala delle Commedie, from 2 *b.* high at the front to 3 *b.* at the rear).[110] We do not have any evidence of the understage mechanism that enabled them to slide laterally on and off the stage along the slots in the stage floor itself. However, it seems likely that each *pedale* was mounted on some kind of carriage with wheels resting on the planks that supported the trestles. The six trees could have been pushed manually (for example, by members of the chorus); they could have been moved by separate rope-and-pulley devices under the stage; or they could have somehow been attached to the central winch that also operated for the change to the Underworld scene and back (as we shall see).[111] Nor is it clear how far into the stage those trees could move (as a means, say, of creating a short stage for the Prologue). However, their position and movement may

[109] It would seem plausible for them to have been positioned between flats 2–3, 4–5, and 6–7 (so we suggest in Fig. 2.10), leaving clear the spaces between the proscenium and flat 1, flats 1–2, and perhaps flats 3–4, for singers to enter and exit. The moveable rocks for the Underworld scene would have emerged differently.

[110] Our reconstruction for the Sala delle Commedie in Fig. 2.11 assumes that the three ranks of trees had a visible height of 5 *b.*, 4.8 *b.*, and 4.5 *b.*

[111] The Rosenwald MS (images 551–52) illustrates a stage with slots/channels to allow for the lateral movement of stage machines such as ships and the like (*Sportelli che si aprono se si havesse a passare barche o altro*). The understage part was mounted on what the Rosenwald MS calls a *castello* (images 555–57), i.e., a carriage-like mechanism (presumably with wheels, although the Rosenwald MS does not show them). Similar devices were available in the Teatro degli Uffizi (e.g., for Amerigo Vespucci's ship in the fourth of the *intermedi* accompanying Michelangelo Buonarroti *il giovane*'s *Il giudizio di Paride* in 1608); compare Pietro Paolo Floriani's mechanism for sliding flats on and off the stage shown in Adami, *Scenografia e scenotecnica barocca tra Ferrara e Parma*, *Tavola* LVII. In the case of *Euridice*, Michele Caccini procured a large number of pulleys, wheels, and so forth, some of which could have been used for this purpose; see note 127.

also have helped obscure the visible change to the Underworld set, which was otherwise a problem (as we shall also see).

In terms of the "look" of the pastoral set, there are some models on which to draw, including Pietro Paolo Floriani's rendering of a pastoral set in the Teatro degli Intrepidi, Ferrara (see Fig. 2.2), seemingly with five flats on either side plus a backdrop, and Cigoli's own sketches for other purposes.[112] Cigoli was also involved in creating other decorations within the Palazzo Pitti, particularly in the guest quarters next to the Sala dei Forestieri on the *piano nobile*, including the Loggetta dell'Allori (painted by Alessandro Allori): some of the pastoral landscapes here might also have a bearing on his design for *Euridice*.[113] Such landscapes, even if not directly linked to any stage designs, provide an excellent example of the use of color to reinforce a sense of perspective, moving away from warmer or richer colors to colder or paler ones.

The Underworld Set

Buonarroti says more about the Underworld set than the pastoral one. Orfeo calls for Euridice "from the mouth of the Inferno" (*dalla bocca dello 'nferno*), led there by Venere (Venus). The scene is made up of "horrendous" and "frightening" boulders that seemed real (*orridi massi … e spaventevoli, che parean veri*), "leafless trees and ash-colored grass" (*sfrondati li sterpi, e livide l'erbe*), and a view, through a gap in a large cliff, of "the city of Dis burning, with tongues of flames licking through openings in its towers, the air around flaring in a color like copper."[114] In Rinuccini's libretto (ll. 398 ff.), Venere notes her and Orfeo's arrival through the dark passage (*L'oscuro varco*) to pallid, sad shores (*rive pallide e meste*), and she tells him to gaze upon the dark plains and the deathly city of the god who reigns over the shades (*Rimira intorno, e vedi / gl'oscuri campi e la Città fatale / del Re che sovra l'ombre ha scettro e regno*). She thereby invites the spectators to "gaze upon" a scene and use their imagination to flesh it out according to her description.

[112] For Cigoli, see, for example, http://arts-graphiques.louvre.fr/detail/oeuvres/15/1438-Dante-dans-la-foret-max.

[113] Padovani, "Il quartiere dei cardinali e principi forestieri," 43–53. Compare also the sketches by Inigo Jones (who was strongly influenced by the Florentines) in Peacock, *The Stage Designs of Inigo Jones*, figs. 97–122.

[114] Buonarroti, *Descrizione delle felicissime nozze*, 18–19: *E là più ad entro per la rottura d'una gran rupe la Città di Dite ardere vi si conobbe, vibrando lingue di fiamme per le aperture delle sue torri, l'aere d'intorno avvampandovi di un colore come di rame.*

Fig. 2.12: Lodovico Cigoli, possible sketch for the Underworld set of *Euridice*. GDSU, 59 P. By permission of the Ministero per i beni e le attività culturali e per il turismo della Repubblica Italiana/Gallerie degli Uffizi.

The seemingly detailed account of the Underworld set in Buonarroti's description has had a significant influence on how scholars have read, or perhaps misread, other evidence we have of it. There are three sketches attributed to Cigoli that have been associated with this part of *Euridice*, all of which clearly show some kind of city in the background (see Figs. 2.12, 2.13, and *CW*Fig.

Fig. 2.13: Lodovico Cigoli, possible sketch for the Underworld set of *Euridice*. GDSU, 60 P. By permission of the Ministero per i beni e le attività culturali e per il turismo della Repubblica Italiana/Gallerie degli Uffizi.

2.20).[115] One of them (*CW*Fig. 2.20) reveals the turrets of Dis belching flames, and Orpheus in the foreground standing near the portal to Hades (bearing the predictable inscription "Lasciate ogni speranza voi ch'entrate"), with a *lira da braccio* almost in playing position, and with Cerberus at his back: this sketch is now in unknown private hands, and the only available image of it was printed in reverse, evidently by mistake.[116] All three sketches figure prominently in their

[115] Two are in GDSU, 59 P and 60 P, and one was sold at auction at Sotheby's (Florence) on 2 February 1987; all three are reproduced in Petrioli Tofani, "L'illustrazione teatrale e il significato dei documenti figurative per la storia dello spettacolo," figs. 15–17, although Petrioli Tofani warns against their being taken literally. The two in GDSU are also given in Testaverde, "Nuovi documenti sulle scenografie di Ludovico Cigoli per l'*Euridice* di Ottavio Rinuccini," figs. 1–2; see also Chappell, *Disegni di Lodovico Cigoli*, 90–92, and Caneva and Solinas (eds.), *Maria de' Medici*, 186–87. However, Testaverde's suggestion that the different orientations of these two images reflects two different designs, one for the Sala delle Statue and the other for the Sala delle Commedie, can be excluded following our measurements of the two rooms. Another sketch by Cigoli that Petrioli Tofani suggests might be connected with *Euridice* would seem, rather, to represent the rape of Persephone/Proserpina (ibid., fig. 18; BNCF, C.B.III.53, fols. 99v–100).

[116] The reverse image is clear from the "Lasciate ogni speranza . . . " inscription. To forestall an obvious objection, it seems most unlikely that Cigoli drew the image in reverse as the model for an engraving (which would end up being printed the right way round).

center Charon rowing his boat across the Styx. The sketch showing Orpheus and the turrets of Dis is closest to the Classical version of the myth overlaid with references to Dante (the inscription), as the singer makes his plea to enter the Underworld:[117] the purpose of the constructions on poles in this image remains unclear – it has been suggested that they are mirrors to enable lighting effects (although we have a slightly different reading of them, below).[118] But while this third sketch comes closest to what Buonarroti describes in terms of the burning city of Dis, it is hard to imagine how it could have functioned on any stage, leaving room for the action. Moreover, although Caronte (Charon) appears in *Euridice*, there is no reference to his boat; nor is there any evidence in Cigoli's invoice or Cresci's inventory of scenic elements that might be linked to it.

For all these reasons, serious doubts must remain about associating any of these sketches with the actual staging of *Euridice*, or indeed, with any theatrical venture. And while Cigoli might initially have envisaged something along one or other of these lines when he first started thinking about the Underworld set, in the end he opted for a much simpler approach, with scenery similar in design and structure to the pastoral one (see Fig. 2.11). Cigoli painted seventeen canvases here, too, representing "large boulders, with gold and silver flecks," and with the same surface area as his *sciena degli alberi* (257 *b.q.*, *Cig6*). Despite those gold and silver flecks, boulders cost less to paint than trees, perhaps because they otherwise involved cheaper colors or less complex design: Cigoli charged only £5 per *b.q.* for them rather than £6 (the city of Dis in the backdrop does not seem to have affected his reckoning).[119] In Cresci's inventory, these canvases are again divided into fourteen flats and a backdrop (*Cres13*, *Cres17*), with the flats 2 *b.* wide, diminishing in height from 7 *b.* to 5 *b.* These had the same dimensions as the pastoral flats – as did the backdrop (measured at 8 *b.* by 4 *b.*) – and, as with them, the surface area falls about 50 *b.q.* short of the amount in Cigoli's invoice; there are also the same apparent discrepancies as with the pastoral set in terms of the canvas provided by Ricoveri (*Ric2–3*). Again, this reflects the fact that Cigoli's original canvases were cut down in the move to the Sala delle Commedie. However, in this case, some of the left-over material may have been used to create the two canvases

[117] It also has clear resonances of Giovanni Stradano's (Jan van der Straet, 1523–1605) illustrations (1587–88) for Dante's *Inferno*, now in Florence, Biblioteca Medicea Laurenziana; e.g., https://commons.wikimedia.org/wiki/File:Stradano_Inferno_Canto_08.jpg.

[118] Petrioli Tofani, "L'illustrazione teatrale e il significato dei documenti figurative per la storia dello spettacolo," 57.

[119] He charged even less for the three panels in the architrave in the Sala delle Commedie (*sc.*2 for each of them in *Cig8*, covering a total of 25.5 *b.q.* according to *Cres6*).

representing boulders (5 *b.q.* each) that were used to extend the parapet at the foot of the stage in the new room (*Cres15*).

Cresci's inventory noted that these flats served to "make the change to the Inferno over the flats [*case*] as woods" and that they had frames at their tops and pulleys to move them down and up (*in giù e 'n su*); he also wrote that they were "in bad condition." The backdrop had a similar frame at the top and so did not slide in from either side (nor would there have been room for it to do so). However, Cresci's wording reversed the motion required for the set change from and back to the pastoral set: there was no room above the stage to hide these flats, and therefore it is clear that the flats and the backdrop were first raised from beneath the stage and then lowered to fold back under it (*in su e in giù*, as it were). As we have seen, this was one of the least favored methods suggested in *Il corago* for changing scenery, as the movement was visible to the audience, but it was the best option for a temporary theatre with limited space in the wings and scant headroom. The mechanism for raising, then lowering, the canvases for the wings appears to have been similar to the one drawn by Pietro Paolo Floriani for similar circumstances, which comprised a box-like sleeve (Floriani calls it a *cassa*) running up and down a square batten attached by rope to a pulley at the top (see Fig. 2.14; *CW*Fig. 2.21).[120] In the case of the flats, Cresci's inventory lists twelve such battens each 8 *b.* high with a *cassa* and pulleys that were "used for the changes to the Inferno" (*Cres18*); two would seem to have been lost. The Underworld canvases were attached to a frame at the top (so *Cres13* notes), but hung loose lower down (so they could fold). These vertical battens were mounted to horizontal ones 11 *b.* long underneath the stage on each side (*Cres19* lists two), which was just over the length of each diagonal side from front to rear. The mechanism also involved sewing concealed ropes to the canvases themselves, for which Ricoveri charged for twenty-four workdays (*giornate*, *Ric14*).[121]

The movement of the Underworld flats was controlled by a long (9 *b.*) winch (*verricello*) with six handles (*manichetti*), and with "fixed wheels" (*ruote ferme*, with grooves around their circumference) along its length, which "served under the stage for the change of scene" (*Cres29*). The winch

[120] Floriani's terminology is clear, although another possible meaning of *cassa* is a container with weights to counterbalance any movement; compare the mechanism in the Rosenwald MS, images 553–54 (including *una cassa piena di sassi*), to facilitate the raising and lowering of a stage curtain.

[121] For *giornate*, see "Money, Accounts, Measurements, Dates, and Time."

Fig. 2.14: Proposed mechanism for raising and lowering the Underworld flats.© Gian Gabriele Bassanello.

was mounted on three braces each 3 *b.* long (five are listed in *Cres31*), and it would have been positioned under the stage longitudinally, from front to back (see *CW*Fig. 2.22).[122] While one would expect those handles to be

[122] For a longitudinal winch with *manichetti* and *ruote ferme* used to operate some movement of the side flats, see Floriani's sketches in Adami, *Scenografia e scenotecnica barocca tra Ferrara e Parma*, 135–36, 139–42, and *Tavole* IX, XI. A latitudinal winch for the backdrop appears to be shown in Lazardig and Rößler (eds.), *Technologies of Theatre*, 317 (fig. 2), and the

positioned at equal distances along the length of the winch (which would be the safest and most efficient way to operate it), it is hard to see how there would have been sufficient height under the stage toward the front to allow for operators positioned there to turn them, even if the trestles allowed access in the first place.[123] But the ropes from the pulley mechanism attached to the battens supporting each flat would have been attached to those fixed wheels, allowing the flats to move up and down in synchronization with each turn of the winch. The mechanism also required fifteen wooden wheels (*carrucole*) with ropes and pulleys (*Cres24*) that were used to "pull" (*tirare*) the set change to the Underworld.

The Underworld backdrop was more complicated than the pastoral one (see Fig. 2.15). Although both backdrops were in three sewn pieces, the central panel of the Underworld one differed significantly from its counterparts on either side (although neither *Cig6* nor *Cres17* notes any distinction) given Buonarroti's claim that it contained a view of the city of Dis (which is confirmed by at least one other source; see Table 3.4).[124] Because the backdrop was freestanding, as it were, it needed a sturdier mechanism to support it, hence the three "guides" and the transverse beam in *Cres20*. The pulley mechanism to raise and lower its elements was probably not dissimilar to the one described by Nicola Sabbatini for lowering a cloud machine containing a person from above the stage.[125] In the case of *Euridice*, however, the entire Underworld backdrop was raised by two small winches, each 3 *b.* long with two handles (*Cres30*; supported by the remaining braces listed in *Cres31*) positioned latitudinally at the rear of the stage, probably one on each side (also shown in *CW*Fig. 2.22).[126] Cresci's

Rosenwald MS (image 552). As some of Floriani's rough drawings suggest, such fixed wheels could be of different diameters to cater for different degrees of movement. The layout of the trestles underneath the stage (compare Fig. 2.9) means that this winch must have been placed off-center. It may or may not be coincidence that, placed thus in the Sala delle Statue, it would have aligned with the door providing access behind the stage.

123 This is true even if one allows for the use in this period of dwarfs (compare P. Fabbri and Pompilio [eds.], *Il corago*, 125) or children as stagehands.

124 For other representations of Dis – on which we have drawn for our reconstruction, although they are more complex – see the engravings representing the sets for the fourth of the 1589 *intermedi* and the second *intermedio* for *La liberazione di Tirreno e d'Arnea* (1617) given, respectively, in Testaverde, *L'officina delle nuvole*, 47, and M. Fabbri *et al.* (eds.), *Il luogo teatrale a Firenze*, 125–26.

125 Sabbatini, *Pratica di fabricar scene, e machine ne' teatri* (1638), 140. A similar mechanism is clear in another drawing attributed to Sabbatini given in Adami, *Scenografia e scenotecnica barocca tra Ferrara e Parma*, 206 (fig. 50).

126 For the winches, Cresci's inventory seems to distinguish between *manichetti* for the long winch operating the flats (*Cres29*) and *manichi* for the two shorter ones for the backdrop (*Cres30*). The former may be rods slotted through the axis of the winch; the latter may be L-shaped handles fixed to each end – both types of handles are shown in contemporary illustrations.

Fig. 2.15: Proposed mechanism for raising and lowering the Underworld backdrop. © Gian Gabriele Bassanello.

inventory further includes additional ropes and similar items no doubt associated with all these mechanisms (*Cres27*).[127]

The central element of the backdrop, with the view of Dis, included turrets with flames emerging from their openings: the illusion was created by the piece of painted wood 6 *b.* long (*Cres22*) positioned at the top of the backdrop and cut to represent a parapet with crenellations (which is probably the meaning of *un pezzo di asse rintornata*), with fireguards behind it (three at 2 *b.* each in *Cres25*). Angelo Ingegneri noted the utility of having "real" flames appear on stage so as to increase the horror of such a scene (*l'incendio accresce l'orrore*), in his case, by setting fire to some material in front of the backdrop.[128] For *Euridice*, however, the effect was probably created by a method similar to that suggested by Nicola Sabbatini, with lit torches held aloft by one or more stagehands standing behind the backdrop; the fireguards would have protected the upper edge of the backdrop, although those carrying the torches would still have needed to be careful to avoid the obvious risk of fire to other elements of the scenery.[129]

Just as the pastoral set had six moveable trees, the Underworld one had five separate boulders standing free on the stage (*Cig5*). Cresci measured them at approximately 2 *b.* by 2 *b.* (*Cres14*) – so, 20 *b.q.*, although Cigoli charged for 16.6 *b.q.* – and says that they were painted on canvas and timber. They were less bulky than the pastoral trees, but they may have served a similar purpose, perhaps also setting off part of the Underworld set (for example, for the opening segment between Orfeo and Venere). Their size was such that they could have moved on wheels on the stage platform itself (rather than by way of some understage mechanism), probably pushed on and off by the five (it seems) Underworld spirits (*ombre*) that appear in the scene (the number and handling of the *ombre* are discussed further in Chapter 3). Any noise made by those wheels could have been

127 Likewise, *GM* 1152 contains numerous invoices submitted by artisans referring to the construction of pulleys, etc., such as on fols. 147 (9 June 1600: twelve *charu[c]hole grosse* with *girelli*), 168 (7 July: twelve *girelli di leg[n]iame d'ulivo 4 cho[n] il chanale e 8 senza [c]hanale servi per la chomedia*, plus eight *girelline pichole* and thirty-six *chaccigluoli* [*sic*]), 225 (28 July 1600: three *girelli*, thirty smaller *girelli*, and thirty-one *charucole grosse* with their *girelli*), 365 (16 September 1600: seven *carucole mezane*). While some of these clearly relate to items in Cresci's inventory, they cannot be matched precisely to them in any useful way.

128 Ingegneri, *Della poesia rappresentativa*, ed. Doglio, 30.

129 Sabbatini, *Pratica di fabricar scene, e machine ne' teatri* (1638), 102–4 (Book 2, Chap. 22: "Come si possa far apparire un'Inferno," and Chap. 23: "Altro modo come si possa mostrare un Inferno"). Both involve men with lit torches who, Sabbatini warns, need to be extremely reliable (*da bene e zelanti dell'onore*) given that such matters should not be undertaken by the stupid and foolish (*però tale attioni non devono essere fatte da persone balorde e sciocche*).

useful in distracting the audience from the change of set. Presumably, these boulders emerged from the *strade* between the flats (perhaps flats 5–6 and behind flat 7) not occupied by the trees; although they were only 2 *b.* high, they would have appeared bigger in the perspective view (that is, in comparison with the size of the vertical elements of the Underworld set positioned upstage).

By the time of Cresci's inventory, those boulders were in so poor a state as to be not worth any reckoning, save to close out an entry in the accounts. Indeed the entire Underworld set was left in bad repair (see also the comments on the flats in *Cres13*). Given that it was more complex than the pastoral set, which remained static, it already seems to have suffered more in the move from the Sala delle Statue to the Sala delle Commedie. It may also have been damaged during rehearsals there: Ricoveri charged for an additional twelve workdays for having "restored and resized" its canvases on the order of Don Giovanni de' Medici (*Ric15*). The actual performance of the opera appears to have caused additional harm to the canvases, which is not surprising given the amount of movement to which these scenic elements were subjected, and the potential pitfalls of keeping the canvas flats folded under the stage when not visible. Some later references to the sets for *Euridice* as they were reused refer only to the pastoral one (see Chapter 4), although presumably the Underworld set was put back into good enough shape for the performance of *Euridice* directed by Giulio Caccini in the Sala delle Commedie in December 1602.

As noted earlier, this manner of changing the set from the pastoral one to the Underworld was not recommended in *Il corago* because of the inconvenience of seeing both sets at the same time, as one gradually covered the other. Nicola Sabbatini in turn suggested various ways of distracting the audience from any such visible stage movement, whether by way of a trumpet fanfare or drumroll, or indeed, just a loud disturbance at the back of the room prompting the spectators to look away from the stage.[130] In the case of *Euridice*, the various movements of the stage machinery in the transition to the Underworld set would hardly have

[130] Sabbatini, *Pratica di fabricar scene, e machine ne' teatri* (1638), 71–72: *che qualche persona confidente messa a bello studio nell'ultimo della Sala, la quale osservando il tempo, che si dovranno tramutare le Scene, mostri di far rumore con altra persona d'accordo, ò veramente (ma potrebbe essere occasione di notabilissimo disturbo) fingere la ruvina, ò rompimento di qualche trave degli Scaloni, overo con un tocco di Tromba, Tamburo, ò d'altro instromento, deviare gli astanti dalla vista delle Scene, et in quel tempo fare la detta operatione dello sparimento, senza che nissuno se ne aveda.* He favors the trumpet fanfare (or something similar from another instrument); he warns against the strategy of faking some collapse of the audience seating, given that it might cause panic. But the main point is to have some

been silent, but to judge by the contemporary stage directions in a copy of the printed libretto (see Table 3.4: the scene changes *con gran rumore in monti ardenti*), there could well have been some additional sound effects in the manner that Sabbatini describes.

Stage Lighting

Buonarroti noted in his description of *Euridice* that by virtue of well-placed illumination, the delightful woods represented in the pastoral set were "full of light as if it were day" (*e per i lumi ben dispostivi, piene di una luce come di giorno*). This lighting was provided by oil lamps and candles placed in reflective tinplate holders or lanterns called *fornuoli* or *frugnoli* (the two terms are synonymous).[131] *Frugnoli* were commonly used for nighttime bird hunting and fishing; by virtue of being closed on three sides, they were able to give off a strong light in a single direction.[132] They were also safer in the theatre, especially when attached to elements of the scenery, by virtue of the flame being mostly enclosed. Cresci's inventory lists sixty *fornuoli di banda stagnata da candele* (*Cres26*), while at least fifty *frugnoli* were provided by Salvadore di Piero, *lanternaio*, from his own stock; Salvadore di Piero also charged £2 for being present on the day of the performance *da le 21 ore insino a le 4 ore di notte* (roughly 3:00 p.m. to 10:00 p.m.).[133] Some

distraction so that *le genti si rivolgano subito verso la Scena, come erano prima acquetandosi, e con maraviglia, e con gusto ammirando il nuovo apparato, che si rappresenta agli occhi loro.*

131 For the relative merits of oil lamps versus candles, see P. Fabbri and Pompilio (eds.), *Il corago*, 124, which notes that candles provided a better light but were expensive, while oil lamps gave off smells and smoke that needed extra ventilation.

132 Geminiano Montanari, *L'astrologia convinta di falso col mezzo di nuove esperienze e ragioni fisico-astronomiche, o sia La caccia del frugnuolo* (Venice: Francesco Nicolini, 1685), 131[*bis*]: *Chiamasi con quello nome di Frugnuolo un certo Fanaletto, che direbbono a Venezia un Ferale, dentro a cui arde una lucerna da olio con lucignolo di bambagia grosso, quanto un dito della mano, onde fa una fiamma poco minore d'una Torcia, tanto più, che il suo vivissimo lume viene accresciuto dal riflesso della parte concava di esso Fanale fatta a tal fine di ferro stagnato, e lucido, che abbaglia fortemente la vista di chi vuol riguardarlo, coprendo in tanto fra l'ombre chi lo porta, e chi seco va accompagnato.* The images of devices for stage lighting in Furttenbach's *Mannhaffter Kunst-Spiegel*, fig. 13 (between 124–25) include such an enclosed lantern (but with a candle inside), as well as more open candle holders that would have diffused the light more broadly. For similar lighting issues in the Teatro degli Uffizi (and larger sources of light given the size of the theatre), see Testaverde, *L'officina delle nuvole*, 183, 196, 202–205, 207, 224, 231.

133 *GM* 1152, fol. 375. The invoice is for 50 *frugnioli a saldatura e bulete e carboni di mio servirno per la comedia de' Pitti da fare lume ale* [sic] *prospetive* (i.e., including nails and pieces of charcoal, the latter presumably to light the candles and oil lamps), plus an entry relating to another sixteen *frugnioli* to be used in the same place. For the time, see "Money, Accounts,

of these lanterns would have been placed as footlights at the front of the stage (partially concealed by the upper edge of the parapet), with others placed or mounted elsewhere on its side elements: Salvadore di Piero's invoice included *bulete* (*bullette*, large-head nails) to hang them. *Il corago* notes the need for lights on the floor at the front of the stage (but placed such that the audience would not see any flame); Leone de' Sommi advised placing lighting in the wings; Angelo Ingegneri suggested behind a coat of arms or any similar device (a *fregio*) and other horizontal elements in the upper proscenium; and Cigoli, toward the rear of the *cielo* so as to illuminate the horizon.[134] In the case of *Euridice*, there was not much space for lighting in the wings, although *frugnoli* could have been attached to the back of the leading edge of the framed pastoral flats, and, we shall see, an additional device was probably used on either side of the rear of the stage (between the final flat and the backdrop) to change the lighting for the Underworld scene. It is true, however, that in proscenium stages of this period, much of the light would have come from the front and sides, with little or none directly overhead save in the case of a *cielo spezzato* (not used for *Euridice*): this has a significant bearing on where the singers would be positioned on the stage for best visibility.

Buonarroti also noted the change of lighting for the Underworld scene: including the flames licking above the towers of Dis and the air all round seeming colored like copper. This would have involved reducing the other lighting of portions of the stage: Ingegneri said that any ghost or shade of the Underworld should make the air dark around it.[135] De' Sommi's

Measurements, Dates, and Time." Salvadore di Piero was also involved in the lighting for the 1589 *intermedi*; see Testaverde, *L'officina delle nuvole*, 205, 212.

[134] P. Fabbri and Pompilio (eds.), *Il corago*, 124: *Dinanzi all'orlo del palco bisognerà metterne qualcheduno come frugnoli coperti dalla banda dell'auditore, con qualche fiore o sasso acciò la fiamma non li dia negli occhi.* De' Sommi, *Quattro dialoghi* . . ., ed. Marotti, 64 (trans. in Blanchard-Rothmuller, "Leone Ebreo de' Sommi's *Four Dialogues on Stage Presentations*," 175) refers to lights, and mirrors to reflect them, placed *dietro alle colonne et dentro per le strade*). Ingegneri (*Della poesia rapppresentativa*, ed. Doglio, 27), recommends placing lights with directional reflectors behind a *fregio* at the center of the proscenium arch. For the *cielo*, see Cigoli, *Prospettiva pratica*, in Camerota, *Linear Perspective in the Age of Galileo*, 239 (advocating at the rear *alcuni piccoli lumi che fanno diventar l'orizzonte naturalissimo*). The Rosenwald MS (images 549–52) has various suggestions for lighting (including in a *cielo spezzato*). For other comments on lighting (by Sabbatini, Furttenbach, etc.), see Hewitt (ed.), *The Renaissance Stage*, 234–38.

[135] Ingegneri, *Della poesia rappresentativa*, ed. Doglio, 30: *per dar maggior verisimiglianza alla conditione dell'ombra, che come cosa infernale, deve far tenebroso l'aere dintorno à sè*. Compare De' Sommi, *Quattro dialoghi* . . ., ed. Marotti, 63 (trans. in Blanchard-Rothmuller, "Leone Ebreo de' Sommi's *Four Dialogues on Stage Presentations*," 174), which recommends dimming any unnecessary lights at tragic moments so as to cause "a most profound horror in the breast of the spectators" (*un profondissimo orrore nel petto degli spettatori*).

recommendation for lights in the wings was developed in *Il corago* to have them mounted on vertical poles between the flats, with the poles able to turn, to allow some shift from a lit stage to a darker one.[136] The Rosenwald MS, on the other hand, suggests rotating little boards (*tavolette*) in front of them.[137] Cigoli might originally have intended something similar for his Underworld scene, at least toward the rear of the stage, given those odd structures he drew in *CW*Fig 2.20 (if that sketch is related to the opera in the first place). However, the two *bilichi* (probably shafts or poles pivoting around their base, with pulleys) listed in *Cres23* measuring 6.5 *b.* in length could have been mounted vertically between the last flat and the backdrop on either side of the stage (in the manner suggested in *Il corago*), allowing any lighting mounted on them to rotate and darken that portion of the set, permitting the flames above the parapet to give a more impressive effect.[138] Such changes in lighting for the Underworld set must also have been reversed, at least to some degree, for the return to the pastoral one, although the timing of the action of the final part of the opera (the shepherd Arcetro notes that day is turning to dusk; ll. 584–87) would probably have prompted less illumination than at its beginning.

We have further documents noting the delivery of candles of various types (of wax and tallow) and sizes, plus six flasks of oil, to Emilio de' Cavalieri's rooms in the Palazzo Pitti (directly behind the Sala delle Commedie) prior to the performance on 6 October 1600.[139] Some of these lighting materials would have been needed for the instrumentalists. The stage lighting would also have been enhanced by the gold and silver flecks that Cigoli used in painting its Underworld elements (the flats, backdrop, and freestanding rocks, *Cig5–6*) in contrast to the pastoral set

[136] P. Fabbri and Pompilio (eds.), *Il corago*, 124. Here the poles are called *correnti*: those lights *che vanno per lo retto dovrannosi porre su un corrente che si possa girare*. Rotating poles in the wings became a common lighting device in later theatres such as at Drottningholm (Mazzoni, *Atlante iconografico*, 272 [fig. 251]) and Český Krumlov; see Baker, *From the Score to the Stage*, 57.

[137] Rosenwald MS, images 553–54, referring to *tavolette in bilico* for a *cielo spezzato*, and *stili* with a rotating *tavola* in the wings. On the other hand, Sabbatini, *Pratica di fabricar scene, e machine ne' teatri* (1638), 85–87 (Book 2, Chap. 12: "Come si possa fare, che tutta la Scena in uno istante si oscuri"), proposes a mechanism for lowering canisters over the candles.

[138] The Rosenwald MS (images 551–52) uses the term *bilichi* in this sense of something rotating around a pivot (here for scenery); compare also Sabbatini, *Pratica di fabricar scene, e machine ne' teatri* (1638), 77–80.

[139] ASF, Carte Strozziane I, 27 (the *memorie* of Giovanni del Maestro), fol. 38; *KirkCM*, 203 n. 79 (*Alla comedia che si fa ne' Pitti addì 6 detto alle stanze del signor Emilio si è dato per ordine del signor Don Giovanni Eccellentissimo e messer Michele Caccini* . . .). This included *6 f[iasch]i d'olio, 6 torcie bianche lb. 27, 70 candelotti, 2 lb. di candele di sego, ½ l.ba di mocholi.*

(although the moveable trees also had gold flecks). In addition, the costumes would have been designed with reflective elements (see Chapter 3). Cigoli added similar flecks to the proscenium arch (*Cig7*), its parapet (*Cig4*), and the coat of arms (*Cig10*): in this case, they were meant to reflect the light from the main floor of the room provided by six torchères on pedestals gilded in silver, each 4 *b.* high (*Cres32*), for which six "white torches" (presumably, very large candles) were delivered to Cavalieri's rooms.[140] One assumes that the windows of the Sala delle Commedie were kept open in order to create a draught allowing any smoke from all these candles, oil lamps, and torches to escape: this was essential in any room temporarily converted into a theatre that did not have any special system allowing the air to circulate, such as was available in the Teatro degli Uffizi.[141]

The Main Floor

We have no indication of where those six torchères were placed on the main floor of the room. Given the measurements of the stage, there would have been some 450 *b.q.* of floor space left for the audience in the Sala delle Statue, and 750 *b.q.* in the Sala delle Commedie (which was longer and wider). Those different dimensions would have had an impact on the location of any raised dais for seating the grand-ducal family and principal guests, in order to achieve the best perspectival view of the stage (see Fig. 2.16).[142] Cigoli's *Prospettiva pratica* suggests that insofar as the audience

[140] De' Sommi, *Quattro dialoghi . . .*, ed. Marotti, 65 (trans. in Blanchard-Rothmuller, "Leone Ebreo de' Sommi's *Four Dialogues on Stage Presentations,*" 177): *qui nella sala non vi aparecchio da porvi altro che dodeci torchie ivi da piedi.* He said that these torches should be placed behind the spectators so as not to obscure their view, and recommended that the audience area should be kept darker than the stage.

[141] See De' Sommi, *Quattro dialoghi . . .*, ed. Marotti, 65 (trans. in Blanchard-Rothmuller, "Leone Ebreo de' Sommi's *Four Dialogues on Stage Presentations,*" 177), on the benefits of leaving windows open, *et pertugiar poscia il suolo della scena.* For the system in the ceiling of the Teatro degli Uffizi, see Testaverde, *L'officina delle nuvole*, 132–34.

[142] There was certainly a raised dais for the principal spectators in the middle of the Sala delle Commedie for the performance of Francesco Cini's *veglia*, *Notte d'Amore*, during the festivities for the wedding of Prince Cosimo de' Medici and Maria Magdalena of Austria on 22 October 1608; see Cesare Tinghi's *Diario di Ferdinando I e Cosimo II granduca di Toscana* (22 July 1600 to 12 September 1615), BNCF, Capponi 261/1, fol. 230 (*Et il luogho del sedere di detti signori fu in mezzo della sala in su un palco di un grado solo et in mezo sedeva la serenissima sposa et manca Madama, poi l'Arciduca, poi il Signore Principe sposo et acanto alla sposa il Cardinale da Este, Farnese, Montealto* [sic], *Sforza et Monte che teneva il primo luogho fra' cardinali come decano*).

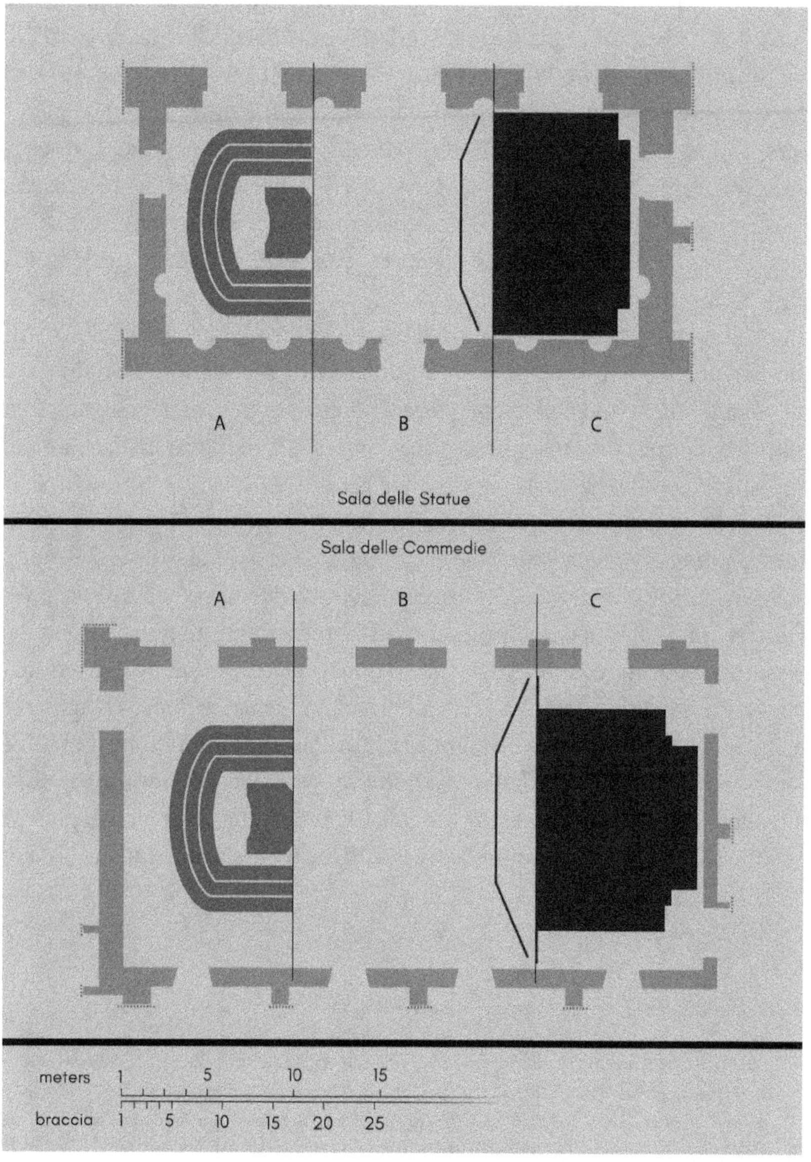

Fig. 2.16: Floor plans of the Sala delle Statue and Sala delle Commedie showing the likely position of the stage and viewing platform, etc. © Gian Gabriele Bassanello.

was concerned, the most perfect view of the stage (*la perfetta veduta*), both in terms of perspective and for ease of seeing and hearing the actors, would be gained at a position as distant from the stage as it was wide measured from the outer edges of the columns supporting the proscenium (compare Fig. 2.1).[143] Given that the stage intended for the Sala delle Statue was 17 *b.* wide, any such dais would have been positioned (11.5 + 17 =) 28.5 *b.* from the east wall, leaving room behind it for seating the other audience members, and a clear space in front of it. This fits the dimensions and proportions of the Sala delle Statue quite well. The greater width of the proscenium in the Sala delle Commedie would have shifted the dais further away from the wall behind the stage, at (13.5 + 22 =) 35.5 *b.*, leaving the same amount of room behind it (46 – 35.5 = 11.5 *b.*) for other seating as there could have been in the Sala delle Statue. This was less good in terms of the perspective. However, the space in front of the platform would have been both longer and wider, therefore with more room for the dancing that followed the performance, unless that dancing took place in the Sala dei Forestieri one floor below (see Chapter 1).

As for the other spectators, there is clear evidence that for later performances in the Sala delle Commedie they were on tiers at the rear of the room, typically for the *gentildonne.*[144] However, no such documentation survives for *Euridice*, and although some manner of tiered seating might plausibly be assumed (as we have in Fig. 2.16), it may not have been needed, given that the opera was done before a relatively small audience. If more chairs were required, however, various inventories of the Palazzo Pitti indicate that there were up to 200 *seggiole da donne alla pistolese* – wooden chairs with rush seats intended for women – available for court functions or other needs, plus 35 painted stools (*sgabelli*) that probably would have been used by men.[145]

* * * * *

143 Camerota, *Linear Perspective in the Age of Galileo*, 237.

144 *SolMBD*, 59 (23 [*recte* 25] November 1610): following a *calcio* in Piazza S. Croce, the grand-ducal family *poi tornono a casa e andorno su alla sala della veglia, dove erano a sedere in mezzo l'arciducessa et Sua Altezza da manritta e l'ambasciatore da mano manca et vi era una gran quantità di gentildonne su' gradi a sedere e fu fatto un ballo nuovo dalle dame della arciducessa, et da' paggi di Sua Altezza.* Similar tiered seating was available for Francesco Cini's *Notte d'Amore* (1608) as described in Camillo Rinuccini, *Descrizione delle feste fatte nelle reali nozze de' serenissimi principi di Toscana Don Cosimo de' Medici, e Maria Maddalena Arciduchessa d'Austria* (Florence: I Giunti, 1608), 32: here the guests *salirono nella sala della foresteria* [sic] *. . . dov'erano ordinati attorno i gradi, per lasciare alquanto di spazio voto per ballare. In una delle teste era una scena bassa à cui si saliva per pochi scalini, e verso il mezzo, il risedio de' Principi, dietr'al quale i gradi ascendevano quasi al palco, per più gente introdurvi.*

145 The 1597 inventory of the Palazzo Pitti in *GM* 422 lists as being stored *nelle stanze della guardaroba* 170 *seggiole da don[n]e alla pistolese* (fol. 38), and 35 *sghabelli di legniame dipinti con arme* (fol. 38v). The 1607 inventory in ibid. lists 200 *seggiole basse di sala pistolese da donne* (fol. 58v) and 36 *sgabelli d'albero tinti de' verde, con arme di Sua Altezza Serenissima* (fol. 59). For *seggiole alla pistolese*, see Thornton, *The Italian Renaissance Interior*, 174–78.

It is clear that despite the remarkable level of detail provided by our documents on the production of *Euridice* – and by our attempts to interpret, rather than merely transcribe, them – not everything is explained clearly: we have had to engage in a degree of guesswork, and some approximations remain, if fewer than we might initially have expected. This is inevitable. There is, however, one more source that we have not yet fully tapped: the opera itself. One consequence of the reconstruction of the stage for *Euridice* proposed here is that it also forces reading Ottavio Rinuccini's libretto and Jacopo Peri's score in a much more practical light than has hitherto been the case. Indeed, viewing *Euridice* in this new context makes one realize, first, just how skillfully Rinuccini anticipated a large number of staging issues in his libretto, and second, how additional problems were faced, and solutions found, as the work went into rehearsal.

3 | *Euridice* in Performance

Despite the status of *Euridice* as the "first" opera to survive complete, it has tended to be treated in the scholarly literature primarily as an academic exercise. In modern eyes, at least, it suffers in comparison with the next new Orpheus opera to reach the stage: *Orfeo* performed in Mantua in February 1607, to a libretto by Alessandro Striggio (the younger), and with music by Claudio Monteverdi. Striggio knew Rinuccini's libretto, and Monteverdi, Peri's score (more than Caccini's, it seems): they each drew significantly upon them, while also seeking – so the argument goes – to improve upon their models in various ways. Striggio was less of a poet than Rinuccini, but he produced a more compact libretto (632 lines rather than Rinuccini's 790, and the text actually set by Monteverdi was shorter). But by way of its poetic variety it offered more opportunities to a professional composer who, in turn, had a far greater musical range than did either Peri or Caccini.[1] Not for nothing does *Orfeo* still have a place in the repertory, whereas performances of *Euridice* are relatively few and far between.

But to treat *Euridice* as just a predecessor of *Orfeo*, or as a mere historical curiosity, misses the point that it, too, was a work of and for the theatre. Indeed, it is far more carefully constructed to that end than any "literary" reading of Rinuccini's libretto might assume. This is clear both in the libretto itself – and in the various layers one can detect in its creation – and still more from what was done in the course of setting it to music. If we can now come closer to reconstructing the staging of *Euridice* in light of the documents discussed in Chapter 2, this also forces a more practical approach to the work itself: that is, to what was mounted on the stage. This approach draws on, and also reveals, the perennial condition of opera as bound by plural creative minds and by performative contingency.

Euridice was certainly more complex in terms of staging than Rinuccini's first libretto, *Dafne*, whether in the latter's original "short"

[1] The libretto of *Orfeo* is in Solerti, *Gli albori del melodramma*, 3: 243–74. Striggio and (perhaps) Monteverdi were present in Florence in 1600 as part of the retinue of the Duke of Mantua; see Carter, *Monteverdi's Musical Theatre*, 38. They would not have seen the actual performance of *Euridice*, but clearly they were familiar with its printed materials, and Monteverdi seems at times to refer directly to Peri's music.

version (with 212 lines of verse) or in the expanded one (445 lines) that was probably performed in the Sala delle Statue on 21 January 1598/99.[2] However, the plot is straightforward enough (line references here [l./ll.] are to the annotated edition of the libretto in Appendix II). Following the prologue delivered by La Tragedia (ll. 1–28), the action is divided into the Classical five sections, each ending in a strophic chorus (with one partial exception): Rinuccini does not explicitly label these sections (we use the Italian "Episodi" in our edition), although they are clear enough.[3] In Episode 1 (ll. 29–100), nymphs and shepherds celebrate the morning of Orfeo and Euridice's wedding in a flower-filled landscape with happy voices and happy songs (ll. 35–36: *e per queste fiorite alme contrade / risuonin liete voci e lieti canti*). Euridice enters with her companions and welcomes these sweet songs (l. 59: *i dolci canti*); she then proposes to go with her friends to a flowery grove near a stream where they can sing and dance. She leaves with them, while those who stay decide to pass the time waiting for Orfeo in happy song.[4] The final chorus, "Al canto, al ballo, all'ombre, al prato adorno," is a summons to the celebrations, including to Diana (the *Selvaggia Diva*) and Venus (*Bella Madre d'Amor*).

Orfeo begins Episode 2 (ll. 101–292), soon joined by his old friend Arcetro, who has just left Euridice and the others at the spring by the laurels (so he later says in l. 172). Orfeo notes how his noble lyre need lament no more because love has won the day, while Arcetro reminds him of his former advice that women's hearts will always soften in the end.[5] Another shepherd, Tirsi, enters singing a song that invites Amor and Hymen to grace the proceedings ("Nel puro ardor della più bella stella"), but as Orfeo thanks him for it, he is interrupted by the sudden appearance

[2] For these versions of *Dafne*, see Fantappiè, "Una primizia rinucciniana."

[3] The term *Episodio* (Episode) has a Classical Greek precedent, which Rinuccini may have been following to some degree. Other commentators use "scenes" but there is a technical problem in that Rinuccini does not follow the practice of contemporary plays by linking them to the entrance of new characters: for example, and as we shall see, Episode 1 would conventionally be separated into at least two scenes, given that Euridice and her companions enter midway through it. Another option, *Quadro* (Tableau), is misleading because Episodes 1–3 and 5 are done on the same set. For the broader issues in contemporary printed librettos, see Riccò, "*Su le carte e fra le scene*", 212–14.

[4] The various entrances and exits noted here and in the rest of the synopsis are not directly indicated in the libretto (which lacks any such stage directions), but we shall see the basis for them, including some in Peri's score.

[5] In most traditional versions of the Orpheus story, Eurydice has resisted his amorous advances until finally giving way. Rinuccini avoids any direct reference to that – presumably because of *Euridice*'s place within the wedding festivities – but makes an indirect one here.

of Dafne,[6] who is eventually persuaded to tell her terrible news: that Euridice was bitten by a snake while dancing across the meadow, and has died in the arms of one of the nymphs. Orfeo is struck dumb (l. 226: *Non piango e non sospiro*) but says he will go to her body to die alongside her; Arcetro decides to follow lest Orfeo should do himself some harm. The nymphs who were with Euridice return (and likewise the shepherd Aminta, so Peri's score directs), and they rue a day in which joy, laughter, and songs have turned into lament. A shepherd warns the nymphs (and thus the female members of the audience) that youth and beauty are but appearances (l. 264: *mirate, donne mie, quel che voi sete*). The chorus laments ("Cruda morte, ahi pur potesti," with the refrain *Sospirate, aure celesti, / lagrimate, o selve, o campi*).

At the beginning of Episode 3 (ll. 292–397), Arcetro returns to tell how he had quickly followed his friend to the site of Euridice's death, where Orfeo threw himself to the ground; let forth such sighs as to prompt lament from the surrounding animals, plants, and flowers; cried out in anguish (Arcetro quotes him); and fell to the ground stained with Euridice's blood. But just as Arcetro was about to approach Orfeo he saw a bright light in the sky, and a divine figure in female form on a sapphire-encrusted chariot led by two doves, descending as gracefully as a swan. On reaching the ground she stepped down, offered Orfeo her hand, and made him appear calmer, at which point Arcetro decided to return to report the news. The chorus offers to sing constant praises to the goddess ("Se de' boschi i verdi onori"), and a shepherd invites them to the temple to raise their voices and hearts singing to heaven (l. 397: *alzian le voci e 'l cor cantando al Cielo*).

Episode 4 (ll. 398–583) takes place in the Underworld. The hitherto unnamed goddess, Venere (Venus), has led Orfeo to the pale and gloomy shores of Hades (l. 407: *rive pallide e meste*) where he can see the dark fields and the deathly city of the king of the shades (ll. 410–11: *gl'oscuri campi e la Città fatale / del Re che sovra l'ombre ha scettro e regno*). She urges him to let loose his noble song to the sound of his golden lyre (ll. 412–13: *Sciogli il tuo nobil canto / al suon dell'aureo legno*), and to pray, sigh, and plead such that the sweet lament that moved the heavens might also sway the Inferno. She leaves, and Orfeo makes his plea ("Funeste piaggie, ombrosi orridi campi," with a refrain inviting the shades of the Underworld to weep at his lament): he asks that the funereal shores should echo his plaint; he describes how he

[6] Rinuccini variously styles her Dafne, Dafne Nunzia, and Nunzia, conflating her identity (seemingly as a close companion of Euridice, just as Arcetro is of Orfeo) and her Classical function (as a "messenger" narrating offstage events).

has been robbed of his beloved and left immobile like a snake in winter; and he calls upon Euridice to witness his cries. Plutone (Pluto) and his bride, Proserpina, appear, accompanied by Radamanto and Caronte (Rhadamanthus and Charon). He asks why a mortal should appear before him, and Orfeo makes his case. Plutone is sympathetic but is constrained by strict law, which Orfeo says any ruler can break, noting that Proserpina and those around appear inclined to favor his cause. Proserpina adds her voice to the argument; Radamanto and Caronte state that a ruler can indeed change the law in the exercise of mercy; and Plutone proclaims his verdict that Orfeo may enter his kingdom to recover his bride, telling him to leave (ll. 546–48: *Scendi, gentil amante / . . . / entro le nostre soglie*). Orfeo celebrates his well-turned laments (l. 552: *o ben versati pianti*) as he does so. Thus we do not see Orfeo leading Euridice from the Underworld (in contrast to Monteverdi's *Orfeo*), presumably to avoid the problem created by Rinuccini's having altered the traditional version of the Orpheus story at this point (the failure of the test set by Pluto for Orpheus not to look back at his bride). But a chorus of Infernal spirits honors his achievement ("Poiché gl'eterni imperi") while warning other mortals (also in the audience) that not all are the offspring of him who rules the sun (Apollo), and that while it might be easy to descend to the Underworld, only the greatest souls are capable of returning.

For Episode 5 (ll. 584–790), the pastoral set returns. Arcetro notes that the day is coming to an end yet Orfeo has not returned; the chorus offers reassurance, but Arcetro is concerned. Aminta suddenly appears, however, to tell the initially incredulous gathering of Orfeo and Euridice's reappearance. As he went to the temple, he thought it more appropriate to go and console Euridice's elderly parents: he joined them as they were surrounded by a group of friendly shepherds; suddenly in a flash Orfeo and his bride came into view, and musical choirs of winged cupids filled the air with sweet songs (l. 676: *dolci canti*). Those assembled are delighted: Aminta's news has made the earth at sunset even more shining, more smiling, and more beflowered than it had been at dawn. Orfeo then appears with his bride and sings a song of rejoicing ("Gioite al canto mio, selve frondose"). Euridice reassures her companions – including the one in whose arms she died – that she has indeed returned, as they can see by her looks and by the sound of her voice (ll. 705–6: *Riconoscete omai gl'usati accenti, / udite il suon di queste voci amiche*). Arcetro asks Orfeo how he prevailed: he answers that it was by way of his sweet song and the sound of his lyre (ll. 712–13: *Dell'alto don fu degno / mio dolce canto e 'l suon di questa cetra*). Orfeo notes the aid of Venere, and how he persuaded Plutone by melodies now sweet, now sad (l. 725: *Modi hor soavi, hor mesti*) such that Euridice was the prize and trophy for his song (l. 730: *fu mercé, fu trofeo del canto mio*). The chorus says that he has excelled himself: he had already moved rocks, rivers, and trees, but now his power has extended to the gods of heaven and to the Inferno. The opera ends with a sung *ballo* ("Biondo arcier, che d'alto monte") praising Apollo, those who embrace the Muses, those who sing for love, the warrior who gains glory in the annals of history, but, above all, Orfeo who went to the Underworld armed only with his lyre.

That final chorus is rather odd given that Orfeo is only mentioned in the final stanza (of eight). The opening invocation to Apollo – the "blonde archer" who makes flow a golden spring (the Permessus from Mount Helicon) – acknowledges Orpheus's father, according to myth, but also tends to be read in Florentine theatrical entertainments as being a reference to the Medici, and in particular the grand duke.[7] However, in the case of *Euridice* it serves other purposes as well, given the connection made with Rinuccini's first opera, which ended with Apollo consecrating himself to art following his failed pursuit of Dafne and her metamorphosis into a laurel. The chorus then goes on to praise those who follow in Apollo's footsteps – therefore including the Florentine artists and intellectuals involved in creating *Euridice* – with music sweeter than that of Philomel or any siren. This music grants eternal honor to any women to whom it is addressed, as well as softening their hearts. Furthermore, it enables the warrior who bravely faces death to gain great glory by way of Clio (the Muse of history, here also served by her sister Muses), just as Orpheus, bearing only his lyre, was victorious over the Underworld. That reference to a "warrior" would probably have been taken as a nod to Don Giovanni de' Medici, who was so closely associated with Rinuccini and Corsi (although, as we shall see, there is a possible reference to King Henri IV).[8]

This final chorus of *Euridice* is in the same poetic meter as the one for *Dafne*, a strophic canzonetta mixing eight- and four-syllable lines in the manner of Gabriello Chiabrera ($a^8a^4b^8c^8c^4b^8$). Rinuccini also uses strophic structures in a range of meters for the other end-of-episode choruses, for the prologue, and, very occasionally, for particular moments within the dramatic action. The rest of his libretto, however, is in a flexible mixture of eleven- and seven-syllable lines that sometimes tends toward *versi sciolti*

[7] Compare Hanning, "Glorious Apollo."

[8] See the remarks on Don Giovanni de' Medici and *Dafne* in Fantappiè, "Una primizia rinucciniana," 211–14. Rinuccini also praised Don Giovanni's military prowess, and associated him with Clio, in the *canzone* "Correndo in ciel le luminose strade" in his *Poesie* (Florence: I Giunti, 1622), 186–87.

and sometimes (by virtue of more regular rhymes) adopt the form and manners of the sixteenth-century madrigal. Rinuccini did the same in *Dafne*: in part the metrical distinctions invoke those of Classical tragedy, and in part they are conceived with particular musical consequences in mind.[9]

This synopsis of *Euridice* has gone into more detail than is customary in accounts of it in order to make a number of preliminary points, one of which is that it has more action than many might assume. Of course, a number of events take place offstage and are typically narrated by "messengers": Dafne on Euridice's death; Arcetro on the appearance of the goddess; Aminta on Orfeo and Euridice's startling return. The episode that has the most dialogue, however, is the one in the Underworld, first between Orfeo and Venere, and then the debate with Plutone: there was good reason for this, we shall see, as there was for the moments where Rinuccini's characters seem to address members of the audience directly. The libretto is also careful to explain when and why characters make an exit (as with Orfeo toward the end of the Underworld episode), and what they are presumed to be doing while offstage (Aminta consoling Euridice's parents). Further worthy of note are the repeated references to the stage setting (the flowery landscape; the pale and gloomy shores of the Underworld with a distant view of Dis) – reinforcing Cigoli's sets – and to music both onstage and off (*canti, voci, suoni*), as well as to the careful passing of time from dawn to dusk within a single day.

That temporal dimension emphasizes Rinuccini's adherence to at least one of the so-called Classical unities (of time), while another (of action) seems granted by the plot.[10] However, the third unity (of place) created more difficulty. In his dedication of the libretto to Maria de' Medici, Rinuccini was anxious to explain why he had altered the traditional ending of the Orpheus story, dropping the test imposed by Pluto that Orpheus should lead Eurydice from the Underworld without looking back (in most versions of the myth, he fails it). This alteration, Rinuccini said, was because of the joyful occasion of the opera's performance, although it also plays into contemporary debates over the greater efficacy of the *lieto fine* in terms of achieving a more positive catharsis on the part of the audience.[11] Rinuccini further sought to justify the change of set from the

9 Fantappiè, "Una primizia rinucciniana," 196–202.

10 Compare Riccò, *Dalla zampogna all'aurea cetra*, 173, 180–84.

11 Fantappiè, "Una primizia rinucciana," 209–10. See also the discussion of Lorenzo Giacomini's view of the *lieto fine* and catharsis in Schneider, *Pastoral Drama and Healing in Early Modern Italy*, 31–33.

pastoral world to the Underworld and back: this was inevitable, he said, if he was to represent the prayers and laments of Orpheus, although he also sought some further Classical precedent in Sophocles's *Ajax* and other plays.[12] This change of set created a structural problem, however. The five-part division of the action of *Euridice* was another typically Classical element, as was the conclusion of each episode with a chorus somehow responding to the prior action, and drawing a moral from it. The chorus toward the end of Episode 3 ("Se de' boschi i verdi onori") fits the pattern well enough: the assembly has just learned from Arcetro of the reversal of Orfeo's fortunes by way of an unnamed goddess, so the moral is that just as spring follows winter, as calm seas follow storms, and as the heavens turn, so do joy and suffering alternate like day and night. But, given the imminent change of set, Rinuccini needs to find a way to get the cast offstage: he tacks on a speech by a shepherd telling everyone to go to the temple to raise their hearts and voices, singing to heaven. Peri and Caccini go one step further by having the chorus repeat the line as they exit, which may have also helped cover the movement of the scenery and any noise created by it.

This was an effective way of leaving the stage vacant for the start of Episode 4 (in the Underworld). However, Rinuccini also needed to consider when, and how, to bring the chorus back on stage to form part of the low-voiced "Choro d'Ombre, e Deità d'Inferno," so he styles it at the end of the episode, while allowing time to change costume. It would seem that only Orfeo and Venere are meant to be onstage at the start of Episode 4, and that Orfeo is on his own once Venere leaves (at l. 417). However, the *ombre* are certainly present onstage at the beginning of Orfeo's plea to the Underworld ("Funeste piaggie, ombrosi orridi campi") given that he addresses them directly in its first section (l. 425: *E voi* . . .), even if Plutone, Proserpina, and their retinue (Rinuccini's deities) arrive slightly later.[13] Having just Venere and Orfeo onstage for the start of Episode 4 would give any members of the chorus present at the end of Episode 3 and needed in Episode 4 some twenty lines of verse for the costume change.

[12] Ottavio Rinuccini, *L'Euridice . . . rappresentata nello sponsalitio della Christianiss. Regina di Francia, e di Navarra* (Florence: Cosimo Giunti, 1600), dedication: *Potrà parere ad alcuno, che troppo ardire sia stato il mio in alterare il fine della favola d'Orfeo, ma cosi mi è parso convenevole in tempo di tanta allegrezza . . . Così parimente ho seguito l'autorità di Sofocle nel l'Aiace in far rivolger la Scena non potendosi rappresentar altrimenti le preghiere, et i lamenti d'Orfeo.*

[13] Rinuccini's distinction between *ombre* and *deità* is not observed by Peri (who allocates the final chorus just to "De[i]tà d'Inferno"), but it makes sense. Peri also reallocates ll. 524–30 to Caronte (Radamanto in the libretto), in addition to Caronte's ll. 535–39, and instead gives Radamanto a solo stanza within "Poiché gl'eterni imperi."

However, Giulio Caccini's involvement in the production of *Euridice*, having "his" singers perform his music rather than Peri's, may have offered a different solution. Peri acknowledges in the preface to his score that Caccini provided the "arias" (*arie*) for Euridice, "some" of the same for "the" shepherd and nymph of the chorus (although there is more than one each, so we do not know which), and the choruses ending Episodes 1, 2, and 4.[14] His use of the term *arie* is imprecise; in the early seventeenth century, an *aria* was a strophic setting of poetry in stanzas, and Euridice does not have any such text; nor do a shepherd (save Tirsi), and a nymph (save in the chorus at the end of Episode 2). But we have seen (in Chapter 1) that this division of labor may have been decided early on (if what Angelo Grillo heard in Florence in spring 1600 had anything to do with *Euridice*). Having different groups of singers perform the choruses at the end of Episodes 3 and 4 meant that Caccini's performers were free to be offstage during Episode 3, and so could reenter at or near the beginning of Episode 4 as silent *ombre*, to be directly addressed by Orfeo and to remain until the end of the scene.[15]

There is a similar issue of exits and entrances on the return to the pastoral set in Episode 5. The singers making up the low-voiced chorus at the end of Episode 4 needed to exit and change costume prior to their reappearance as shepherds (although having Caccini's singers as a separate group for that chorus would have avoided this problem as well). This is presumably why Rinuccini begins Episode 5 with Arcetro expressing to the "Choro" his concerns about Orfeo's continued absence, and, in turn, why

[14] Jacopo Peri, *Le musiche . . . sopra L'Euridice* (Florence: Giorgio Marescotti, 1600 [= 1601]), preface: *Non dimeno Giulio Caccini (detto Romano) il cui sommo valore è noto al Mondo, fece l'arie d'Euridice, et alcune del Pastore, e Ninfa del Coro, e de' Cori, "Al canto, al ballo," "Sospirate," e "Poi che gli eterni imperi."* Giulio Caccini, *L'Euridice composta in musica in stile rappresentativo* (Florence: Giorgio Marescotti, 1600), assigns numbers to these choruses, and to the one ending Episode 5 (so that was Caccini's as well?), but not the one ending Episode 3 (which was presumably Peri's). This numbering (*Coro Primo*; . . . *e comincia il coro 2*; *Coro Quarto*; *Coro V*) suggests that the manuscript that Caccini sent to the printer combined materials that had been created separately, i.e., that he had copies of those numbered choruses (as prepared for the 6 October performance) that were inserted into his manuscript score for the rest of the opera. The printer then typeset the numbering, even though it did not make much sense to do so.

[15] It is not entirely clear that this could have occurred, however. The issue hinges in part on which of the "arias" for a shepherd and a nymph were by Caccini, and how this might bear on his assigning to a single tenor or soprano voice speech that Rinuccini labeled just "Choro." As noted in Appendix II, these assignments quite often differ from Peri's, particularly in Episodes 3 and 5. But in Episode 3, Caccini generally favors a tenor (in contrast to Peri's soprano), perhaps meaning that at least one of "his" singers remained onstage even though a tenor would have been needed for the Episode 4 chorus. Caccini also creates confusions in Episode 5 in terms of who enters when.

Peri (unlike Caccini) assigns the response of the "Choro" to a nymph (C1 clef) as part of a female group (also including Dafne) that, so it is implied, has stayed with Arcetro while events in the Underworld were taking place.[16] Rinuccini seems to suggest, and Peri (but again, not Caccini) makes it clear, that the shepherds are a separate group that Aminta encountered consoling Euridice's parents (l. 644: the *schiera di pastori amici*). While Rinuccini might have planned for these shepherds to enter with Aminta (at l. 597), Peri seems to delay matters still further: certainly one shepherd (C4 clef: Tirsi?) enters with Aminta (he is allocated ll. 654–56, logically enough), but, for the rest, Peri assigns all of Rinuccini's "chorus" speeches responding to Aminta either to a nymph or to Arcetro, meaning that the other shepherds need only accompany the entrance of Orfeo and Euridice at l. 684.

Rinuccini's, then Peri's, attention to such matters is clearly a result of careful forethought and practical experience. Caccini's score of *Euridice* is much less logical in this regard, and is therefore harder to stage as it stands. But the comparison with Striggio and Monteverdi's *Orfeo* is more striking still. Striggio, at least, was a relative novice in theatrical terms, and even Monteverdi's score (as it was published in 1609) raises a number of staging issues. *Orfeo* is in five "acts," but with two situated in the Underworld (Acts 3–4). Perhaps surprisingly, however, it has less action than *Euridice*, and more plot holes: for example, there is no explanation of how Orfeo first encounters Speranza (the equivalent figure to Venere in *Euridice*) who leads him to the gates of the Underworld, leaving him there alone (as Dante required), or how Plutone and Proserpina actually manage to hear Orfeo's plea delivered there in Act 3 (they appear only in Act 4). Striggio is also far less careful than Rinuccini to explain the entrances and exits of his characters: we are not told when Euridice leaves in Act I; how Orfeo returns at the beginning of Act 2 (even though Striggio, unlike Rinuccini, has him already present in Act I); and indeed where Orfeo might be during the bulk of Act 4, given that he does not interact directly with Plutone and Proserpina (itself a strange omission). Any stage director of *Orfeo* needs to solve these kinds of problems. Rinuccini and Peri already do so for *Euridice*, although

[16] Clefs at the beginnings of musical staves are indicated by way of pitch and line: the C1 clef (also known as the soprano clef) has "middle" C (*c′*) on the first line from the bottom of the stave. The modern treble clef is a G2 clef, and the bass clef, F4. C3 indicates the alto clef and C4 the tenor clef. It is important to remember, however, that these clefs do not necessarily reflect specific voice types (a "soprano" voice could sing a part notated in the G2, C1, or even C2 clef) nor the gender of the singers (a male castrato could have music notated in G2, C1, C2, or C3 clefs). Thus it is true that a part in C1 clef could be for a castrato shepherd, but that would not be consistent with the typical nymph (C1) and shepherd (C4) assignments in the opera.

understanding how requires a more careful reading of the sources than they have been given to date.

The Performers

In the preface to his score, Peri provides some information on the singers involved in the performance of *Euridice* during the 1600 wedding festivities, listing those who took the roles of Aminta (Francesco Rasi), Arcetro (Antonio Brandi), and Plutone (Melchiorre Palantrotti), plus, in what seems an afterthought, Dafne, played by Jacopo Giusti (also styled a "fanciulletto Lucchese"); in fact, Giusti had been Peri's young student since February 1598/99, also lodging in his house.[17] Rasi and Palantrotti were late arrivals in the cast (as we shall see). Antonio di Francesco Brandi, also called "Il Brandino," was a male contralto who appeared in other music-theatrical works with music by Peri, and the role of Arcetro seems to have been designed by Rinuccini, and extended by Peri, particularly with him in mind.[18]

Peri's preface also notes the instrumentalists who provided the accompaniment: Signor Jacopo Corsi (harpsichord), Signor Don "Grazìa" Montalvo (chitarrone), Messer Giovanbattista (Jacomelli) dal Violino (*lira grande*), and Messer Giovanni Lapi (a *liuto grosso*).[19] This is a typical combination of continuo instruments, although we shall see that the *lira grande* (presumably what we now call a *lira da gamba* or a *lirone*) probably has a special resonance. As for other roles, we have seen that Peri states that some were taken by singers attached to Giulio Caccini, who therefore performed his music rather than Peri's. Caccini's intervention has tended to place him in a bad light in modern eyes, but it also made some sense in terms of how singers of the time were generally taught by rote rather than

[17] Carter and Goldthwaite, *Orpheus in the Marketplace*, 277–78.

[18] For Brandi, see *KirkCM*, 347–48; Carter and Goldthwaite, *Orpheus in the Marketplace*, 296. He was also the messenger (Tirsi) narrating the metamorphosis of Dafne in Marco da Gagliano's setting (1608) of Rinuccini's revised libretto of his first opera, and it is tempting to suggest that he took the same role in Peri and Corsi's earlier version in the late 1590s: the surviving music ("Qual nova meraviglia") is in the same C3 clef (see Porter, "Peri and Corsi's *Dafne*," 180–81).

[19] However, Peri does not provide any details for the upper instrumental line needed for the ritornellos in the prologue and the final *ballo*, nor for Tirsi's *triflauto* in Episode 2. For the instrumentalists he names, see Carter and Goldthwaite, *Orpheus in the Marketplace*, 116–18. Garzía (*sic*) Montalvo was a nobleman who figures in some later Medici entertainments; Jacomelli was in court service (*KirkCM*, 256–61). They and Lapi were well connected with Corsi.

from notated music (not all singers could read it) and in the presence of a *maestro* or his assistant.

This was almost certainly the case for one role in *Euridice*. Caccini's illegitimate son, Pompeo, was commissioned by Jacopo Corsi and Ottavio Rinuccini to teach the prologue (delivered by La Tragedia) to the young Ginevra di Piero *mazziere* (she was nicknamed "L'Azzurrina").[20] We do not know if he taught her Peri's music or Caccini's; it may have been the latter, even though Caccini himself disapproved of Ginevra's involvement in the opera (and subsequent events may explain why Peri does not include the prologue in his list of the portions of *Euridice* performed to Caccini's music).[21] But he disapproved still more of Pompeo's pursuing an illicit relationship with her, making her pregnant. Pompeo promised to marry her after the end of the festivities, but his father threw him out of the house in disgrace (which may also have been an expedient to avoid the consequences of his actions), forcing Ginevra's mother, Camilla, to take the case to the Magistrati degli Otto di Guardia e Balìa in early 1601.[22] On 12 February 1600/1, Pompeo was judged by default (*in contumacia*, meaning that he was not present) and given the standard penalty (a fine of £100 and the requirement to pay Ginevra a dowry of *sc.*75 unless he married her), although the case dragged on. Pompeo and Ginevra did in fact marry on 25 January 1602/3.[23] However, she does not seem to have continued any

[20] McGee, "Pompeo Caccini and *Euridice*," which needs some revision in light of the information presented here. Ginevra was being taught the *prologo della comedia* at the request of Corsi and Rinuccini (so probably the prologue of *Euridice* rather than that of *Il rapimento di Cefalo*). Her father was Piero di Francesco Giannetti: the term *mazziere* indicates a profession (mace-bearer). He married Camilla di Andrea Bindi in May 1571 (Florence, Archivio Arcivescovile, RPU 51.1, no. 691), and Ginevra was born on 30 November 1580 (Florence, Archivio dell'Opera del Duomo, Battesimi femmine, Registro 236, fol. 159v, http://archivio.operaduomo.fi.it/battesimi/visualizza_carta.asp?id=236&p=261&ricdir=a&Submit=Visualizza). As McGee suggests (at 91–92), Pompeo Caccini was "illegitimate" because he may have been sired by Vincenzo Gonzaga in the rather sordid matter of proving his virility prior to marrying Eleonora de' Medici in 1584.

[21] In testimony delivered on 12 March 1600/1, Gian Jacopo Cini said that Pompeo feared his father's anger concerning Ginevra *perché contro sua voglia recitava il prologo*; McGee, "Pompeo Caccini and *Euridice*," 94–95 (doc. 3).

[22] McGee, "Pompeo Caccini and *Euridice*," 93–94 (doc. 1: Camilla's petition of 27 February complaining about the leniency of the penalty applied to Pompeo): *Essendo poi stato ritenuto et sviato fuora da suo padre, acciò 'l matrimonio non seguisse.* On 26 June 1601, Giulio Caccini petitioned the grand duke for relief from the fine of £100 (saying that he was willing to pay the dowry of *sc.*75 on the occasion of Ginevra's marriage, whenever that might be) now that he desired to repatriate his son (*Hora desiderando ripatriare detto suo figlio*): ibid., 95–96 (doc. 5). A number of associated documents refer to events taking place during the "time" of the wedding of Maria de' Medici but not in any more specific terms.

[23] Florence, Archivio Capitolare di S. Lorenzo 4475 (Matrimoni 1575–1621), by date.

association with the *concerto di donne* run by Giulio Caccini: the Ginevra who is mentioned in connection with the Caccini family during its visit to Paris in 1604–5 was Ginevra di Lorenzo Bartolini, wife of Giovan Paolo di Niccolò Rinuccini (and a lady-in-waiting to Christine of Lorraine), who moved that year to France to serve Maria de' Medici. Nor is it clear whether Ginevra di Piero Giannetti actually sang during the wedding festivities.

Finding sufficient singers to provide the large forces needed for princely wedding festivities was always a problem for the Medici and their peers in northern Italy:[24] on 11 May 1600, one day after the appointment of the five *deputati* taking charge of arrangements for the 1600 wedding, Grand Duke Ferdinando wrote to the Bishop of Padua seeking to recruit an Augustinian friar known to have an excellent castrato voice for both the chamber and the church (*un frate ... eunuco con voce buonissima per la musica, et cappella*), specifically to meet his needs for the forthcoming celebrations.[25] It is also clear that adjustments were made in the allocation of singers to theatrical roles as preparations for such festivities were underway so as to juggle the various demands of rehearsal and eventual performance. For example, further information on one cast of *Euridice* is provided by the handwritten annotations made (it seems) by Michelangelo Buonarroti *il giovane* in a surviving copy of Rinuccini's printed libretto (see Fig. 1.6). These annotations have been assumed to reflect some later performance of a version of the opera, and even, perhaps, the one directed by Giulio Caccini in the Palazzo Pitti on 5 December 1602, although the presence in this list of Jacopo Giusti makes it implausible (he otherwise disappears from the record in late 1600). Rather (so we argued in Chapter 1), they probably reflect Buonarroti's attempt to gain information on the casting of the opera prior to its performance on 6 October 1600, without his knowledge of the eventual participation of Rasi and Palantrotti.

Combining all that information with musical details of the principal roles gives a clear sense of the issues of casting the opera (see Table 3.1).[26]

24 For the case of festivities in Mantua and Florence in 1608, see Carter, "A Florentine Wedding of 1608."

25 See the *copialettera* in *MdP* 294, fol. 179v, which refers to *un frate dell'ordine di Santo Augustino* and the desire *perché con questa occasione dello sponsalitio di mia nipote et della venuta dell'Illustrissimo signor Cardinale Aldobrandino io me ne possa far honore con li conserti degli altri miei musici*. The grand duke had made a similar approach to Cardinal Sauli for the same singer on 7 April, with a view to lodging him in the monastery of S. Spirito and having him sing in the choir there; *MdP* 294, fol. 168v. We do not know who this was, or whether the grand duke's efforts were successful.

26 Table 3.1 draws on *KirkCM*, 207, which in turn refers to Palisca's account of this copy of the libretto (University of Illinois at Urbana-Champaign, Rare Book and Manuscript Library, Italian Plays 0520) in "The First Performance of *Euridice*." This copy reflects the first state of the

Table 3.1: The casting of Peri's *Euridice*

Role (clef: range)	*Buonarroti's(?) annotations*	*Peri's score*	*Notes*
La Tragedia (C1: *e*♭′–*c*″)	Giovannino del signor Emilio [Giovanni Boccherini]		Ginevra di Piero Giannetti *mazziere* was taught the role but probably did not sing it in October 1600.
Euridice (C1: *d*′–*e*♭″)	Cog[na]ta di Giulio	Caccini dependent	Probably Margherita Gagnolanti, Caccini's sister-in-law by his first wife.
Orfeo (C4: *d*–*f*′)	Zazzerino		Jacopo Peri
Arcetro (C3: *g*–*b*′)	Brandino	Antonio Brandi	
Tirsi (C4: *g*–*e*′)			
Aminta (C4: *e*–*e*′)	Pompeo di Giulio [Caccini]	Francesco Rasi	
Dafne Nuntia (C1: *d*′–*e*″)	Jacopino lucchese	Jacopo Giusti	
Venere (C1: *d*′–*d*″)	Castrato del signor Emilio		Probably Fabio Fabbri
Choro di ninfe e pastori (C1, C1, C3, C4, F4)		Some Caccini dependents	
Plutone (C4: *c*–*c*′)	[Aldobrando Trabocchi da] Pienza	Melchiorre Palantrotti	
Proserpina (C1: *e*′–*d*″)	Quel che fece Venere [He who played Venere]		Probably Fabio Fabbri
Radamanto (C4: *c*–*b*♭)	Ms. [probably *Messer*] Pier Mon		
Caronte (C4: *c*–*d*′)	Frate della Nuntiata		
Choro di ombre, e Deità d'Inferno (C2, C3, C4, F4 // C3, C4, C4, F4)		Caccini dependents	Chorus is in two groups; the top part in group 1 (C2 clef) has range *c*′–*b*♭′

Of the singers in the annotated list, the two singers identified as "del signor Emilio" (de' Cavalieri) – Giovanni Boccherini and Fabio Fabbri – were in Medici service and formed the *concerto de' castrati*, which Peri then directed from late 1600 to 1603.[27] Aldobrando Trabocchi, from Pienza, entered the roll of court musicians in August 1602, although his

edition of the libretto. The list of roles follows the order given in the initial list of "Interlocutori" in Rinuccini's libretto.

27 Carter and Goldthwaite, *Orpheus in the Marketplace*, 258–59.

recruitment was under discussion in June 1598, given his abilities as a virtuoso bass singer as well as an ordained priest.[28] The singer named "Ms. Pier Mon" (perhaps French; that is, Pierre Monne or Mont) and the friar from SS. Annunziata have not otherwise been securely identified.[29]

The fact that the annotated list has Giovanni Boccherino taking the role of La Tragedia in the prologue (singing Peri's music) rather than Ginevra di Piero Giannetti (singing Caccini's?) may be due to circumstance. If the judgment in her mother's favor delivered on 12 February 1600/1 was made after the birth of the child, conception would likely have taken place in late April or early May 1600, and Ginevra is unlikely to have been onstage five months later. This affair may also have had an impact on Pompeo Caccini's ability to perform in *Euridice* (the annotated list gives him as Aminta), although according to Michelangelo Buonarroti's description of the 1600 festivities, he certainly took part in *Il rapimento di Cefalo*.[30] However, Jacopo Corsi may also have seen an opportunity to make use of a different, and better, tenor whom he had known since 1592, if not before. Francesco Rasi (1574–1621), from Arezzo, was well known in Florence but was currently employed by Duke Vincenzo Gonzaga of Mantua: Grand Duke Ferdinando I requested his services for *Il rapimento di Cefalo* and he arrived in Florence (somewhat late in the day, it was felt) in mid-August 1600.[31] Similar patronal connections may also have operated in the case of another apparent substitution in the cast of *Euridice*: Melchiorre Palantrotti was at the time a singer in the Papal Chapel in Rome and associated with Cardinal Montalto, and he, too, was requested for *Il rapimento di Cefalo* (he was perhaps among the Roman singers who arrived in Florence in early July 1600).[32] Neither Rasi nor Palantrotti can have been involved in the early stages of preparing *Euridice*. Indeed, Peri seems to

28 *KirkCM*, 296–99. There was some discussion in 1603 about whether Trabocchi, as a priest, could legitimately take part in secular court entertainments; see Carter and Goldthwaite, *Orpheus in the Marketplace*, 221 n. 26. It is not clear how this might have affected his participation in *Euridice* (which did not occur).

29 But the "Frate della Nuntiata" may have been the bass singer Fra Filippo Maria di Ranieri Corona (mentioned in *KirkCM*, 347).

30 Carter, "Rediscovering *Il rapimento di Cefalo*," paras. 5.4–5.

31 For Rasi, see *KirkCM*, 556–603. He wrote to the Duke of Mantua on 14 August 1600 noting his arrival in Florence and the excellent treatment he was receiving there; *KirkCM*, 566. His prior connections with Corsi are noted in Carter, "Music and Patronage in Late Sixteenth-Century Florence," 73, 100 n. 91.

32 *KirkCM*, 565 n. 83. For Palantrotti, see Hill, *Roman Monody, Cantata, and Opera from the Circles around Cardinal Montalto*, 25; Carter, "Rediscovering *Il rapimento di Cefalo*." He was certainly present in Florence in late August when *Il rapimento di Cefalo* was being rehearsed every morning; *SolMBD*, 23.

have written the role of Plutone for a different singer: the part is low (as befits the character) but still in the tenor clef (C4), whereas Caccini's music for Palantrotti in *Il rapimento di Cefalo* is in the bass clef (F4) with a much wider and deeper range.[33] In the case of Aminta, however, Peri and Rinuccini probably expanded the role when Rasi came on board (so we shall see).

Table 3.1 identifies twelve named roles in *Euridice*, two of which seem to have been taken by a single singer (Venere and Proserpina, requiring a quick costume change). Only Euridice was played by a woman (absent Ginevra Giannetti for the prologue), although one or more of Caccini's *donne* would have been nymphs in the chorus.[34] This was not unusual: Monteverdi's *Orfeo* had an all-male cast in 1607, with castrati taking the female roles. In addition to these eleven singers, others were needed to fill out the chorus of nymphs and shepherds in the pastoral episodes, and the Infernal spirits in the Underworld. The latter episode seemingly requires the largest number of performers onstage at one time (ten or eleven in all): Orfeo, Plutone, Proserpina (also as Venere), plus Caronte, Radamanto, and an additional five or six low-voice spirits to make up the two four-part choruses at the end.[35] The pastoral episodes variously require Aminta, Arcetro, Dafne, Euridice, Orfeo, and Tirsi, plus a five-part chorus from which two separate nymphs take solo roles (we shall see how and why), as do at least one shepherd and perhaps two. One of those nymphs could have been the singer who played La Tragedia. One of the shepherds could have taken the role of Caronte: the "Pastore del Coro" taking the lowest part in the three-voice setting (two sopranos and a tenor) of the final stanza of the chorus ending Episode 2 ("Ben nocchier costante e forte") has a very similar vocal range, unlike the other "Pastore del Coro" who begins Episode 1. The final chorus of the opera ("Biondo arcier, che d'alto monte") has internal stanzas set for three sopranos (probably Dafne and two nymphs) and three shepherds (Aminta, Tirsi, and one of the

33 Caccini included some of the music for *Il rapimento di Cefalo* in his *Le nuove musiche* (Florence: I Marescotti, 1601 [= 1602]). In his own score of *Euridice*, the part for Plutone is also in the F4 clef, but not as wide-ranging or deep.

34 Compare Ottavio Rinuccini's comment on the casting of Monteverdi's *Arianna* for Mantua in 1608 (letter to Alessandro Striggio, 20 December 1607), in *KirkCM*, 338: *In quanto a quello che appartiene al rappresentarsi l'Arianna, non ci veggo difficoltà, se non che io avevo fatto gran capitale su 'l Brandino, su la Settimia per Venere, nel resto delle donne di Giulio per i cori, ornamento di grande importanza.*

35 The issue hinges on whether Plutone sang in the final chorus alongside Caronte and Radamanto. This might seem implausible in casting terms (Plutone should stand apart, if he has not already exited), but it could have been fudged.

shepherds). Additional singers for the choruses (but not allocated solo roles) include one soprano (perhaps the one who played Venere and Proserpina), one mezzo-soprano, one alto for the pastoral chorus and an additional one for the Infernal spirits, and two basses. The total number of singers needed is sixteen or seventeen, although they are not all are onstage at the same time; even just the maximum ten or eleven singers for the Underworld scene would have had to squeeze into a relatively small performance space. But that total number is surprisingly large: Monteverdi's *Orfeo* was designed to be done with ten or so singers, if with a much bigger group of instruments.[36]

Although Peri acknowledged Caccini's intervention in the October performance of *Euridice*, his score published in February 1600/1 included his own music, not Caccini's, for the portions of the opera he mentions. The fact that Caccini's score issued in December 1600 contains very few of the revisions made to the text of the opera as it went through rehearsal (and therefore entered Peri's score) is also significant: clearly it did not benefit from that part of the creative process, and it has far more practical problems as a result. Most of those revisions occurred in the roles taken by the singers named in Peri's preface, and who were therefore situated in his camp rather than Caccini's. This is what one would expect. Aminta is a revealing case in point, however. The annotated cast list assigns the role to Pompeo Caccini, who would presumably have sung his father's music. That libretto also does not indicate a performer for Tirsi, who is present as a named character only in Episode 2. Pompeo Caccini may instead have taken that role, if he was still available (see above).[37] Indeed, at one point, the plan may have been to have Tirsi and Aminta played by the same singer: this is certainly possible in Caccini's score, which removes Aminta from Episode 2 (Caccini has him present only in Episode 5). However, Rasi's late casting as Aminta gave Peri the opportunity to reclaim that part of the opera and to make significant additions to it, none of which entered Caccini's version of *Euridice*.

From Page to Stage

This discussion of the singers for *Euridice* starts to suggest the kinds of changes made to the work as it moved from conception to performance.

36 Carter, *Monteverdi's Musical Theatre*, 96–99.

37 Although if he was, he did not sing his father's music. Peri's score is clear that Tirsi's "Nel puro ardor della più bella stella" with the *triflauto* was indeed performed as he wrote it (*e con tale strumento fu sonata*). Caccini's score does not have any *obbligato* instrument here.

The three principle sources for *Euridice* as it was presented during the 1600 festivities are all printed: the libretto by Rinuccini (dedicated to Maria de' Medici in October 1600, with the day left blank); the score by Caccini (dedicated to Giovanni de' Bardi on 20 December 1600); and the one by Peri (dedicated to Maria de' Medici on 6 February 1600/1). Each of these sources must derive from manuscripts delivered to the printer that are now lost, but given that typesetters tended to reproduce what was in front of them as closely as possible – with little or no editorial interference save perhaps in matters of layout – one can plausibly assume that most problems or oddities in a printed edition will derive from such prior sources (or from the typesetter's ability to interpret them). The obvious exception is where the typesetter himself has made mistakes, whether or not sufficient to warrant the author insisting on him redoing his work. But in the case of the libretto, Rinuccini was not well served by his printer, Cosimo Giunti: the typesetting is poor, and there are some bad errors in terms of the foliation.[38] He also appears to have required Giunti to reset the first signature (A), which survives in two different states, with slight differences in terms of typography and layout (see Fig. 3.1), and elsewhere, there is some evidence of stop-press corrections. But the whole would have benefited from closer proofreading: a few mistakes get corrected by hand in all the copies we have examined – meaning that the correction was probably made prior to the release of those copies – and another is likewise emended in some.[39] Giorgio Marescotti did a much better job printing the libretto of *Il rapimento di Cefalo*, which he issued in two separate editions (one with the text in roman type and the other in italic) on two types of paper, one of better quality than the other.[40]

Aside from such typographical issues, however, one also needs to interrogate the materials and circumstances that led to a print's creation. For example, our three sources each have a different relationship to the performance of *Euridice* on 6 October 1600. We shall see that the printed

[38] The foliation of signature C runs 5, 5, 7, 7 (which is perhaps a problem caused by standing type). A number is missing for fol. 9 (signature D[1]r). Folio [D3]r is numbered 12 in some copies, corrected to 11 in others.

[39] See Appendix II for further details of the copies we have examined, and exemplars reflecting the two states. The manuscript corrections can be seen in the online versions cited there. They include: l. 120, *Venga deh venga* for *Vaga deh venga*; l. 211, *sì spaventoso* for *che spaventoso*; l. 253, *momento* for *tormento*. An incorrect character identifier for l. 521 ("Orf.") is corrected by hand to "Plut." in a few surviving copies. These corrections were adopted in the edition of *Euridice* included in the posthumous edition of Rinuccini's *Poesie*, 12–39, but with only a very few exceptions, this follows the version printed in 1600, repeating numerous textual errors therein.

[40] Carter, "Rediscovering *Il rapimento di Cefalo*," n. 1.

L'EVRIDICE
D'OTTAVIO
RINVCCINI
RAPPRESENTATA
NELLO SPONSALITIO
Della Christianiss.
REGINA
DI FRANCIA, E DI
NAVARRA.

IN FIORENZA, 1600.
Nella Stamperia di Cosimo Giunti.
Con licenza de' Superiori.

L'EVRIDICE
D'OTTAVIO
RINVCCINI,
RAPPRESENTATA
NELLO SPONSALITIO
Della Christianiss.
REGINA
DI FRANCIA, E DI
NAVARRA.

IN FIORENZA, 1600.
Nella Stamperia di Cosimo Giunti.
Con licenza de' Superiori.

Fig. 3.1: Ottavio Rinuccini, *L'Euridice . . . rappresentata nello sponsalitio della Christianiss. Regina di Francia, e di Navarra* (Florence: Cosimo Giunti, 1600), title page. (Left) The first state of the first signature (University of North Carolina at Chapel Hill, Music Library, UNC Italian Opera Libretto Collection). (Right) The second state: note the corrected position of the apostrophe in the title of the opera, the comma at the end of line 3, the different position of line 5, etc. (Venice, Fondazione Giorgio Cini, Fondo Rolandi, ROL.0101.06).

libretto reflects a relatively early version of Rinuccini's text. Caccini's score clearly contains some of the music used in October, including the role of Euridice and those three choruses (ending Episodes 1, 2, and 4), plus whatever else of the music for the nymphs and shepherds of the chorus might have been by him. But we cannot tell how much of the rest of Caccini's score was composed before October (and therefore was available for use even if it was not adopted) or after. There is a similar problem with Peri's score. He seems to have been anxious for it to be read as an accurate reflection of what was done in October: he declared on the final page that *Euridice* was performed as "described" here (*E con questo ordine, che s'è descritta, fù Rappresentata*). However, it is unclear whether his music for the passages allocated to Caccini was written before the performance (and therefore conceived for it) or after (therefore added for the sake of completeness).

Peri's concern for accuracy extends to the stage directions in the score, which are unusually detailed for the period (see Table 3.2).[41] Typically, they are in the present tense and therefore occupy a space midway between prescription and description, but we cannot tell when they were added to Peri's manuscript that eventually was sent to the typesetter, whether after the fact or as annotations made during rehearsal. Either way, they clearly reflect decisions that were necessarily made as *Euridice* headed onto the stage. Some of them, inevitably, were already implicit in Rinuccini's libretto: for example, and as we have seen, the poet had already considered how to handle the transitions from Episode 3 to 4, which involved finding a way for the chorus to exit the stage, and from Episode 4 to 5 (in terms of when the shepherds reenter). Not surprisingly, however, other such issues only came to light as *Euridice* started to come off the page. This is entirely typical of any opera, or for that matter of any theatrical production of any period.

In the case of Rinuccini's *Dafne*, we know that he first created a short version of the libretto, which was set to music to make a simple test of the power of modern song, so Rinuccini said in the dedication of the libretto of *Euridice* (*per far una semplice prova di quello, che potesse il canto dell'età nostra*).[42] He then expanded his text – giving it a "better form" (*miglior forma*) – for the performance before the grand duchess and Cardinals del Monte and Montalto, probably in Carnival 1598/99: that expansion doubled the text in length (from 212 to 445 lines of verse).[43] We do not have any first-draft materials for *Euridice*.[44] Nevertheless, some ghostly evidence of them might survive in the final version: for example, the clumsy repetition of l. 312 in l. 333, and of l. 494 in l. 498, might suggest late

41 The score of Monteverdi 's *Orfeo* (Venice: Ricciardo Amadino, 1609) has a quite large number of directions concerning the music (e.g., which instruments play when), but very few regarding the onstage action.

42 Peri used exactly the same wording about *Dafne* in his own preface to *Le musiche . . . sopra L'Euridice*.

43 See Fantappiè, "Una primizia rinucciniana," for the discovery of the first version.

44 The contrast with Michelangelo Buonarroti *il giovane* is striking, given that drafts for his theatrical works survive in abundance, replete with revisions, stage directions, and the like that got filtered out in their printed versions; see Testaverde, "Michelangelo Buonarroti il Giovane e le didascalie sceniche per il *Giudizio di Paride*." However, there is no known Rinuccini "archive" that might contain such materials. The principal exception is his *Narciso* (never set to music), which survives in two manuscripts (a third was lost during or just after World War II), one of which, an autograph, is in two layers (so they reveal three separate stages of creating the libretto).

Table 3.2: Stage directions in Peri's score of *Euridice*

After line	*Direction*	*Notes*
84	*Partesi Euridice, e Dafne con altre Ninfe del Coro.*	Euridice and Dafne exit with other nymphs.
143	*Viene in scena sonando la presente Zinfonia con un Triflauto, e canta la seguente stanza; salutando Orfeo di poi s'accompagna con gli altri del Coro, e con tale strumento fu sonata.*	Tirsi enters playing a sinfonia on a *triflauto*, greets Orfeo, and then joins the other members of the chorus.
161	*Dafne ritorna in Scena Sola.*	Dafne returns alone.
246	*Qui tornano le compagne di Euridice con Aminta.*	Euridice's companions return with Aminta.
292	*Torna Arcetro, e dice.*	Arcetro returns.
397	*Finito questo a v. il Coro si parte, e la Scena si muta in Inferno.*	After the five-part statement of "Alziam le voci e 'l cor cantando al Cielo" the chorus exits, and the scene changes to the Underworld.
417	*Venere si parte, e lascia Orfeo nell'Inferno.*	Venere exits, leaving Orfeo in the Underworld.
583	*Qui torna la scena come prima.*	The (pastoral) scene returns as before.
683	*Qui torna Orfeo con Euridice.*	Orfeo returns with Euridice.
742	*Ballo à 5. Tutto il Coro insieme cantano, e Ballano.*	The entire chorus sings and dances the final *ballo* (with a ritornello repeated several times and danced by two members of the chorus).

insertions in the text, with Rinuccini failing to delete one occurrence of the repeated line (although l. 312 was removed in Peri's score). Likewise, other evidence of drafting in the printed libretto seems apparent in Rinuccini's shifts in the styling of the messenger reporting Euridice's death as "Nunzia" and as "Dafne" (or some combination of the two).[45]

[45] She is styled "Daf. Nunzia" at her entrance (l. 162), then "Daf." (l. 176), "Nun." (l. 182), then "Daf." (l. 188) thereafter. The "Nun." for l. 182 cannot be a typesetting error: it must reflect an inconsistency in Rinuccini's manuscript (as he was still considering a name for the messenger?).

It is clear that the version of the libretto sent to the Giunti press was subject to several stages of subsequent revision that therefore are not apparent in the printed edition. This may or may not tell us anything about the chronology of the printing itself. But the text that both Peri and Caccini had in front of them when setting it to music already had one layer of changes that might broadly be categorized as "literary" in scope: in other words, Rinuccini made some initial improvements to the text to satisfy poetic requirements rather than any actual or anticipated musical ones (all these differences are noted in Appendix II). For example, when in Episode 1 Euridice says how her joy increases because of her companions, the printed libretto has their faces shining with "laughter and delight" (l. 76: *dal bel guardo seren riso, e diletto*) whereas both Peri and Caccini have the more elegant "joy and delight" (*gioia, e diletto*). Likewise, in the choral lament concluding Episode 2, both scores revise an obscure subjunctive (l. 274: *oscura* for the libretto's *oscuri*) and avoid a typographical error (l. 288: *nell'ira* for *nell'ora*). These are demonstrable improvements; they also come from passages in the libretto where we know Caccini's music was used on 6 October. But there are similar variants shared between Peri and Caccini's scores in sections where Caccini's music was not so used, including passages for Orfeo (for example, l. 189: *l'alma turbata* for *l'alma dubbiosa*), Plutone (l. 457: *Sì dolci preghi* for *Sì dolci note*), and also (though not consistently) for Aminta.[46] There are additional cases where Caccini's settings used in October do not contain variants found in Peri's, including Euridice's two speeches in Episode 5. This is troublesome but does not vitiate the broader argument emerging here: that the version of *Euridice* that Rinuccini made available to Peri and to Caccini already had some revisions to the manuscript that had been (or would be) submitted to the printer. Any literary edition of Rinuccini's libretto might need to take them into account.

However, the libretto was revised still further, and in quite substantial ways. Caccini has just one variant from readings shared by the libretto and Peri's score, in a passage (l. 654) that he sets for a shepherd of the chorus who might therefore have been another of his singers. In general, however, Caccini does not seem to have had access to the libretto as Rinuccini worked further on it in collaboration specifically with Peri. Clearly a number of decisions had to be made as soon as Peri put pen to music

[46] Both Peri and Caccini also adopt *Alziam le voci e 'l cor cantando al Cielo* at the end of Episode 3 (l. 397) rather than Rinuccini's *Alzian*. This is also one of the few changes made to the 1600 text in the 1622 edition of the libretto.

paper, not least in terms of who would sing what, in cases where Rinuccini had left matters open, and here we see him favoring the singers under his, rather than Caccini's, control. Arcetro, for example, was sung by Antonio Brandi, with whom Peri is known to have worked later in other contexts. The character is prominent enough in Episode 2 (Arcetro has twenty-eight lines, plus two reallocated by Peri from the chorus) and still more in Episode 3 (seventy-nine lines, largely because of his narration of Orfeo's rescue by Venere), but he takes a back seat in Episode 5 in the libretto with only eleven lines, which Peri expands to thirty by giving him text assigned by Rinuccini to the chorus. Likewise, the role of Aminta (at least, after it was allocated to Francesco Rasi) was expanded from a total of sixty-eight lines in the libretto to ninety-two, by way of reallocating speeches in Episode 1 (ll. 65–72) and in Episode 5 (ll. 731–42; although Aminta loses two lines to Dafne at ll. 721–22); the latter episode also includes five lines for Aminta not present in the printed libretto (ll. 604a–e).[47] Another of Peri's singers, Jacopo Giusti, also saw changes to, and a slight expansion of, his role as Dafne.

Other decisions needed to be made in terms of the staging, not least with regard to the allocation of speeches to individual "nymphs" or "shepherds" of the chorus and what that might mean for any movement they needed to make. In Episode 1, Rinuccini is fairly systematic in terms of who says what (see Table 3.3). As the libretto progresses, however, he becomes increasingly more casual in labeling speeches just for "Choro," with no allocation to any shepherd or nymph. It is unclear whether this shift in the text reflects the limited extent of discussions between Rinuccini and Peri by the date of the manuscript from which the libretto was printed (that is, they had already formed some kind of plan for Episodes 1 and 2, but matters were less firm from Episode 3 on). But whatever the case, for the later episodes Peri is forced to choose, whether because of the ways in which the singers were distributed or for the sake of greater musical variety. Caccini had to make similar decisions, too, and the fact that he and Peri often differ in this regard raises further questions about which parts of their scores were predicated upon performance and which not.

[47] It is slightly odd that Aminta is given before Dafne in the list of "Interlocutori" in Rinuccini's printed libretto – which lists them in order of appearance – even though he appears after in the text itself (but before in Peri's score). However, this may just because he is bracketed with Arcetro and Tirsi as "Pastori." In Peri's case, however, the first speech assigned to "Aminta Pastore del coro" (Episode 1, ll. 65–72) may reflect a revision on his own behalf: i.e., he originally gave it to a "Pastore del coro" but then wrote "Aminta" above the part without deleting the original, such that the typesetter reproduced the double assignation.

Table 3.3: The allocation of roles in *Euridice*, Episode 1

Lines	*Rinuccini*	*Peri*
29–41	CHORO [addressing *Ninfe*]	Pastore del Coro
42–44	Ninf[a] del Cho[ro]	Ninfa del Coro
45–49	Past[ore]	Pastore del coro
50–53	Ninf.	Ninfa del Coro [with l. 53 then repeated by *Pastore del coro*, by Arcetro, and by *tutto il coro* in five vocal parts]
54–60	Eur[idice]	Euridice
61–72	Past.	ll. 61–64: Ninfa del Coro
		ll. 65–72: Aminta Pastore del coro
73–81	Eur.	Euridice
82–84	Cho.	Choro [but a single line in C1 clef]
85–100	CHORO [for end of episode]	[No initial label, but the first stanza is set for five vocal parts, recurring as a refrain, with subsequent stanzas set for *Ninfa del Coro*, *Pastore del Coro*, and *Altra Ninfa del Coro*]

The role of the chorus in pastoral drama was a matter of some discussion. Its place in tragedy was clear by way of Classical precedent in terms of representing a group observing the action and granting some space for the authorial voice (to comment or draw some moral), as well as to articulate the five-part division of the drama. Comedies and pastorals were a different matter, however, given their typical subjects and settings. As we saw (in Chapter 1), Angelo Grillo praised in particular Rinuccini's handling of the pastoral chorus as giving the lie to the common opinion that it was inessential to the genre. The contemporary playwright and stage director, Angelo Ingegneri, explained matters further in his *Della poesia rappresentativa et del modo di rappresentare le favole sceniche* (1598):

Choruses can also be given to pastorals and comedies, but not out of necessity, as in tragedies, for these two types of poetry imitate private actions which take place in the town and in the wood, with no one else having knowledge of, or curiosity about, the events except those who take part in them. . . . Therefore, if choruses are to be placed in pastorals, it will not be enough, as some are wont to do, to place the word "Choro" at the end of each act and provide a canzona for them to sing. Rather, it will be best to find an opportunity to introduce them into the action, such as, for example, festivities, weddings, dances, games, outdoor pastimes, amusements, or other entertainments. . . .

> Once these choruses have been introduced at a suitable occasion, they can be either stable or mobile, as the occasion itself demands, and can intervene to speak with the actors or not. . . . The author will do well if, wanting a chorus in his play, he handles it in such a manner that it enters and leaves realistically, and even better if he makes it divide the acts with short and charming *canzoni* . . .[48]

Here Ingegneri is typically concerned with issues of verisimilitude in terms of who can plausibly be on stage at any given moment. He also makes a distinction for pastoral plays between a "stable" and "mobile" chorus: by "stable" he seems to mean a chorus that remains a constant presence onstage and that also provides the *canzoni* between the "acts" on the stricter model of tragedy, although Ingegneri is more flexible about the role of end-of-act choruses in comedies and pastorals. He further allows some freedom in terms of whether either any such chorus might or might not address the principal characters. He does not say, although it seems implied, that such address would most likely come from individual members of the chorus. This explains Rinuccini's nymph and shepherd *del coro*, although as we have seen, Peri quite often redistributes such remarks to named characters (Arcetro, Dafne, etc.).

Although Ingegneri allows significant freedom for the role of the chorus in pastorals (in contrast to tragedies), Rinuccini follows the tragic model, at least to some degree: hence the choruses at the end of each episode. In *Euridice*, the most obvious example of the "stable" chorus comes in Episode 4 (in the Underworld). As we have seen, there is a question of whether at least some spirits (*ombre*) are present silently onstage from the beginning of this episode as an essential part of the scenery, as it were. These spirits certainly form part of Rinuccini's final "Choro d'Ombre, e Deità d'Inferno." However, they do not address the principal characters but, rather, serve to pronounce the moral at the end of the sequence.

Matters are more complicated in the pastoral episodes. In Episode 1 (Table 3.3), Rinuccini allocates the initial ll. 29–41 to the "Choro" (styled in the upper

[48] Ingegneri, *Della poesia rappresentativa*, ed. Doglio, 11: *Alle pastorali e alle commedie ancora si possono dare i cori; ma non si danno loro di necessità, come alle tragedie, perché queste due sorti di poesia imitano azioni private, le quali si fanno nelle città e nei boschi, senza che n'abbia né cognizione, né curiosità altra persona che quelle medesime che v'intravengono. . . . Laonde, se si vorrano mettere i cori nelle pastorali, non basterà, come alcuni sono usati di fare, il dire nella fine di ciascun atto questa parola "coro" e porvi una canzona da cantare, ma converrà trovare occasione d'introdurgli, per essempio, festività, nozze, balli, giuochi, freschi, diporti od altri simiglianti trattenimenti. . . . Questi cori introdotti la prima fiata con occasione, potranno poi esser stabili e mobili, secondo che l'istessa occasione il richiederà, e intromettersi a parlare con gli istrioni e non vi si intromettere . . . gran giudicio sarà dell'autore se, volend'egli pure il coro nella sua favola, ve 'l porterà in modo tale ch'egli entri, ed esca verisimilmente a suo beneplacito; e molto maggiore s'ei gli farà divider gli atti con brevi e leggiadre canzoni . . .*

case that he also uses for the end-of-episode chorus), perhaps because he viewed it as the equivalent of Aristotle's "parodos" (the first entrance of the chorus after the prologue).[49] This speech has to perform the various functions typical of any such opening: to establish the time at the start of a happy day (l. 41: *oh dì felice*); the place amid a flowery landscape (l. 35: *queste fiorite alme contrade*); and the subject, the wedding of Orfeo and Euridice (ll. 37–41). It must also perform a task specific to opera, justifying the presence of joyful songs (l. 36: *risuonin liete voci e lieti canti*). The speech is directly addressed to beautiful nymphs (l. 29: *Ninfe ch'i bei crin d'oro*) – presumably also in honor of the female members of the audience – which is why Peri assigns it to a singular shepherd, although the chorus is in effect inviting itself to participate in what Ingegneri required of it in pastorals: "festivities, weddings, dances, games, outdoor pastimes, amusements, or other entertainments."

Rinuccini then allocates other speeches to a single nymph and a shepherd; they might or might not be the same ones each time, though in at least one case they are not. In ll. 42–44 a nymph continues the general theme, invoking Apollo; a shepherd then calls upon other celestial divinities as benign witnesses (ll. 45–48); and a nymph invites other nymphs to affirm that the sun has never seen so fine a pair of lovers (l. 53: *Non vede un simil par d'amanti 'l Sole*) – her final line is a quotation from Petrarch (*RVF* 245: "Due rose fresche e colte in paradiso"),[50] and Peri has it repeated by a shepherd, by Arcetro, and then by the full chorus in harmony (Caccini gives the repetition to a shepherd, a nymph, and the chorus). In all these cases, the chorus is talking to itself. Euridice's first speech (ll. 54–60), however, changes the dynamic. A shepherd makes a convoluted response that makes its way toward a direct address to her at l. 65, with the imperative *Credi, ninfa gentile* (the "ninfa" is clearly Euridice, given what follows). Peri clarified Rinuccini's rather complex syntax by breaking the shepherd's speech into two clear units, the first (ll. 61–64) set for a nymph, and second (at the imperative: ll. 65–72) for "Aminta Pastore del coro." Euridice responds in general terms of gratitude (ll. 73–76) but then issues a direct instruction (ll. 77–81): her beloved companions (*compagne amate*) should join her in a flowery grove where they can sing and dance to the sound of a burbling stream. Rinuccini then switches terms: the "Choro" speaks for itself to issue another imperative (l. 82: *Itene liete pur . . .*) – Euridice and her female companions should indeed leave, while "we" (the chorus) will

49 Compare Aristotle's *Poetics*, part 12. To follow the Aristotelian model, the choruses ending Episodes 1–4 therefore would each be some version of a "stasimon" (although as we shall see, the one ending Episode 2 is a "kommos").

50 Rinuccini quite often makes such literary references and allusions: compare Saino, "Più dolci affetti."

stay (. . . *noi qui fra tanto*) in anticipation of Orfeo's arrival, passing the time in happy song. This *lieto canto* becomes the end-of-episode chorus ("Al canto, al ballo, all'ombre, al prato adorno") in the manner recommended by Ingegneri. We have already seen that according to a stage direction in Peri's score, Euridice, Dafne, and other nymphs make their exit after *Itene liete pur* (hence the gendered *liete*). Now the stable chorus explicitly orders shepherds to join them by the stream (ll. 86–87: *alle bell'onde e liete / tutti, o pastor, correte*). Rinuccini does not offer any indication of which shepherds are to leave at this point – indeed, the whole of Episode 1 has largely been about the nymphs – and Peri needs at least two or three of them for the five-voice chorus ("Al canto, al ballo").[51] But his reallocation of Rinuccini's speeches in Episode 1 now starts to make some directorial sense. In the libretto, both Arcetro and Aminta first appear (at different times) in Episode 2. But given that Peri (though not Rinuccini or Caccini) brings them into Episode 1, they need to leave the stage as well.[52] One imagines that this is the kind of issue that could only emerge as rehearsals were underway and matters of staging therefore started to come to the fore.

Treating the chorus's instruction to the shepherds as an implicit stage direction rather than just a generic statement of celebration is one benefit of the type of close reading of *Euridice* rendered possible by situating it, precisely, in its theatrical framework. However, Rinuccini's distinction in Episode 1 between a stable chorus present from beginning to end (and performing the final chorus), and a mobile one associated with Euridice, creates another staging issue that is resolved by a handwritten set of stage directions in one surviving copy of the 1600 libretto, which seem to have been inserted at some time close to, even prior to, the first performance (see Fig. 3.2).[53] Some of these

[51] To forestall an obvious question, a chorus with separate musical lines for five "voices" (in the case of "Al canto, al ballo," for C1, C1, C3, C4, and F4 clefs) needs at least five singers, although it could have been done by more (doubling one or more of those musical lines).

[52] It is clear from later in the libretto that Arcetro was with Euridice by the stream but left before her misfortune with the snake (ll. 171–72: *Pur hor tutta gioiosa / al fonte degl'allor costei lasciai*). Peri later has a stage direction saying that Aminta returns with Euridice's companions when Dafne tells Arcetro to go and comfort Orfeo (after ll. 244–46).

[53] Rolandi, "Didascalie sceniche in un libretto dell'*Euridice* del Rinuccini"; the libretto (with signature A in its second state) now survives in Venice, Fondazione Giorgio Cini, Fondo Rolandi, ROL.0101.06. The annotations are of uncertain date, and some were truncated when the copy was bound, but they seem directly linked to the staging in 1600 or preparations for it. They are also clearly made in connection with a version of Peri's score: one of them mentions the *triflauto* used in Episode 2 – if in the wrong place – that is not mentioned either in the libretto or by Caccini. Given the reference to the curtain dropping at the beginning, these directions also seem to reflect the performance done in the Sala delle Commedie (as we have seen, the curtain would have moved differently in the Sala delle Statue). As Rolandi notes, the spelling of "Orphœo" with the ligature indicates a classically trained mind.

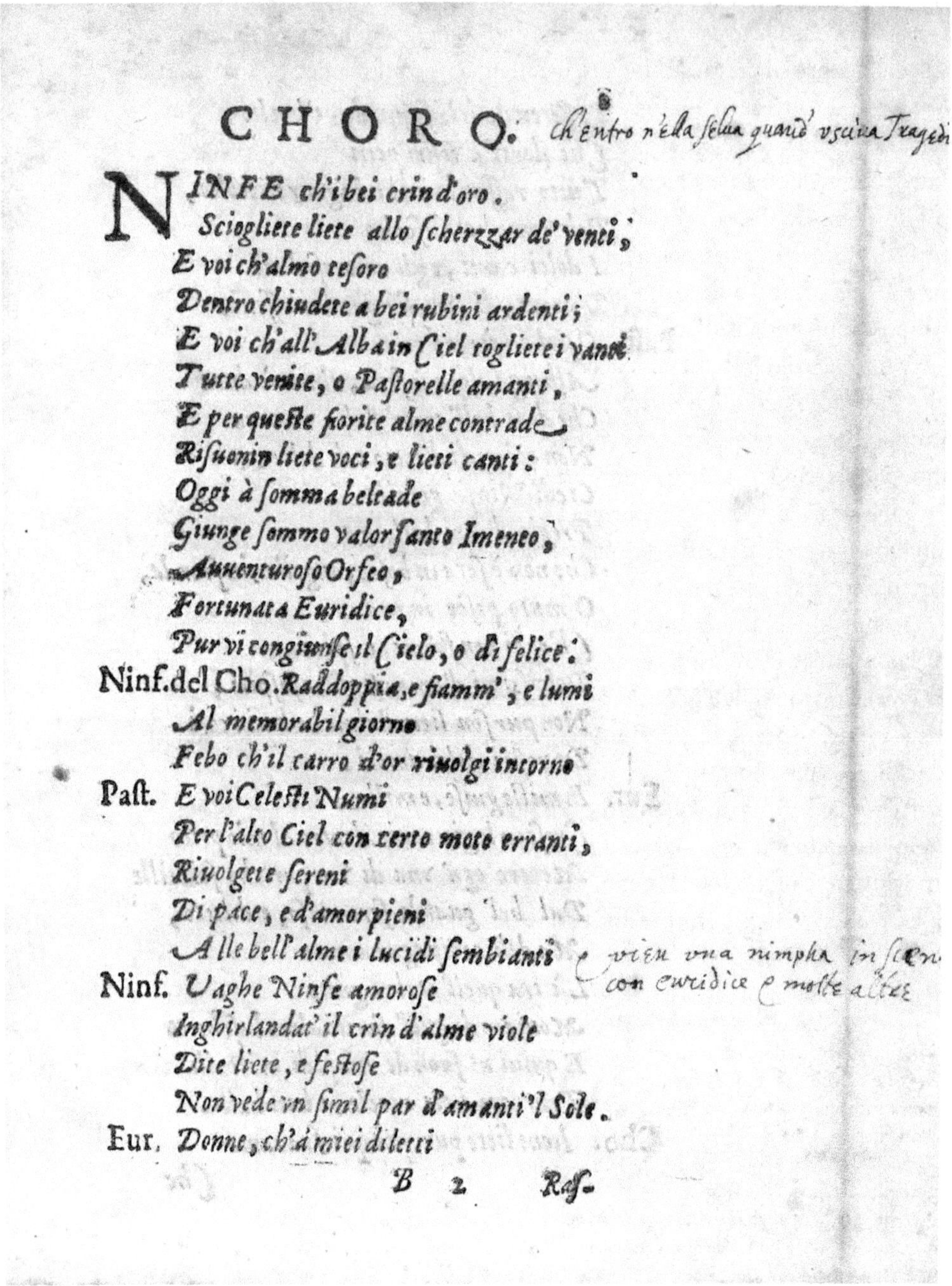

CHORO. ch'entro nella selva quand' usciva Tragedi

NINFE ch'i bei crin d'oro,
Sciogliete liete allo scherzzar de' venti;
E voi ch'almo tesoro
Dentro chiudete a bei rubini ardenti;
E voi ch'all'Alba in Ciel togliete i vanti.
Tutte venite, o Pastorelle amanti,
E per queste fiorite alme contrade
Risuonin liete voci, e lieti canti:
Oggi à somma beltade
Giunge sommo valor santo Imeneo,
Avventuroso Orfeo,
Fortunata Euridice,
Pur vi congiunse il Cielo, o dì felice:

Ninf. del Cho. Raddoppia, e fiamm', e lumi
Al memorabil giorno
Febo ch'il carro d'or rivolgi intorno

Past. E voi Celesti Numi
Per l'alto Ciel con certo moto erranti,
Rivolgete sereni
Di pace, e d'amor pieni
Alle bell'alme i lucidi sembianti. e vien una nimpha in scena con euridice e molte altre

Ninf. Vaghe Ninfe amorose
Inghirlandat' il crin d'alme viole
Dite liete, e festose
Non vede un simil par d'amanti 'l Sole.

Eur. Donne, ch'à miei diletti

B 2 Rass-

Fig. 3.2: Ottavio Rinuccini, *L'Euridice . . . rappresentata nello sponsalitio della Christianiss. Regina di Francia, e di Navarra* (Florence: Cosimo Giunti, 1600), fol. B2r: copy with added stage directions. Venice, Fondazione Giorgio Cini, Fondo Rolandi (ROL.0101.06).

directions are in the past tense (so, reflecting a performance) and some in the present (which might still reflect a prior performance if the tense is somehow used in the "historic" form). One of them affects Episode 1 (see Table 3.4). While Peri's score makes it clear that Euridice and her female companions exit before "Al canto, al ballo," it says nothing about when they first enter. However, our unknown director marked this to occur at l. 50, where a

Table 3.4: Stage directions in an annotated copy of the libretto of *Euridice*

Line	*Direction*	*Notes*
	Bottata giù la tela restò la scœna in foggia di selva mirabilment' illuminata, la quale riesce felicissimamente in p[er]spectiva	After the curtain dropped, the set revealed a wonderfully illuminated wood that is very effectively shown in perspective.
1	[La Tragedia] *La quale venne sola ne [. . .]*	La Tragedia appeared alone.
29	[CHORO beginning Episode 1] *ch'entrò n'ella selva quand'usciva Tragedia*	The chorus entered the wood as La Tragedia exited.
50	*e vien una nimpha in scena con euridice e molte altre*	A nymph enters with Euridice and many others.
82	*Et vanno via le nimph[. . .]*	The nymphs leave (at *Itene liete pur*).
101	*e viene orphœo d'una banda cantand[. . .]*	Orfeo enters from one side, singing.
123	*e vienne arcetro de l'altra banda, son[ando . . .] triplo flauto, e cantando*	Arcetro entered from the other side, playing a triple flute and singing (but in Peri's score, Tirsi enters later playing the *triflauto*).
236	*e va via orphœo*	Orfeo leaves on the final line of "Non piango e non sospiro" (*Io venga o cara vita, o cara morte*).
	[Added to stage direction at the end of Episode 3: . . . *e la Scena si tramuta*] *con gran rumore in monti ardenti >ingresso de l'i[nferno]< con una prospettiva in mezo de la cita fatale de l'inferno*	The set changes with great noise to fiery mountains, the entrance to the Inferno, with a view in the middle of the deathly city (of Dis).
417	*e va via venere*	Venere leaves at the end of her speech.
436	*[vengo]no d'una banda [. . .] de l'altra pluto [ne e prose]rpina d'e l'altra*	[?Radamanto and Caronte] enter from one side of the stage, and Plutone and Proserpina from the other, at the start of the third section of Orfeo's "Funeste piaggie, ombrosi orridi campi."
553	*e se ne va d'onde vene plutone*	At the end of his final speech, Orfeo enters the Underworld from where Plutone came.
684	*vien orphœo ed' euridice a mano*	Orfeo enters with Euridice on his arm (for "Gioite al canto mio, selve frondose").

nymph calls on other nymphs (*Vaghe ninfe amorose*) to place garlands in their hair and to praise the lovers (the quotation from Petrarch). Thus Euridice is not present from the beginning of the episode, and the nymph who accompanies her therefore belongs to the mobile chorus and addresses the stable one. This mobile chorus also includes Dafne (so Peri's score suggests in his own direction for the exit), which makes sense given that she will return as the messenger relating Euridice's sad fate.

The mixing of stable and mobile members of the chorus – and their separate entrances and exits – pertains elsewhere in *Euridice* as well. The next handwritten stage direction clarifies the beginning of Episode 2 (l. 101). Having Orfeo appear here, rather than earlier (as in Monteverdi's *Orfeo*), is clearly intended for theatrical effect. He makes a striking entrance on his own from one side of the stage, although the stable chorus remains present, if silent – it has already said that it will wait until he arrives – and presumably reacts to what he says with appropriate gestures and movements (we shall see Marco da Gagliano's recommendations on such matters). Orfeo delivers his quite long monologue (ll. 101–22) about how his former laments have turned to joy, and then invokes first Apollo (l. 113: *Padre cortese*) and then Venus (l. 117: *Bella Madre d'Amor*) as he hopes that day will quickly pass into night. Our unknown stage director has Arcetro enter toward the end of this speech (just before l. 123), and from the other side of the stage – by theatrical convention, from somewhere different from Orfeo (Arcetro has been with Euridice and her companions) – although this annotation seems to reflect some earlier plan given that it has Arcetro playing the *triflauto* rather than Tirsi slightly later in Peri's score. Arcetro and Orfeo then engage in dialogue (ll. 123–43) prior to Tirsi's entrance with a song to the *triflauto* ("Nel puro ardor della più bella stella"). Tirsi then moves to join the other members of the chorus already present onstage (so Peri's stage direction instructs; see Table 3.2): once he receives Orfeo's thanks for his good wishes, he stays silent.

This leaves Orfeo and his friend, Arcetro, as the two principal characters onstage engaging with the abrupt entrance of Dafne on her own to deliver her terrible news (at l. 162; she is "alone" according to Peri's stage direction). After the questions posed to her by Arcetro and Orfeo, and Orfeo's and then Arcetro's instruction that she should reveal all, Dafne begins her narration; Orfeo reacts and then leaves (at l. 236, the end of "Non piango e non sospiro"), soon followed by Arcetro (l. 246, as Dafne tells him to go). The stable chorus remains silent throughout: significantly, Peri allocates ll. 186–87 to Arcetro rather than Rinuccini's "Choro." Dafne remains on stage, at which point, according to Peri's stage direction, Euridice's companions enter along with Aminta. A nymph from the stable chorus asks one of those arriving with Aminta whether it is indeed true that they are returning without Euridice (ll. 247–49). Aminta replies, and another nymph (also from the stable chorus, it seems) notes how the happy day has taken a dark turn, with joyful songs turned into complaints and laments. Rinuccini then has a shepherd respond by warning the nymphs – and the audience – of the impermanence of beauty (ll. 260–64). This cues the end-of-episode chorus ("Cruda morte, ahi pur potesti").

However, a decision seems to have been made in rehearsal here. Peri's score has the shepherd's admonition set for a tenor voice (C4 clef) but with the label "Ninfa," meaning that in practice the music would have had to have been transposed up an octave. This is a typical kind of annotation in a performance score that then gets accidentally carried over into the printed one (which, in principle, should either have ignored it or have renotated the music).[54] Peri therefore made a late decision to have a nymph, not a shepherd, respond to the nymph, maintaining a dialogue between mobile and stable chorus members (respectively, Euridice's companions who returned with Aminta, and the nymphs and shepherds on stage from the beginning of Episode 2). This dialogue carries through into "Cruda morte, ahi pur potesti," the structure of which now makes more sense as Peri (but not Caccini) chose to set it. Rinuccini provides seven four-line stanzas ($a^8b^8a^8b^8$); the last two lines of the first stanza are also marked to return as a refrain after each subsequent one (*Sospirate, aure celesti, / lagrimate, o selve, o campi*). One clue to Rinuccini and Peri's thinking, however, lies in the second stanza, which refers specifically to cruel death (the *Cruda morte* invoked in stanza 1) having left Euridice's beautiful face deprived of all color (I. 269: *Quel bel volto almo fiorito*), a comment that can only be made by a nymph who was with her at her death. Thus Peri sets stanza 1 for a solo soprano (marked "Coro," from the stable chorus), then stanza 2 for the mobile "Ninfa del Coro" and stanza 3 for the stable one. These two nymphs alternate again for stanzas 4 and 5; the mobile nymph has stanza 6 (referring to the snake); and for the final stanza (where the ability of a skilled helmsman to steer a boat through a storm is contrasted with the inability of mortals to escape death), the two nymphs together are joined by a shepherd for a three-voice setting. Each stanza is separated by the refrain set for five voices. By having the stanzas alternate between a "stable" and a "mobile" nymph, Rinuccini and Peri make this chorus conform more closely to the

[54] For a similar case, see Carter, "Some Notes on the First Edition of Monteverdi's *Orfeo*," 510–12.

model of Aristotle's *kommos* (*Poetics*, part 12: "a dirge shared between chorus and actors").

Toward the end of Episode 2, it seems that Arcetro leaves the stage on his own, following Dafne's instruction at ll. 244–46 (*Va pur* . . .). But even if he were accompanied both on his exit and on his return by, say, some of the shepherds, none of them shares in his recounting at the beginning of Episode 3 of what he has just seen. Thus the active members of the chorus in Episode 3 are those present on stage at the end of Episode 2.[55] Arcetro addresses its nymphs (l. 295: *donne*) as he tells of Orfeo's weeping at the site of Euridice's death and the appearance of the unnamed goddess to rescue him. Peri – but not Caccini – responds correctly by having the chorus's three interventions in Arcetro's narrative each set for a single female voice: two labeled "Coro" (a single vocal line in C1 clef: ll. 298–301; l. 337) and one allocated to Dafne (l. 323).[56] Only after Arcetro has finished does Peri allow a shepherd to speak (one is also present onstage since Episode 2, it seems), who says that praises should be sung to the goddess; the same or another shepherd then issues the instruction after the "final" chorus, "Se de' boschi i verdi onori," that everyone should go to the temple, thereby enabling the cast to exit for the set change.

In the final pastoral episode (5), however, the procedure is similar to Episodes 1 and 2, with, in effect, a chorus present from the beginning and a separate group entering later. Peri has the "Coro" (a nymph) speak with Arcetro and then note Aminta's return with a happy look on his face. At that point, the dialogue is split between, on the one hand, Arcetro and those present with him at the beginning of Episode 5, and on the other, Aminta and at least one shepherd entering with him. Arcetro (not Rinuccini's "Choro") speaks to Aminta directly and adds interjections to the latter's account of Orfeo and Euridice's return.[57] The shepherd who then fleshes out that account by noting the surprise and delight of seeing them (l. 654: *Pensa di qual stupor, di qual diletto*) must have been with Aminta. Arcetro (again, not Rinuccini's "Choro") notes that the day now shines more brightly at dusk than it did at dawn (ll. 682–83: *e più ride la terra, e più s'infiora, / al tramontar del dì ch'in su l'aurora*). But when Orfeo and

[55] At least, this is how Rinuccini and Peri seem to handle matters. In the actual performance on 6 October 1600, Caccini's singers, who sang the chorus at the end of Episode 2, may have left the stage (given that Peri's singers sang the chorus at the end of Episode 3) to change costume for the spirits of the Underworld in Episode 4.

[56] Peri seems to associate the label "Coro" with the stable chorus; compare his treatment of ll. 82, 265.

[57] However, there is a slip in Peri's score: he assigns ll. 614–17 to Arcetro but the music is notated in the C1 clef (i.e., for a nymph).

Euridice appear on stage (probably with additional companions),[58] the chorus already present takes a more active role. In ll. 691–93, the nymph in whose arms Euridice had died says that it is indeed her, and a different (it seems) nymph says that she hardly believes her eyes (ll. 697–99). Then, when it comes to asking direct questions of Orfeo and Euridice, Dafne (rather than Rinuccini's "Choro"), Arcetro, and Aminta take the lead in soliciting more information on events in the Underworld. This leads to the final chorus ("Biondo arcier, che d'alto monte"), which alternates stanzas for five voices and for three, for the "whole" chorus together ("Tutto il Coro insieme cantano, e Ballano"). There is no longer any need to label them as nymphs or shepherds, or to view them as stable or mobile: this is, in effect, what Aristotle would have called the "exodos," which may also be why its content seems somewhat detached from the drama itself.

Not all of these and other stage movements are indicated by specific directions in Peri's score or in the annotated libretto, although those directions offer sufficient clues to prompt the close reading of the libretto and score that has enabled the deciphering of such movements. However, the annotated libretto also contains two other directions worthy of note, both in Episode 4 in the Underworld. First, the Underworld deities (as distinct from the *ombre*) are cued to enter for the last third of Orfeo's plea at the gates of Hades ("Funeste piaggie, ombrosi orridi campi"). When Orfeo reaches the most powerful moment in his plea, directing his remarks to Euridice (l. 436: *E tu* . . .), one group (presumably including Radamanto and Caronte) enters from one side of the stage, and Plutone and Proserpina from the other (again, therefore from different places): clearly they (and in particular, Proserpina) have already been listening, but now they are prompted to appear.[59] The subsequent stage movement follows logically enough. In his final speech (ll. 540–50), Plutone notes the triumph of mercy in the Underworld, instructs his ministers to reveal Orfeo to Euridice, and invites Orfeo to cross his threshold (*Scendi, gentil amante*) and to bring his wife back to the living. Orfeo celebrates his good fortune and then exits on the side of the stage from where Plutone came

[58] As we have seen, having just one or two shepherds enter with Aminta (at l. 597) but more with Orfeo and Euridice (at l. 684) would allow still more time for any shepherds who had played spirits in Episode 4 to change costume.

[59] This annotation was badly truncated when the libretto was bound, and it is confusingly worded. Having the Underworld divinities on two sides makes for easier entrances on a stage with scant space between the side flats. But it also raises a question left unanswered by Rinuccini: how Orfeo manages to cross the River Styx. Striggio and Monteverdi made much more of this issue in their *Orfeo*.

(so the annotation says),[60] immediately prior to the end-of-episode chorus of spirits and Infernal deities ("Poiché gl'eterni imperi").

However, there remains the question of those other spirits and when they appear. As we have seen, there are, in effect, two options (at least, if we bring Caccini's singers into the mix): they are present from the beginning of Episode 4, or they enter as Orfeo begins his plea to the Underworld at "Funeste piaggie, ombrosi orridi campi" (given Orfeo's direct address to them). Either way, they are separate from Plutone, Proserpina, Radamanto, and Caronte. But they certainly remain present for the discussion between Orfeo and Plutone: Orfeo notes the spirits and dark divinities that seem to be moved by his grief and tears (l. 499: *quest'ombre intorno, e quest'oscuri numi*). Angelo Ingegneri makes a number of recommendations for the appearance of an *ombra* on any stage: it should enter upstage so as to seem larger than life (by virtue of the perspective) therefore making it appear more horrendous; it should be covered entirely in black silk, not revealing its face, hands, or feet; it should move on wheels rather than seeming to walk normally; and it should be in constant motion when speaking.[61] It is very tempting to suggest that the five free-standing rocks (moving on wheels) that Cigoli created for the Underworld set were intended to facilitate the appearance of five spirits, one behind each of them, and presumably (following Ingegneri) toward the rear of the stage.

Regardless of precisely when these spirits entered, the stage direction in the annotated version of Rinuccini's libretto make it clear that the Underworld deities (Radamanto and Caronte on the one hand, and Plutone and Proserpina on the other) were on opposite sides of the stage, at least when they entered. Some such spatial separation (therefore probably of the spirits as well) is also explicit in both Peri's and Caccini's settings of the final chorus, "Poiché gl'eterni imperi," for two four-voice groups in alternation. In Peri's case (and Caccini follows), the first of its five stanzas is

[60] It might seem likely that Plutone and Proserpina leave with Orfeo (although Radamanto and Caronte do not), although as noted earlier, the final chorus of Episode 4 may have needed Plutone's voice. In Peri's setting, the C2 part in the first chorus goes down to *c'*, two notes below the range of Proserpina (*e'–d''*) and one below that of Venere (*d'–d''*, with the role taken by the same singer), so she, too, could possibly have joined in if she does not exit with Orfeo.

[61] Ingegneri, *Della poesia rappresentativa*, ed. Doglio, 30: *Il suo sito io direi poscia ch'egli havesse ad essere l'ultima parte della principale prospettiva per due ragioni; la prima, perché secondo la proportione de gli edifici quivi posti, l'ombra vicina a loro e in lor paragone sembra di grandezza straordinaria, il che aita assai l'orribilità . . . La qual ombra devrebbe essere tutta coperta, più che vestita, di zendale ovvero altra cosa simile, pur di color nero, e non mostrar né volto, né mani, né piedi e sembrare insomma una cosa informe, movendosi più tosto sopra a picciole ruote che mutando i passi, over caminando ordinariamente . . . e mentre ella ragionerà, esser continoamente inquieta, né giamai punto fermarsi . . .*

delivered by the "De[i]tà d'Inferno Primo Coro a 4" (Caccini just labels it "Primo Coro"), and the second is response from a second chorus (Peri marks it "Risposta Secondo Coro"). The third stanza is allocated by Peri to Radamanto, perhaps in recompense for his prior speech having been allocated to Caronte (Caccini gives it to "Una delle Deità"); the fourth stanza is for the "first" chorus; and, for the fifth, both choruses join in singing the music previously allocated to the "second."

Peri's two four-voice choruses seem to be made up of different voices (although they sing together at the end): the first has parts in C2, C3, C4, and F4 clefs, and the second, in C3, C4, C4, F4 ones. This would suggest that Radamanto and Caronte (two C4 roles) were joined in the second chorus by two spirits (an alto and a bass), while the first chorus had three spirits plus (it seems likely) Plutone.[62] Thus Rinuccini's designation in the libretto is entirely correct: this is a chorus of *ombre* (at least five) and *deità* (probably three) of the Underworld. But whatever the distribution of the singers, their position seems to change as the chorus proceeds. The subject of the first three stanzas is Orfeo himself and his triumph over the Underworld. However, there is a striking rhetorical shift in the middle of the fourth stanza, with a direct address to the "sons of the earth," in effect the audience (l. 574: *O figli della terra*), who should not expect similar treatment. That address continues in the fifth and final stanza, when both Peri and Caccini have the two separate groups join together musically, and, one assumes, physically, although there remains the question of how to handle their exits from different parts of the stage at the same time as the change back to the pastoral set for Episode 5.

"Speaking" and "Singing"

Striggio and Monteverdi introduced both Orfeo and Euridice in Act I of their opera. However, Rinuccini's decision to focus first on Euridice – as befits the title of his work – and to save Orfeo's entrance until the beginning of Episode 2 makes dramatic sense:[63] it allows members of the stable chorus to stay onstage for the end of Episode 1 precisely, so they say, because they are waiting for Orfeo to arrive. So too, of course, is the audience, who in

[62] Caccini's two choruses each have the same clefs (C3, C4, F3, F4) so the disposition of the deities is less clear (his Caronte is a C4 role and Radamanto and Plutone are F4 ones); the solo section for the unnamed deity who sings the third stanza is in C4 clef.

[63] Striggio and Monteverdi therefore ended up with the problem of having Orfeo make a "new" entrance at the beginning of their Act 2.

addition is expecting him to do what, according to myth, he does best: to sing. Indeed, the handwritten stage direction has Orfeo enter singing ("cantando") as he contrasts his former laments with his happier state now that Euridice has returned his love. But this is odd, because everything up to this point has also been done *cantando*. It also raises the question of what distinguishes Orfeo's "Antri ch'a' miei lamenti" as something "sung" in the first place.[64]

Much has been made of the fact that the first operas took as their subjects famous mythological musicians: Apollo in the case of *Dafne*, and then his son, Orpheus. As we have seen (in Chapter 1), early opera positioned itself as an attempt to recreate the reputed power of music in Classical Antiquity. But the genre also demonstrated significant anxieties, not least concerning its patent lack of verisimilitude to be mitigated, first, by its pastoral environment, and second, by finding plausible occasions where singing might be justified. Episode 1 of *Euridice* is full of musical references – *lieti canti* (l. 36), *dolci canti* (l. 59), *liete carole e lieti balli* (l. 81), and passing the time *con lieto canto* (l. 84) – prior to the final chorus that invites further singing and dancing ("Al canto, al ballo . . . "). All these allusions to music onstage suggest a typical degree of nervousness about its plausibility as a dramatic medium. But when the nymph orders her companions to declare how the sun has never seen so fine a pair of lovers, she tells them to "say" it (l. 52: *dite liete e festose*). Peri has the quotation from Petrarch – *Non vede un simil par d'amanti 'l Sole* – duly repeated by a shepherd, by Arcetro, and even by a five-part chorus, but whether they are "singing" in Rinuccini's or Peri's mind is another matter altogether.

In his preface to the score of *Euridice*, Peri tried to lessen the problem by reference to the opinion held by "many" that the ancient Greeks and Romans had sung their tragedies throughout: in other words, music was an essential condition for, and medium of, dramatic performance. But Peri also realized that he was walking a tightrope. His task, he said, was to imitate speech in song because, without doubt, no one ever spoke singing. He therefore made another assumption about Classical practice: that the ancient Greeks and Romans used a type of harmony that went beyond ordinary speech but fell short of the melody of song, so as to take some form in between the two.[65] He then went on at some length to explain the

[64] For a discussion of similar issues in Striggio and Monteverdi's *Orfeo*, see Carter, "In questo lieto e fortunato giorno."

[65] Peri, *Le musiche . . . sopra L'Euridice*, preface: *Onde veduto, che si trattava di poesia Dramatica, e che però si doveva imitar col canto chi parla (e senza dubbio non si parlò mai cantando) stimai, che gli antichi Greci, e Romani (i quali secondo l'openione di molti cantavano su le Scene le*

operation of his new form of lyrical declamation midway between the slow, suspended movements of song and the fluent, faster ones of speech (*un temperato corso tra i movimenti del canto sospesi, e lenti, e quegli della favella speditii, e veloci*) by way of matching melodic movement and harmonic shifts to verbal accent (important words, stressed syllables, etc.), and taking into account the emotional content of the text according to whether it expressed grief, joy, or the like. He then retreated somewhat from his prior position: even though he would not claim that this is the type of song that was adopted in Greek and Roman plays, it was the only option within "our" music to accommodate "our" speech.[66]

We now tend label this style of musical declamation "recitative," although the later connotations of that term do not do justice to the expressive range of its early seventeenth-century predecessor. In his account of *Il rapimento di Cefalo*, Michelangelo Buonarroti *il giovane* referred to Giulio Caccini's noble imitation of naked speech which did not obscure by way of harmony the understanding of the words.[67] This, too, downplays the expression and nuance that Peri managed to achieve in his music, even as he struggled to explain it in his preface. Rinuccini certainly provided a broad emotional canvas with his day of joy, laughter, and song turning to complaints and lament (ll. 258–59: *O gioie, o risi, o canti, / fatti querele e pianti*), then back again. He also used a wide variety of words as characters describe their own or others' utterances, ranging from speech (*dire, parlare, ragionare*) to song (*cantare, temprare*), with various expressive points in between (*gioire, godere, piangere, sospirare*). In general, however, he favors the notion of them existing in a "speaking" environment where the role of music is to bring out the hidden qualities of words themselves. Euridice's comment to her companions on her return from the Underworld captures the ambiguities perfectly: she asks them to recognize her customary accents and to hear the sound of her friendly words (ll. 705–6: *Riconoscete omai gl'usati accenti, /*

Tragedie intere) usassero un'armonia, che avanzando quella del parlare ordinario, scendesse tanto dalla melodia del cantare, che pigliasse forma di cosa mezzana. Peri here somewhat typically (for the period) confuses the Classical terms *armonia* and *melodia* (the latter properly meaning the entire musical work, i.e., the *melos*).

[66] *E però, (sì come io non ardirei affermare questo essere il canto nelle Greche, e nelle Romane favole usato), così ho creduto esser quello, che solo possa donarcisi dalla nostra Musica, per accomodarsi alla nostra favella.* For a fuller account of the origins and operation of the new style, see Palisca, "Peri and the Theory of Recitative."

[67] Michelangelo Buonarroti (*il giovane*), *Descrizione delle felicissime nozze . . . della Cristianissima Maestà di Madama Maria Medici, Regina di Francia e di Navarra* (Florence: Giorgio Marescotti, 1600), 21: Caccini had the opportunity *di far conoscere di quanta efficacia fosse la musica, che imitante nobilmente il nudo parlare, non asconde sotto armonia la intelligenza significativa delle parole.*

udite il suon di queste voci amiche). While her use of *accenti*, *suon*, and even *voci* (depending on how one chooses to translate the last) might seem musical in the narrow sense of the term, Rinuccini was seeking something broader about the nature of language and what we hear within it.

Here we need to consider a more complex set of variants between the libretto and Peri's score, where words, phrases, or even lines are altered. Some just reflect the correction of copying errors (or their creation) and standard orthographical differences.[68] The latter also seem to betray Peri's (and not Caccini's) personal mannerisms, such as *viddi* for Rinuccini's *vidi* in the past tense of *videre*, *inpero* for *impero*, *spene* for *speme*, *inmortal* and *inmortali* (for *imm-*), and frequently, but not consistently, *lacrime* for *lagrime* (and its derivatives). But far more of these variants reflect a conscious process of revision, first by Rinuccini on his own (in the case of those few variants also adopted by Caccini) and then when he continued (we assume) to work on the text as it took musical shape in the hands of Peri and his performers. Although it would no doubt be foolish to attempt to account for every single variant in the manner adopted below, there are enough consistencies among them to reveal various criteria in play. In one case, Rinuccini (or Peri) realized that a line had accidentally been used twice (ll. 312, 333) and so removed its first appearance (Caccini does not). Elsewhere, Rinuccini worried about the choice of words, such as whether Arcetro's account of Orfeo's weeping where Euridice died was a *lagrimosa vista* or a *miserabil* one (l. 323); whether a stone (to which Arcetro compares Orfeo) can be can be *insensibil[e]* or *insensata* (l. 332);[69] whether doves leading the chariot of a goddess would have *penne* or *piume* (l. 352); or if it was better to describe Euridice's parents as being "old" (*vecchi*) or "sad" (*mesti*, l. 642 – a reading shared by Caccini). In some such lexical cases, however, Rinuccini makes a more emphatic choice (l. 629: *in sì mortal dolore* for *nel mortal dolore*) or a more elegant one: when Orfeo asks Plutone that he might recover Euridice, she is his "soul" (*ch'io ricovri da te l'anima mia*, l. 467) rather than his "lady" (*la donna mia*).[70] In others, he seems to have realized that he had not got things quite right in his first

[68] One obvious copying error within the score is in the final chorus at l. 758, where Peri's *alma felice* in the fourth line of the third stanza (for Rinuccini's *alma corona*, which fits the rhyme scheme) accidentally reverts to l. 746, the fourth line of the first stanza. Peri's handling of l. 75 (*scintilli* for *scintille*) and l. 197 (*o dall'acute spine* for the printed libretto's *e dall'acute spine*) may also be copying or typographical errors; there is scant apparent benefit to them.

[69] Rinuccini chooses the latter, perhaps preferring to avoid the comparison with Ariosto, *Orlando furioso* I: 39.8 (*che par cangiato in insensibil pietra*).

[70] Rinuccini's original *donna mia* has echoes of Dante (*Vita nova*, 26: *Tanto gentile e tanto onesta pare / la donna mia, quand'ella altrui saluta*). Given that Rinuccini's Underworld is not much

version: Orfeo takes Venere's right hand (*la destra ei prese*, l. 365) rather than offering her his own (*ei porse*); it made more sense in the context of the plot to have Aminta describe Orfeo and Euridice (on their return) as "fortunate lovers" (*felici amanti*) rather than "faithful" ones (*fedeli amanti*, l. 599); and Euridice tells her companions to rid themselves of grief (*Sgombrate ogni dolor, donzelle amate*, l. 695) rather than fear (*ogni timor*). Rinuccini also sought to improve the clarity of his syntax for the sake of easy comprehension by way of reordering a sentence to bring the main verb closer to its beginning (ll. 160–61: *E per te, Tirsi mio, rimeni il Sole / sempre le notti e i dì lieti e ridenti*, for *E per te, Tirsi mio, liete e ridenti / sempre le notti e i dì rimeni il Sole*), or sacrificing other poetic niceties: the "pitiless" force that Arcetro invokes in l. 241 (*ove l'empia n'assal*) is the envious, cruel death treated as vocative in l. 237 (*Ahi morte invida e ria*) but it is too far away and grammatically separate to make the connection, so Peri has Arcetro adopt a more straightforward repetition (*ove morte n'assal*).[71]

These are matters that Rinuccini or Peri might have identified when hearing the text rather than just reading it. They also opt for greater theatrical impact by introducing a greater number of deictic locutions focusing the attention on the who, what, where, and when of the action.[72] We have already seen that early in Episode 1 the libretto refers directly to the pastoral location (l. 35: *e per queste fiorite alme contrade*), thereby bringing the set more to life in the mind's eye. In the case of the Underworld episode, however, Rinuccini adopts a different tactic. In the libretto, Orfeo asks Venere a double question, the first concerning the murky path on which he finds himself, and the second, where he might see Euridice again (ll. 404–5: *per qual fosco sentier mi scorgi, e dove / rivedrò quelle luci alme e serene?*). In the score, that question becomes both simpler and more urgent by way of a double "dove" (*Dove mi scorgi, dove / rivedrò* . . .) – turning an eleven-syllable line into a seven-syllable one – leaving Venere to note (ll. 406–7) the "dark passage" (*L'oscuro varco*) and the pale, gloomy shores (*rive pallide e meste*). There are other such added cases of deixis as well. Orfeo refers to Love instilling sweetness in "me" (*che*

influenced by Dante (in contrast to Striggio and Monteverdi's *Orfeo*), his more Petrarchan revision may be revealing.

71 Orfeo's comment to Plutone about how the spirits of the Underworld seem moved to pity is another case in point: the libretto (ll. 498–501) has *Mira, Signor, deh mira / . . . / vedi come al mio duol, come al mio pianto / par che ciascun si strugga e si consumi*. For l. 500, Peri's score removes the *vedi* (it is redundant), but gains further advantage by claiming that the spirits seem moved by great pity (*come d'alta pietà vint'al mio duolo*).

72 Compare the discussion of deixis in Calcagno, "Imitar col canto chi parla."

di dolcezza Amor nel cor mi stilla, l. 129) rather than just distilling it (*nel cor distilla*). When Arcetro describes Orfeo's suffering at the site of Euridice's death, he adds a demonstrative "there" (l. 311: *Ivi, con tanto affanno*) rather than having him just being overcome (*Vinto da l'alto affanno*). And as the chorus questions Euridice on her return, it reemphasizes the temporal span of the action "today" (l. 708: *Com'oggi nell'Inferno* instead of the original *Forse il gran regno Inferno*).

Rinuccini could well have made these changes on his own. Others, however, seem to have been more influenced by the music, or even by the singers. There is not much difference between *in questo allegro dì, gentil donzella* (l. 175) and Peri's *in così lieto dì, gentil donzella* save that the latter has fewer clashing consonants and is easier to sing. Other such revisions are also easier to deliver: *scolorito il bel volto e i bei sembianti* instead of *scolorito il bel viso ...* (l. 221);[73] *così turbi d'amor gl'almi diletti* rather than *gl'almi contenti* (l. 239); *a questo cor dolente* for *a questo sen dolente* (l. 468); *e vivo e spir'anch'io* for *e spiro e vivo anch'io* (l. 701);[74] and even just *darle aita* instead of *dargli* (l. 337). No less "musical" is the incorporation in the score of phatic expressions that can, in turn, be given sonic weight: the score adds the *ahi* to Dafne's *quand'ahi ria sorte acerba* (l. 203; the libretto has *quando, ria*), and, in the case of Orfeo's pleas in the Underworld, the text set by Peri is less concerned with where Plutone does not seem to feel any spark of pity – his heart (l. 485: *scintilla di pietà non senti al core*) – than with the fact that the absence of pity is cause for an "alas" (*scintilla di pietà non senti, hai lasso*), anticipating the exclamation that Rinuccini provides at the beginning of the next line. It does not seem to matter that in this case, as in a few others, the change means losing a rhyme (*dolore/core*). Peri as composer – and no doubt as singer – prefers to revel in the immediate repetition across the lines (*hai lasso* and *ahi lasso*).[75] So would any musician of this period.

These clear indications that Rinuccini's original libretto was subject to both dramatic and musical intervention should come as no surprise. In most cases, the variants are created within the framework of the original poetry, preserving its metrical integrity on a line-by-line basis: a word may

[73] *Volto* and *viso* are in effect synonymous, but Rinuccini tends to use *volto* in tragic moments and *viso* in happier ones. Peri's vocal preference for *volto* here seems to outweigh the clash with *volti* in the previous line.

[74] The fact that l. 701 is from a speech for Euridice (a role taken by one of Caccini's singers) is revealing: clearly Peri's music for the role had the benefit of additional intervention from Rinuccini.

[75] In this context, *hai* and *ahi* are interchangeable (i.e., "ah!").

be altered within, or added to, a seven-syllable line but it retains seven syllables. We have already seen one case, however, where an eleven-syllable line is shortened to seven syllables, and there is one example of the reverse: Arcetro's first line in Episode 2, praising Love for Orfeo's good fortune (l. 123: *Sia pur lodato Amore*) is expanded to include heaven in the reckoning (*Sia pur lodato il Ciel, lodato Amore*), whether for reasons of pious propriety or to allow the singer a bit more time to establish his entrance. More significant, however, are those cases where new lines are added to the libretto. There are three, each of which seems to require different explanation.

The first is probably the most straightforward. Dafne appears abruptly in the middle of Episode 2 (l. 162) to interrupt Orfeo, Arcetro, and Tirsi. She is filled with fear and pity, and she bemoans the drastic turn taken by fate. Arcetro wants to know what has happened, given that he had just recently left her in happy mood at the spring (where Euridice and her companions were singing and dancing). Orfeo then asks Dafne directly what bad news has made her look so grim on this joyful day. Peri's score adds a line for Dafne between Arcetro's and Orfeo's speeches: "Oh day full of anguish and full of woes" (l. 172a: *O giorno pien d'angoscia, e pien di guai*). Rinuccini slots it in nicely enough: Dafne's *guai* rhymes with Arcetro's *già mai* and *lasciai*. Presumably he did so to direct Orfeo's – and the audience's – attention away from Arcetro back to her (hence Orfeo's direct question). It also, of course, increases the pathos of the scene.

The second such addition to the libretto – an extra line (464a) in Orfeo's exchange with Plutone – raises more complex questions. Earlier in Episode 4, Venere had issued a clear set of instructions to Orfeo at the entrance to the Underworld (ll. 412–17):

Sciogli il tuo nobil canto
al suon dell'aureo legno:
quanto morte t'ha tolto ivi dimora.
Prega, sospira e plora:
forse avverrà che quel soave pianto
che mosso ha il Ciel pieghi l'Inferno ancora.

[Let loose your noble song / to the sound of the golden lyre: / what death has taken away from you is there within. / Pray, sigh, and plead: / perhaps it will come to pass that the sweet lament / which has moved heaven will also sway the Inferno.]

Venere leaves, and Orfeo begins his plaint ("Funeste piaggie . . . "), which Rinuccini structures in three sections of unequal length, each in the form of a madrigal ending with what becomes a one-line refrain (*Lagrimate al mio pianto, ombre d'Inferno*). As we have seen, Plutone, Proserpina, and their retinue enter at the third section, summoned, it seems, precisely by this *pianto*.

Rinuccini originally had Plutone state that Orfeo's "so sweet notes and so suave accents" (l. 457: *Sì dolci note e sì soavi accenti*) would not be in vain if plaints or laments were able to arouse pity in his kingdom. This is changed (by both Peri and Caccini) to the more forceful "so sweet prayers and so suave accents" in the score (*Sì dolci preghi* . . .). The shift then seems reinforced by the new line for Orfeo later in the episode as he seeks to soften Plutone's resolve by reminding him of his love for Proserpina. In the original libretto, Orfeo expresses the hope that the sweet song of his noble lyre will serve to recover Euridice (ll. 465–66: *vagliami il dolce canto / di questa nobil cetra*). But Peri's score (and not Caccini's) prefaces this with a separate plea: that Plutone be moved by the sad sound of his sighs (l. 464a: *movat'il tristo suon de' miei sospiri*). The added *preghi* (l. 457) and *sospiri* (l. 464a) are precisely what Venere urged upon Orfeo in the first place (l. 415: *Prega, sospira e plora*). But they again force the question of what, if anything, in Orfeo's *canto* constitutes a "song" in any formal sense of the term.

We have seen this issue arise in the case of Orfeo's initial entrance in Episode 2 (at "Antri ch'a' miei lamenti"), and it seems to reflect a dilemma on Rinuccini's part, and therefore in *Euridice* as a whole. We might argue over whether Orfeo's plea to the Underworld, "Funeste piaggie, ombrosi orridi campi," counts as what opera scholars would call a diegetic song (that is, an actual song acknowledged as such by the characters or articulated in ways to be heard thus by the audience). But there are four other, more explicit diegetic moments in the opera: the choruses ending Episodes 1 and 3, Tirsi's "Nel puro ardor della più bella stella" in Episode 2 (with its "Zinfonia" for *triflauto*), and Orfeo's "Gioite al canto mio, selve frondose" in Episode 5. The work is also framed by what one can assume are explicit songs: the prologue delivered by La Tragedia (who twice refers to herself as singing), and the final *ballo*, "Biondo arcier, che d'alto monte." All of these texts are structured as one would expect of "songs" in this period, that is, in regular stanzas and sometimes in poetic meters other than the looser combination of eleven- and seven-syllable lines that designate some form of recitative. Such stanzaic and metrical structures imply a more structured and tuneful musical style. Tirsi's "Nel puro ardor" is a little unusual, given that each of its two stanzas consists of four eleven-syllable lines and one five-syllable one, although there are strong internal rhymes that break the longer lines into two. More typical are the chorus toward the end of Episode 3, "Se de' boschi i verdi onori," in eight-syllable lines ($a^8b^8c^8a^8b^8c^8$), and the final "Biondo arcier, che d'alto monte," in eight- and four-syllable lines ($a^8a^4b^8c^8c^4b^8$), both common patterns of the Chiabreran canzonetta. Likewise, the prologue is constructed in the standard four-line stanzas of eleven-syllable lines (*abba*). In all these cases – as in Orfeo's "Gioite al canto mio," we shall see – the same music is repeated from stanza to stanza.[76]

However, although La Tragedia invites the audience to lend its ear to the singing of Orfeo (l. 28: *del Tracio Orfeo date l'orecchia al canto*), Rinuccini and then Peri seem to have been uncertain about how best to represent it. Inevitably given his role in the opera – and his authority as the greatest of mythical musicians – Orfeo is often in the musical spotlight, as at his entrance in Episode 2 ("Antri ch'a' miei lamenti"), his response to news of the death of Euridice in Episode 3 ("Non piango e non sospiro"), and then his plea at the gates of the Underworld ("Funeste piaggie . . . "). In each of these three cases, Rinuccini mixes eleven- and seven-syllable lines loosely organized by way of rhyme in the manner of the sixteenth-century poetic madrigal (plus in the case of "Funeste piaggie," a refrain at the end of each of its three madrigal-like sections). Rhyme also serves to provide closure for each passage or its subdivisions, whether by way of a couplet (. . . *zz*) or some alternation (. . . *yzyz*; . . . *yzzy*). This invites a flexibly expressive, lyrical musical response. But absent more regular poetic structures – and in the case of the music, the typical signifiers of vocal virtuosity (such as extensive ornaments) – it can be hard to distinguish the musical setting here from the more routine declamation by which the action in *Euridice* proceeds. Orfeo needs to stand apart from the other characters onstage in terms of his own musical singing or speaking, but neither Rinuccini nor Peri necessarily provides sufficient means for him to do so save by way of his prominence in the drama as a whole.

While shepherds and nymphs might plausibly sing songs, whether separately or together, Rinuccini seems to have felt that Orfeo, the greatest musician of Classical Antiquity, could not descend to that level: his songs had to be not-songs, as it were. The issue seems to come to a head in Orfeo's last set-piece moment: his entrance with Euridice in Episode 5 on their return from the Underworld. This is to all intents and purposes a diegetic song:

[76] In this repertory, end-of-episode/act choruses tend to be strophic anyway, but while the one ending Episode 2 ("Cruda morte, ahi pur potesti," also in eight-syllable lines) might also count as a particular type of song – a diegetic lament on the model of Aristotle's *kommos* – Episode 4's "Poiché gl'eterni imperi" (in sevens) does not.

Gioite al canto mio, selve frondose,
  gioite, amati colli, e d'ogni intorno
  Eco rimbombi dalle valli ascose.

Risorto è il mio bel sol di raggi adorno,
  e co' begl'occhi onde fa scorno a Delo
  raddoppia foco all'alme e luce al giorno,
  e fa servi d'Amor la terra e il Cielo.

[Rejoice in my song, leafy woods, / rejoice beloved hills, and all around / let Echo resound from the hidden valleys. // My fair sun has come back adorned with rays, / and with fair eyes that put Apollo to shame / she redoubles the fire within souls, and light to the day, / and makes the earth and heaven servants of love.]

Given its function, Rinuccini has to handle this differently from Orfeo's other texts in *Euridice*, but nor can he give Orfeo a simple Chiabreran canzonetta. Therefore he turns to a model that he had already adopted in a parallel situation in *Dafne*, if in a quite different dramatic context.

In Rinuccini's earlier libretto, Apollo responds to Dafne's metamorphosis into a laurel with "Non curi la mia pianta o fiamma o gelo," a text in three stanzas in eleven-syllable lines (*aba // bcb // cdcd*). The form has sometimes been identified as *terza rima* given the interlocking rhyme and the concluding quatrain (or two distichs), but it is more properly to be associated with the Trecento madrigal, which often consists of two tercets and a concluding "ritornello" (usually a distich): Petrarch's "Non al suo amante più Diana piacque" (*RVF* 52) is an example.[77] One assumes that Rinuccini intended the formal archaicism, perhaps also with a sideways glance at Sannazaro's *Arcadia* (which uses longer *terza rima* structures in *versi sdruccioli*; compare Ergasto's complaint at his unyielding lover in "La pastorella mia spietata e rigida" ending Egloga 1). He may also have been influenced by Torquato Tasso, who sometimes uses the Trecento form.[78] The surviving setting of "Non curi la mia pianta," attributed to Jacopo Corsi, has music just for the first stanza, to be repeated for the second and third: it repeats the final line of stanza 1, therefore also

[77] Although Petrarch's madrigals vary in the rhyme scheme adopted in the tercets; see Bausi and Martelli, *La metrica italiana*, 104. For "Non curi la mia fiamma" as *terza rima*, see Porter, "Peri and Corsi's *Dafne*," 182, and Palisca, "Aria Types in the Earliest Operas," para. 6, but compare Fantappiè, "Una primizia rinucciniana," 200. Poems (*capitoli*, *eglogi*, etc.) in *terza rima* (as used in Dante's *Divina commedia*) are usually much longer.

[78] Drago, "Nell'officina di un 'poeta-faber'," 109–17.

providing the music for the additional line in stanza 3.[79] This is typical of the musical *arie da cantar terza rima* (suitable for any such text of whatever length) that proliferated in printed and manuscript collections of our period.

Orfeo's "Gioite al canto mio" is a more compressed version of the same structure (*aba // bcbc*). Both Peri and Caccini treat the text strophically (with the same music for stanza 2 as for stanza 1, although Caccini applies some variation to the second stanza), and both follow the musical model of repeating the final line of stanza 1 – here creating a rather nice musical pun as Echo resounds from the valleys – which therefore creates the music for the additional line ending stanza 2. Both also set the text in triple time, Peri explicitly so, and Caccini implicitly (by virtue of the rhythmic patterns). In terms of metrical accents, eleven-syllable lines are not well suited to dance-like triple time, but the melodic style and the strophic repetition make this Orfeo's most songful moment in *Euridice.*

Nevertheless, there remains a constant tension between "singing" and "speaking" that is typical of early opera: musical speech is the more plausible medium – once one accepts the irrational premise on which it is founded – but song constantly seeks to intervene. The third case in *Euridice* where lines were added to the original libretto seems to illustrate matters perfectly (see Fig. 3.3). In Episode 5, Aminta enters bearing good news, the chorus hopes that it concerns Orfeo, and Aminta issues a clear instruction to the nymphs (ll. 605–13):

Non più, non più lamenti,
dolcissime compagne,
non fia chi più si lagne
di dolorosa sorte,
di fortuna o di morte. Il nostro Orfeo,
il nostro Semideo,
tutto lieto e giocondo,
di dolcezza e di gioia
nuota in un mar che non ha riva o fondo.

[Lament no more, no more, / sweetest companions, / let no one complain anymore / of sad fate, / of fortune, or of death. Our Orfeo, / our demigod, / all happy and gay, / swims in a sea of sweetness and joy that has no shore or bottom.]

[79] Porter, "Peri and Corsi's *Dafne*," 180–82. Porter's transcription of "Non curi la mia pianta" marks a repeat of the first two lines, which is incorrect.

These seven- and eleven-syllable lines are clearly designed for recitative (and Caccini follows). Peri, however, sets them in a song-like style starting in triple time – although it is not notated as such – prompted, one assumes, by the celebratory tone and also, perhaps, by the grammatical imperative (not to lament) plus the vocative (*dolcissime compagne*). However, there is a clash between the need for celebration and the important information that this text conveys. Thus Peri precedes it with five added lines (ll. 604a–e):

Se de' tranquilli petti
il seren perturbò nuntia dolente,
messaggiero ridente,
la torbida tempesta e i fosch'orrori
ecco disgombro, e rassereno i cori.

[If in your calm breasts / a grieving bearer of news disturbed the peace, / [as a] smiling messenger, / the turbid storm and gloomy horrors / now do I dispel, and make your hearts serene.]

The syntax is obscure (that sudden *messaggiero ridente*), suggesting that these new lines were a last-minute addition made on the hoof. But in them, Aminta contrasts his role as a joyful messenger against Dafne's earlier one reporting the death of Euridice; he also urges the chorus to be cheerful once more (hence his subsequent shift to triple time to that effect). Turning Aminta's subsequent lines (at *Non più, non più lamenti*) into some manner of song rather than sung speech may have been to do with Francesco Rasi's taking the role. But with that decision made, Peri seems to have felt that it needed some manner of introduction, whether to allow for stage movement or just to make clear the point of the song itself.

For the rest, not everyone appreciated the long passages of recitative in early opera. Emilio de' Cavalieri reported the view circulating in Rome that in the case of *Euridice* and *Il rapimento di Cefalo*, the music was tedious and too redolent of chanting the Passion (*che le musiche sono state tediose; et che li è parso sentir cantar la passione*).[80] Cavalieri was not without some bias, and his comments need placing in juxtaposition with other, more favorable reports of *Euridice* (see Chapter 1). But the notion that recitative led to boredom placed significant pressure on the genre in its early history, as indeed it did later as well.

[80] *KirkCM*, 205–6.

Fig. 3.3: Jacopo Peri, *Le musiche . . . sopra L'Euridice* (Florence: I Marescotti, 1600 [= 1601]), 42. Bologna, Museo Internazionale e Biblioteca della Musica.

Costumes, Movement, Gesture

Treating the libretto and score of *Euridice* in all these pragmatic theatrical lights gives the opera a surprising physicality and presence, even if that is nothing more than Rinuccini and Peri were required to do by staging it in the first place. Other aspects of the production are more difficult to recover, however, in terms of what information survives. For example, the libretto makes it clear that the nymphs of the chorus are meant to have blonde hair (l. 29: *Ninfe ch'i bei crin d'oro*) left loose or tied with ribbons, but it reveals nothing more about what they are wearing. Likewise, while Peri (but not Caccini) has Tirsi enter in Episode 2 playing a *triflauto* – presumably a fake "antique" instrument with its sound supplied by three offstage recorders[81] – he would have been marked as a shepherd in other ways as well. Costumes would have played a significant role in enabling such identification, and according to Cigoli's nephew, the artist had a significant say in their design.[82] However, we have no direct evidence of how those for *Euridice* might have looked.

Orpheus was represented often enough in Medieval and Renaissance art, meaning that there was a significant iconographical tradition on which any costume designer could draw to represent the character on the stage. The representation in Giovanni Andrea dell'Anguillara's *Le metamorfosi di Ovidio … ridotte in ottava rima* (1584) – linked to Ovid's *Metamorphoses*, book 10 – is typical enough (see *CW*Fig. 3.5). But there were dangers in transferring any iconography from painting to the theatre. One of the few images that we have of Orpheus in a theatrical context is the sketch by Alessandro Allori for *La genealogia degli dei*, a *mascherata* staged in Florence for the long-running festivities celebrating the wedding of Grand Duke Francesco and Johanna of Austria in 1565–66. This is in pencil but also has annotations indicating colors: a red cloak, a short habit, and

[81] In the 1610s, Roberto del Beccuto was well known in Florence for making extravagant instruments in the ancient manner; see *SolMBD*, 99, 107. Emilio de' Cavalieri provided at the end of the score of his *Rappresentatione di Anima, et di Corpo* (Rome: Nicolò Mutii, 1600) a rather strange short piece headed "Aria Cantata, et Sonata; al modo Antico" with two instrumental parts (C1 clef) and a vocal line (C4). The first of those parts is directed to be played by a "Flauto" (meaning a recorder), and the second by a "Flauto ò vero dalle Sordelline," the latter seemingly meaning a bagpipe or musette. Cavalieri also seems to indicate a preference for both instrumental parts being played on the *sordelline* should that be possible (which it was, on some such instruments). The text ("Io piango Filli il tuo spietato interito") consists of four lines of *versi sdruccioli*, clearly a pastoral meter (on the basis of Sannazaro).

[82] See Chapter 1, note 69.

buskins in the Classical style (see CWFig. 3.6).[83] It shows Orpheus carrying a *violone* in his left hand and its bow in his right, although as dell'Anguillara's image suggests, he would more often be represented playing a *lira da braccio*, a bowed string instrument that in the iconographical tradition often stood for a Greek lyre (a plucked instrument), which is what Cigoli chose for one of his sketches for the Underworld scene (if it was; see CWFig. 2.20). This is also how Orfeo was represented in *L'Argonautica*, the naval battle on the Arno staged during the festivities celebrating the wedding of Cosimo de' Medici and Maria Magdalena of Austria in October–November 1608, at least as represented in an engraving by Remigio Cantagallina (see CWFig. 3.7).

In the libretto to *Euridice*, Rinuccini is ambiguous on the instrument he associates with Orfeo. He tends to prefer *cetra* (ll. 106, 466, 567, 573, 713, 787) to *lira* (l. 740), and even suggests that its strings are somehow plucked with a plectrum (l. 566: *Or di soave pletro*).[84] How others interpreted these terms, however, remains a matter for debate. In the performance notes that Marco da Gagliano – a colleague and friend of Peri – provided for his own setting of Rinuccini's *Dafne* (staged in Mantua in late February or early March 1608), what the poet called Apollo's *nobil cetra* (l. 368) was to be represented by a bowed *lira da braccio*: Gagliano even went so far as to explain how Apollo should pretend to play this instrument onstage, matching his bow strokes to the sound supplied by four players of actual string instruments in the wings.[85] As for *Euridice*, one assumes that Orfeo carried some instrument at appropriate points in the action: on his return from the

83 The extensive series of costume sketches for this entertainment is discussed in Riccò *et al.*, "La mascherata della 'Genealogia degli dei'."

84 Rinuccini also associates the *lira* with Apollo in the final chorus of *Euridice* (l. 757), which he further suggests has "golden strings" that are "struck" (ll. 762–63; *l'auree corde / sì soave indi percote*). Riccò, *Dalla zampogna all'aurea cetra*, 197–202, argues in favor of a Florentine preference for the plucked lyre, even while acknowledging representations of Orpheus with the bowed *lira da braccio* such as Cristoforo Stati's statue (at www.metmuseum.org/art/collection/search/198764) commissioned shortly after the performance of *Euridice* by Jacopo Corsi (see Carter and Goldthwaite, *Orpheus in the Marketplace*, 118). However, we argue that the situation was somewhat more fluid.

85 Marco da Gagliano, *La Dafne . . . rappresentata in Mantova* (Florence: Cristofano Marescotti, 1608), preface: *Non voglio anche tacere, che dovendo Apollo nel canto de' terzeti "Non curi la mia pianta, o fiamma, o gielo" recarsi la lira al petto (il che debbe fare con bell'attitudine) è necessario far apparire al Teatro, che dalla lira d'Apollo esca melodia piu che ordinaria, però pongansi quattro Sonatori di viola (abbraccio, o gamba poco rilieva) in una delle strade più vicina, in luogo dove non veduti dal popolo veggano Apollo, e secondo che egli pone l'arco su la lira suonino le tre note scritte, avvertendo di tirare l'arcate pari, acciò apparisca un'arco solo. Questo inganno non può essere conosciuto, se non per immaginazione da qualche intendente, e reca non poco diletto.*

Underworld he refers to the success of the sound of "this lyre" (l. 713: *e 'l suon di questa cetra*). Whether he pretended to play it is a separate issue, although the fact that the instrumentalists accompanying the opera included Giovanni Battista Jacomelli playing a *lira grande* is highly suggestive: any mismatch, if there was, between Orfeo holding one type of lyre and the sound of another might or might not have mattered in the context of a theatrical performance.

In other cases, the iconographies adopted in paintings and similar images tended to be simpler than what was typical for theatrical use. Bernardo Buontalenti's costume sketches for the *intermedi* to *La pellegrina* (1589), or those by Alessandro Allori for *La disperazione di Fileno* (1590 or early 1591), appear much richer in terms of clothing (and the material used for it), footwear, and additional decoration (tiaras, necklaces, bracelets, etc.).[86] Allori's shepherds and nymphs provide a good example even in the case of relatively simple characters (see *CW*Figs. 3.8–3.9). The shepherds may wear animal skins and furs, just as Leone de' Sommi required for pastoral characters, but they also have shirts with elaborate collars and cuffs.[87] Likewise Allori's nymphs have opulent dresses decorated with intricate lace, covered with costume jewelry to reflect the light. Thus the female singers in the performance of *Euridice* directed by Giulio Caccini in December 1602 had dresses with elaborate collars in white voile and silk trimmings, studded with pieces of black glass.[88] This tendency toward embellishment is clear also in the case of divinities such as Venus – often shown semi-nude in paintings but richly clothed on stage – and Pluto, the latter seen in regal garb in one of Alfonso Parigi's engravings of sets for Marco da Gagliano and Jacopo Peri's opera, *Flora*, performed in Florence in 1628 during the festivities for the wedding of Margherita de' Medici and Odoardo Farnese, Duke of Parma.[89]

86 See the discussion, and illustrations, in Riccò, *Dalla zampogna all'aurea cetra*, 87–109, 235–45. The images included in Vincenzo Panciatichi's *Gli amorosi affanni* (Venice: Gio. Battista Ciotti, 1605 [= early 1606]), the revision of his *L'amicizia costante* (1600), also provide some useful ideas; see the reproductions in Riccò, *L'arcadia "in mano"*, 2: 251–57.

87 De' Sommi, *Quattro dialoghi in materia di rappresentazioni sceniche*, ed. Marotti, 51–52; Blanchard-Rothmuller, "Leone Ebreo de' Sommi's *Four Dialogues on Stage Presentations*," 143–47.

88 Four such collars were worn by Caccini's female singers, *GM* 235, fol. 63left: *quattro colletti di velo biancho da donne a crivelletti, increspati minuti fatte a llattughe, guarniti tutti pieni di bisantini di vetro neri e napettine di seta, rimasti questo mese di novembre 1603 alle donne di Giulio Romano musiche che recitorno alla commedia musichale fatta per la venuta del Cardinale Montalto.*

89 Blumenthal, *Giulio Parigi's Stage Designs*, vol. 2, fig. 48, also available at https://research.britishmuseum.org/research/collection_online/collection_object_details.aspx?objectId=1457112&partId=1.

Movement and gesture would also have had a significant impact on how *Euridice* looked in performance. We have already referred to the use of different sides of the stage for particular entrances and exits, and to the various distinctions between the "stable" and "mobile" members of the chorus that would have determined how they were positioned. Marco da Gagliano, in the preface to the score of his *Dafne* (1608), offered quite detailed instructions on how to handle the "stable" chorus (although one of a much bigger size than would have been possible on the stage for *Euridice*). After the prologue, he says,

> let the chorus appear onstage, which will be formed by nymphs and shepherds, more or fewer according to the capacity of the stage . . . When half of the chorus has entered – that is, six or seven shepherds and nymphs (for the chorus should not be made up of less than sixteen or eighteen persons) – the First Shepherd, turning to his companions, should begin speaking, and thus singing and moving should arrive at the position where he is to stop. And with the chorus having formed a half-moon on the stage, the others, whether shepherds or nymphs, should follow the song as it regards them, gesturing according to the requirements of the subject.[90]

He also notes that any individual member of the chorus participating in the dialogue should step forward and then back as appropriate, and he repeatedly insists on the need for the chorus to give the impression of paying close attention to the action with appropriate facial expressions and gestures:

> Tell the shepherd who recounts the victory of Apollo to Dafne to move two or three paces in front of the others, and to imitate with gestures the attitudes adopted by Apollo in the battle. But when the shepherd comes to bring the news of the transformation of Dafne, let those who are at the ends of the chorus all seek to move back to that part of the stage where they can look the Messenger in the face, he placing himself somewhat forward, and above all they should demonstrate attention and pity in hearing the sad news.[91]

[90] Gagliano, *La Dafne*, preface: *esca il coro in scena, il quale sarà formato di Ninfe, e di Pastori più o meno seconda la capacità del palco . . . il primo Pastore, come sia uscito la metà del Coro, cioè sei o sette tra Pastori, e Ninfe (che non vorrebbe esser formato, il Coro di manco, che di Sedici, o disciotto persone) volto a' compagni cominci a parlare, e cosi cantando e movendosi arrivi al luogo, ove dee fermarsi; e formato il Coro una meza luna su la Scena, gl'altri o Pastori, o Ninfe seguitino il canto, che tocca loro gesteggiando secondo che ricerca il suggetto . . .*

[91] *Avvertisca quel Pastore che racconta la vittoria d'Apollo a Dafne d'avanzarsi due, o tre passi avanti gli altri, e d'imitare co' gesti l'attitudini usate da Apollo nel combattimento. Ma venendo quel Pastore a portar la nuova della trasformazione di Dafne, procurino coloro, che sono su le teste del Coro di ritirarsi tutti su quella parte del palco, dove possano rimirare in viso il Nunzio facendosi alquanto avanti, e sopra tutto mostrino attenzione, e pietà nell'ascoltare la dolorosa novella.*

Gagliano's positioning of the chorus in a half-moon is a Classical gesture, but it somewhat belies the impression otherwise presented his instructions that the performers onstage should remain in motion. However, his instructions for the prologue (in *Dafne*, delivered by "Ovid") set up a nice distinction between stasis and movement:

Before the curtain falls, to make the listeners attentive, one should sound a sinfonia made up of various instruments which serve to accompany the choruses and to play the ritornellos. After fifteen or twenty bars, let the Prologue appear, that is, Ovidio: note that he should match his step to the sound of the sinfonia, not, however, with affectation as if he were dancing but with gravity, in such a manner that the steps are not discordant with the sound. When he has arrived at the position where it seems appropriate to him to begin, let him commence without other movements; and above all let the song be full of majesty, gesturing more or less according to the elevation of the conceit, noting, however, that every gesture and every step should fall on the beat of the sound and of the song. He should rest after the first quatrain, taking three or four steps, that is, for as long as the ritornello lasts, but always in time. Note that the movement should begin on the accent on the penultimate syllable; let him begin again in the position where he finds himself. He could sometimes join together two quatrains to show a certain *sprezzatura*. The costume should be that which is appropriate to a poet, with the laurel crown on the head, lyre at his side, and bow in hand.[92]

Gagliano's score for *Dafne* does not include the music for any opening sinfonia – nor does *Euridice* – though one could be added easily enough. However, Gagliano's instructions for Ovidio could work equally well for Peri's La Tragedia.[93]

Save for such more static moments, however, the main aim is to keep the action moving, so as also to maintain the audience's attention (the latter is

[92] *Innanzi al calar della tenda, per render attenti gli uditori, suonisi una Sinfonia composta di diversi istrumenti, quali servono per accompagnare i Cori e sonare i ritornelli; alle quindici o venti battute esca il Prologo cioè Ovidio avvertendo d'accompagnare il passo al suono della Sinfonia, non però con affettazione come se ballasse; ma con gravità di maniera tale ch'i passi non siano discordanti dal suono; arrivato al luogo, dove gli par conveniente di dar principio, senz'altri passeggiamenti cominci, e sopra tutto il canto sia pieno di maiestà più ò meno secondo l'altezza del concetto gesteggiando, avvertendo però ch'ogni gesto, e ogni passo caschi su la misura del suono e del canto, respiri fornito il primo quadernario passeggiando tre o quattro passi, cioè quanto dura il ritornello, pur sempre a tempo; avvertisca di cominciare il passeggio su la tenuta della penultima sillaba, ricominci nel luogo, dove si trova; Puossi tal volta congiugnere due quadernarii per mostrare una certa sprezzatura; L'abito sia qual conviensi a Poeta con la corona d'Alloro in testa, la lira al fianco, e l'arco nella mano . . .*

[93] It is somewhat odd, however, that the first stanza of Rinuccini's prologue to *Euridice* is not a complete syntactic unit (rather, it chiefly contains a relative clause), meaning that separating it from the second by way of an instrumental ritornello (as both Peri and Caccini do) and stage movement obscures the meaning.

another of Gagliano's repeated concerns). One of the striking differences between Peri's and Caccini's scores for *Euridice* is the way in which Peri handles the endings and beginnings of speeches as they transition from one to the other; Caccini demarcates them much more clearly. Even granting that musical recitative is not to be delivered according to a strict metrical beat, Peri creates within his notation a quite subtle system whereby speeches end on a half note (minim), a whole note (semibreve), or a double whole note (breve, which is Caccini's regular practice, although how he would have performed it is another matter). In the first case, the next speech begins quickly; the third, which is particularly prominent in the Underworld episode, prompts a quite long pause for some kind of reflection or reaction, whether or not matched by a gesture. Further nuance is added according to whether bass notes (indicating the harmony) are tied across speeches; whether or not there is a harmonic disjunction between speeches; and whether a subsequent speech starts close to the sounding of its accompanying bass note or sometime thereafter (indicating a still more pregnant pause for reaction).

A brief passage from Episode 2 reveals all this in operation (see Fig. 3.4). Dafne has just been wondering how she can reveal the terrible news of Euridice's death. Peri has Arcetro jump in on the upbeat with the bass tied over (*Di' pur . . .*), telling her to speak out because the fear of doing so can often be worse than what needs to be said; Dafne gives a quick but measured response that in this case the reverse is true (*Troppo più . . .*), maintaining Arcetro's final harmony but with a minor rather than major triad; Orfeo quickly interjects (*Ah, non sospender più . . .*), over another tied bass note, saying that she should not keep him in a state of turmoil; and Dafne begins her narration (*Per quel vago boschetto*) over a quite different harmony from that on which Orfeo ended, and in a monotone over a long sustained chord. That monotone clearly stems from Dafne's attempt to assert a matter-of-fact tone. But Peri has also made another choice here: one might have expected Dafne to pause so as to gather herself before beginning her tale, but she starts (too?) quickly, as if any such pause would make her lose her courage to continue.

Gagliano also had advice for the role of the messenger in *Dafne* describing Apollo's pursuit of Dafne, her resistance, and then her metamorphosis into a laurel (the role was played in Mantua by the singer who played Arcetro in *Euridice*):

The part of this Messenger is most important: it requires expression of the words above everything else. Here I would like to be able to draw from life how it was sung

Fig. 3.4: (Upper) Jacopo Peri, *Le musiche . . . sopra L'Euridice* (Florence: I Marescotti, 1600 [= 1601]), 14, systems 4–5 (Bologna, Museo Internazionale e Biblioteca della Musica). (Lower) Giulio Caccini, *L'Euridice composta in musica* (Florence: Giorgio Marescotti, 1600), 13, systems 3–4 (Bologna, Museo Internazionale e Biblioteca della Musica).

by Signor Antonio Brandi, otherwise called "Il Brandino" . . . for he sang it in such a way that I do not believe one can desire more. His voice is a most exquisite contralto, the delivery and grace of his singing marvelous, and not only does he make you understand the words, but also with gestures and with movements it seems that he insinuates in the spirit a certain something more.[94]

[94] *. . . la parte di questo Nunzio è importantissima ricerca espressiva di parole oltre ad ogn'altra. Qui vorrei poter ritrarre al vivo, come fu cantata dal signor Antonio Brandi,*

Here Gagliano notes that although correct delivery of the words (*pronuntiatio*) is essential, it is not sufficient, and must be accompanied by appropriate gestures and movements that would have conveyed meaning in ways that can be difficult to recover today. But some insight into how they did so can be gained from the gestural codes operating in contemporary painting, from some descriptions of actors of the time that move beyond just generic praise or blame, and from contemporary treatises on acting, perhaps the most notable of which is *Il corago*. The last has two chapters on the manner of performing theatrical works with music and without (emphasizing hand gestures over other bodily actions), plus another two on the handling of the chorus and its movements, including choreography.[95] Much of this advice is commonsensical, including the need both for individual characters and (in general) for the chorus to stay downstage so that they can be heard, and for them not to turn their back to the audience. In terms of gesture, the general principle is that such actions must clarify and emphasize the content of the text without laboring or somehow replacing it. In the case of musical recitative, gestures will be more measured, given that the delivery of the text itself its slower, meaning that they must be carefully controlled and done more broadly to match the pace of the words.[96] A slight exception is made for deities (particularly Infernal ones), who might use gestures more frequently and with greater nuance; while in the case of messengers reporting an offstage death, their actions must also convey those of the person involved at the time.[97]

altrimenti il Brandino . . . per ciò che egli la cantò talmente, ch'io non credo, che si possa desiderar più, la voce, è di contralto esquisitissima, la pronunzia, e la grazia del cantare maravigliosa, ne solo vi fa intendere le parole ma co' gesti, e co' movimenti par che v'imprima nell'animo un non sò che da vantaggio.

95 P. Fabbri and Pompilio (eds.), *Il corago*, 89–102 (Chap. 15, "Del modo di recitare in musica"; Chap. 16, "Del modo di recitare semplice"; Chap. 17, "Dei cori"; Chap. 18, "Dei balli e passeggi").

96 P. Fabbri and Pompilio (eds.), *Il corago*, 90: *Come che il recitar cantando va più adagio che il recitar parlando, è forza che anche il gestire vada più tardo sì che la mano non finisca prima della voce al che sarà di vuopo di muoverla dal bel principio molto tardo et il gesto deverà esser largo.* Ibid., 96: *Devesi sempre generalmente osservare che il gesto finisca con il periodo e con il concetto che l'uomo dice poiché dà più grazia e fa maggiormente imprimere nelli ascoltanti quello di che si parla, intendendo sempre che non si devino fare che il gesto sia per accompagnamento delle parole e non le parole accompagnamento del gesto, dovendosi sempre regolare da quelle e fare or più presto or più tardi secondo la pronunzia della parole avvertendo che non sieno anco tanto frequenti che impedischino il recitare, se però non dovessino essere tali per l'occasione che bene spesso si porge di rappresentare qualche parte ridicola come nelle commedie spessissimo accade.* That greater flexibility allowed to comic characters is typical.

97 Ibid., 92: for deities, *non disdirà né sarà indecenza il gestire un poco più frequente e con maggiore finezza più e manco secondo la materia di che favellano.* Ibid., 95: for messengers, *Tal volta*

At times, the advice in *Il corago* is reminiscent of Marco da Gagliano's for his *Dafne*: for example, performers taking individual roles should not move while singing so as to preserve a consistent vocal delivery, but only during pauses covered by instrumental music (Gagliano suggests the same for the prologue).[98] At others, it is just obvious: any singer performing successfully on the stage must also be a good actor, and singers lacking such ability, however excellent in other ways, are generally less well received than perfect actors with only average singing voices and musical training.[99] But this also echoes Vincenzo Galilei's advice in his *Dialogo della musica antica, et della moderna* (1581) that those seeking to create the best musical declamation would be well advised to imitate the skilled actor in terms of inflection and pacing.[100] The well-known case of Virginia Andreini (née Ramponi), one of the best actors of her generation, also proves the point: she was able to take the title role in Rinuccini and Monteverdi's *Arianna* (1608) at a late stage (as a replacement for the young singer Caterina Martinelli, who died prematurely) with great success and to universal praise. Indeed, it seems likely that the role was expanded – not least by way of an extended lament – precisely to take advantage of Andreini's abilities.[101]

Pictorial representations, possibly of Virginia Andreini, also provide some hints of the vocabulary of gestures. Domenico Fetti's *Bacchus and Ariadne on Naxos* (1611–13?) is generally associated with her performance in Monteverdi's opera: here Ariadne gestures upward with her right hand, her left hand across her chest; and her downward gaze meets that of

accaderà narrare la morte di qualche eroe et il modo, nel qual caso sarà necessario rappresentare i gesti di colui del quale narra la morte.

98 Ibid., 91: *Se nel recitare commune si deve evitare il parlare caminando, massime con velocità, tanto più si deve fuggire nel canto, quale notabilmente si altera e guasta con il moto.* As for stage movement, *i passeggi si devono di quando in quando tramezzare al canto, nel qual tempo si doverebbe sonare, o ritornello deve fare a proposito . . .*

99 Ibid., 91: *Sopra tutto per esser buon recitante cantando bisognerebbe esser anche buono recitante parlando . . . così al co[mun]e del teatro sodisfazione maggiore hanno dato i perfetti istrioni con mediocre voce e perizia musicale.* Compare also Leone de' Sommi's comment that bad plays could be redeemed by good actors, but even the best plays would fail in the hands of unskilled ones; De' Sommi, *Quattro dialoghi* . . ., ed. Marotti, 39 (trans. in Blanchard-Rothmuller, "Leone Ebreo de' Sommi's *Four Dialogues on Stage Presentations*," 127).

100 Vincenzo Galilei, *Dialogo della musica antica, et della moderna* (Florence: Giorgio Marescotti, 1581), 89; Galilei, *Dialogue on Ancient and Modern Music*, 224–25.

101 See Carter, "Lamenting Ariadne"; Monteverdi's opera is now lost save for Arianna's lament on being abandoned by Teseo (Theseus), which had a wide dissemination at the time. For a broader discussion of *commedia dell'arte* actors and their musical abilities, see Wilbourne, *Seventeenth-Century Opera and the Sound of the Commedia dell'Arte.*

Bacchus, whose left arm is the active one.[102] This matches the advice in *Il corago* (in Chapter 16: "Del modo di recitare semplice") on using gestures to represent various emotional states (anger, entreaty, grief, despair, etc.): the arms and hands should not move both in the same way, and one side of the body (normally the right) should always take the lead. Fetti also emphasizes the importance of the gaze and facial expressions (*Il corago* is silent on both), and, especially in the case of Ariadne, how the line of sight (she looks downward) can act as a counterpoint to gesture (she points upward). Such finely tuned details may not have been noticed in the case of the actual performance of *Arianna* (done before a large audience), but they would certainly have made an impact in the much smaller theatrical spaces typical of many courtly performances, including, of course, *Euridice.*

This seems to have been the case in the performance of a sacred dialogue by Ottavio Rinuccini in the chapel of Archduchess Maria Magdalena, the wife of Grand Duke Cosimo II, in 1619. The performance by the singer Arcangela Paladini was described by the poet and playwright Jacopo Cicognini, who was familiar enough with best theatrical practice:

> She represented St. Cecilia in action and in song with so graceful and devout a manner, given that not only with the sound of her truly angelic voice, but also with superhuman gestures and movements, she expressed the words and their conceits. At times she let forth pure rays of humility and devotion by raising her gaze upwards; at others, she seemed to burn with seraphic love by way of her ardent countenance; and at others still – as the subject of her song required – her face made apparent a serene and iridescent saintly joy. Thus, with sweet force did she so vividly impress upon hearts each emotion that the astonished listeners seemed transported from their bodies.[103]

Il corago applies similar rules to the handling of the chorus as used in tragedies and pastoral plays: the hands, face, and eyes are responsible for

[102] Wilbourne, *Seventeenth-Century Opera and the Sound of the Commedia dell'Arte*, 56–58, 87–89. Fetti's painting is readily available at https://commons.wikimedia.org/wiki/File:Arianna_e_Bacco_nell%27isola_di_Nasso_by_Domenico_Fetti_1611.jpg.

[103] From Jacopo Cicognini 's dedication (dated 22 April 1619) to *Versi sacri cantati nella cappella della Serenissima Arciduchessa d'Austria G. Duchessa di Toscana del Signor Ottavio Rinuccini* (Florence: Zanobi Pignoni, 1619), given in Solerti, *Gli albori del melodramma*, 2: 337–38: *la quale con sì graziosa e devota maniera rappresentò con l'azione e col canto Santa Cecilia . . . perciocché non solo col tuono di voce veramente angelica, ma con gesti e movimenti sovraumani esprimeva le parole e concetti spirando talora da gli occhi sollevati in alto purissimi raggi d'umiltà e devozione; talora infiammata nel sembiante pareva che ardesse di serafico amore, e, secondo che la materia del canto richiedeva, talora se li rimirava la fronte d'una santa letizia serena e scintillante, di maniera che con dolce forza imprimeva ne' cuori qualunque affetto sì vivamente che gli ascoltanti, attoniti, rassembravano rapiti fuori di sé stessi . . .*

underlining the text and revealing precise emotional states. The chief difference is that its members must preferably act in unison as if they were a single person, each making the same gesture at the same time (*il medesimo gesto e nel'istesso tempo*).[104] When the main characters speak to the chorus, they should gesture not to any individual but, rather, to the group, using two hands and turning the head and the body while keeping the feet in one place.[105] However, *Il corago* also allows a similar distinction to Angelo Ingegneri's between a "stable" chorus and a "mobile" one. In the latter case, some members of the chorus separate themselves from the group and therefore have greater freedom of action until they switch back into place, but if they sing together, they should still gesture in similar ways so as to preserve a sense of movement in harmony.[106] The same is true if the chorus is required to dance, as a whole or in groups, as would have been the case at the end of *Euridice* in "Biondo arcier, che d'alto monte." Indeed, choreographing the movements of the chorus both within the dramatic action or in any final *ballo* was a matter of significant concern: *Il corago* devotes an entire chapter to it (18: "Dei balli e passeggi") explaining how to create a sense of synchronization on the one hand, and variety on the other, in terms of the chorus's position on the stage (at the front, back, or on either side), and in its various entrances and exits.[107] However, the relatively small stage designed by Cigoli must have posed some challenges in this regard.

Rinuccini would probably have been the original stage director for *Euridice*. He also needed to be concerned with coordinating movement backstage no less than with what was done in view of the audience. This was particularly the case given that Peri's score, unlike Monteverdi's for *Orfeo*, contains no purely instrumental music to provide additional flexibility for actors entering or leaving the stage, or for the two changes of set; nor is it clear how any could have been improvised given Peri's very limited

[104] P. Fabbri and Pompilio (eds.), *Il corago*, 98.

[105] Ibid., 96: when a single actor *parla con molti, sì come accade nelle tragedie che bene spesso parla con i cori, non deve gestire verso uno solo ma con ambe le mani volgendo destramente la testa e la vita intorno senza però muovere i piedi.*

[106] Ibid., 91: *I cori quando faranno le parti d'attore useranno e gesti e moti più naturali e frequenti che quando imitano quelli che cantano e darà non poca grazia se quando più persone vengano cantando insieme in un medesimo sentimento et affetto, averanno anche i gesti simili, perché così ancora si vedrà l'armonia dei gesti.*

[107] Ibid., 99: *Compariscono i cori in scena più volte e perciò sarà uffizio del corago il fare che non sempre faccino la medesima uscita e la medesima entrata; potrà dunque farli uscire talora tutti dalle strade vicine al foro seguendo l'un dreto all'altro mentre cantano; talora da tutte le strade, talora tutti a un tempo con aprire il foro, talora in un modo, talora in un altro secondo la varietà delle figure che dovranno fare nei passeggi et il numero di essi . . .*

number of instruments (primarily forming the continuo group) that he describes in his preface, unless (to follow a suggestion in *Il corago*) they simply arpeggiated a single chord for as long as was needed.[108] In the case of those set changes, however, there may have been other ways to cover them. As we have seen in Table 3.4, the anonymous stage directions added to one surviving copy of the libretto note that the Underworld set appeared with "great noise" (*con gran rumore*), in part, no doubt, from the movement of the scenery but also, it seems, in a manner also suggested by Nicola Sabbatini as a way of distracting the audience (see Chapter 2). Add to that the movement of the chorus prior to exiting the stage at the ends of Episodes 3 and 4, and the audience's attention may have been sufficiently diverted from the otherwise rather obvious set changes forced by Cigoli's design of the stage.

Reading *Euridice*

Any entertainment presented as part of a royal wedding celebration was bound to have messages, both private and public. Consequently, there was more to *Euridice* than just moving its audience by way of powerful narratives or fine singing. The libretto's repeated references to *diletto, gioia, riso, stupore* or their opposites (*pietà, spavento, terrore*) were clearly designed to dictate a range of responses across a wide emotional spectrum. However, there are also passages where the characters onstage seem to speak across the footlights, as it were, such as when the shepherd warns against the impermanence of youth and beauty (l. 264: *mirate, donne mie*), or the Infernal spirits say that not everyone can be an Orpheus (l. 574: *O figli della terra*). The most obvious example of such address occurs, of course, in the prologue. As in most such cases in the early history of opera, La Tragedia provides both an explanation and an excuse for the novelty of the genre, making it clear that she is not here to sing of tragic subjects on sad and tearful stages. Such things should be banished from royal roofs (l. 9: *Lungi, via lungi pur da' regii tetti*) – that is, the Palazzo Pitti – because she has come to arouse sweeter emotions (*più dolci affetti*) such that everyone inspired by Apollo will follow in her new path. Cigoli's design for *Euridice* may have represented ancient ruins on the proscenium arch,

108 Ibid., 91. The advice (cited above) to have stage movement covered by instrumental music calls for an appropriate ritornello, or other music, or at least arpeggiating gracefully above a single bass note (*nel qual tempo si doverebbe sonare, o ritornello deve fare a proposito, o altre note o almeno arpeggiare su la medesima corda con grazia*).

but, clearly, a new model of Classical drama was being played out beneath them.[109] La Tragedia then speaks directly to Maria de' Medici (l. 17: *Vostro, Regina, fia cotanto alloro*), whose brow will be adorned by laurels greater than ever seen in ancient Athens or Rome. As she turns to her (l. 21: *Tal per voi torno*), she says that on the occasion of the royal nuptials she tempers her songs to happier strings so as to cause sweet delight (*dolce diletto*). While the Seine prepares her crown, robes, and thrones, Maria should give her ear to Orfeo's song. But the question now is what Maria was meant to hear within it.

La Tragedia's reference to Apollo is reinforced by Orfeo in his opening speech, "Antri ch'a' miei lamenti" (in Episode 2). After celebrating the fact that he need lament no more, he urges on the day (ll. 113–19):

Sferza, Padre cortese,
a' volanti destrier le groppe e 'l dorso.
Spegni nell'onde omai,
spegni o nascondi i fiammeggianti rai.
Bella Madre d'Amor, dall'onde fora
sorgi, e la nott'ombrosa
di vaga luce scintillando indora.

[Kind father, whip / the shoulders and back of the flying steeds. / Now extinguish in the waves, / extinguish or hide the flaming rays. / Fair mother of Amor, up from the waves / now rise, and gild shadowy night / sparkling with beautiful light.]

His appeal to Apollo, guiding the chariot of the sun, and then Venus (*Madre d'Amor*) as the night-bearing moon, reflects a typical eagerness to consummate his marriage. Rinuccini may also have been thinking of the original intended location of the performance of *Euridice*, in the Sala delle Statue, which contained statues of Apollo and Venus.[110] But these two deities had a very particular place within nuptial iconographies that also situate *Euridice* very clearly within the 1600 festivities as a whole. Indeed, the entire sequence of entertainments staged in Florence, from the banquet in the Salone dei Cinquecento to *Il rapimento di Cefalo* – passing through *Euridice* and the *festa* in the Riccardi gardens – worked according to a scheme that had strong narrative and iconographical traditions that need to be deciphered with some care.

[109] See also the comments on the prologue to *Euridice* in Riccò, *Dalla zampogna all'aurea cetra*, 139–56.

[110] Saladino, "L'arredo statuario della Sala delle Nicchie."

The mythological archetype for such celebrations was the wedding of Peleus, one of the Argonauts, and the sea-goddess, Thetis.[111] She is successfully wooed, and tamed, by a mortal into a union that mixed divine and human bloodlines; their wedding is attended and celebrated by the Olympians; and they bear a son, the great hero Achilles. The bones of the story are found in Homer (*Iliad* 24: 59–63), and it had a rich tradition thereafter. Thus it offers one underpinning for Annibale Carracci's (1560–1609) grand fresco cycle in the vault of the gallery of the Palazzo Farnese in Rome, done between 1598 and 1600 (so recent thinking mostly goes): it is commonly, though not universally, agreed that this was created in association with the wedding of Duke Ranuccio I of Parma (*r.* 1592–1622) and Margherita Aldobrandini (1588–1646) – the niece of Cardinal Pietro Aldobrandini and great-niece of Pope Clement VIII – which took place on 7 May 1600 after long negotiations. In the center of the vault is a large-scale representation of the triumph of Bacchus and Ariadne, paired on either side by representations – done by Annibale's brother, Agostino (1557–1602) – of Aurora and Cephalus (see *CW*Fig. 3.10), and, by one reading, of Thetis being transported across the sea for her wedding to Peleus.[112] Other frescoes and related images in the vault deal with different mythical lovers and related subjects: Diana and Endymion, Venus and Anchises, Polyphemus and Galatea, Jove and Europa, Jove and Ganymede, Hero and Leander, Perseus and Andromeda, and, of course, Orpheus and Eurydice. The stories associated with Ariadne and with Cephalus – as with some others represented here – might seem problematic for weddings: Ariadne had just been abandoned by Theseus, and Cephalus was attached to Procris. The notion that such mortal relationships were a minor inconvenience to be trumped by divine intervention certainly played a role in the choice of *Il rapimento di Cefalo* for the 1600 festivities, we shall see. But there were other messages to be conveyed as well.

The central prominence in the Galleria Farnese of Bacchus and Ariadne stems from Catullus's (d. 54 BCE) Poem 64. This begins with the story of how Peleus first saw and fell enamored of Thetis on his voyage with the

[111] For a longer version of the following discussion of mythological archetypes and their role in the epithalamic tradition, see Carter, "Epyllia and Epithalamia."

[112] For the conflicting identifications, see Ginzburg, *La Galleria Farnese*, 16 (and n. 63). The subject has been interpreted as Galatea (which all art historians now refute), as Glaucus and Scylla, as Thetis led to her wedding (e.g., by Proteus or Nereus), and as Venus carried by a Triton to the same or a different wedding. The reading as Thetis stems from Valerius Flaccus, *Argonautica* 1: 130–33, and it is endorsed in Colonna, *La galleria dei Carracci in Palazzo Farnese a Roma*, plate 13, although it remains a matter of contention. Robertson, *The Invention of Annibale Carracci*, 143, notes the problem but prefers to sit on the fence.

Argonauts, thereby establishing the main scene, their wedding. All Thessaly has come to Peleus's palace, leaving the fields unplowed and cattle untended, and the populace admires its rich decoration with the royal marriage bed at its heart. This prompts Catullus into a long digression (ll. 50–264) describing the bed's coverlet, embroidered with the story of Ariadne's desertion by Theseus, his ill-fated return to Thebes, and Bacchus's arrival to rescue the maid. This digression is an *ekphrasis* – a vivid description of a work of art – which, in turn, invokes rhetorical devices associated with *enargeia*, that is, bringing a scene to life in the minds of listeners as if they were actually present at what is being described or narrated. After the inset-tale, Catullus then returns to his main subject (ll. 265–383). The Thessalians leave the palace: the poet compares their flocking through the doors with the waves stirred up by Zephyr as Aurora (dawn) heralds the day (ll. 269–77). They are replaced by the gods – Chiron, Peneus, Prometheus, Jove, and Juno – arriving at the celebrations. While they feast, the Three Fates address Peleus and announce the impending arrival of the bride that very evening to consummate the marriage (ll. 323–37), and they sing of the future birth of Achilles and of his triumphs in the Trojan War (ll. 338–83).

Catullus uses Poem 64 to contrast the Golden Age – when the gods would celebrate with mortals – with that of Iron (ll. 384–408), when hideous crimes have spoiled the land, and the gods have deserted mankind. That depressing ending would inevitably be reversed in subsequent epithalamia (in honor of weddings) or similar poetry where the marriage being celebrated, its consummation (and the bride's loss of virginity), and its procreative consequences, offer the prospect of a new age of peace and prosperity.[113] The Florentines were eager enough to take advantage of the rhetoric in 1600 in extolling the virtues and benefits of a Medici Queen of France, and signs of rich fecundity were apparent on all sides during the festivities.[114] Bringing entertainments into the scheme, however, brought into play various strands apparent in other Classical epithalamia drawing on Peleus and Thetis, such as the one written for the marriage of the Roman Emperor Honorius and Maria (daughter of Flavius Stilicho) in or around

[113] Ketterer, "Classical Sources and Thematic Structure in the Florentine *intermedi* of 1589," 219–20, notes the reversal in Virgil's fourth *Eclogue*, the Golden Age rhetoric of which was appropriated in particular by the Medici in the fifteenth and sixteenth centuries.

[114] Even the libretto of *Euridice* printed by Cosimo Giunti may have elaborated the allegory. The lily in the central woodblock on the title page has its petals closed, but the much larger device on the *verso* of the final printed page (which also appears in earlier Giunti prints) has them open, dropping seeds that are gathered by *putti*.

398 CE by Claudian (*c.* 370–404 CE). Its preface sets the stage as the feasting at the Olympian wedding: Chiron offers the loving-cup to Jove, Peneus turns water into nectar, Terpsichore joins the celebration – leading the dance – and on the seventh day, Apollo sings of the birth of Achilles. In the epithalamium itself, Honorius laments his too-long wait for his bride; (l. 46) Amor, moved by the plaint, summons Venus from the palace of Vulcan; (l. 122) she orders a Triton to take her to the wedding, accompanied by cupids and nereids;[115] (l. 180) she arrives in Milan and banishes the god of war given that this should be a time of peace and joy; (l. 202) she consecrates the union, invoking Hymen and the Three Graces, and offers instructions on decorating the marriage bed with a canopy richer than the one Lydia (the country) made for Pelops (presumably, for his wedding to Hippodameia) or the Bacchae for Lyaeus (Bacchus); (l. 228) she acts as *pronuba* (a female attendant leading the bride to the groom) to bring Maria from her home, praising her beauty ("Redder than roses thy lips . . . Pinker thy fingers than Aurora's . . . If Bacchus, Ariadne's lover, could transform his mistress' garland into a constellation how comes it that a more beauteous maid has no crown of stars?");[116] and as Honorius takes Maria to her new abode, (l. 295) a chorus of soldiers consoles the father of the bride with thoughts of grandchildren. The text is also full of other mythological references, most of which will be familiar by now: to Jove and Europa, Apollo and Daphne, Diana and Endymion, and so on.

Claudian's text sanctioned the conflation of the marriage of a late Roman emperor with that of Peleus and Thetis – the basis for similar comparisons in Renaissance princely weddings – and the presence of a deity (Venus) aiding a mortal union. But it also provided a convenient set of mythological subjects, and even a potential iconographical program, appropriate for nuptial celebrations. These epithalamia further explain the frequent references to Aurora in these wedding entertainments, with the bride as beautiful as the rose-tinted dawn, whose cheeks flush less from timidity than to mark potential sexual fulfillment. No less important, however, is Claudian's bringing another element into the mix: he follows Homer by having Apollo sing at the wedding of Peleus and Thetis, and Pindar by including the Muses; this differs from Catullus, who has only the Fates perform their prophesy of glorious progeny.

[115] Hence the Venus (rather than Thetis) reading of Agostino Carracci's fresco in the Galleria Farnese.

[116] To use Maurice Platnauer's translation (in the Loeb Classical Library).

The purpose of the cast of mythological characters that appeared in the 1600 Florentine festivities – as elsewhere in the north Italian courts in the early modern period – now becomes clearer, as do their roles in entertainments that function as inset-tales, as it were, within the broader epithalamic narrative created by the entire celebration. If Apollo and Terpsichore were present at the wedding of Peleus and Thetis – so Claudian has it – this opened the door to all the arts acting in the service of celebrating princely nuptials, including drama, music, and dance. For example, the banquet on the evening of the wedding ceremony took place in a richly decorated Salone dei Cinquecento that included two grottoes, one containing statues of Hymen and Lucina (the latter the goddess of childbirth), and the other of Apollo and Mnemosyne (mother of the Muses), with six other niches holding statues representing the virtues (Glory, Justice, Peace, etc.). At the end of the banquet, two chariots emerged from those grottoes, one containing Juno and the other Minerva. In a dialogue – to a text by Battista Guarini with music by Emilio de' Cavalieri – Juno disputed Minerva's claim that she is a fitting *pronuba* for Maria de' Medici at the nuptials (a role usually taken by Venus, as we have seen): these are not matters for a military goddess, Juno says. However, the two eventually agree to set their differences aside so as to join forces in honor of the Queen of France, predicting that she will bear a famous conqueror of the Orient who will recover the lost empire and extend the boundaries of the French kingdom (*Da te sorga un famoso / domator d'Orïente, che l'impero / perduto acquisti e spieghi il regno augusto*).[117]

A similar prediction was made during the *festa* in the gardens of the Palazzo Riccardi on Sunday 8 October. Here a group of Tuscan peasant girls presented fruits of the harvest to the queen, singing prettily; various military exercises and games were also introduced by singers representing Pindar and Poliziano, performing to the sound of instrumentalists hidden in the trees.[118] Pindar was an obvious Classical choice given his panegyrical victory odes, while Poliziano harked back to the fifteenth-century Florentine "golden age" of Lorenzo "Il Magnifico" (the poet also provided a precedent for *Euridice*, we shall see). Then came Diana to preface a hunt: she compares Maria de' Medici's beauty with that of Aurora, says that she embodies the (military) virtues of Bellona and Minerva, and predicts that her marriage will bring illustrious offspring who will extend the glory of

[117] The text of the dialogue is given in *SolMBD*, 231–38.

[118] For the texts, see *SolMBD*, 239–59 (although the attribution to Chiabrera is incorrect; see Chapter 1, note 46).

Tuscany and France from north to south, and east to west, while also (she emphasizes) seeking to tame the Ottoman Empire and recover Jerusalem for the Christians. This explains the similar reference in the *Dialogo di Giunone e Minerva* done three days earlier, and perhaps also the reference to the brave "warrior" in the penultimate stanza of the final chorus of *Euridice*. Such comments were apposite: it was widely felt that Henri IV had too close a relationship with the Turks and was not filled with sufficient Christian zeal to undertake a crusade.[119]

Gabriello Chiabrera's text for *Il rapimento di Cefalo*, the opera that concluded the festivities, builds on these themes. His choice of subject was clearly influenced by Pierre de Ronsard's (1524–85) poem *Le Ravissement de Cephale, divisé en trois poses* (no. 17 in his fourth book of Odes, first published in 1550), where the Aurora/Cephalus story is presented as an inset-tale (told by Naïs) in an epithalamic context associated with the wedding of Peleus and Thetis.[120] Like Ronsard, Chiabrera fudges the presence of Cephalus's mortal beloved, Procris (who is dead in Ronsard's account and barely mentioned by Chiabrera), even though she appears prominently in the standard versions of the myth (for example, Ovid, *Metamorphoses* 7: 661–862). The prologue to *Il rapimento* is delivered by La Poesia (Poetry), surrounded by Apollo and the Muses. In contrast to her mute representation in Cigoli's design for the proscenium arch of *Euridice*, here she speaks, praising Maria de' Medici's beauty, which is so great as to draw jealous complaint from Thetis in the sea, Iris in the clouds, and even Hesperus in the night sky. La Poesia also predicts military glory for Maria's sons, as did Minerva at the banquet and Diana in the Riccardi gardens. Within the opera itself, and in addition to Aurora's exchanges with Cefalo, Titone (Tithonus) laments his abandonment by Aurora; Oceano complains to Febo/Apollo that the sun has not yet risen (because Aurora has abandoned her duties); Amore explains that he has wounded Aurora as proof of his valor; Notte (Night) objects to the non-appearance of dawn and will seek Giove's (Jove's) counsel; the earth-goddess Berecintia grumbles about the absence of sunlight and is reassured by Amore; Amore is then summoned to a council of the gods and urged to set matters right (by having Cefalo reciprocate Aurora's love), which he does; and Aurora tricks Cefalo to give her his hand, whereupon she whisks him into the heavens. A final chorus of hunters praises the power of love

119 For an overview, see Isom-Verhaaren, *Allies with the Infidel*.

120 Pierre de Ronsard, *Les Quatre Premiers Livres des odes* (Paris: Guillaume Cavellart, 1550), fols. 127–133v. Ronsard's rather odd term, "pose," appears to relate to the strophe, antistrophe, and epode typical of the Pindaric ode.

(Cefalo is silent), with a refrain celebrating the ineffable ardor that summons the heart into heaven's domains (ll. 608–9: *Ineffabile ardore, / ch'a gli alberghi del Ciel richiama il core*). Michelangelo Buonarroti *il giovane* struggled in his description of the 1600 festivities to find a moral to fit: Cefalo discovers that all things on earth have their origins from the gods, and that it is not a worthy place for noble souls, who can only achieve their just desserts and happiness in heaven.[121] It is not clear whether the Florentines took greater pleasure in another possible allegory, given that Maria de' Medici (as rose-tinted Aurora) had succeeded in gaining the hand of Henri IV (Cefalo) only after his official divorce from Marguerite de Valois and the death of his mistress, Gabrielle d'Estrées.

These epithalamic contexts offer new insight into *Euridice* in terms of its place both within the Florentine festivities and in the broader literary tradition. Orpheus is connected with Peleus by virtue of being a fellow Argonaut (according to Apollonius of Rhodes). The story of his relationship with Eurydice also functions as an inset-tale in the two main sources with which Rinuccini was clearly familiar: in Virgil's *Georgics* 4: 453–527, the context is Aristaeus and his bees (he pursues Eurydice, causing her death); while in Ovid's *Metamorphoses* 10: 1–85, Orpheus's wedding is contrasted with the happier one of Iphis and Ianthe, where Hymen does a better job of making a successful union. Another source, however notional, for Rinuccini was Poliziano's *Fabula di Orfeo* (1479–80), rich in Florentine resonances if only by way of its author. However, he needed to deal with the problems of the ending of the myth, given the circumstances in which *Euridice* was performed. He also inserted a number of new elements typical of the epithalamic tradition: hence the (unusual) choice of Venere to lead Orfeo to the Underworld; the invocations to Amore and Imeneo (Hymen); the repeated references to Apollo, including the final chorus ("Biondo arcier, che d'alto monte") that spends far more time extolling the "blonde archer" and his creation of the Muses than it does Orfeo's achievement; and even, perhaps, the military reference in that chorus's penultimate stanza. And while Orfeo and Euridice's return from the Underworld occurs toward the end of the day represented by the time span of the opera, Rinuccini also invokes what is now a familiar set of images: Euridice had been as pale as a lily at her death but now has rose-red cheeks (ll. 664–69: *qual palidetto giglio / dolcemente or languia la bella sposa, / or qual*

[121] Buonarroti, *Descrizione delle felicissime nozze . . .*, 34: *Imperò che diede a conoscere per questa guisa il Poeta nella figura di Cefalo, le terrene bellezze avere dal Cielo lor dependenza, e de gli animi singolari, e gentili non essere il basso mondo stanza accettevole, o degno albergo.*

purpurea rosa / il bel volto di lei venia vermiglio), while the earth smiles and grows more beflowered than at any dawn (ll. 682–83: *e più ride la terra, e più s'infiora, / al tramontar del dì ch'in su l'aurora*).

Another of Rinuccini's elaborations is no less significant. For both Virgil and Ovid, it is Orpheus's failure of the test to lead Eurydice from the Underworld without looking back at her that is the most significant element of the story. Virgil describes Orpheus's descent to the Underworld and the impact of his singing there; he also says that Eurydice's return was granted by Proserpina (Pluto is barely mentioned), and when Orpheus fails the test, Virgil comes up with Eurydice's words of accusation and regret. Ovid devotes much more space to Orpheus's own plea to Pluto and Proserpina, which he invents in powerful rhetorical terms: Orpheus seeks to assure them that he has come only to rescue his bride; he invokes Pluto's own love for Proserpina; and he says that if he is unsuccessful, he is resolved to die so as to stay at Eurydice's side. Ovid then relates how the gods of the Underworld were moved to tears, and that Pluto and Proserpina could not refuse his request. Orpheus's failure of the test and his second loss of Eurydice take up fewer lines, while Eurydice is granted only a single word: "Farewell."

What Rinuccini adds, however, is the extended debate between Orfeo and Plutone, then involving Proserpina, Radamanto, and Caronte. Plutone asks Orfeo why he is there; Orfeo says that he has come lamenting and weeping so as to seek mercy (ll. 454–56: *per impetrar mercede, / . . . / volsi piangendo e lagrimando il piede*); Plutone admits that his singing and accents would not be in vain if laments and tears could gain mercy in his kingdom; and Orfeo reminds Plutone of his love of Proserpina and asks that he might once more see the light of Euridice's eyes and hear the sound of her sweetest words (ll. 470–71: *a queste orecchie il suono / rendi delle dolcissime parole*). Plutone then admits that he is moved by some new emotion (l. 477–78: *non so qual novo affetto / m'intenerisce il petto*) – no doubt a hint at the power of Peri's "new" music – but that Orfeo's prayers are butting against a too-harsh law sculpted in unyielding diamond (ll. 479–80: *Ma troppo dura legge, / legge scolpita in rigido diamante, / contrasta a' preghi tuoi, misero amante*).

Thus far Rinuccini's text is a plausible elaboration of Ovid. But Plutone's repetition of *legge* prompts Orfeo to take an entirely unexpected turn: he who governs and rules others is free of all law (ll. 482–83: *Ahi che pur d'ogni legge / sciolto è colui che gl'altri affrena e regge*). Orfeo seems to realize that he has crossed a line: he quickly reverses course (l. 484: *Ma tu . . .*) back to the question of pity (an emotion that can be aroused by poetry and music), and to the fact that Plutone has himself been in love. He also tells Plutone to observe (l. 494: *Mira, Signor, deh mira*) how Proserpina is sighing and weeping at Orfeo's tears, and likewise (l. 498: *Mira, Signor, deh mira* – an unusually awkward repetition) how the other spirits around them seem moved to an extreme. Proserpina intervenes directly, begging Plutone for his love for her to ease Orfeo's lament: the lesson would not have been lost on Maria de' Medici in terms of how to make a royal husband bend to her will. Orfeo, in turn, asks if Plutone can still deny mercy, then says that it surely matters little if Euridice is released, given that they will soon be back at the time of their death (Ovid has Orpheus make exactly the same point). Plutone, however, returns to the issue of the law. Radamanto (Caronte in Peri's score) intervenes: just as Jove rules the heavens and Neptune the sea, so should Plutone have free dominion over the Inferno. Given that Rhadamanthus was one of the judges of the Underworld, he speaks with some authority. But this forces Plutone to get to the heart of the matter (ll. 531–32):

Romper le proprie leggi è vil possanza;
anzi reca sovente e biasmo e danno.

[To break one's own laws is a contemptible power; / indeed it often brings both blame and injury.]

Orfeo counters in perfect *stychomythia* (ll. 533–34):

Ma degl'afflitti consolar l'affanno
è pur di regio cor gentil usanza.

[But to console the suffering of the afflicted / is indeed the noble custom of a royal heart.]

Caronte seals the deal: Plutone can make the law as he pleases (l. 539: *fa' pur legge, o gran Re, quanto a te piace*). The decision is made, and Plutone announces that Orfeo may indeed enter the Underworld to regain his bride.

The fact that this action in the Underworld is played in sight of the audience makes it stand out in an opera where so much else takes place offstage and is instead conveyed, conventionally enough, by way of narration (as with Euridice's death, Venere's intervention, and Orfeo and Euridice's eventual return). No less striking is that Orfeo actively participates in this exchange: Striggio and Monteverdi handled things in quite another way (Orfeo is absent from the debate between Plutone and Proserpina), which may say something about the channels of communication between ruler and ruled in Florence versus Mantua. Of course, Rinuccini has little choice but to invent dialogue for Plutone, Proserpina, Radamanto, and Caronte, given that there is no other witness who could narrate Orfeo's encounter with them. However, his own decision – against all the sources – to turn this encounter into a political debate about a ruler's prerogative in matters of law makes this episode central to any messages that *Euridice* conveyed.

Many of the arguments in the Underworld scene in *Euridice* can be linked to recent debates in the Accademia degli Alterati promoted by Lorenzo Giacomini, who argued in favor of the political and civic utility of tragedy: that arousing pity among those in power prompts justice and thence what Plutone grants to Orfeo – clemency.[122] Rinuccini's framing this debate within an antique genre, and Cigoli's between statues of Poetry and Painting on a proscenium also figuring ancient ruins – to be renewed, in effect, by the drama played out on the stage – emphasizes the point still more by virtue of transforming an old genre into something quite new, an achievement bringing significant credit to both poet and composer, and to their princely patrons. It also vitiates the need to create more direct analogies between the characters in *Euridice* and those actually or figuratively present in the audience (for example, the grand duke as Plutone or, in some readings, Orfeo; Proserpina as the grand duchess or Maria de' Medici; Euridice as Florence; and so on).[123] The Medici or their guests did not need to identify with any individual character in any of the entertainments staged during the 1600 festivities to perceive their broader messages about sovereignty, power, and the responsibilities they entailed.

122 Lorenzo Giacomini, *De la purgazione de la tragedia: discorso fatto . . . ne l'Academia degli Alterati ne l'anno MDLXXXVI*, in Weinberg (ed.), *Trattati di poetica e retorica del Cinquecento*, 3: 349: *la misericordia è affetto laudevole, sì che a la divinità è attribuita et essa sola come onnipotente ne la sua estrema perfezione è appropriata, ed attiene alla giustizia che rettamente ci dispone verso gli altri.* For the broader issues, see Bertini, *"Havere a la giustizia sodisfatto"*, 313–36.

123 These kinds of analogies tend to lie at the heart of the readings of *Euridice* proposed in, for example, Bujić, "Figura poetica molto vaga"; De Caro, *"Euridice"*; Harness, "*Le tre Euridici.*" Blocker, "The Accademia degli Alterati and the Invention of a New Form of Dramatic Experience," however, tends to resist them, although we probably disagree on her narrower reading of the opera as a political statement on the part of the Alterati, just as we would on her view of *Euridice* as somehow marginal (both conceptually and physically) within the 1600 festivities.

4 | Conclusions and Consequences

Our inquiry into *Euridice* and its staging has led us down multiple paths. It also opens up further ones both for our understanding of Florentine theatrical practice around 1600, and for ways in which we might best engage with reconstructing this practice today, whether for the benefit of scholars or for broader audiences within or beyond the theatre. The following discussion proceeds down both those paths while also considering some broader issues that emerge from the kind of inquiry undertaken here.

Later Entertainments in the Sala delle Commedie

Every single item in Cresci's inventory of the stage for *Euridice* – and in Cigoli's and Ricoveri's invoices – has been accounted for in our reconstruction of it. Moreover, the materials that Michele Caccini placed in storage near the Teatro degli Uffizi in late August or early September 1601 were reasonably complete. However, the inventory notes that several elements of the sets were in bad condition (the Underworld drops and the moveable rocks; *Cres13–14*) or were declared missing (half the parapet; *Cres7*), while at least one other entry suggests some additional loss (*Cres18*, with twelve rather than fourteen *correnti* used to change the set to and from the Underworld scene). Other parts of the stage construction had also been diverted for other uses once the stage itself was dismantled, notably for the *stanzino* constructed in one of the rooms in the grand duchess's apartment (*Cres 36–42*). Such losses would have needed to be remedied before these materials could be employed again either in their current form or remodeled for some other theatrical purpose. Nevertheless, it was clearly intended that they should be kept available for reuse in some way: otherwise there was no point storing them alongside other stage properties. This would have been entirely normal for most theatres of our period (and later), where the same sets and machines could often reappear (with or without cosmetic changes) in successive entertainments. Indeed, Cigoli's nephew and biographer, Giovanni

Battista Cardi, noted that the sets for *Euridice* were kept and adapted in whole or in part until they went beyond repair.[1]

The Sala delle Commedie seems to have differed from other formal rooms in the Palazzo Pitti (such as the Sala delle Statue) by being used less frequently for other functions; the same is true of the other nearby rooms on a floor of the palace that remained relatively private for the Medici household. In the first decade of the seventeenth century, the main spaces for receiving and lodging guests in the Pitti were on the west wing of the *piano nobile* around the Sala (Grande) dei Forestieri, with the nearby Sala delle Statue being used for official banquets and receptions on special occasions, and for welcoming particularly prominent guests. The ground floor was also treated as a more public space, particularly during the hot summer months.[2] The third floor of the palace and its attics, however, remained largely devoted to rooms for the princes and princesses, and in its more remote corners, for some functionaries (also with storage space for the Guardaroba): guests were accommodated there only in cases of significant demand, as in the 1600 and 1608 wedding festivities.[3] Thus the carpenter Camillo di Benedetto Pieroni dismantled the *Euridice* stage only sometime after 8 February 1600/1, and possibly later in the spring or summer prior to

[1] See Battelli (ed.), *Vita di Lodovico Cardi Cigoli*, 27, and Camerota, *Linear Perspective in the Age of Galileo*, 106: *Sopraggiungendo le nozze della regina di Francia fece la scena, la qual fu così stimata che ancora in questi tempi fu conservata, sebbene o di tutta o di parte alcuna volta servendosene, il tempo e gli uomini l'han disfatti e condotta alla fine.*

[2] From 1600 to 1609, Cesare Tinghi often referred to guests being housed on the *piano nobile* in the *stanze solite de' forestieri*; see his *Diario di Ferdinando I e Cosimo II granduca di Toscana* (22 July 1600 to 12 September 1615), BNCF, Capponi 261/1, fols. 63v, 65v, 77v, 86, 90v. He also uses the term *le stanze de' forestieri principi* (fols. 160v, 239v, 278). In the same period, guests could also be housed on the ground floor in *le camere terrene della segreteria vecchia* (fols. 36, 36v, 63v, 189v, 191v); *le camere terrene di Don Giovanni* (fols. 13v, 16v, 63, 95v, 142v); and the *camere terrene* next to those occupied by the grand duke (fols. 135, 135v, 138, 138v, 155v, etc.).

[3] In October 1600, the Duke and Duchess of Mantua were lodged in the rooms on the third floor near Maria de' Medici's, with two chambers and a drawing-room formerly occupied by Don Antonio de' Medici; see the records of Giovanni del Maestro, the *maestro di casa*, in ASF, Carte Strozziane I, 27, fols. 28, 38[*bis*]v (*nelle stanze di contro alla Regina; e se li danno 2 camere et il salotto nel apartamento del Signor Don Antonio*). This would have placed them close to the Sala delle Commedie. For the 1608 festivities, Cardinal d'Este had *le stanze dette già del Signor Don Giovanni [de' Medici] sopra Madama Serenissima*, Cardinal Farnese was placed *sopra alla sala delle fighure in luogo dove stavano già la principessa di Francia* (i.e., Maria de' Medici's former suite above the Sala delle Statue), and Don Giovanni de' Medici had *due camere in su la sala della comedia*; see Tinghi, *Diario di Ferdinando I e Cosimo II*, BNCF, Capponi 261/1, fol. 224. In 1609 various visitors (many on the death of Grand Duke Ferdinando), were lodged *su ad alto nelle stanze dette di Don Antonio, nelle soffitte de' paggi, nelle soffitte dette del Signor Don Giovanni, nelle camere della sala della comedia*, and *nelle camere delli altri anbasciatori in sulla sala della comedia* (ibid., fols. 238v, 248, 251v, 264, 266v).

Michele Caccini's transferring it to the Teatro degli Uffizi.[4] One assumes that it was then reconstructed – and Cigoli's scenery reused – in December 1602, when Giulio Caccini directed a performance of *Euridice* in the Sala delle Commedie (on 5 December), in the presence of Cardinals del Monte and Montalto (neither of whom were present in Florence in October 1600).[5] Again, that stage stayed in place for a fair while, at least until sometime in the middle of 1603, when Camillo Pieroni removed its lanterns (*fornuoli*).[6]

However, some decision was then made to repurpose its materials: on 3 September 1604, Lodovico Cigoli and Giulio Parigi prepared an estimate of the expenses and materials needed to make a new set for comedies (*una sciena da Comedia*) that could be placed over the pastoral set (*sopra la scena a boscaglia*) of *Euridice*. The wording suggests that this new set would replace the Underworld set that (we have seen) was already in disrepair when Michele Caccini placed it in storage in the Teatro degli Uffizi; however, the pastoral set would remain available for use. Cigoli and Parigi estimated a total cost of *sc.*100 for the necessary materials, including *sc.*50 for painting and supplies (*per la pitura e spese del pittore di colori e altro*), plus *sc.*30 for canvas (unless old material could be reused), *sc.*10 for wooden frames (*telai*) for the flats, and another *sc.*10 for ironmongery. Grand Duke Ferdinando signed the order for this work to be done the next day, and on 14 September, Michele Caccini requisitioned wood and canvas for the project from the Fortezza da Basso: his 300 *b.* of canvas was close to what Francesco Ricoveri sewed for the Underworld set of *Euridice* (252 *b.* in *Ric2* and half of the 80 *b.* in *Ric3*).[7] Some of the wording in

4 *SFF* 72, fol. 30: *per la disfacitura della Commedia cioè palcho e prospettiva ch[']era nella sala de' Pitti a tetto.* This is in a series of entries for work done from 8 February 1600/1 to 17 December 1601, for which payment was made on 15 March 1601/2.

5 It has been assumed that this was the premiere of Caccini's full version, although it is possible that it combined Peri's and Caccini's music in a manner similar to, though not necessarily the same as, what was done in October 1600: Cesare Tinghi's diary entry for 5 December 1602 (*SolMBD*, 30) says only that *Euridice* was *ghuidata da Giulio Caccini romano*, although given the seemingly greater presence in the cast of "his" singers, it seems likely that more of Caccini's music was used. Luti, *Don Antonio de' Medici e i suoi tempi*, 127, is incorrect in saying that this performance took place in Don Antonio de' Medici's theatre in the Casino di S. Marco (though the sequence of entertainments for the two cardinals did indeed include comedies performed there): Tinghi is clear that the gentlemen and ladies ascended the stairs (of the Palazzo Pitti) into the room that was (still) called Don Antonio's (*montorno su nella sala detta del Signor Don Antonio*). For this and subsequent performances in the Sala delle Commedie, see also Fantappiè, "Sale per lo spettacolo a Pitti," 140–50.

6 *SFF* 72, fol. 52: *per haver levato i fornuoli alla prospettiva della Commedia nel palazzo.* Pieroni was paid on 10 December 1603 for work done since 26 May 1603.

7 *SFF* 123 (*Memoriale e ricordanze*, 1604–12), fol. 5, is a copy of a document dated 3 September 1604 listing a *Nota di spese e robe che bisognia a fare una sciena da comedia sopra la scena a boscaglie del[']erudice nel palazo de' Pitti tutto per detto di messer Lodovico Cigoli e messer*

Caccini's requisition concerning the wood (for *usci*, *tetti*, and ornamental *regoli*) suggests that this comic set was more architectural in design (and with various three-dimensional elements) than the hanging canvases of the sets for *Euridice*. But replacing the Underworld set with a *sciena da Comedia* made Cigoli's original construction more useful, given that it now catered for two of the three typical stage types long established by Sebastiano Serlio: the pastoral and the comic.

As for the pastoral set, it was presumably used for the revival of Rinuccini's *Dafne* performed on 26 October 1604 for the visit of Duke Ranuccio Farnese of Parma:[8] the work requires a single *scena boschereccia* without any change, and the only special effect is the appearance of the Python (represented as a dragon). But the new *sciena da Comedia* was probably ready in time for the performance in the Sala delle Commedie on 9 December 1604 of an improvised comedy staged by Florentine youths in the manner of *commedia dell'arte* characters (*a uso di zanni et pantalone*), *La inconstanza d'amore*, and then on 13 December, another comedy, *La pazzia di Lelio*, performed by the Compagnia degli Uniti (including Giovanni Battista Andreini), which was followed by one hour of dancing.[9]

The Sala delle Commedie had very little furniture in it when an inventory of the Palazzo Pitti was prepared in the summer of 1607.[10] However, as plans started heating up for the festivities for the next major Medici wedding, of Prince Cosimo and Maria Magdalena of Austria (eventually held in October–November 1608), the grand duke ordered (on 13 July 1607) that various arrangements be put in place for staging comedies, which (by November 1607) involved disassembling and rebuilding the stage and scenery that had been used in the Palazzo Pitti, with, in addition, the provision of new elements for *intermedi*.[11] During the 1608 festivities

Giulio Parigi pittori (i.e., an estimate of likely costs, prepared in consultation with Cigoli and Parigi), with, at the end, the grand duke's order to prepare the set dated 4 September. Ibid., fol. 5v, contains a copy of the list of materials (wood, canvas, etc.) requisitioned by Michele Caccini from the Fortezza da Basso, dated 14 September 1604. The 3 September document is noted in Testaverde, "Nuovi documenti sulle scenografie di Ludovico Cigoli per l'*Euridice* di Ottavio Rinuccini," 318.

[8] For the libretto, a new first signature (A) was printed (Florence: Cristofano Marescotti, 1604), and hence a new title page, to replace the one in otherwise leftover copies of the 1600 edition.

[9] *SolMBD*, 34–35; Burattelli *et al.* (eds.), *Comici dell'arte*, 1: 63, 66, 89. Andreini was also active as a poet and playwright in Florence during this period: his tragedy *La Florinda* was performed in 1603 by the Accademia degli Spensierati (to which he also dedicated his poem *La divina visione* in 1604), and his *La saggia egiziana* (1604), a dialogue in verse in praise of the theatre, was dedicated to Don Antonio de' Medici.

[10] *GM* 422, fol. 65r–65v.

[11] *SFF* 123, fol. 64 (an order to the *depositario*, Vincenzo Medici, to pay *sc.*500 to Cresci *per fare alcuni accomodamenti di scene per comedie e preparamenti pur di comedie*); fol. 73 (Cresci's

themselves, the Sala delle Commedie was the location for Francesco Cini's *veglia*, *Notte d'Amore* (on 22 October). This required three separate sets: the *Cascine* on the western edge of Florence, with mountains in the distance; a garden with flowering trees, loggias, and fountains; and a fantastical land- and seascape (*castelli in aria, mari, monti, rupi, edifizi ardenti e rovinanti*).[12] It also required clouds and flying machines, including (at the end) the characters Aurora and Aura descending from a sky containing a *coro di stelle, e d'Amori*. All this was clearly more elaborate than anything that had been done in the Sala delle Commedie to date. These new sets appear to have been designed by the Florentine artist and engraver Remigio Cantagallina, who constructed a model of them.[13] Cantagallina or his colleagues probably also took advantage of this opportunity to reconfigure the stage itself. The proscenium was presumably extended closer to the full width of the room (22 or 23 *b.*), allowing more space for action. The stage floor also seems to have been lower: a *veglia* involved dramatic episodes separated by communal dancing, so there needed to be a more direct connection between the stage and the main floor of the room by way of steps leading from one to the other.[14] But it is still very hard to imagine how any elaborate machines might have operated within and above the stage itself.

The main play of the 1608 festivities, Michelangelo Buonarroti *il giovane*'s *Il giudizio di Paride*, was performed in the Teatro degli Uffizi (on 25 October) with spectacular *intermedi* in a way that deliberately harked back to the 1589 set for *La pellegrina*.[15] *Notte d'Amore*, however, was closer in function to *Euridice* in 1600, even if it clearly exceeded Rinuccini and Peri's opera in terms of scenic spectacle, and reflected a significant change in taste as to what such entertainments were now required to do. It was repeated the day after its first performance, then on 25 January 1608/9 for

request for more money to pay the cost *per disfare la prospetiva che era nel salone de' Pitti e per rifarla di nuovo sì la prospetiva e palcho così nuovi intermedi*). Cresci then asked for additional payments for the 1608 entertainments in the way he had done in 1600.

12 Camillo Rinuccini, *Descrizione delle feste fatte nelle reali nozze de' serenissimi principi di Toscana Don Cosimo de' Medici, e Maria Maddalena Arciduchessa d'Austria* (Florence: I Giunti, 1608), 32–35. The text was printed as *Notte d'Amore* . . . (Florence: Cristofano Marescotti, 1608), given in *SolMBD*, 261–79.

13 *SFF* 123, fol. 110 (part of an accounting of expenses of the 1608 festivities dated 20 August 1609) includes a payment to Cantagallina of £165 for the model.

14 Rinuccini, *Descrizione delle feste fatte nelle reali nozze*, 32, refers to *una scena bassa a cui si saliva per pochi scalini*.

15 Carter, "A Florentine Wedding of 1608." *Il giudizio di Paride* was then repeated in the Teatro degli Uffizi on 19 November 1608 for the visit of Duke Vincenzo Gonzaga of Mantua (who had missed the October festivities); *SolMBD*, 54.

the visit of the Duke of Nevers, and probably (at least in part) on 25 November 1610 for that of the Spanish ambassador, Don Ferrante Borgia.[16] It further established a pattern that became increasingly common for entertainments in the Palazzo Pitti in the 1610s. But both *Il giudizio di Paride* and *Notte d'Amore* each in their own way reflect a general discomfort with opera in the north Italian courts in the early seventeenth century, in part because it was considered too passive an experience for princely spectators, whose notion of cutting a *bella figura* required something more active by way of dancing or jousting. Entertainments also became longer: *Notte d'Amore* lasted for five hours, whereas *Euridice* took less than two (though in October 1600 it was followed by communal dancing).[17] The increasing amount of spectacle, and the machines needed to create it even in a "temporary" theatre, also reveal other expansionary pressures in the hyper-inflating currency of conspicuous consumption. For the Farnese ambassador in 1600, *Euridice* could still be "very beautiful," despite the simplicity of its staging; in the case of *Notte d'Amore* in 1608, the Modenese Alfonso Fontanelli was impressed, rather, by "beautiful clouds, chariots in the air, and other unusual sights."[18] The administrators of the Ufficio di Monte e Soprassindaci appear to have been concerned about the escalating costs: when they sought to reconcile the finances of the 1608 festivities, they also (it seems) requested sight of the 1600 accounts for purposes of comparison.[19]

There were hardly any entertainments in Carnival 1609/10 because of the one-year period of mourning following the death of Grand Duke Ferdinando I on 3 February 1608/9. But as the court returned to carnival entertainments in 1611 under the new grand duke, Cosimo II, Cresci and his colleagues continued to be involved in providing stages and associated materials for theatrical events, whether in the Palazzo Pitti (for a *balletto* with a text by Ottavio Rinuccini, performed in the *sala detta delle commedie* on 14 February 1610/11), the Palazzo del Parione occupied by Don Giovanni de' Medici (for a staging of *Dafne*, probably Marco da Gagliano's setting, on 9 February 1610/11), or Don Antonio de' Medici's Casino di S. Marco.[20]

[16] *SolMBD*, 45, 57, 59 (the last has an incorrect reference to 23 November 1610).

[17] *SolMBD*, 30 (the performance of *Euridice* directed by Giulio Caccini on 5 December 1602), 45 (*Notte d'Amore*).

[18] *SolMBD*, 45: *bellissime nuvole e carri per l'aria ed altre cose di vista peregrina.*

[19] On 16 March 1610, Cresci sent his various accounts and associated documents for each of the 1608 entertainments, *E più se li è rimandato i libri e le listre della Commedia e banchetto fatto al tempo della Cristianissima di Francia*; *SFF* 123, fol. 116v.

[20] *SFF* 123, fol. 135v has copies of various orders from the grand duke: (21 December 1610) *di far fare la scena de' Pitti per fare una commedia questo Carnevale per loro Altezze Serenissime*; (6 February 1610/11) *per fare accomodare la scena in casa del Illustrissimo et Eccellentissimo*

Those in the Sala delle Commedie tended to follow the pattern of *Notte d'Amore*, alternating dramatic scenes on an elaborate stage with opportunities for communal dancing: Ottavio Rinuccini's *Mascherata di ninfe di Senna* (1613), Michelangelo Buonarroti *il giovane*'s *Balletto della Cortesia* (1614), Gabriello Chiabrera's *Veglia delle Grazie* (1615), and Ferdinando Saracinelli's *Ballo delle zingare* (1615) all involved movement between the stage and the auditorium. The principle also became adopted in entertainments in the Teatro degli Uffizi, as in the case of the *barriera* and *mascherata* done there on 17 February 1612/13, or Andrea Salvadori's spectacular *veglia*, *La liberazione di Tirreno e d'Arnea* (6 February 1616/17).[21] As for entertainments on a simpler scale elsewhere in the Palazzo Pitti, in 1618, Giulio Parigi was commissioned by Grand Duke Cosimo II to create "a little comic set" with its stage made as light as possible, enabling it to be moved easily from place to place.[22] So far as the Sala delle Commedie was concerned, however, it is clear that whatever survived of Cigoli's stage and sets for *Euridice* had long been changed beyond all recognition. So had the aesthetic principles on which they were founded.

In part because of the pressures for increasing spectacle, the Sala delle Commedie eventually outlived its usefulness, at least as a theatrical space: it seems to not have been served for any such purpose after 1626.[23] This is also clear from the list of the festivities in Florence celebrating the wedding of Margherita de' Medici and Duke Odoardo Farnese of Parma in October 1628: a banquet in the Sala delle Statue; a *festino da ballo* in the Sala dei Forestieri; an opera, *Flora*, in the Teatro degli Uffizi; and

Signor Don Giovanni Medici; (8 February 1610/11) *per fare accomodare la scena al Casino*. An order had already been given on 29 October 1610 *di far rassettare la scena della commedia de' Pitti*; ibid., fol. 128.

21 Giovanni Villifranchi, *Descrizione della barriera, e della mascherata, fatte in Firenze a' XVII et a' XIX di febbraio MDCXII al Serenissimo Signor Prencipe d'Urbino* (Florence: B. Sermatelli, 1612 [= 1613]). For *La liberazione di Tirreno e d'Arnea* (and the relationship between the stage and the auditorium), see the well-known engraving by Jacques Callot of its first *intermedio* at www.britishmuseum.org/research/collection_online/collection_object_details.aspx?objectId=1585865&partId=1.

22 Landolfi, "Su un teatrino mediceo e sull'Accademia degli Incostanti a Firenze nel primo Seicento," 70 n. 39 (citing *MdP* 1848, fol. 347): *una scenina d'una commedia portatile da gangherarsi con suo palco fatta con la maggiore leggerezza possibile*. Such a portable stage was probably useful because Grand Duke Cosimo II de' Medici was now frequently bedridden with illness.

23 The following discussion draws on Fantappiè, "Sala per lo spettacolo a Pitti," 167–80. It is also worth noting (to avoid confusion) that by the 1620s, at least, Cesare Tinghi might call the Teatro degli Uffizi the *sala delle comedie* even while the Sala delle Commedie in the Palazzo Pitti was still in use: compare *SolMBD*, 178 (28 January 1624/25), 179 (29 January), listing entertainments in two different spaces.

tournaments or similar exercises in outdoor locations both in the Boboli Gardens and in the Villa del Poggio Imperiale. After 1628, the Teatro degli Uffizi also fell into disuse, but the Medici still needed a theatre. Plans to build a new one next to the Palazzo Pitti were initiated around 1630, but by 1637 they seem to have failed, given that the "new room for comedies" (*lo stanzone nuovo delle commedie*) was treated as a storage space for wood.[24] A similar project was proposed by Alfonso Parigi in the early 1640s but was finally abandoned in the early 1650s: thus for the wedding of Grand Duke Ferdinando II and Vittoria Della Rovere in July 1637 – and in the absence both of an appropriate indoor space within the palace and of the Teatro degli Uffizi – the main entertainment, *Le nozze degli dei*, was done in the courtyard of the Pitti. The Sala delle Statue and the Sala dei Forestieri continued to be available for festive gatherings and the like, and the Salone dei Cinquecento in the Palazzo Vecchio was occasionally used as a theatrical space. Eventually, the Medici adopted the Teatro della Pergola (begun in 1652 and opened in 1657) as its preferred location for grander theatrical performances, as with the production of Giovanni Andrea Moniglia's opera *Ercole in Tebe* celebrating the wedding of Prince Cosimo de' Medici (later Grand Duke Cosimo III) and Marguerite Louise d'Orléans in 1661.[25]

Somewhat similarly, as the trend shifted in favor of more spectacular and more participatory kinds of indoor and outdoor entertainments supported by the Medici, the ennobling Classical ideals adopted in *Dafne* and *Euridice* appear to have fallen by the wayside, and likewise their ambitions for high-minded forms of musical theatre that would be of civic benefit above and beyond the need for princely entertainment and propaganda. In effect, *Euridice* did indeed belong in the space originally intended for it, the classically inspired Sala delle Statue, rather than any *sala delle commedie.* But while the Florentine playwright Andrea Salvadori may still have wished to claim in 1625 that it brought no little glory to the Tuscan name that under the Medici grand dukes the musical practice of ancient Greek drama had been revived in Florence, there was no longer much direct interest in its consequences save on the part of theorists such as Giovanni Battista Doni.[26] Although Rinuccini participated in, and even facilitated, this shift,

[24] Fantappiè, "Sala per lo spettacolo a Pitti," 172 n. 190.

[25] However, the Medici did later have a private theatre in the Villa di Pratolino that, while permanent, bore a number of similarities in terms of its dimensions to the Sala delle Commedie; see Garbero Zorzi, "I teatri di Pratolino."

[26] Andrea Salvadori, preface to *La regina Sant'Orsola, recitata in musica nel teatro del Serenissimo Gran Duca di Toscana* (Florence: Pietro Ceconcelli, 1625), given in Carter and Goldthwaite,

with works in the vein of his 1611 *balletto* or his *Mascherata di ninfe di Senna*, there is a certain air of regret in the prologue he wrote for a performance of *Dafne* in the residence of Don Giovanni de' Medici (probably the one on 9 February 1610/11). Here La Musica laments the fact that while she had once been allowed to represent the glories of Apollo, Orpheus, and (in one version of this prologue) Ariadne under royal roofs, she has now been banished from them by a crowd that she does not deem worthy of naming (ll. 27–28: *Turba, di cui ridir non degno il nome, / tolsemi ogni mio pregio, ogni mio vanto*).[27] As a result (ll. 29–32):

E poteo sì che dal reale albergo,
ove d'or mi credea rinnovar gli anni,
per sottrarmi d'invidia a' fieri inganni,
volsi, sdegnando, disprezzata il tergo.

[And they [the crowd] were so powerful that from the royal dwelling / where I once believed I would renew the ages, / in order to distance myself from the harsh stratagems of jealousy, / did I, scorned, turn my back in disdain.]

La Musica's point is that she has perforce found a better place in the palace of Don Giovanni de' Medici, the "sun" who stands at the head of noble knights (l. 37: . . . *o sol de' cavalier più degni*).

The Medici did not entirely abandon opera: obvious examples include Marco da Gagliano's collaborations with Jacopo Peri on *Lo sposalizio di Medoro ed Angelica* (performed in the Sala dei Forestieri in the Palazzo Pitti on 25 September 1619) and *Flora* (Teatro degli Uffizi, 14 October 1628, for the Medici–Farnese wedding). But what scholars have traditionally called "court opera" – perhaps wrongly, it now appears – and similar entertainments in this period tended to move (or return) primarily to private households, whether of princes rather than (grand) dukes, of patricians (Domenico Belli's *Orfeo dolente* of 1616 for Ugo Rinaldi, in the operatic style but acting as *intermedi* for a performance of Tasso's *Aminta*), or in the case of Rome, of prelates (Filippo Vitali's *Aretusa*, performed in the house of Monsignor Ottavio Corsini in 1620; Domenico Mazzocchi's *La catena d'Adone* of 1626, commissioned by Cardinal Ippolito Aldobrandini). The most typical exception was when they could be attached to court

Orpheus in the Marketplace, 4. Salvadori was using the point to argue that things had now moved on by bringing sacred dramas to the stage.

27 Two versions of this prologue are given in Solerti, *Gli albori del melodramma*, 2: 103–4. One of them refers to "Alba" (probably Aurora in *Il rapimento di Cefalo*), following the same stanza included in the prologue (delivered by Giulio Caccini) in Rinuccini's *Narciso*. The other, however, invokes Rinuccini's *Arianna* (Mantua, 1608).

entertainments on the chivalric model, as with Francesca Caccini's *La liberazione di Ruggiero dall'isola d'Alcina*, performed in the Villa del Poggio Imperiale in 1625 as the preface to a *balletto*, followed by a *balletto a cavallo*.

Although Peri's score of *Euridice* was reprinted in Venice in 1608 (by Alessandro Raverii) – with only very minor variants in the music and text – its only other known performance fits the new pattern. In April 1616 both Peri and Rinuccini were in Bologna at the invitation of Cardinal Luigi Capponi to stage *Euridice* (on 27 April) as part of a series of entertainments (including a joust, a *palio*, and a play by Jacopo Cicognini) that Capponi was staging in honor of Cardinals Giovanni Battista Leni, Bonifazio Bevilacqua, and Domenico Rivarola. It did not go well: the poet and the composer fell out over the latter's desire to cancel the performance because of the lack of time for rehearsal and the poor quality of the singers.[28] According to Andrea Barbazza's report to the Duke of Mantua, Peri felt that Rinuccini was somewhat ridiculously pretending to be more a musician than a poet (*il Zazzerino dice che il Signor Ottavio fa più da musicho che da poeta onde è cosa ridicolosa*), that is, he was interfering in musical matters beyond his domain. Almost seven years later, Pierfrancesco Rinuccini included the libretto near the front of the posthumous collection of his father's *Poesie* that appeared in early 1622 (dedicated to Louis XIII of France), with a preface addressed to the Accademia degli Alterati noting the poet's fame for having pioneered the practice of sung tragedies (*nelle Tragedie da cantarsi*), moving audiences in noble theatres to marvel and delight by way first of *Dafne* and then of *Euridice* (*Fu la sua Dafne la prima, e poi L'Euridice, che ne' nobili Teatri empiè gli spettatori di maraviglia, e di diletto*) such that others were inspired by so sweet a style (*sì dolce maniera di comporre*) to follow in his footsteps. Even before his death, Rinuccini had been the subject of an extraordinary *elogio* by Sillano di Francesco Licino, a *dottor di legge* and member of the Council of Bergamo, praising him to the skies with all the attributes of Orpheus himself.[29]

[28] *KirkCM*, 208–9; Carter and Goldthwaite, *Orpheus in the Marketplace*, 268–70.

[29] Sillano Licino, *Elogio del Molto Illustre Signor Ottavio Rinuccini* (n.p., n.d.), fol. [A1]v: *et a chi daremo finalmente la palma di esser salito tant'alto, oltre cioè le strade del Sole, e del Tempo, anzi dell'eternità (se tanto può dirsi) et non la daremo con voti concordi al Signor Ottavio Rinuccini? Nume (e certo non m'inganno) divino, Intelligenza altissima, Orfeo celeste, ò pur del Cielo un'Eccho, e stupor di natura e d'arte? che ferma il corso de' fiumi, dà il moto a i sassi, placa l'ira alle fiere, acqueta le procelle in mare, e ritira l'huomo dalla selvatichezza alla vita civile, da gli odii all'amore, dalla crudeltà alla pietà, e dai vitii, alle virtù.* The sole (it seems) surviving copy of Licino's *Elogio*, in the Biblioteca Nazionale Marciana, Venice, is bound in with a copy of Rinuccini's *Poesie* (1622). Given its reference to Orazio del Monte (1570–1614) as *Governator*

Rinuccini's libretto for *Euridice* continued to have some resonance throughout the seventeenth century and beyond; it even gets quoted in Carlo Francesco Badini's libretto for Joseph Haydn's *L'anima del filosofo, ossia Orfeo ed Euridice* (1791). Peri's music, however, was soon buried in the music-history textbooks as a matter of purely academic interest, if that.

Euridice Today

Any study such ours devoted to the reconstruction of a music-theatrical performance should seek to move beyond the bounds of academe to reach, on the one hand, those practitioners who could bring such an event to life, and on the other, the public that might attend it. This assumes – as we must – that either constituency will be willing to treat the theatrical and musical practices of a distant past as warranting something more than just archeological interest. It also forces the obvious observation that the traditional location for displaying and contextualizing earlier *objets d'art* – the museum or gallery – will scarcely suffice for works meant to be seen and heard in a given space and time, a historical "there and then" that might or might not relate to any "here and now." As a result, a number of tensions will inevitably arise in terms of what the possible consequences of our work might be.

The first public display of the fruits of the research presented in this book took place in the context of an exhibition entitled *Firenze e la nascita dell'Opera: fra documenti ritrovati e ricostruzioni virtuali* (*Florence and the Birth of Opera: Documents and Virtual Reconstructions*) held in the Casa Buonarroti, Florence, from 3 April to 15 May 2019 (see *CW*Fig. 4.2a; *CW*Fig. 4.2b contains the exhibition catalog).[30] This served as a laboratory, as it were, for us to test our findings, aided by a group of graduate students in museum studies, whose enthusiastic engagement in unfamiliar musical and theatrical worlds gave us further confidence in the utility of our work. Of course, such exhibitions on Medici entertainments are not unknown in Florence: indeed, our study has drawn on the catalogs

meritissimo della Città di Bergamo, it seems to date from between 1605 and 1610, and it reads like a statement advocating or celebrating Rinuccini's admission to an academy.

30 See www.casabuonarroti.it/firenze-e-la-nascita-dellopera-fra-documenti-ritrovati-e-ricostruzioni-virtuali/. This was also part of a year-long project undertaken by students on the Marist College M.A. in Museum Studies program at the Istituto Lorenzo de' Medici (directed by Maia Wellington Gathan). The exhibition was linked to a conference and a concert (see our Preface).

prepared for such well-known ones as *Il luogo teatrale a Firenze*, *La scena del principe*, and *Teatro e spettacolo nella Firenze dei Medici* (Palazzo Medici Riccardi, 1975, 1980, 2001), plus two designed to celebrate the 400th anniversary of *Euridice* in 2000 – *Lo "spettacolo maraviglioso"* (Archivio di Stato) and *"Per un regale evento": spettacoli nuziali e opera in musica alla corte dei Medici* (Biblioteca Nazionale Centrale) – and, more recently, the one on the banquet celebrating the 1600 wedding (*Dolci trionfi e finissime piegature*, Palazzo Pitti, 2015).[31] Like them, our exhibition included a curated selection of manuscript and printed documents, drawings and engravings, and so forth, in our case also drawing on the rich collection of the Casa Buonarroti itself (which has a large set of original documents associated with Michelangelo Buonarroti *il giovane*). It moved chronologically and thematically from the 1589 *intermedi* through the musical pastorals of the 1590s, then *Dafne* and *Euridice*, to the 1608 festivities and *La liberazione di Tirreno e d'Arnea* of early 1617. And we included the typical mixture of sources needed to reflect the multifaceted nature of any theatrical venture in our period: letters, diaries, printed descriptions, librettos, musical scores (some with matching audio examples), costume sketches, set designs, and the like.

The main difference, however, was that we were able to take advantage of new digital technologies to create virtual renditions of various theatrical moments within our period, including aspects of the stage for *Euridice*. These included a sequence breaking down and recombining the various elements of its proscenium as designed for the Sala delle Statue and reworked for the Sala delle Commedie, plus another – intended as a *coup de théâtre* – demonstrating in real time the change from the pastoral to the Underworld set and vice versa, including the mechanisms by which it was achieved. Indeed, our working with multimedia designers, including Gian Gabriele Bassanello, gave us a remarkable opportunity to experiment with the various possible readings of Lodovico Cigoli's invoice for creating the scenery, and Gianbattista Cresci's inventory of the stage, trying out different solutions to what might have seemed at the start to be intractable problems. Visitors to the exhibition were genuinely curious about, and captivated by, these renditions and their moving parts. The results formed the basis for some of the images in this book, while those digital sequences in the exhibition further served as a proof of concept, as it were, of the

[31] M. Fabbri *et al.* (eds.), *Il luogo teatrale a Firenze*; M. Fabbri *et al.* (eds.), *La scena del principe*; Garbero Zorzi and Sperenzi (eds.), *Teatro e spettacolo nella Firenze dei Medici*; De Angelis *et al.* (eds.), *Lo "spettacolo maraviglioso"*; Bartoli Bacherini (ed.), *"Per un regale evento"*; Giusti and Spinelli (eds.), *Dolci trionfi e finissime piegature*.

potential for an actual reconstruction of *Euridice* in a staged production based on the physical evidence and its theatrical and musical consequences that we have explored here.

An exhibition of this kind might usefully prepare an audience to see a performance of an unfamiliar opera such as *Euridice*, and for obvious reasons, a multimedia one is certainly better than one without such technological wizardry. But it remains a poor substitute for an actual production of the work. If we were to attempt any staging of *Euridice* within the Palazzo Pitti according to Cigoli's original design, it could only be done in the Sala delle Statue: the Sala delle Commedie no longer survives in its original form, and while the present-day Sala Bianca (formerly the Sala dei Forestieri) has the same horizontal dimensions as the room one floor higher, it would not suit Cigoli's modifications for the lower ceiling.[32] The documents we have presented would certainly bring us closer to realizing such a staging than the court diaries, printed descriptions, and related materials that would normally provide a basis for it, precisely because our materials have forced us to engage with nitty-gritty matters at a level of detail lost in higher-level records or those designed for other purposes. However, there are a number of practical questions, and even philosophical ones, that would first need be addressed. Presenting a historical reconstruction of *Euridice* somehow close to what was done in 1600 is one thing, but staging it in a manner appropriate for the twenty-first century is another that would involve all manner of compromises typical of any music-theatrical endeavor. Some are inevitable, such as finding singers for the castrato roles; others, however, reflect obvious conflicts between any search for historical accuracy – whatever that might mean – and present-day relevance. Opera is particularly fraught terrain so far as these kinds of debates are concerned: even if historical accuracy is rarely high on any agenda for modern opera houses, questions remain about the need for intelligent productions that somehow respect the dramatic and structural integrity of the work being performed.[33]

Despite the rise of so-called Historically Informed Performance and its widespread acceptance in most musical circles, save for a few institutional pockets of resistance, its place within the world of opera production remains troubled. It would seem that with only a few obvious exceptions,

[32] The Sala delle Statue (now called Sala delle Nicchie) is part of the typical itinerary through the Palazzo Pitti; the Sala Bianca tends to be reserved for temporary exhibitions, concerts, etc. Other spaces commonly used for operatic performances are the main courtyard and the Boboli Gardens.

[33] Petrobelli, "La regia dell'opera," 954.

the scholarship supporting such performance has had greater impact in musical spheres than in theatrical ones. But while musicians are moving increasingly in favor of "original" performance practices, it is patently absurd to exert the great effort required to have performers play on historical instruments or sing in an appropriate stylistic way within a staging of an opera that bears scant relation to its original intent or even content. The current fashion for *Regietheater* (Director's Theatre), however, makes this a common enough artistic strategy, or just a marketing one.[34] The typical arguments are that this is necessary to cater for the presumed tastes of modern audiences, for whom the theatre is not the place for academic exercises, and that the universal truths presumed to lay at the heart of the genre should not be limited to a particular time and place but demand perpetual reinvention. However, it also reflects the economic and other realities of an opera industry that focuses on a relatively narrow range of "products" (repeat performances of a tiny percentage of the vast number of operas produced over the past four centuries) that therefore must be dressed in different guises to set them apart. But while a bizarre treatment of an operatic warhorse might not do much harm if others will soon follow along more or less conventional lines, works that are rarely staged do not have the luxury of multiple productions to compare one against the other. Further dilemmas arise when one enters the unfamiliar world of seventeenth-century opera, with its musical styles and theatrical practices that do not appear to fit conventional operatic norms, and coming from a period that often seems misunderstood as one of political, economic, and cultural decline.[35]

A survey of performances of Peri's *Euridice* over the past fifty years or so (there have been fewer of Caccini's) reveals a typical mixture of quasi-"historical" or "modern" settings.[36] Three productions in Florence are worth considering in more detail. Franco Zeffirelli's for the 1960 Maggio Musicale Fiorentino (repeated in 1965), staged in the Boboli Gardens, sought what Zeffirelli called "a historical and emotionally moving interpretation of the text" (*interpretazione storica ed emotiva del testo*) based, he said, on as faithful as possible reconstruction of the visual aspects of the

34 For an overview, see P. Fabbri, "Di vedere e non vedere"; Baker, *From the Score to the Stage*, 320–81; Müller, "*Regietheater*/Director's Theater" (with an extensive bibliography); Junod, "Au fil du temps." Beaussant, *La Malscène*, is particularly acute on the irreconcilable (it seems) tendencies of Historically Informed Performance and the all-powerful modern-day opera director.

35 See the essays in Candiard and Gros de Gasquet (eds.), *Scènes baroques d'aujourd'hui.*

36 There is a useful, if partial, list of these productions at https://operabaroque.fr (under Peri, *Euridice*), with some images and a few links to video and audio recordings.

Fig. 4.1: *Euridice* (directed by Franco Zeffirelli) at the 23rd Maggio Musicale Fiorentino, Boboli Gardens, Florence, 28–30 June 1960. By kind permission of the Archivio Storico della Fondazione Maggio Musicale Fiorentino.

work while still paying attention to modern taste (see Fig. 4.1).[37] Zeffirelli himself studied visual materials related to the 1589 *intermedi*, and Piero Tosi's costumes drew on late sixteenth-century paintings. The set design was also relatively straightforward – a series of steps leading up to a reproduction of Buontalenti's grotto in the background, surrounded by fountains, vases, *putti*, and statues – save for its grand scale that required a large number of dancers and extras to fill the space. The choreography was done by Ani Radošević, who had some interest in early dance, and who had just worked with Zeffirelli on his production of Handel's *Alcina* for the Teatro La Fenice in Venice (February 1960, with Joan Sutherland in the title role). But the music did not exhibit the same degree of historical rectitude: Bruno Rigacci conducted an ensemble that included a group of

[37] Bucci and Monti (eds.), *Orfeo in Toscana*, 58. A model of the set is on display at the Museo Fondazione Franco Zeffirelli (Florence); the Fondazione's archive also contains a number of photographs of Buontalenti's sketches for the 1589 *intermedi* which Zeffirelli himself appears to have procured for the project. Tosi was also well known as a costume designer who paid close attention to historical accuracy.

early instruments (the Complesso di strumenti antichi Rolf Rapp–Nives Poli), but Vito Frazzi's "transcription" of the score required modern ones as well, and made a number of cuts and additions, as well as adding richer accompaniments all in a manner typical of the treatment of early operas going back to Vincent d'Indy's and Giacomo Orefice's handling of Monteverdi in the first decades of the twentieth century.[38]

By 1996, the renowned early-music conductor Alan Curtis was able to take a more responsible approach to Peri's score in a production presented in two performances before invited guests in the gardens of the former Medici villa at Pratolino (now attached to the Villa Demidoff). The director, Luciano Alberti, took advantage of the outdoor location – with its obvious pastoral associations – to have the actors and audience move from place to place to match the dramatic action. He also exploited the principal landmarks of the garden, including Giambologna's *Appennine Colossus* and the lily pond at its feet, and the nearby stables. La Tragedia and Orfeo entered on carriages drawn, respectively, by a black horse and a white one; nymphs and shepherds did indeed sing and dance in a meadow; Dafne emerged from the grotto underneath the dragon behind the *Colossus*; Orfeo sang "Funeste piaggie, ombrosi orridi campi" on a carriage moving in front of the stables, with devils and other creatures of the Underworld leaning out of the building's windows; he arrived at Plutone's and Proserpina's thrones positioned at the edge of the pond, on which floated Caronte's barque; Euridice appeared on a smaller boat; and the soloists, chorus, and dancers resumed their pastoral guise for the final episode. But while that open-air staging was not particularly "authentic," Alberti's handling of the drama was certainly respectful of its content, as one might expect of someone of his stature not just as a director but also as a scholar and critic. Moreover, the fact that the choreography was done by Flavia Sparapani, another expert in early dance, reminds us of the importance of Historically Informed Performance in this realm as well.[39]

That 1996 production was done in front of a niche audience, as was the one that celebrated the 400th anniversary of *Euridice* in the Palazzo Pitti on 6–8 October 2000 (given the size of the room and the high price of the

[38] Carter, *Monteverdi's Musical Theatre*, 5–7. Even what is often regarded as the "best" scholarly edition of *Euridice* (edited by Howard Mayer Brown) has additional instrumental parts accompanying the voices in places.

[39] Bucci and Monti (eds.), *Orfeo in Toscana*, 84–86. The production was in honor of the meeting of the European Council in Florence on 21–22 June 1996. Caccini's *Euridice* had been staged at the Teatro della Pergola in June 1980 (as part of the Maggio Musicale), directed by Giorgio Marini, conducted by Raffaello Monterosso, and with choreography by Barbara Sparti (yet another expert in historical dance); ibid., 70–71.

tickets). But those involved in the latter should probably have known better. This production took place in the Sala Bianca, proclaimed to be the room in which the work was first performed, with a minimal set. The musical director, Aníbal Cetrangolo, had already released a historically plausible recording of the opera (in 1997, using the period-instrument Ensemble Albalonga) – with only a few additions of other music of the time – and he probably did not deserve the negative comments made on that aspect of the performance in 2000. However, the Florentine stage director Riccardo Massai took a decidedly avant-garde approach to the production: according to one reviewer, "Bucolic delights were transformed into a slick, millennium wedding, with a catholic priest officiating and guests in Armani-style suits swilling champagne. The only scenery was an olive tree, whence Euridice, raped by Pluto, was borne away to work as a prostitute in an underworld, urban Hell of hookers, drugdealers, and pimps astride red Lambrettas."[40] The audience booed loud and strong.

In the fashion of their times, Zeffirelli's approach was more historicizing than historical, while Massai's was overtly (post)modernist; Alberti's, on the other hand, took the middle road, as it were. Paradoxically – if also typically – the handling of the music went in the opposite direction. But while Zeffirelli paid close attention to the text and the broader traditions into which it inserted itself, Massai instead sought greater legitimacy in the act of reinterpretation for modern audiences. In some such cases, the influence is Brechtian, while in others it is simply a product of an opera industry struggling to maintain its relevance in difficult cultural and economic times. One danger revealed by the patent failure of the Massai production is that an audience unfamiliar with a given opera is left no less confused than those who might know it well. The search for relevance, however, also demonstrates a patent reluctance to trust operas as being sufficient on their own terms, ignoring the possibility that we might find it within *Euridice*'s original time and place.

In the case of the 2000 production, there was a clear disagreement between the stage director (Massai) and the musical one (Cetrangolo). As we have seen, Rinuccini and Peri, serving in similar capacities, also disagreed over the performance of *Euridice* in Bologna in 1616. Such creative tensions are not unusual within a genre that purports to be collaborative but often tends to the competitive in terms of the primacy of its constituent

[40] See Jean Grundy Fanelli 's review in *17th-Century Music: The Newsletter of the Society for Seventeenth-Century Music*, 10/2 (spring 2001), 4–5 (https://sscm-sscm.org/17CM/vol%2010%20no%202.pdf).

elements. We do not know how Rinuccini and Peri resolved their differences, if they did, but at least they did not have to engage in more modern debates concerning the merits of creation versus re-creation and the impact of one on the other.[41] Yet one assumes that they still sought some manner of consistency within the production based on a close reading of the text and music, and within the constraints of an early seventeenth-century stage.

Our own aim might be no different. There is no single solution to the problems raised here, not least in light of the obvious paradox of Historically Informed Performance: that while it might be plausible for a modern audience to be historically informed, we can never see or hear a work through period eyes and ears. Nor will what one might call an archeological approach to reconstructing early modern theatres necessarily produce the same impact as those spaces would have made on their original audiences, save by reorienting current notions of spectacle. Yet as many working in musical fields (if fewer in theatrical ones) have come to realize, the apparent constraints of using early performance styles also bring a great deal of freedom to move within them: it is a great mistake to think that a historically informed performance must inevitably be dogmatic in historical terms, or arid in the result. The question therefore rests on the extent to which one feels able to trust the work. We have seen that Rinuccini, Peri, and Cigoli clearly had some kind of coherent vision for *Euridice* both for itself and in its context, even if that vision was modified according to circumstance (the move from the Sala delle Statue to the Sala delle Commedie) or as practical issues emerged during rehearsal. We have also seen, in light of our close examination here, that the opera has a surprisingly strong dramatic rhythm based on contrasting physical locations, emotional situations, and the reversals associated with them. Whether or not one goes to the extreme of reproducing the original sets – though that would not be so "extreme" – it is clear that *Euridice* is best done on an intimate scale as regards the staging and any instrumental ensemble (it is not Monteverdi's *Orfeo*), with singer-actors in costumes appropriate to the type and status of their characters, and paying close attention to the delivery of the text in word and gesture. When read closely, the libretto itself is transparent enough on the structure and content of the drama, and on the messages it is meant to convey about political necessity on the one hand, and the power of art on the other. The music supports rather than dominates the poetry, and it is not amenable to significant

[41] Compare Gousset, "Comment recréer dans l'esprit de . . . ?"

embellishment, which is not to say that it should not be sung well. Both the libretto and the score are much clearer than one might expect in terms of handling the entrances and exits of the main characters and the chorus. Probably the most significant constraints – which might, in turn, be treated as an opportunity – are the surprisingly small area of the original stage, which would prompt some careful choreography of the action, plus the need for a lighting scheme to replicate the effect of candles and oil lamps illuminating its (brighter) pastoral scenes and (darker) Underworld one. But with a creative designer of the sets and a stage director willing to work with, rather than against, the text, it seems likely that any performance of *Euridice* that paid at least some attention to the issues we have developed in this book would be more likely to succeed than not.

Appendix I: Documents

A Lodovico Cigoli's Invoice for Designing and Painting the Stage and Scenery for *Euridice*

Source: GM 1152, fol. 445 (document dated 14 October 1600). This is headed "N° 221 / messer Lodovicho Cigholi / Comedia de' Pitti" (no. 221 is the original numbering in the sequence of documents here relating to the 1600 entertainments). Information in the far left-hand column is editorial.

The complete document is reproduced as *CW*Fig. 1.3a–b. It is also transcribed in Testaverde, "Nuovi documenti sulle scenografie di Ludovico Cigoli per l'*Euridice* di Ottavio Rinuccini," 319–20.

Fol. 445r		Il Serenissimo Gran Duca		The Most Serene Grand Duke
		De' dare a me Lodovico Ciardi detto Il Cigoli questo dì 14 di ottobre 1600 per le apiè cose descritte, et tutto è servito per la sciena de' Pitti servite alle feste della Regina. Il qual conto è dato a braccia quadre fuori del arme et dei 6 alberi tutti dintornati et dei tre pezzi di travate che ricorrono infra l'una et l'altra trave.		owes me, Lodovico Ciardi called Il Cigoli, this day, 14 October 1600, for the items listed below, and everything was used for the stage in the Pitti used for the festivities of the queen, the which account is given in *braccia quadrate* save for the coat of arms and the six trees in the round, and the three pieces [as] cross-pieces that run below the one and the other main beam.
Cig1	*b.q.* 225	Et imprima tutta la centina del cielo a £2 il braccio [quadrato] somma £450 cioè scudi	*sc.*64 £2	And first, the whole arch of the sky at £2 per *b.q.*; in sum £450
Cig2	*b.*[*q.*] 257	Et di più la sciena degli alberi non contando gli alberi dintornati pezzi 17 a £6 il braccio quadrato somma in tutto £1542 cioè	*sc.*220 £2	And further, the scene of the trees not including the trees in the round; 17 pieces at £6 per *b.q.*; in sum in total £1,542
Cig3	*b.*[*q.*] 52½	Il parapetto della sciena tocha d'oro et argento et sue rivolte a £5 il braccio quadrato somma £262.10*s.* cioè	*sc.*37 £3.10*s.*	The parapet of the stage, with gold and silver flecks, and its turned ends at £5 per *b.q.*; in sum £262.10*s.*
Cig4	*b.*[*q.*] 104½	Il piano del palcho a £1 il braccio [quadrato] somma £104.10*s.*	*sc.*14 £6.10*s.*	The floor of the stage at £1 per *b.q.*; in sum £104.10*s.*
Cig5	*b.*[*q.*] 16⅗	E' massi picholi sopra il palcho sono pezzi 5 e tochi d'oro et argento a £5 somma £80.12*s.* cioè	*sc.*11 £3.12*s.*	And the small boulders on the stage numbering 5 pieces, and with gold and silver flecks, at £5 [per *b.q.*]; in sum £80.12*s.*

Cig6	*b.*[*q.*] 257	E' massi grandi tochi d'oro et argento sono pezzi diciasette a £5 somma £1285 cioè	*sc.*183 £4	And the large boulders, with gold and silver flecks, numbering 17 pieces, at £5 [per *b.q.*]; in sum £1,285
Cig7	*b.*[*q.*] 228⅙	Tutta la facciata (fuori del arme, et i tre pezzi che sono fra le travate) cioè i duoi telai degli angoli nei quali è finto i festoni et aria con alquanto di rovina, i duoi pezzi di centina nei quaili [*sic*] è finto in panno di lacha fine et tocho d'oro, et sotto i duoi pilastri con due femine l'una rapresentando la poesia, et nel altra la pittura e perspettiva, et sotto a ciascuna un basso rilievo, et pilast[r]i nel muro per finimento della sciena a lire £4 il braccio [quadrato] somma £912.13*s.*4*d.* cioè	*sc.*130 £2.13*s.*4*d.*	The whole facade (except the coat of arms, and the three pieces that are between the beams), i.e., the two framed canvases in the corners in which are feigned festoons and sky with a few ruins; the two pieces in an arch in which is feigned cloth in fine lacquer and with gold flecks; and under [them] the two pilasters with two women, one representing poetry and the other painting and perspective; and under each one a bas relief; and pilasters against the wall so as to finish off the stage; at £4 per *b.q.*; in sum £912.13*s.*4*d.*
			*sc.*662 £3.5*s.*4*d.* [total for page]	
Fol. 445v				
Cig8	Pezzi 3	che vanno per riempiere i tre vani sopra la facciata davanti che fanno ricorrere li membri degli sfondati della arcitravata cioè scudi 2 del l'uno sommano	*sc.*6	[Three pieces] which serve to fill the three spaces above the facade in front that act to cover over the parts with gaps[?] in the architrave; i.e., *sc.*2 each

(*cont.*)

Cig9	Pezzi 6	E più sei alberi tutti dintornati et tochi d'oro i quali si movano di sul palcho alti l'uno per l'altro braccia 5½ raguagliati a scudi cinque del l'uno	*sc.*30	And further, six trees all in the round, and with gold flecks, which move on the stage, the one and the other averaging 5½ *b.* high; at *sc.*5 each
Cig10	Pezzi 1	E più l'arme sopra la sciena nella quale v'è l'arme della Regina, computti [= con putti] maggiori del naturale messa d'oro fine >e campi< et tocha di oro alta braccia 7 et larga braccia 5 in circha et di tanto deve dare scudi 35	*sc.*35	And further, the coat of arms above the stage in which is the arms of the queen, with *putti* larger than life, with fine gold >in its fields< and with gold flecks, 7 *b.* high and 5 *b.* wide or thereabouts, and for this is owed *sc.*35
Cig11		E per il danno riceuto della risoluzione fatta da Sua Altezza del locare la sciena in altro salone più basso et più largo che per dove era fatta, il che per ridurla proporzionata al detto luogho di e spesa e tempo pretendo scudi 25	*sc.*25	And for the damage caused by the decision made by His Highness to locate the stage in another *salone* lower and wider than the one for which it was made, such that for the expense and time to remake it proportional to the said space, I claim *sc.*25
		Nella quale domanda, et prezzo tutto sopra et di là detto, è compreso tutte le spese di colori, oro, et manifattura aspettante al pittore et tanto somma in tutto scudi *sc.*758 £3.5*s.*4*d.*	[*sc.*]96 [total for page] [*sc.*]662 £3.5*s.*4*d.* [carried over] ——— [*sc.*]758 £3.5*s.*4*d.*	In the which request and price all given above and there said is included all the costs of colors, gold, and manufacturing pertaining to the painter, and the whole amounts in total to *sc.*758 £3.5*s.*4*d.*
		[in the hand of Michele Caccini] Rischontro tutte li sudetti capi e misure per me Michele Caccini ministro presente detto messer Lodovicho questo dì 14 di ottobre 1600, e tutto è a dovere		I, Michele Caccini *ministro*, compare all the said entries and measurements in the presence of the said Messer Lodovicho this day 14 October 1600, and everything is as it should be.

B Gianbattista Cresci's Inventory of Materials for *Euridice*

Source: GM 1152, fols. 463r–464v (document dated 18 September 1601). This is headed "N° 228," i.e., the original numbering in the sequence of documents here relating to the 1600 entertainments. Save for the final date, closing salutation, and signature (and a final entry by Michele Caccini), this document is in the hand of Matteo Chelli, *scrivano di castello*. Information in the far left-hand column is editorial.

The complete document is reproduced as *CW*Fig. 1.11a–d. It is also partially transcribed (up to and including *Cres24*) in Testaverde, "Nuovi documenti sulle scenografie di Ludovico Cigoli per l'*Euridice* di Ottavio Rinuccini," 320–21.

Fol. 463r	Molto Magnifico messer Michele Caccini		Very Magnificent Messer Michele Caccini
	E vi si è dato credito a libro della reale comedia fattasi l'anno passato d'ottobre nell Salone sopra gli Ufizi per le feste e nozze della Cristianissima Regina di Francia a carte 219, 220 dell'appiè robe quale avete tratte della prospettiva e apparato di una comedia fattasi nell Palazzo de' Pitti per dette nozze, e si è riscontrato una vostra poliza fatta sotto dì 4 stante e si è messa nella filza delle scritture della reale comedia sotto n° 219 et se n'è fatto uno inventario e acomodate nelle stanze che sono sul detto salone dove è altra munizione cioè		And you have been given credit in the account book of the royal comedy done in October of the past year in the *salone* above the Uffizi for the festivities and wedding of the Most Christian Queen of France at pages 219, 220, of the following items that you have handled regarding the perspective and apparatus of a comedy done in the Palazzo Pitti for the said wedding, and a comparison has been made with your memorandum done on the 4th inst., and it is placed in the file of documents for the royal comedy as no. 219, and an inventory has been made from it, and they have been placed in the rooms that are next to the said *salone* where there is other equipment, i.e.:
Cres1	Quattordici telai dipinti sulla tela a boscaglie che fanno le strade della sciena da dua bande, alta la maggiore braccia sette, la minore braccia cinque, larghe braccia 2 l'una incirca	n° 14	Fourteen frames painted on canvas as woods that make the streets of the stage on two sides; the tallest 7 *b.* high and the smallest 5 *b.*, about 2 *b.* wide
Cres2	Un pezzo di foro simile lungo braccia otto alto braccia quattro	n° 1	A similar backdrop, 8 *b.* long, 4 *b.* high
Cres3	Dua triangoli di tela dipinti che insieme fanno un quadro di braccia 7½ per ogni verso servono a riquadrare la facciata dinanzi alla sciena rasente il palco dell salone grande delle stanze de' forestieri dove s'è recitata	n° 2	Two triangles of painted canvas that together make a square of 7½ *b.* on each side, which serve to square off the facade in front of the set, next to [i.e., above] the stage of the *salone grande* of the Stanza dei Forestieri where it was performed
Cres4	Dua pilastri di legniame e tela dipinti con dua fi[g]ure di chiaro scuro, alti l'uno braccia otto, larghi braccia tre servono a detta facciata	n° 2	Two pilasters of timber and canvas painted with two figures in *chiaroscuro*, each 8 *b.* high, 3 *b.* wide, which serve for the said facade
Cres5	Dua panni di tela dipinti a broccato rosso con sua telai e drappelloni che fanno mezzo tondo che mettano in mezzo l'arme di detta facciata lunghi l'uno braccia dieci larghi braccia sette nell mezzo sono in disordine	n° 2	Two cloths of canvas painted in red brocade with their frames and drapes that make a half oval, in the middle of which is placed the arms of the said facade, each 10 *b.* long, 7 *b.* wide in the middle; they are in disorder
Cres6	Tre pezzi di fregi dipinti a sfondato dell palco dell salone di legniame e coperti di tela lunghi in tutto braccia diciasette andante, larghi braccia 1½	n° 3	Three pieces of friezes painted *a sfondato* of [i.e., above] the stage of the *salone*, of timber and covered in canvas, with a total length of 17 *b.a.*, 1½ *b.* wide

Cres7	Telaio di tela dipinto a massi lungho in tutto braccia otto ½ alto braccia 2, servì al parapetto dell palco in terra. Per la vostra poliza dite essere dua di braccia 17 andante e per non se n'essere trovato se non uno vi si dà credito solo d'uno	n° 1	Frame of canvas painted as boulders, in total 8½ *b.* long, and 2 *b.* high; served as the parapet of the stage on the ground. According to your memorandum you say that there are two making 17 *b.a.*, and given that only one of them was found, you are given credit only for one
Cres8	Una tela senza telai dipinta a aria servita per il cielo della scena lunga braccia diciasette larga braccia tredici ½ raguagliata	n° 1	A canvas without frames painted as a sky, used for the sky of the stage; 17 *b.* long, and 13½ *b.* wide on average
Cres9	Alberi di carta pesta dipinti a frutti e foglie lunghi braccia 7 con il pedale larghi ne' rami braccia dua l'uno	n° 6	Trees of *papier-mâché* painted with fruits and leaves, 7 *b.* long [= high] with the base, each 2 *b.* wide in its branches
	segue di là		continues overleaf
Fol. 463v			
	E più l'appiè tele tratte dell piano dell palco, e prima		And further, the following canvases taken from the floor of the stage, and first
Cres10	Un pezzo lungo braccia dodici, largo braccia dua braccia ventiquattro quadre	*b.*[*q.*] 24	One piece 12 *b.* long, 2 *b.* wide; 24 *b.q.*
Cres11	Un lungo braccia otto e largo braccia 6 che è braccia quarantotto quadre	*b.*[*q.*] 48	One 8 *b.* long and 6 *b.* wide, which is 48 *b.q.*
Cres12	Tre pezzuoli in tutto braccia sette quadre	*b.*[*q.*] 7	Three little pieces, in total 7 *b.q.*
Cres13	Quattordici tele dipinte a massi che fanno la muta dell'Inferno sopra le case a boscaglia, lunghe le più alte braccia 7 e le più basse braccia cinque larghe l'una braccia dua con lor' telai nelle teste e pulleggie da tirarle in giù e 'n su, sono male in essere	n° 14	Fourteen canvases painted as boulders that make the change to the Inferno over the flats [painted] as woods, the highest ones 7 *b.* long [= high], and the lowest ones 5 *b.*, each 2 *b.* wide, with their frames at the top and pulleys to pull them down and up; they are in bad condition
Cres14	Cinque pezzi di scogli dipinti sulla tela e legniame lunghi braccia 2 larghi braccia dua incirca serviti per scogli sul palco. Questi sono tutti cattivi che non si sono inventariati né datovene credito, però gli potrete fare tratti e finiti.		Five pieces of rocks painted on canvas and timber, 2 *b.* long, 2 *b.* wide, or thereabouts, used as rocks on the stage. These are all bad such that they are not inventoried, nor has credit been given to you for them; however, you can treat them as dealt with and done.

(*cont.*)

Cres15	Dua telai dipinti a massi lunghi braccia 2½, larghi braccia dua servirno appiè del palco	n° 2	Two framed canvases painted as boulders, 2½ *b.* long, 2 *b.* wide; they were used at the foot of the stage
Cres16	Una tenda di tela verde servita per turare la scena dinanzi lungha braccia ventidua larga braccia sedici	n° 1	A curtain of green canvas used to close the stage in front; 22 *b.* long, 16 *b.* wide
Cres17	Un foro per la muta dello Inferno in tela senza telaio dipinta a scogli lungo braccia otto largho braccia quattro incirca con un'armadura di legnio da capo	n° 1	A backdrop for the change to the Inferno on canvas without a frame, painted as rocks, 8 *b.* long, 4 *b.* wide, or thereabouts, with a wooden framework at the top
Cres18	Correnti d'Abeto numero dodici di braccia otto l'uno con lor' puleggie e cassa di legnio attaccata serviti alle mute dell'Inferno	n° 12; *b.* 96	Battens of fir, twelve in number, 8 *b.* each, with their pulleys and wooden case attached, used for the changes to the Inferno
Cres19	Numero dua di detti di braccia undici per le guide	n° 2; *b.* 22	Two in number of the said [battens] of 11 *b.* for the guides
Cres20	Numero tre guide con dua correnti l'una di braccia 4 larghe l'una con sua traverse tutto braccia 24 andante di correnti	n° 3; *b.* 24	Three in number guides with two battens each, each 4 *b.* long with its traverse; in all 24 *b.a.* of battens
Cres21	Quattro centine d'asse d'albero di ½ tutte braccia 26 andante larghe ½ braccio	n° 4; *b.*[*a.*] 26	Four arches [made] of planks of ½-thick wood; in all 26 *b.a.*, ½ *b.* wide
Cres22	Un pezzo di asse rintornata dipinta per il foro lunga braccia sei	n° 1	One piece of crenellated[?] plank painted for the backdrop; 6 *b.* long
Cres23	Bilichi di legniame con più puleggie lunghi braccia 6½ l'uno	n° 2	[Two] wooden shafts with several pulleys; each 6½ *b.* long
Cres24	Carrucole piccole di legno con lor' puleggie e corde per tirare la muta dell'Inferno numero quindici	n° 15	Small grooved wheels of wood with their pulleys and ropes to pull the change to the Inferno, fifteen in number
Fol. 464r			
Cres25	Parafuochi di banda stagniata lunghi braccia dua l'uno largha ½ braccia, sono numero tre	n° 3	Fireguards of tinplate, each 2 *b.* long, ½ *b.* wide; there are three in number
Cres26	Forniuoli di banda stagniata da candele per prospettive numero sessanta	n° 60	Tinplate candle lanterns for stages, sixty in number
Cres27	Fune e sustre libbre[?] dieci in più pezzi di queste non vi se ne dà credito perché non si sono trovate nell' riscontrare, tutto per aviso		Cords and ropes, ten pounds[?] in several pieces; for these you have not been given credit because they were not found in the comparison; all as a matter of note

Cres28	Tavole d'abeto traforate in più luoghi numero cinque lunghe braccia sei larghe braccia dua ½ l'una in circa, servite al piano dell palco	n° 5	Boards of fir with slots in several places, five in number; each 6 *b.* long, 2½ *b.* wide, or thereabouts; used for the floor of the stage
Cres29	Un fuso da verricello d'abeto lungo braccia nove con più ruote ferme e sei manichetti da girare servito sotto il palco alla muta della scena	n° 1	A winch-spindle of fir, 9 *b.* long, with several fixed wheels and six short handles to turn; used under the stage for the change of scene
Cres30	Dua fusi da verricello d'abeto lunghi braccia tre l'uno con più ruote fermi [*sic*] e dua manichi per uno	n° 2	Two winch-spindles of fir, each 3 *b.* long, with several fixed wheels and two handles each
Cres31	Cinque coscie d'asse d'albero di ⅓ lunghe braccia tre l'una in circa, servite per dette verricelli	n° 5	Five braces [made] of planks of ⅓-thick wood, each about 3 *b.* long; used for the said winches
Cres32	Torciere di legnio con piedistallo appiramidato inargentato, alto di tutto braccia quattro l'una in circa	n° 6	[Six] torchères of wood with a pyramid-shaped pedestal gilded in silver; each in total about 4 *b.* high
	E di tutto vi si è dato credito. E queste che seguono appiè non vi se ne dà credito atteso che per la vostra dite avere rese a Piero guardaroba de' Pitti che l'aveva prestate per detta Comedia		And everything has been credited to you. And those [items] that follow below have not been credited to you given that in your [memorandum] you say that you have delivered them to Piero, *guardaroba* of the Pitti, who had lent them for the said comedy
Cres33	Tavole d'abeto vecchie numero undici lunghe braccia cinque larghe braccia dua l'una in circa, che parte traforate	n° 11	Old boards of fir, eleven in number; each 5 *b.* long, 2 *b.* wide, or thereabouts, some with slots
Cres34	Capre d'albero e d'abeto numero dieci, che numero quattro lungha braccia dieci l'[un]a e numero sei lunghe braccia tre l'una, alte tutte braccia 2½ l'una incirca	n° 10	Trestles of wood and fir, ten in number; of which four in number are each 10 *b.* long, and six in number are each 3 *b.* long, all around 2½ *b.* high
Cres35	E similmente delle sette capre d'abeto lunghe braccia 3 et alte braccia 2½ che accettasti dalla fabricha de' Pitti, et né dell'arme grande di Francia che è rimasta sul ricetto delle scale sopra la porta che entra nela loggia in mezzo al piano di Sua Altezza Serenissima anco di questa non vi s'è dato credito, ma se n'è fatto nota appiè di detto inventario per ricordo di ritrovare dette robe se mai Sua Altezza Serenissima volessi fare rimettere insieme detta prospettiva per recitare detta comedia.		And likewise for the seven trestles of fir, 3 *b.* long and 2½ *b.* high, that you accepted from the building-office of the Pitti; nor for the large coat of arms of France that has remained at the head of the stairs above the door that leads to the loggia in the middle of the floor of His Most Serene Highness – this, too, has not been credited to you, but a note has been made at the foot of the said inventory as a memorandum to recover the said items if ever His Most Serene Highness should wish to put back together the said stage to perform the said comedy.

segue di là

continues overleaf

(*cont.*)

Fol. 464v			
	Ancora vi si è dato credito al libro di detta Comedia a 219 delle appiè legniame ritratto dell <palco della prospettiva> armadura dello cielo e altro di detta scena che ce ne darete debito per conto dela reale comedia che non vi se n'è dato credito per conto della comedia de' Pitti e apresso ne abbiano dato debito alla fabrica de' Pitti per essere servito a fare uno stanzino in camera di Madama Serenissima dall bosco delli Allori, et è lo appresso legniame		Further, you have been credited in the account book of the comedy at [page] 219 with the following timber taken from <the floor of the stage> the framework of the sky and elsewhere in the said stage for which you are given a debit on the account of the royal comedy and for which you have not been credited in the account of the comedy in the Pitti, and now it has been debited to the building-office of the Pitti for having been used to make a small room in Most Serene Madama's chamber on the side of the Bosco degl'Allori, and it is the following timber
Cres36	Piane d'albero pezzi tre, braccia tre l'una, braccia nove andante	n° 3; *b.*[*a.*] 9	Planks of wood, three pieces, each 3 *b.* [making] 9 *b.a.*
Cres37	Correnti d'abeto braccia ottantaquattro andante in pezzi nove	n° 9; *b.*[*a.*] 84	Battens of fir; 84 *b.a.*, in nine pieces
Cres38	Correnti simili pezzi dua di braccia tredici l'uno, pezzi 2, braccia 26	n° 2; *b.* 26	Similar battens; two pieces each of 13 *b.*; two pieces; 26 *b.*
Cres39	Asse d'abeto di ⅓, braccia 6⅓ quadre, pezzi tre	n° 3; *b.*[*q.*] 6⅓	Planks of ⅓-thick fir; 6⅓ *b.q.*; three pieces
Cres40	Asse d'albero di ⅓, braccia dodici quadre, pezzi sette	n° 7; *b.*[*q.*] 12	Planks of ⅓-thick wood; 12 *b.q.*; seven pieces
Cres41	Mezzi legni d'abeto sottile numero [4], braccia 13 l'uno, braccia 52	n° 4; *b.* 52	Half planks of fine-grained fir; [four] in number; each 13 *b.*; 52 *b.*
Cres42	Pianoni d'abeto numero sette, braccia 10 l'uno	n° 7; *b.* 70	Large planks of fir; seven in number; each 10 *b.*
	E questo è il fine di detto legniame, imperò ce ne darete debito conforme al presente avviso acciò si vadi d'accordo con la scrittura. Et altro non fa dirne. Dio vi dia ogni contento.		And this is the end of the said timber. However, you will be debited with it in conformance with the present advisory so that everything matches in writing. And there is nothing more to tell you. May God give you every contentment.
	Questo dì 18 di settembre 1601 Di Vostra Signoria, molto magnifica Aff[ezionatissi]mo Gianbatista Cresci		This day, 18 September 1601 Your Very Magnificent Lordship's Most affectionate [servant] Gianbatista Cresci
	[Note in Caccini's hand] Fatto debitore detto dì commedia reale e creditore commedia de' Pitti delle sudette robe come sopra a libro delle feste a 174		[Note in Caccini's hand] This day, the royal comedy was made debtor, and the comedy in the Pitti creditor, of the said items as above in the account book of the festivities, at [page] 174

C Francesco Ricoveri's Invoice for Sewing Canvas, etc. for *Euridice*

Source: GM 1152, fols. 427v, 429r (fol. 428 is a separate insert). This is part of a long list of work done since 20 May prepared sometime after the festivities (the account was settled on 10 November 1600). Measurements are mostly what seem to be in *braccia andante.* Ricoveri largely charges for the sewing of canvas (at £1 per 10 *b.a.*), although *Ric14–15* are reckoned by *giornate* (workdays) at £3.10*s.* per *giornata.* The information in the far left-hand column is editorial.

The relevant extracts from this document are reproduced as *CW*Fig. 1.12a–b.

Fol. 427v			
Ric1	14 tele nel Palazo de' Pitti di braccia sei l'uno che v'è braccia 18 di cucito per telaio, tutto braccia 252 monta	£25.4*s.*	Fourteen canvases in the Palazzo Pitti, each 6 *b.* [high], which is 18 *b.* of sewing for each frame, in all 252 *b.*
Ric2	14 tele servirno per i massi son braccia 252 monta	£25.4*s.*	Fourteen canvases [that] were used for the boulders are 252 *b.*
Ric3	Per dua fori uno dipinto li alberi e l'altro i massi alti braccia 5 e lungi braccia 8½ che v'è in tutto braccia 80 [*sic*] monta	£8	For two backdrops, one painted with trees and the other with boulders, 5 *b.* high and 8½ *b.* wide, which is in total 80 *b.* [*sic*]
Ric4	Braccia 80 del piano del palcho che s'ebbe allungare monta	£8	80 *b.* for the floor of the stage, which had to be lengthened
Ric5	Per dua bandinelle dalli illati del palcho che hanno auto cresciere e poi isc[e]mare braccia tutto dugento monta	£20	For two banners on the sides of the stage, which had to be increased in size and then reduced; 200 *b.* in total
Ric6	Per il cielo numero 8 teli braccia centocinquanta monta	£15	For the sky, canvases eight in number; 150 *b.*
Ric7	Per la tela che tura dinanzi il palcho braccia 20	£2	For the canvas that closes the stage in front; 20 *b.*
Ric8	Per l'archo che sta sopra il palcho braccia 150 monta	£15	For the arch that stands above the stage; 150 *b.*
Ric9	Per l'arme che va sopra deto braccia 20	£2	For the coat of arms that goes above the aforesaid; 20 *b.*
Ric10	Per dua tele a triangolo braccia 52	£5.4*s.*	For two triangular canvases; 52 *b.*
Ric11	Per dua tele per dua nichie braccia 40	£4	For two canvases for two niches; 40 *b.*
Ric12	Per la tenda dinanzi braccia 100	£10	For the curtain in front; 100 *b.*
Ric13	Una tenda verde braccia 200	£20	A green curtain; 200 *b.*
Fol. 429r			
Ric14	Per aver cucito le corde a massi e inpastato le istricie di tela intorno che sono giornate 24 in tutto	£84	For having sewn together the cords for the boulders and pasted the strips of canvas around them: 24 workdays in total
Ric15	Per avere ristaurato e ritagliato le tele de' massi secondo la volontà del Signor Don Giovanni [de' Medici] che sono giornate 12	£42	For having restored and resized the canvases for the boulders according to the wish of Signor Don Giovanni [de' Medici]: 12 workdays
Ric16	Per la pasta per inpastare le striscie	£2	For the paste to paste the strips
Ric17	Per il giorno della commedia	£7	For the day of the comedy

Works Cited

Adami, Giuseppe, "Nel segno di Aleotti: materiali per lo sviluppo della tradizione ferrarese del Seicento" in C. Cavicchi *et al.* (eds.), *Giovan Battista Aleotti e l'architettura*, 253–65

Scenografia e scenotecnica barocca tra Ferrara e Parma (1625–1631) (Rome: L'Erma di Bretschneider, 2003)

Adorni, Bruno, "Il Teatro Farnese a Parma" in C. Cavicchi *et al.* (eds.), *Giovan Battista Aleotti e l'architettura*, 205–26

Aiazzi, Giuseppe, *Ricordi storici di Filippo di Cino Rinuccini dal 1282 al 1460 preceduti dalla storia genealogica della di lui famiglia e dalla descrizione della cappella gentilizia in Santa Croce con documenti ed illustrazioni* (Florence: Piatti, 1840)

Alberti, Leon Battista, *L'architettura*, edited by Giovanni Orlandi and Paolo Portoghesi, 2 vols. (Milan: Il Polifilo, 1966)

Alonge, Roberto and Guido Davico Bonino (eds.), *Storia del teatro moderno e contemporaneo*, vol. 1, *La nascità del teatro moderno: Cinquecento e Seicento* (Turin: Einaudi, 2000)

Armellini, Mario, "Musica e musicisti nei *Marmi* di Anton Francesco Doni" in Giovanna Rizzarelli (ed.), *I "Marmi" di Anton Francesco Doni: la storia, i generi e le arti* (Florence: Olschki, 2012), 331–52

Assonitis, Alessio, "The Birth of Maria de' Medici (26 April 1575): Hearsay, Correspondence, and Historiographical Errors" in Brendan Dooley (ed.), *The Dissemination of News and the Emergence of Contemporaneity in Early Modern Europe* (Farnham, U.K. and Burlington, Vt.: Ashgate, 2010), 83–94

Attolini, Giovanni, *Teatro e spettacolo nel Rinascimento* (Rome: Laterza, 1988)

Baker, Evan, *From the Score to the Stage: An Illustrated History of Continental Opera Production and Staging* (Chicago and London: University of Chicago Press, 2013)

Baldini Giusti, Laura, "Il salone da ballo e la sala della musica: nuovi percorsi nel Quartiere da Inverno di Palazzo Pitti" in Carlo Sisi and Ettore Spalletti (eds.), *Ottocento e Novecento: acquisizioni 1974–1989* (Florence: Centro Di, 1989), 15–21

Baldinucci, Filippo, *Vocabolario toscano dell'arte del disegno, nel quale si esplicano i propri termini e voci, non solo della pittura, scultura et architettura, ma ancora di altre arti a quelle subordinate, e che abbiano per fondamento il disegno* ... (Florence: Santi Franchi, 1681), http://barocchi.sns.it/dizionario/FB_V

Barbaro, Daniele, *La pratica della perspettiva ... opera molto utile a' pittori, a scultori et ad architetti* (Venice: Camillo and Rutilio Borgominieri, 1569; facs. Bologna: Forni, 1980)

Bartoli Bacherini, Maria Adelaide (ed.), *"Per un regale evento": spettacoli nuziali e opera in musica alla corte dei Medici* (Florence: Centro Di, 2000)

Bastogi, Nadia, "Per una ricostruzione della biografia e dell'attività pittorica di Alessandro Pieroni" in Anna Maria Bernacchioni (ed.), *Alessandro Pieroni dall'Impruneta e i pittori della Loggia degli Uffizi* (Florence: Edifir, 2012), 27–50

Battelli, Guido (ed.), *Vita di Lodovico Cardi Cigoli, 1559–1613* (Florence: Barbèra, 1913)

Battistelli, Franco, "Scenografia, scenotecnica e teatri: Sabbatini e Torelli" in *Arte e cultura nella provincia di Pesaro dalle origini a oggi* (Venice: Marsilio, 1986), 377–86

Bausi, Francesco and Mario Martelli, *La metrica italiana: teoria e storia* (Florence: Le Lettere, 1993)

Beaussant, Philippe, *La Malscène* (Paris: Fayard, 2005)

Bertelli, Sergio, "Palazzo Pitti dai Medici ai Savoia" in Anna Bellinazzi and Alessandra Contini (eds.), *La corte di Toscana dai Medici ai Lorena: atti delle giornate di studio, Firenze, Archivio di Stato e Palazzo Pitti, 15–16 dicembre 1997* (Florence: Ministero per i Beni e le Attività Culturali, 2002), 11–109

Bertelli, Sergio and Renato Pasta (eds.), *Vivere a Pitti: una reggia dai Medici ai Savoia* (Florence: Olschki, 2003)

Bertini, Fabio, *"Havere a la giustizia sodisfatto": tragedie giudiziarie di Giovan Battista Giraldi Cinzio nel ventennio conciliare* (Florence: Società Editrice Fiorentina, 2008)

Bevilacqua, Mario, *I progetti per la facciata di Santa Maria del Fiore (1585–1645): architettura a Firenze tra Rinascimento e barocco* (Florence: Olschki, 2015)

Bianconi, Lorenzo, "Il libretto d'opera" in Sandro Cappelletto (ed.), *Il contributo italiano alla storia del pensiero: musica* (Rome: Treccani, 2018), 187–208

Blanchard-Rothmuller, Catherine Anne, "Leone Ebreo de' Sommi's *Four Dialogues on Stage Presentations*: A Translation with Introduction and Notes" (PhD diss., Indiana University, 1973)

Blocker, Déborah, "The Accademia degli Alterati and the Invention of a New Form of Dramatic Experience: Myth, Allegory, and Theory in Jacopo Peri's and Ottavio Rinuccini's *Euridice* (1600)" in Katja Gvozdeva, Tatiana Korneeva, and Kirill Ospovat (eds.), *Dramatic Experience: The Poetics of Drama and the Early Modern Public Sphere(s)* (Leiden: Brill, 2017), 77–117

Blumenthal, Arthur, *Giulio Parigi's Stage Designs: Florence and the Early Baroque Spectacle*, 2 vols. (New York: Garland, 1986)

Bosisio, Paolo, *Teatro dell'Occidente: elementi di storia della drammaturgia e dello spettacolo teatrale*, 2 vols. (Milan: LED, 2006)

Bourbon del Monte Santa Maria, Guidobaldo, *I sei libri della prospettiva ... dal latino tradotti e commentati*, edited by Rocco Sinisgalli (Rome: L'Erma di Bretschneider, 1984)

Bucci, Moreno and Raffaele Monti (eds.), *Orfeo in Toscana: il Maggio Musicale e la nascita del melodramma* (Florence: S.P.E.S., 1999)

Bujić, Bojan, "'Figura poetica molto vaga': Structure and Meaning in Rinuccini's *Euridice*," *Early Music History*, 10 (1991), 29–64

Buonarroti *il giovane*, Michelangelo, *Opere varie in versi ed in prosa*, edited by Pietro Fanfani (Florence: Le Monnier, 1863)

Burattelli, Claudia, Domenica Landolfi, and Anna Zinanni (eds.), *Comici dell'arte: corrispondenze*, 2 vols. (Florence: Le Lettere, 1993)

Calcagno, Mauro, "'Imitar col canto chi parla': Monteverdi and the Creation of a Language for Musical Theater," *Journal of the American Musicological Society*, 55 (2002), 383–431

Camerota, Filippo, "La scena teatrale" in *Nel segno di Masaccio: l'invenzione della prospettiva* (Florence: Giunti, 2001), 149–53

Linear Perspective in the Age of Galileo: Ludovico Cigoli's "Prospettiva pratica", Biblioteca Galilæana 1 (Florence: Olschki, 2010)

Candiard, Céline and Julia Gros de Gasquet (eds.), *Scènes baroques d'aujourd'hui: La mise en scène baroque dans le paysage culturel contemporain*, Théâtre et société 5 (Lyons: Presses Universitaires de Lyon, 2019)

Caneva, Caterina and Francesco Solinas (eds.), *Maria de' Medici (1573–1642): una principessa fiorentina sul trono di Francia* (Livorno: Sillabe, 2005)

Cantelli, Giuseppe, *Francesco Furini e i Furiniani*, Studi d'arte e collezionismo 1 (Florence: GL Arte Collezionismo, 2010)

Capecchi, Gabriella *et al.* (eds.), *Palazzo Pitti: la reggia rivelata* (Florence: Giunti, 2003)

Carter, Tim, "A Florentine Wedding of 1608," *Acta musicologica*, 55 (1983), 89–107; reprinted in Carter, *Music, Patronage and Printing in Late Renaissance Florence*

"Epyllia and Epithalamia: Some Narrative Frames for Early Opera," *The Italianist*, 40, no. 3 (2020), 382–99

"'In questo lieto e fortunato giorno': 'parlare' e 'cantare' nell'*Orfeo* di Monteverdi" in Luca Liana Püschel and Rossetto Casel (eds.), *In questi ameni luoghi: intorno a "Orfeo"* (Turin: Associazione Arianna, 2018), 29–42

Jacopo Peri (1561–1633): His Life and Works, 2 vols. (New York: Garland, 1989; modified reprint of PhD diss., University of Birmingham, 1980)

"Lamenting Ariadne," *Early Music*, 27 (1999), 395–405

Monteverdi's Musical Theatre (New Haven, Conn. and London: Yale University Press, 2002)

"Music and Patronage in Late Sixteenth-Century Florence: The Case of Jacopo Corsi (1561–1602)," *I Tatti Studies: Essays in the Renaissance*, 1 (1985), 57–104; reprinted in Carter, *Music, Patronage and Printing in Late Renaissance Florence*

Music, Patronage and Printing in Late Renaissance Florence, Variorum Collected Studies Series CS682 (Aldershot, U.K. and Burlington, Vt.: Ashgate, 2000)

"Music-Printing in Late Sixteenth- and Early Seventeenth-Century Florence: Giorgio Marescotti, Cristofano Marescotti and Zanobi Pignoni," *Early Music History*, 9 (1989), 27–72; reprinted in Carter, *Music, Patronage and Printing in Late Renaissance Florence*

"New Light on Monteverdi's *Ballo delle ingrate* (Mantua, 1608)," *Il saggiatore musicale*, 6, no. 1 (1999), 63–90

"*Non occorre nominare tanti musici:* Private Patronage and Public Ceremony in Late Sixteenth-Century Florence," *I Tatti Studies: Essays in the Renaissance*, 4 (1991), 89–104; reprinted in Carter, *Music, Patronage and Printing in Late Renaissance Florence*

"Rediscovering *Il rapimento di Cefalo*," *Journal of Seventeenth-Century Music*, 9, no. 1 (2003), https://sscm-jscm.org/v9/no1/carter.html

"Some Notes on the First Edition of Monteverdi's *Orfeo* (1609)," *Music and Letters*, 91 (2010), 498–512

Carter, Tim, and Richard A. Goldthwaite, *Orpheus in the Marketplace: Jacopo Peri and the Economy of Late Renaissance Florence* (Cambridge, Mass.: Harvard University Press, 2013)

Cavicchi, Adriano, "Appunti sulle tipologie teatrali dell'Aleotti" in C. Cavicchi *et al.* (eds.), *Giovan Battista Aleotti e l'architettura*, 227–42

Cavicchi, Costanza, Francesco Ceccarelli, and Rossana Torlontano (eds.), *Giovan Battista Aleotti e l'architettura* (Reggio Emilia: Diabasis, 2003)

Chappell, Miles L., *Disegni di Lodovico Cigoli (1559–1613)*, Gabinetto Disegni e Stampe degli Uffizi 74 (Florence: Olschki, 1992)

"Lodovico Cigoli: Essays on His Career and Painting" (PhD diss., University of North Carolina at Chapel Hill, 1971)

Ciancarelli, Roberto, *Il progetto di una festa barocca: alle origini del teatro Farnese di Parma (1618–1629)* (Rome: Bulzoni, 1987)

Cigoli, Lodovico Cardi, *Trattato pratico di prospettiva . . . : manoscritto Ms 2660A del Gabinetto dei Disegni e delle Stampe degli Uffizi*, edited by Rodolfo Profumo (Rome: Bonsignori, 1992)

Cole, Janie, *Music, Spectacle and Cultural Brokerage in Early Modern Italy: Michelangelo Buonarroti il Giovane*, 2 vols., Fondazione Carlo Marchi: Quaderni 44 (Florence: Olschki, 2011)

Colonna, Stefano, *La galleria dei Carracci in Palazzo Farnese a Roma: Eros, Anteros, Età dell'Oro* (Rome: Gangemi, 2007)

Cormier, Maxime, "Marie de Médicis vue par les observateurs italiens (1597–1624)" (MA thesis, Université Rennes 2, 2012), https://dumas.ccsd.cnrs.fr/dumas-00713161

Covoni, Pierfilippo, *Don Antonio de' Medici al Casino di San Marco* (Florence: Tipografia Cooperativa, 1893)

Cox, Virginia, *The Prodigious Muse: Women's Writing in Counter-Reformation Italy* (Baltimore, Md.: The Johns Hopkins University Press, 2011)

D'Amia, Giovanna, "Giovan Battista Aleotti e la storiografia dell'architettura teatrale" in C. Cavicchi *et al.* (eds.), *Giovan Battista Aleotti e l'architettura*, 197–204

Danti, Ignazio, *Les Deux Règles de la perspective pratique de Vignole (1583)*, translated by Pasqual Dubourg Glatigny (Paris: CNRS, 2003)

Daolmi, Davide, "La drammaturgia al servizio della scenotecnica: le 'volubili scene' dell'opera barberiniana," www.examenapium.it/barberini (a shorter version is in *Il saggiatore musicale*, 13, no. 1 (2006), 5–62)

De Angelis, Marcello, Elvira Garbero Zorzi, Loredana Maccabruni, *et al.* (eds.), *Lo "spettacolo maraviglioso": il Teatro della Pergola; l'opera a Firenze* (Florence: Pagliai Polistampa, 2000)

De Caro, Gaspare, *"Euridice": momenti dell'umanesimo civile fiorentino* (Bologna: Ut Orpheus Edizioni, 2006)

De Luca, Francesca, *Le nozze di Maria de' Medici con Enrico IV: Jacopo da Empoli per l'apparato di Palazzo Vecchio* (Florence: Edizioni Polistampa, 2006)

De' Sommi, Leone, *Quattro dialoghi in materia di rappresentazioni sceniche*, edited by Ferruccio Marotti (Milan: Il Polifilo, 1968)

Deutsch, Catherine, "'Jamais il n'y eut Musique si harmonieuse': Regards français sur les festivités florentines du mariage de Marie de Médicis et Henri IV," *Le Verger: Bouquet*, 6 ("La fête à la Renaissance", November 2014), http://cornucopia16.com/blog/2014/11/30/catherine-deutsch-jamais-il-ny-eut-musique-si-harmonieuse-regards-francais-sur-les-festivites-florentines-du-mariage-de-marie-de-medicis-et-henri-iv

Dooley, Brendan, *A Mattress Maker's Daughter: The Renaissance Romance of Don Giovanni de' Medici and Livia Vernazza* (Cambridge, Mass.: Harvard University Press, 2014)

Drago, Samuele, "Nell'officina di un 'poeta-faber': repertorio metrico dei madrigali tassiani," *Stilistica e metrica italiana*, 17 (2017), 107–53

Dubost, Jean-François, *Marie de Médicis: La reine dévoilée* (Paris: Payot et Rivages, 2009)

Durante, Elio and Anna Martellotti, *Don Angelo Grillo O.S.B. alias Livio Celiano: poeta per musica del secolo decimosesto* (Florence: S.P.E.S., 1989)

Evangelista, Anna, "L'attività spettacolare della Compagnia di San Giovanni Evangelista nel Cinquecento," *Medioevo e Rinascimento*, 18/n.s. 15 (2004), 299–366

Fabbri, Mario, Elvira Garbero Zorzi, and Anna Maria Tofani (eds.), *Il luogo teatrale a Firenze: Brunelleschi, Vasari, Buontalenti, Parigi; spettacolo e musica nella Firenze medicea* (Milan: Electa, 1975)

La scena del principe: Firenze e la Toscana dei Medici nell'Europa del Cinquecento (Florence: Edizioni Medicee, 1980)

Fabbri, Paolo, "'Di vedere e non vedere': lo spettatore all'opera," *Il saggiatore musicale*, 14, no. 2 (2007), 359–67

Fabbri, Paolo and Angelo Pompilio (eds.), *Il corago, o vero Alcune osservazioni per metter bene in scena le composizioni drammatiche*, Studi e testi per la storia della musica 4 (Florence: Olschki, 1983)

Fabretti, Alessandra, "Il teatro della Sala Grande a Ferrara e i tornei aleottiani," *Musei ferraresi*, 12 (1982), 183–208

Facchinetti, Fiorella, "Le vicende costruttive" in Marco Chiarini (ed.), *Palazzo Pitti: l'arte e la storia* (Florence: Nardini, 2000), 20–39

Fagiolo, Maurizio, *La scenografia dalle sacre rappresentazioni al futurismo* (Florence: Sansoni, 1973)

Fantappiè, Francesca, "La celebrazione memorabile: potere, arte e spettacolo nelle memorie di corte di Ferdinando I Medici," *Arte, musica e spettacolo*, 2 (2001), 203–40

"La chiesa di San Lorenzo tra due dinastie: le pubbliche cerimonie dai Medici ai Lorena" in Robert W. Gaston and Louis A. Waldman (eds.), *San Lorenzo: A Florentine Church* (Cambridge, Mass.: Harvard University Press, 2017), 542–66

"Sale per lo spettacolo a Pitti (1600–1650)" in Bertelli and Pasta (eds.), *Vivere a Pitti*, 135–80

"Saracinelli, Ferdinando" in *Dizionario biografico degli italiani*, vol. 90 (Rome: Treccani, 2017), 569–73, www.treccani.it/enciclopedia/ferdinando-saracinelli_(Dizionario-Biografico)

"Strozzi, Piero Vincenzo" in *Dizionario biografico degli italiani*, vol. 94 (Rome: Treccani, 2019), 451–54, www.treccani.it/enciclopedia/piero-vincenzo-strozzi_(Dizionario-Biografico)

"Una primizia rinucciniana: la 'Dafne' prima della 'miglior forma'," *Il saggiatore musicale*, 24, no. 2 (2017), 189–222

Farneti, Fauzia, "La Sala delle Nicchie: un apparato decorativo ritrovato" in Capecchi *et al.* (eds.), *Palazzo Pitti*, 110–23

Fenlon, Iain, "A Golden Age Restored: Pastoral Pastimes at the Pitti Palace" in Massimilano Rossi and Fiorella Gioffredi Superbi (eds.), *L'arme e gli amori: Ariosto, Tasso and Guarini in Late Renaissance Florence*, 2 vols. (Florence: Olschki, 2004), 2: 199–229

Ferrone, Siro, *Attori, mercanti, corsari: la commedia dell'arte in Europa tra Cinque e Seicento* (Turin: Einaudi, 1993)

Formichetti, Gianfranco, "Crogi, Passitea" in *Dizionario biografico degli italiani*, vol. 31 (Rome: Treccani: 1985), 227–29, www.treccani.it/enciclopedia/passitea-crogi_(Dizionario-Biografico)

Galilei, Vincenzo, *Dialogue on Ancient and Modern Music*, translated by Claude V. Palisca (New Haven, Conn. and London: Yale University Press, 2003)

Gambuti, Alessandro, "Lodovico Cigoli architetto," *Studi e documenti di architettura*, 2 (1973), 37–136

Garbero Zorzi, Elvira, "I teatri di Pratolino" in Alessandro Vezzosi (ed.), *Il giardino d'Europa: Pratolino come modello della cultura europea* (Milan: Mazzotta, 1986), 93–98

Garbero Zorzi, Elvira and Mario Sperenzi (eds.), *Teatro e spettacolo nella Firenze dei Medici: modelli dei luoghi teatrali* (Florence: Olschki, 2001)

Garbero Zorzi, Elvira and Luigi Zangheri (eds.), *I teatri storici della Toscana: censimento documentario e architettonico*, vol. 8, *Firenze* (Venice: Marsilio, 2000)

Giazzon, Stefano, "Vincenzo Panciatichi da *L'amicizia costante* (1600) a *Gli amorosi affanni* (1605): una pastorale 'in viaggio' fra Firenze e Venezia" in Daria Perocco (ed.), *Tra boschi e marine: varietà della pastorale nel Rinascimento e nell'età barocca* (Bologna: Archetipolibri, 2012), 311–51

Ginzburg, Silvia. *La Galleria Farnese: gli affreschi dei Carracci* (Milan: Electa, 2008)

Giuliani, Maria Carla, "'La Mascara' di Hercole Bottrigari: dibattito teorico e nuove proposte per il teatro del '500 in un trattato inedito di prospettiva scenica," *Antichità viva*, 24, no. 4 (1985), 26–33; 25, no. 2–3 (1986), 60–66

Giusti, Giovanna and Riccardo Spinelli (eds.), *Dolci trionfi e finissime piegature: sculture in zucchero e tovaglioli per le nozze fiorentine di Maria de' Medici* (Livorno: Sillabe, 2015)

Glixon Beth L. and Jonathan E. Glixon, *Inventing the Business of Opera: The Impresario and His World in Seventeenth-Century Venice* (New York and Oxford: Oxford University Press, 2006)

Goldthwaite, Richard A. and Giulio Mandich, *Studi sulla moneta fiorentina (secoli XIII–XVI)* (Florence: Olschki, 1994)

Gonzáles Román, Carmen, *Spectacula: teoría, arte y escena en la Europa del Renacimento* (Málaga: Universidad de Málaga, 2001)

Gousset, Jean-Paul, "Comment recréer dans l'esprit de . . .? Expériences de trois restitutions au théâtre de la Reine, à Trianon et à l'Opéra royal de Versailles" in Jean-Noël Laurenti (ed.), *Restitution et création dans la remise en spectacle des œuvres des XVIIe et XVIIIe siècles: Actes du colloque international (Versailles–Nantes, 2008)*, Annales de l'Association pour un Centre de Recherche sur les Arts du Spectacle aux XVIIe et XVIIIe siècles 4 (Villejuif: ACRAS, 2010), 36–40

Hanning, Barbara Russano, "Glorious Apollo: Poetic and Political Themes in the First Opera," *Renaissance Quarterly*, 32 (1979), 485–513

Harness, Kelley, *Echoes of Women's Voices: Music, Art, and Female Patronage in Early Modern Florence* (Chicago and London: University of Chicago Press, 2006)

"*Le tre Euridici*: Characterization and Allegory in the *Euridici* of Peri and Caccini," *Journal of Seventeenth Century Music*, 9, no. 1 (2003), https://sscm-jscm.org/v9/no1/harness.html

Hénin, Emmanuelle, "Le rideau de théâtre: Prélude et substitut au spectacle scénique" in Véronique Lochert and Jean de Guardia (eds.), *Théâtre et imaginaire: Images scéniques et representations mentales (XVI*[e]*–XVIII*[e] *siècle)* (Dijon: Éditions Universitaires de Dijon, 2012), 151–70

Hewitt, Barnard (ed.), *The Renaissance Stage: Documents of Serlio, Sabbatini, and Furttenbach*, translated by Allardyce Nicoll, John H. McDowell, and George R. Kernodle (Coral Gables, Fla.: University of Miami Press, 1958)

Hill, John Walter, *Roman Monody, Cantata, and Opera from the Circles around Cardinal Montalto*, 2 vols. (Oxford: Clarendon Press, 1997)

Ingegneri, Angelo, *Della poesia rappresentativa e del modo di rappresentare le favole sceniche*, edited by Maria Luisa Doglio (Modena: Panini, 1989)

Isom-Verhaaren, Christine, *Allies with the Infidel: The Ottoman and French Alliance in the Sixteenth Century* (London and New York: I. B. Tauris, 2011)

Johnson, Eugene J., *Inventing the Opera House: Theater Architecture in Renaissance and Baroque Italy* (Cambridge and New York: Cambridge University Press, 2018)

Junod, Philippe, "Au fil du temps: Réflexions sur la mise en scène à l'opéra," *Revue musicale de Suisse Romande*, 71, no. 4 (December 2018), 30–37

Ketterer, Robert C., "Classical Sources and Thematic Structure in the Florentine *intermedi* of 1589," *Renaissance Studies*, 13 (1999): 192–222

Kirkendale, Warren, *Emilio de' Cavalieri, "gentiluomo romano": His Life and Letters, His Role as Superintendent of All the Arts at the Medici Court, and His Musical Compositions*, "Historiae musicae cultores" biblioteca 86 (Florence: Olschki, 2001)

The Court Musicians in Florence during the Principate of the Medici, with a Reconstruction of the Artistic Establishment, "Historiae musicae cultores" biblioteca 61 (Florence: Olschki, 1993)

Landolfi, Domenica, "Su un teatrino mediceo e sull'Accademia degli Incostanti a Firenze nel primo Seicento," *Teatro e storia*, 6 (1991), 57–88

Lavin, Irvin, "Lettres de Parmes (1618, 1627–28) et débuts du théâtre baroque" in Jean Jacquot (ed.), *Le Lieu théâtral à la Renaissance* (Paris: Centre National de la Recherche Scientifique, 1964), 105–58

Lazardig, Jan and Hole Rößler (eds.), *Technologies of Theatre: Joseph Furttenbach and the Transfer of Mechanical Knowledge in Early Modern Theatre Cultures*, Zeitsprünge: Forschungen zur Frühen Neuzeit 20, no. 3–4 (Frankfurt am Main: Vittorio Klostermann, 2016)

Litchfield, R. Burr, *Emergence of a Bureaucracy: The Florentine Patricians, 1530–1790* (Princeton, N.J.: Princeton University Press, 1986)

Florence Ducal Capital, 1530–1630 (New York: ACLS Humanities E-Book, 2008), http://hdl.handle.net/2027/heb.90034.0001.001

Luti, Filippo, *Don Antonio de' Medici e i suoi tempi*, Fondazione Carlo Marchi: Quaderni 27 (Florence: Olschki, 2006)

McGee, Timothy, "Pompeo Caccini and *Euridice:* New Biographical Notes," *Renaissance and Reformation*, 26 (1990), 81–99

Malanima, Paolo, "Corsi, Iacopo" in *Dizionario biografico degli italiani*, vol. 29 (Rome: Treccani: 1983), 574–77, www.treccani.it/enciclopedia/iacopo-corsi_res-5512502d-87eb-11dc-8e9d-0016357eee51_(Dizionario-Biografico)

Mamone, Sara, *Firenze e Parigi: due capitali dello spettacolo per una regina Maria de' Medici* (Milan: Silvana Editoriale, 1987)

Marinazzo, Adriano, "La Sala delle Nicchie: una ricostruzione virtuale," in Capecchi *et al.* (eds.), *Palazzo Pitti*, 124–27

Marotti, Ferruccio, *Lo spazio scenico: teoria e tecniche scenografiche in Italia dall'età barocca al Settecento* (Rome: Bulzoni, 1974)

Mazzoni, Stefano, *Atlante iconografico: spazi e forme dello spettacolo in occidente dal mondo antico a Wagner* (San Miniato: Titivillus, 2003)

L'Olimpico di Vicenza: un teatro e la sua perpetua memoria (Florence: Le Lettere, 1998)

Mazzoni, Stefano and Ovidio Guaita, *Il teatro di Sabbioneta* (Florence: Olschki, 1985)

Mersmann, Jasmin, *Lodovico Cigoli: Formen der Wahrheit um 1600* (Berlin and Boston: De Gruyter, 2016)

Migliarisi, Anna, *Renaissance and Baroque Directors: Theory and Practice of Play Production in Italy* (New York, Ottawa, and Toronto: Legas, 2003)

Milesi, Francesco (ed.), *Giacomo Torelli: l'invenzione scenica nell'Europa barocca* (Fano: Fondazione della Cassa di Risparmio di Fano, 2000)

Milstein, Joanna, *The Gondi: Family Strategy and Survival in Early Modern France* (Farnham, U.K. and Burlington, Vt.: Ashgate, 2014)

Mohler, Frank, "Medici Wings: The Scenic Wing Change in Renaissance Florence," *Theatre Design and Technology*, 44, no. 4 (Fall 2008): 58–64 (see also https://spectacle.appstate.edu/)

Morolli, Gabriele (ed.), *Siena 1600 circa: dimenticare Firenze. Teofilo Gallaccini (1564–1641) e l'eclisse presunta di una cultura architettonica* (Siena: Protagon Editori Toscani per Santa Maria della Scala, 1999)

Müller, Ulrich, "*Regietheater*/Director's Theater" in Helen M. Greenwald (ed.), *The Oxford Handbook of Opera* (Oxford and New York: Oxford University Press, 2014), 582–605

Murata, Margaret, *Operas for the Papal Court (1631–1668)* (Ann Arbor: UMI Press, 1981)

Nagler, Alois Maria, *Theatre Festivals of the Medici, 1539–1637* (New Haven, Conn. and London: Yale University Press, 1964)

Newcomb, Anthony, *The Madrigal at Ferrara, 1579–1597*, 2 vols. (Princeton, N.J.: Princeton University Press, 1980)

Nicoll, Allardyce, *The Development of the Theatre: A Study of Theatrical Art from the Beginnings to the Present Day*, 5th ed. (New York: Harcourt, Brace,

1966), translated by Clelia Falletti as *Lo spazio scenico: storia dell'arte teatrale* (Rome: Bulzoni, 1971)

Orlando, Angela, *Le Grand Parti: fiorentini a Lione e il debito pubblico francese nel XVI secolo* (Florence: Olschki, 2002)

Padovani, Serena, "Il quartiere dei cardinali e principi forestieri" in Marco Chiarini (ed.), *Palazzo Pitti: l'arte e la storia* (Florence: Nardini, 2000), 43–53

Palisca, Claude V., "Aria Types in the Earliest Operas," *Journal of Seventeenth-Century Music*, 9, no. 1 (2003), https://sscm-jscm.org/v9/no1/palisca.html

"Musical Asides in the Diplomatic Correspondence of Emilio de' Cavalieri" (1963), in *Studies in the History of Italian Music and Music Theory*, 389–407

"Peri and the Theory of Recitative" (1989), in *Studies in the History of Italian Music and Music Theory*, 452–66

Studies in the History of Italian Music and Music Theory (Oxford: Clarendon Press, 1994)

"The Alterati of Florence, Pioneers in the Theory of Dramatic Music" (1968), in *Studies in the History of Italian Music and Music Theory*, 408–31

"The First Performance of Euridice" (1964), in *Studies in the History of Italian Music and Music Theory*, 432–51

The Florentine Camerata: Documentary Studies and Translations (New Haven, Conn. and London: Yale University Press, 1989)

Parenti, Adonella Barbara, *Pietro Accolti e "Lo inganno de gl'occhi": tradizione e rinnovamento nella letteratura prospettica di primo Seicento* (Montevarchi: Accademia Valdarnese del Poggio, 2011)

Parigino, Giuseppe Vittorio, *Il tesoro del principe: funzione pubblica e privata del patrimonio della famiglia Medici nel Cinquecento*, Accademia Toscana di Scienze e Lettere "La Colombaria": Studi 180 (Florence: Olschki, 1999)

Payne, Alina, *The Telescope and the Compass: Teofilo Gallaccini and the Dialogue between Architecture and Science in the Age of Galileo* (Florence: Olschki, 2012)

Peacock, John, *The Stage Designs of Inigo Jones: The European Context* (Cambridge: Cambridge University Press, 1995)

Pegazzano, Donatella, *Committenza e collezionismo nel Cinquecento: la famiglia Corsi a Firenze tra musica e scultura*, Le voci del museo 22 (Florence: Edifir, 2010)

Peri, Jacopo, *"Euridice": An Opera in One Act, Five Scenes*, edited by Howard Mayer Brown, Recent Researches in the Music of the Baroque Era 36–37 (Madison, Wisc.: A-R Editions, 1981)

Petrioli Tofani, Annamaria, "L'illustrazione teatrale e il significato dei documenti figurative per la storia dello spettacolo" in Elizabeth Cropper, Giovanna Perini, and Francesco Solinas (eds.), *Documentary Culture: Florence and Rome from Grand Duke Ferdinando I to Pope Alexander VII; Papers from a Colloquium Held at the Villa Spelman, Florence, 1990*, Villa Spelman Colloquia 3 (Bologna: Nuova Alfa Editoriale, 1992), 49–62

Petrobelli, Pierluigi, "La regia dell'opera: lettura storica o interpretazione attuale?" in Jean-Jacques Nattiez (ed.), *Enciclopedia della musica*, vol. 4, *Storia della musica europea* (Turin: Einaudi, 2004), 951–55.

Pinelli, Antonio, *I teatri: lo spazio dello spettacolo dal teatro umanistico al teatro dell'opera* (Florence: Sansoni, 1973)

Pirrotta, Nino, *Li due Orfei: da Poliziano a Monteverdi* (Turin: ERI, 1969; rev. 1975); translated by Karen Eales as *Music and Theatre from Poliziano to Monteverdi* (Cambridge: Cambridge University Press, 1982)

Porter, William V., "Peri and Corsi's *Dafne*: Some New Discoveries and Observations," *Journal of the American Musicological Society*, 18 (1965), 170–96

Povoledo, Elena, "Origini e aspetti della scenografia in Italia dalla fine del Quattrocento agli intermezzi fiorentini del 1589" in Pirrotta, *Li due Orfei* (1975), 335–460; translated as "Origins and Aspects of Italian Scenography (from the End of the Fifteenth Century to the Florentine *intermedi* of 1589)" in Pirrotta, *Music and Theatre from Poliziano to Monteverdi*, 281–383

Riccò, Laura, *"Ben mille pastorali": l'itinerario dell'Ingegneri da Tasso a Guarini e oltre* (Rome: Bulzoni, 2004)

Dalla zampogna all'aurea cetra: egloghe, pastorali, favole in musica (Rome: Bulzoni, 2015)

La "miniera" accademica: pedagogia, editoria, palcoscenico nella Siena del Cinquecento (Rome: Bulzoni, 2020)

L'arcadia "in mano": illustrazioni editoriali della favola pastorale (1583–1678), 2 vols. (Rome: Bulzoni, 2012)

"Su le carte e fra le scene": teatro in forma di libro nel Cinquecento italiano (Rome: Bulzoni, 2008)

Riccò, Laura *et al.*, "La mascherata della 'Genealogia degli dei' (Firenze, carnevale 1566): le ricerche in corso; atti della giornata di studi, Firenze, 2 dicembre 2011," special issue of *Studi italiani*, 25, no. 1–2 (January–December 2013)

Rinaldi, Alessandro, "Nigetti, Matteo" in *Dizionario biografico degli italiani*, vol. 78 (Rome: Treccani, 2013), 555–58, www.treccani.it/enciclopedia/matteo-nigetti_(Dizionario-Biografico)

Ripa, Cesare, *Iconologia*, edited by Sonia Maffei (Turin: Einaudi 2012)

Robertson, Clare, *The Invention of Annibale Carracci* (Milan: Silvana, 2008)

Rolandi, Ulderico, "Didascalie sceniche in un libretto dell'*Euridice* del Rinuccini (1600)," *Rivista musicale italiana*, 23 (1926), 21–27

Rossini, Francesco, "Corrispondenti strozziani (Magliabechiano VIII, 1399): le lettere di Angelo Grillo" in Clizia Carminati (ed.), *"Testimoni dell'ingegno": reti epistolari e libri di lettere nel Cinquecento e nel Seicento* (Bergamo: Edizioni di Archilet, 2019), 185–230

Saino, Stefano, "'Più dolci affetti': la lingua dei melodrammi di Ottavio Rinuccini," *La lingua italiana: storia, strutture, testi*, 10 (2014), 121–35

Saladino, Vincenzo, "L'arredo statuario della Sala delle Nicchie" in Capecchi *et al.* (eds.), *Palazzo Pitti*, 128–37

Saslow, James M., *The Medici Wedding of 1589: Florentine Festival as "theatrum mundi"* (New Haven, Conn. and London: Yale University Press, 1996)

Schneider, Federico, *Pastoral Drama and Healing in Early Modern Italy* (Farnham, U.K. and Burlington, Vt.: Ashgate, 2010)

Serlio, Sebastiano, *L'architettura: i libri I–VII e Extraordinario nelle prime edizioni*, edited by Francesco Paolo Fiore (Milan: Il Polifilo, 2001)

Solerti, Angelo, *Gli albori del melodramma*, 3 vols. (Milan: Sandron, 1904; repr. Bologna: Forni, 1976)

Musica, ballo e drammatica alla corte medicea dal 1600 al 1637: notizie tratte da un diario con appendice di testi inediti e rari (Florence, 1905; repr. New York: Broude, 1968; repr. Bologna: Forni, 1989)

Spinelli, Riccardo, "Feste e cerimonie tenutesi a Firenze per le 'felicissime nozze': nuovi documenti" in Caneva and Solinas (eds.), *Maria de' Medici*, 130–40

Sternfeld, Frederick W., "The First Printed Opera Libretto," *Music and Letters*, 69 (1978), 121–38

Surgers, Anne, *Scénographies du théâtre occidental* (Paris: Nathan, 2000)

Tabacchi, Stefano, *Maria de' Medici* (Rome: Salerno, 2012)

Talbot, Michael, "*Ore italiane*: The Reckoning of the Time of Day in Pre-Napoleonic Italy," *Italian Studies*, 40 (1985), 51–62

Tamburini, Elena, *Due teatri per il principe: studi sulla committenza teatrale di Lorenzo Onofrio Colonna (1659–1689)* (Rome: Bulzoni, 1997)

Gian Lorenzo Bernini e il teatro dell'arte (Rome: Bulzoni, 2012)

Il quadro della visione: arcoscenico e altri sguardi ai primordi del teatro moderno (Rome: Bulzoni, 2004)

Tamburini, Elena (ed.), *Scenotecnica barocca: "Costruzione de' teatri e machine teatrali" di Fabrizio Carini Motta (1688) e "Pratica delle machine de' teatri" di Romano Capecchia (1689–91)* (Rome: E&A Editori, 1994)

Testaverde, Anna Maria, "L'avventura del teatro granducale degli Uffizi (1586–1637)," *Drammaturgia*, 12/n.s. 2 (2015), 45–69

(as Annamaria Testaverde Matteini), *L'officina delle nuvole: il Teatro Mediceo del 1589 e gli intermedi del Buontalenti nel memoriale di Girolamo Seriacopi*, Musica e Teatro: Quaderni degli Amici della Scala 11–12 (Milan: Edizioni degli Amici della Scala, 1991)

"Michelangelo Buonarroti il Giovane e le didascalie sceniche per il *Giudizio di Paride*" in Stefano Mazzoni (ed.), *Studi di storia dello spettacolo: omaggio a Siro Ferrone* (Florence: Le Lettere, 2011), 166–79

"Nuovi documenti sulle scenografie di Ludovico Cigoli per l'*Euridice* di Ottavio Rinuccini (1600)," *Medioevo e Rinascimento*, 17/n.s. 14 (2003), 307–21

"San Lorenzo 'cantiere teatrale'" in Monica Bietti (ed.), *La morte e la gloria: apparati funebri medicei per Filippo II di Spagna d'Austria* (Livorno: Le Sillabe, 1999), 75–79

Thornton, Peter, *The Italian Renaissance Interior, 1400–1600* (New York: Harry N. Abrams, 1991)

Tognetti, Sergio, *I Gondi di Lione: una banca d'affari fiorentina nella Francia del primo Cinquecento* (Florence: Olschki, 2013)

Vène, Magali, *Bibliographia serliana: Catalogue des éditions imprimées des livres du traité d'architecture de Sebastiano Serlio (1537–1681)* (Paris: Picard, 2004)

Weinberg, Bernard (ed.), *Trattati di poetica e retorica del Cinquecento*, 4 vols. (Bari: Laterza, 1972)

Wilbourne, Emily, *Seventeenth-Century Opera and the Sound of the Commedia dell'Arte* (Chicago and London: University of Chicago Press, 2015)

Zorzi, Ludovico, *Il teatro e la città* (Turin: Einaudi, 1977)

Index

Page references in italics refer to footnotes.

Accademia degli Alterati, 2, 5, 18, 42–43, 197, 207
Accademia degli Intronati (Siena), 88
Accademia degli Spensierati, 18, *201*
Accademia della Crusca, *41*
Accademia Fiorentina, 5
Accolti, Marcello, *14*, 35, 37, *39*
Accolti, Pietro, 72
account books, 21, 23, 24, 27, 29–30, 33–36, *87*, 203
  moneys of account, 29
Alberti, Leon Battista, *69*
Alberti, Luciano, 213, 214
Albizzi, Eleonora degli, 5
Aldobrandini, Ippolito (cardinal), 206
Aldobrandini, Margherita, 189
Aldobrandini, Pietro (cardinal), 39, 41, 189
  at 1600 wedding, 6–8, 13, 16, 53, 56, 60, *141*
Aleotti, Giovan Battista, 76, 78
Allori, Alessandro, 27, *28*, 113
  costume sketches, 176–77, 178
Altoviti, Ridolfo, *12*
Ambrogiana (Medici villa), *41*
Andreini, Giovanni Battista, 201
Andreini (née Ramponi), Virginia, 184
Anguillara, Giovanni Andrea dell', 176
Antella, Donato dell', *12*, *18*, 23, 24–25, 28
Apollonius of Rhodes, 194
Archilei, Vittoria, *37*
Ariosto, Ludovico, *97*, *166*
Aristotle, 154, 160, 161, *171*

Baccellini, Matteo, *42*, *43*
Badini, Carlo Francesco, 208
Baglioni-Orsini, Francesca, *8*
Barbaro, Daniele, 68
  perspective, 70
  rustic sets, 107–8
Barbazza, Andrea, 207
Barberini, Taddeo, *76*
Bardi, Giovanni de', 2, 14–15, *45*, 146
  1608 wedding festivities, 15
  his "Camerata," 2
  L'amico fido, *13*, 17
Bargagli, Girolamo. *See* La pellegrina
Barozzi da Vignola, Giacomo, 69
Bartolini, Ginevra di Lorenzo, 141
Bassanello, Gian Gabriele, 209
Bati, Luca, 17
Beccheria, Alessandro, *4*, *11*, *13*
Beccuto, Roberto del, *176*
Bella, Stefano della, *84*
Bellegarde, Roger de (Monsieur le Grand), 53, 60
Belli, Domenico, 206
Benevoli della Scala, Margherita, 43
Bentivoglio, Marchesa, *41*
Bergamo, 207
Bernardi, Leonora, 3
Bertozzi, Adamo, *16*
Bevilacqua, Bonifazio (cardinal), 207
Bindi, Camilla di Andrea, *140*
Boccherini, Giovanni, 142
Bologna, *94*
  Euridice performed in, 207, 214
Bolsi, Girolamo, *88*, 89
Borgia, Don Ferrante, 203
Bottrigari, Ercole, 71
Bourbon, Catherine de, *6*
Bourbon del Monte Santa Maria, Guidobaldo, 71–72
braccia andante, 32, *106*, *110*
Brandi, Antonio di Francesco ("Brandino"), 139, *144*, 151, 182
Bronzino, Agnolo, *69*
Brown, Howard Mayer, *213*
Buonarroti, Michelangelo *il giovane*, 2, *43*, *148*, 209
  annotates libretto of *Euridice*, 54–56, 141
  Balletto della Cortesia (1614), 204
  Descrizione delle felicissime nozze (1600), 2, 6, *9*, 14, 15–17, *18*, 19, 80

Il giudizio di Paride (1608), 1, 75, *112*, 202–3
on *Euridice*, 17, 19–20, *60*, 61–63, 81, 93, 97, 108, 113–14, 116, 119, 123–24
on *Il rapimento di Cefalo*, 2–3, 61, 143, 165, 194
on the banquet, *6*
on the wedding ceremony, 7–8
Buontalenti, Bernardo, 17, 27, *53*
and *periaktoi*, 70, 74, 77
argues with Don Giovanni de' Medici, 5, 14, *61*
costume sketches, 178, *212*
grotto (Boboli Gardens), 212
intermedi (not used) for 1600 festivities, 13–14, 50
portable stage for the Pitti, 40
Buontalenti, Eufemia, *13*
Butteri, Giovanni Maria, *28*

Caccini, Francesca, 43, 207
Caccini, Giulio
and Angelo Grillo, 42–44, 45, 47
and *Dafne*, 45–46
and *Narciso*, *206*
and the "Camerata," 2
banishes his son, 140
his *Euridice* performed in 1602, *20*, 122, 141, 178, 200, *203*
his singers at court, 46, 51, 61, 141
his singers in *Euridice*, 44, 45, 137, 139, 144, *160*, 162, *168*
Le nuove musiche (1602), *17*, 44, *144*
modern stagings of his *Euridice*, 211, *213*
music praised, *3*, 37, 43, 165
not mentioned in 1600 description of *Euridice*, 62
publishes *Euridice*, 44–45, 59, *137*, 145, 146
reinstatement in Medici service, 5–6, 51
score probably not known by Monteverdi, 130
supported by Jacopo Corsi, 51
See also Euridice; Il rapimento di Cefalo
Caccini, Michele, 25, 39, 50, 198
and *Euridice*, 27–30, 32, 33, 52–53, 54, 56, 85, *102*, 106, *110*, *112*, *125*, 200
new scenery for the Sala delle Commedie, 200–1
Caccini, Pompeo
and *Euridice*, 140, 143, 145
and Ginevra Giannetti, 45, 140–41
Caccini, Settimia, 43, *144*
"Camerata" (Florentine), 2
See also Bardi, Giovanni de'
Cantagallina, Remigio, 177, 202
canvas
sewing, 31–33, *106*
telo (*tela*, *telaio*), 32–33, 74, 78, 94, 105, *110*, 117, 200
types of, 32, 106
See also braccia andante; Ricoveri, Francesco
Cappello, Bianca (grand duchess), 5
Capponi, Luigi (cardinal), 207
Cardi, Giovanni Battista, *27*, 176, 198–99
Cardi, Lodovico ("Il Cigoli"). *See* Cigoli, Lodovico
Carini Motta, Fabrizio, *78*
Carlo Emanuele I (Duke of Savoy), 9, 12
Carracci, Agostino, 189, *191*
Carracci, Annibale, 189
Casa Buonarroti (Florence), 208–9
Castro, *69*
Catullus, 189–90, 191
Cavalieri, Emilio de'
comments on the 1600 festivities, *13*, 14–15, 61, 81, 111, 174
complains about Corsi and Rinuccini, 37, 39
"his" *Euridice*, *14–15*, 20, 58
his singers, 142
Rappresentatione di Anima, et di Corpo, 39, *176*
rooms in the Pitti, *48*, 57, 58, 84, 125–26
sidelined, 5–6, 37
superintendent of the Galleria dei Lavori, 20
See also Dialogo di Giunone e Minerva; Il giuoco della cieca; Il satiro: La disperazione di Fileno
Cayet, Pierre Victor, *16*, *60*
Cecchi, Giovanni Maria, *69*
Celiano, Livio. *See* Grillo, Angelo
Cesis, Anna Maria, *88*
Český Krumlov, 67, *125*
Cetrangolo, Aníbal, 214
Charon, 116, 133, 213
Château d'If, 10
Chelli, Matteo, 29, *110*
Chiabrera, Gabriello
and the canzonetta, 134, 171, 172
festa in the Riccardi gardens, *16*, *192*
Veglia delle Grazie (1615), 204
See also Il rapimento di Cefalo
Chiaramonti, Scipione, 72
Chimenti da Empoli, Jacopo, 6–9, 15, *28*
Christine of Lorraine, 8, 12, 16, 19, 46, 49, 52, 60, 141, 197
and *Dafne*, 4, 38–39, 46, 148

Christine of Lorraine (*cont.*)
Corsi's "comedy" (spring 1600), 39–41, 47, 48–49, 50
favoring France, 2, 6, 9, 10
her wedding (1589), 1, 11, 14, 18, *25*, 65, 77, *91*
rooms in the Pitti, 30, *53*, 87
support for entertainments, 3, *20*, 50–51, 97
Cicognini, Jacopo, 185, 207
Cigoli, Lodovico (Cardi), 25–27, 215
designs costumes for *Euridice*, *27*, 176
invoice for *Euridice*, 25, 27–29, 31, 54, 85, 89, 96, 116, 198
new comic set for the Pitti, 200–1
other works, 36, 89, 91, 113
Prospettiva pratica, *27*, 72, *93*, 98, 101, 102, 106, *124*, 126–28
sketches for *Euridice*, 91, 114–16, 125, 177
See also Euridice (stage)
Cini, Francesco
Notte d'Amore (1608), *58*, *60*, *126*, *128*, 202–3
Cini, Gian Jacopo, *140*
Cini, Giovan Battista, 69
Claudian, 191–92
clefs (musical), *138*, 142
Clement VIII (Pope), 6, 189
Compagnia degli Uniti, 201
Compagnia di S. Alberto Bianco, *51*
Compagnia di S. Giovanni Evangelista, 69
Concini, Giovanni Battista, *61*
Corona, Fra Filippo, *143*
Corsi, Bardo, 10
Corsi, Jacopo, 2, 19, 140, *177*
and Angelo Grillo, 42–43
and Don Giovanni de' Medici, 5, 134
and Francesco Rasi, 143
and the Alterati, 2, *43*
costumes, 20, 34
criticized by Cavalieri, 37
helps finance 1600 wedding, 10, 19, 51
his "comedy" (spring 1600), *35*, 39–51
his costs for *Euridice*, 19, 20, 34
ode by Rinuccini, 38
performs in *Euridice*, 59, 139
residence in Florence, 3, *4*, 11–12, 46
shares costs of other entertainments, 18, 19
supports Caccini, *5*, 51
supports Peri, 51
villa in Sesto Fiorentino, 42
See also Dafne (Corsi and Peri), Euridice
Corsini, Ottavio, 206
Cresci, Gianbattista, 24–25, 56, 77, *201–2*, 203
inventory of stage for *Euridice*, 29–31, 36–37, 85–87, 98, 110, 116, *121*, 198
monitors costs of 1600 festivities, *14*, 28, 33–35, 61
See also Euridice (stage)
Crogi, Passitea, 8
Curtis, Alan, 213

Dafne (Corsi and Peri), 3–4, 47, *55*, *134*, 207, 209
and Classical Antiquity, 37–38, 43, 164, 205
Corsi's music for, 3, 46, 172
costs for, *21*, 50
experimental, 64, 148
first version, *4*, 130–31, 148
music by Caccini(?), 45–46, 61
performed 21 Jan. 1598/99, 4, 19, 37, 39, *40*, 50, 51, 83, 131, 148
performed 26 Oct. 1604, 2, 50, 201
poetic structures, 134–35, 172–73
possible performance in spring 1600, 40, 50
printed librettos, *18*, 38, *201*
reference in *Euridice*, 38, 39
simple scenery, 54, 79
Dafne (Marco da Gagliano, 1608), *139*, 177
performed 9 Feb. 1610/11, *46*, 203, 206
preface to, 177, 179–83
Dal Pozzo, Carlo Antonio (Archbishop of Pisa), 11
Dante Alighieri, 64, 116, 138, *166–67*, *172*
Danti, Ignazio, 68–70, 71, *81*
Della Rovere, Vittoria (grand duchess), 205
Dialogo di Giunone e Minerva (1600), 14, 16, *28*, 41, 192–93
Doni, Anton Francesco, *69–70*
Doni, Giovanni Battista, 205
Drottningholm, 67, *125*

Eleonora of Toledo, 1
Empoli, 6, 27
epithalamia, 189–92, 193, 194
Este, Cesare d' (Duke of Modena), 1, *13*, 17, 52
Estrées, Gabrielle d', 10, 194
Euridice (1600)
addressing the audience, 132, 133, 135, 154, 159, 163, 171, 188
allegorical readings, 187–88, 190, 194–97
altering the myth, 64, 133, 135, 194–96
attributed to Cavalieri, *14–15*, 20, 58
Caccini's music in, 44–45, 137, 139–40, 147, 150, *163*, 181
Caccini's score lacks revisions, 145, 150–51, 166
chorus: final one odd, 134, 193, 194

chorus: stable versus mobile, 153–55, 158-61, 163, 179, 186
choruses: end of episodes, 44–45, 131, 137, 144–45, 147, 152–53, *154*, 155, 162–63, 170–71, *177*, 186
Classical models, 2–3, 43, 97, 131, *132*, 135–36, 153, *154*, 160, 161, 164–65, *171*, 187–88, 197, 205
Classical unities, 64, 135, 194
compared with Monteverdi's *Orfeo*, 130, 133, 138, 145, 158, *161*, 163, *167*, 186, 196–97, 215
Corsi's role in, 2, 19, 20, 34, 37, 46, 50, 59, 139, 140, 143
cost of, *14*, 20–21, 33–34, *35*, 36
dancing after, 60, 128, 203
dancing in, 134, 149, 161, 186
diegetic song, 131, 133, 134, 155, 158, 170–74, 177–78
five episodes, 131, 136, 152
funding shared, 20–21
messengers in, *132*, 135, 149, 151, 158, 174, 181, 196
modern performances, *60*, 211–16
musical references in, 131–34, 164–66
Orfeo's lyre, 131, 132, 133, 134, 169, 170, 177–78
performed in Bologna (1616), 207, 214
Peri's and Caccini's settings compared, 45, 144, *155*, 159, 160, 162–63, 166, 170, 173, 174
poetic meters, 134–35, 167, 169, 170–71, 173, 174
plot, 131–35
preview in spring 1600(?), 40, 50, 56
printed libretto, *4*, *18*, 38–39, 54–56, 141, 146–47, 149, 150, 155, *190*
reception (critical), 14–15, 61, 81, 111, 174
reception (favorable), 60–61, 81, 174, 203
recitative, 164–66, 170, 171, 173, 174, 181
revisions during rehearsals, 54, 150–51, 166–70, 173–74
triflauto, *139*, *145*, *155*, 158, 170, 176
Euridice (production)
chorus (handling of), 136–38, 144–45, 153–55, 158–63, 179–80, 183, 185–86, 187, 216
costume changes, 136, 137, 144, *160*, *161*
costumes, 19, 20, *27*, 34, 176–78, 215
entrances and exits, 102, 111, *112*, *131*, 135, 136-38, *144*, 155, 157–63, 169, 171, 179, 186, 187, 216
gesture, 158, 179–86, 215
instruments, 59, 102–4, 125, 139, 176, 177–78, *180*, 186–87, 215
moved to the Sala delle Commedie, 53–54, 56, 80, 83–85, 87, 116, 122
singers, 34, 54–56, 137, 139–40, 141–45, 150–51, *160*, 162–63, 168, 174
stage directions, 64, *131*, 148, 155–58, 161–62, 164, 187
Euridice (stage)
artisans present at performance, 32, 36, 123
audience seating, 59–60, 80, 83, 111, 126–28
backdrops, *53*, 87, 98, 106, 107, 110, 117, 119–21, 124–25
coat of arms, 30, 89, 91–92, 94, 96, 97, 126
curtain, 62, 87, 97, 103, *155*
dimensions (Sala delle Commedie), 58, 79, 84–85, 91, 94, 98, 102, 107, 126, *205*
dimensions (Sala delle Statue), 52, 79, 82–83, 91, 93, 98, 102, 107, *110*, 126–28
flats, *33*, 79, 85, 87, 99, 102, 110–11, 112, 116–19, 122, 124–25, *161*
floor (platform), 31, 32, 85, 86, 87, 91, 93–96, 98–104, 107, 112, 121
framing, 86–88, 91, 105, 106
lighting, 32, 54, 106, 108, 121, 123–26, 216
materials go to the Teatro degli Uffizi, 29–30, 85–86, *88*, 198, 200
parapet, 91, 93–96, 97, 101, 102–3, 117, 124, 126
pastoral set, 62, 64, 79, 85, 90, 95, 107–13, 117, 123, 200, 201
proscenium, 62, 83, 85, 87, 88–97, 102, 106, 126, 128, 187, 193, 197, 209
rake, 101, 107, 111–12
references in the libretto, 108, 113, 135, 154, 167
scenery in bad condition, 30, *92*, 102, 117, 122, 198, 200
scenery reused, 198–99, 200, 201
scenery "unfinished," 14, 81
"sky," 32–33, 36, *53*, 85, 87, 104–6, 107, 111, 124
space behind, 58, 83, 98, 101, 102, 117–21, *119*, 125
trestles, 30, 86, 87, 98–101, 112, 119
Underworld set, 62, 64, 79, 85, 109, 111, 113–23, 124–25, *161*, 162, 187, 198
winches, 112, 117–21
Eurydice, *131*, 189, 194, 195

Fabbri, Fabio, 142
Farnese, Odoardo (Duke of Parma and Piacenza), *76*, 78, *100*, 178, 204

Farnese, Pier Luigi (Duke of Parma and Piacenza), *69*
Farnese, Ranuccio I (Duke of Parma and Piacenza), 201
Ferrara, *41*, *42*, 76
  theatres, *76*, 78, 88, *97*, 113
Ferrucci, Andrea, 93
festa in the Riccardi gardens (1600), 9, 16, 18, *19*, 54, *60*, 188, 192–93,
Fetti, Domenico, 184–85
Firenze e la nascita dell'Opera (exhibition, 2019), 208–10
Florence
  Casino di S. Marco (Don Antonio de' Medici), 17, *19*, 58, *200*, 203
  Duomo (Opera del), 9, 16, 17, 86
  Fortezza da Basso, *13*, 24–25, 31, 33, 53, 86, *87*, 200
  Fortezza del Belvedere, 5, 25
  Loggia de' Tornaquinci, 91
  Palazzo Corsi, *91*
  Palazzo del Parione (Don Giovanni de' Medici), 17, 203
  Palazzo Riccardi (Via Gualfonda), 9, 16, 192
  Palazzo Strozzi, *91*
  Palazzo Vecchio (Salone dei Cinquecento), 6, 16, 17, 31, 36, *61*, 69, 86, 205
  Piazza della Signoria, 17
  Piazza S. Croce, *128*
  S. Gaggio, 91
  S. Giovanni Battista, 17
  S. Lorenzo (Cappella dei Principi), 5, 14, *53*
  SS. Annunziata, 11, 143
  S. Spirito, *141*
  S. Trinita, 11
  Teatro del Cocomero, *61*
  Teatro della Dogana, 18
  Teatro della Pergola, *61*, 205, *213*
  Uffizi (Galleria), 6, 17, 27, 51, *53*; *see also* Teatro degli Uffizi
  See also Palazzo Pitti
Floriani, Pietro Paolo, 76, *101*
  set designs, 76, 78–79, 113
  stage machinery, *112*, 117, *118*
Fontanelli, Alfonso, 203
Franceschi, Lorenzo, *16*
Frazzi, Vito, 213
Furttenbach, Joseph (the Elder), 48, 51, 52, 58, 84, 103, *124*
  Architectura civilis (1628), 47, 49, 82–83
  Architectura recreationis (1640), 75, *78*
  Mannhaffter Kunst-Spiegel (1663), *75*, *78*, *123*
  manuscript notebook, 75, *118*
Gagliano, Marco da, *4*
  Dafne (1608), *46*, *139*, 177, 203
  Flora (1628), 178, 204, 206
  Lo sposalizio di Medoro ed Angelica (1619), 206
  on staging, 158, 177, 179–83, 184
Gagnolanti, Margherita, 142
Galilei, Vincenzo, 2, 184
Gallaccini, Teofilo, 72, *89*
Galluzzi, Riguccio, *10*
Gatti, Oliviero, 88
Ghorini, Francesco, *86*
Giacomini, Lorenzo, 2, *135*, 197
Giambologna, 213
Giannetti, Ginevra di Piero ("L'Azzurrina"), 45, 140–41, 143, 144
Giannetti, Piero di Francesco, *140*
Ginevra di Piero *mazziere*. *See* Giannetti, Ginevra di Piero
giornate, 117
Giovannini, Baccio, 10, 12
Giugni, Vincenzo, 23
Giunti, Cosimo, *4*, *18*, 38, 146, 150, *190*
Giunti, Filippo, 18–19
Giusti, Jacopo, 139, 141, 151
Gondi, Girolamo, 9, 10, 11
Gondi, Piero (cardinal), 9
Gonzaga, Ferdinando (cardinal, later Duke of Mantua), *97*, 207
Gonzaga, Vincenzo (Duke of Mantua), 9, 54, *130*, *140*, 143, *202*
Grillo, Angelo (Livio Celiano), 42–47, 137, 152
Gualterotti, Raffaello, *43*
Guarini, Battista (Giovanni Battista), *13*, 41
  Il pastor fido, 3
  See also Dialogo di Giunone e Minerva
Guidiccioni Lucchesini, Laura, 3
  See also Il giuoco della cieca; Il satiro; La disperazione di Fileno
Guidotti, Alessandro, 39
Guitti, Francesco, 76, *97*, *100*

Handel, George Frideric, 212
Haydn, Joseph, 208
Henri II (King of France), 6, 11
Henri IV (King of France), 1, 11, 41
  and Ottoman empire, 193
  delays wedding, 11–13
  demands for dowry, 10
  "messages" to, 134, 193, 194
  not present in Florence, 6
  political circumstances, 2, 9–10, 12
Henri II of Lorraine, *6*

Historically Informed Performance, 210–11, 213, 215
Homer, 189, 191

Il corago, 70, 73–74, 75
author of, *70*
changing sets, 72, 74, 79, 117, 122
instrumentalists, 103–4, 187
lighting, *123*, 124–25
movement and gesture, 183–84, 185–86
pastoral sets, *108*
raked stage, 101
stagehands, *119*
stage measurements, 107
Il giuoco della cieca (1595), 3, 37
staged in Jan. 1598/99, 4, *37*, *40*, 51
Il rapimento di Cefalo (1600), 1, 24, 46, *140*, *206*
allegory, 188, 189, 194
and Caccini's reinstatement, 5–6
and Don Giovanni de' Medici, 14
Buonarroti on, 2–3, 17, 61, 165, 194
cast, 51, 55, 143, 144
composers, 17
confused with *intermedi*, 1, 14
cost, 21, 33–34
costumes, *34*
criticisms of, 14–15, 61, *81*, 174
draws on Ronsard, 193
open rehearsal, 16, *60*
order to prepare, 14, 25, 51
plot, 193–94
printed libretto, *18*, *38*, 146
recitative, 165, 174
replaces a comedy with *intermedi*, 13–14, 50
sketches for, *13*
staging, *13*, 81, *86*
surviving music, *144*
Il satiro (1590 or 1591), 3
Indy, Vincent d', 213
Ingegneri, Angelo, 71
choruses, 152–53, 155, 186
lighting, 124
pastoral sets, 108
Underworld scenes, 121, 124, 162
intermedi, 1, 17, *19*, 51, *76*, 79, 201, *204*, 206
for 1589 wedding, 1, *13*, 14, 17, 77, *119*, *124*, 178, 202, 212
for 1608 wedding, 15, 75, *112*, 202
planned for 1600 wedding, 13, 50

Jacomelli, Giovanni Battista ("dal Violino"), 139, 178
Johanna of Austria (grand duchess), 1, 9, 176
Johnson, Eugene J., 64
Jones, Inigo, *88*, *113*

La disperazione di Fileno (1590 or 1591), 3, 178
Lanci, Baldassare, *69*
La pellegrina (1589), 1, 17, *39*, 202
costumes, 178
production notes on, 14, 77
sets, 77
See also intermedi
Lapi, Giovanni, 139
Latini, Cosimo, *52*
Leni, Giovanni Battista (cardinal), 207
L'Estoile, Pierre de, *19*
Licino, Sillano, 207
Ligozzi, Jacopo, 28, *91*
Livorno, 5, *11*, 16
Lottini, Giovanni Agnolo, *38*
Louis XIII (King of France), 207
Lyons, 10, 12, 13

Maestro, Giovanni del, *9*, *11*, *12*, *13*, *19*, 47, *54*, *58*, *60*, *125*, *199*
Maggio Musicale Fiorentino, 211–13
Mantua, *41*, *46*, 71, 130, *141*, *144*, 177, 181, 197, *206*
Marescotti, Giorgio, *18*, 38, 146
Marguerite de Valois (Queen of France), 9–10, 194
Marguerite Louise d'Orléans (grand duchess), 205
Maria Magdalena (Archduchess of Austria), 185
See also wedding of Cosimo de' Medici and Maria Magdalena of Austria (1608)
Marini, Giorgio, *213*
Marino, Giambattista, *42*
Marmi, Giacinto (Iacinto) Maria, 47, 48, *53*, 57, 59, *60*, 84
Marotti, Ferruccio, 65
Marseilles, 10, 12–13, 16
Martinelli, Caterina, 184
Massai, Riccardo, 214
Mattei, Matteo, *36*
Matteo *imbiancatore*, 36, 56
Mattias (Archduke of Austria), 10
Mazzocchi, Domenico, 206
Medici, (Don) Antonio de', 5, 8, 12, 58, *201*
moves to Casino di S. Marco, 17, *200*, 203
See also Palazzo Pitti
Medici, Caterina de' (Queen of France), 6, 9, 10, 11, *28*

Medici, Cosimo I de' (duke, then grand duke), 1, 5, *9*, 10, 17, 51, 69
Medici, Cosimo II de' (grand duke), 1, 8, 185, 203–4
See also wedding of Cosimo de' Medici and Maria Magdalena of Austria (1608)
Medici, Cosimo III de' (grand duke), 205
Medici, Eleonora de' (Duchess of Mantua), 8–9, 12, 54, 60, *140*, *199*
Medici, Ferdinando I de' (grand duke), 1, 40–41, 48, *60*, *71*, 200, 201
and 1600 wedding, 2, 6, 9–13, *14*, *18*, 19, 22, 25, 34, 52, 141, 143
death, *200*, 203
entertainments addressed to, 134, 197
family relations, 5, 8, *9*, 16, 48, 52
his wedding (1589), 14, 18, *25*, 65, 77, *91*
privy purse, 21
rooms in the Pitti, 11, *53*, 83, 84, *199*
Medici, Ferdinando II de' (grand duke), 205
Medici, Filippo de', 16
Medici, Francesco I de' (grand duke), 1, 5, 9, 176
Medici, Giovan Carlo de', *84*
Medici, (Don) Giovanni de', 2, 5, 6, 8, 12, *72*, *199*
and *Euridice*, 35, 122, *125*, 134
and Jacopo Corsi, 3, *4*, 5, 19
and Ottavio Rinuccini, 5, *134*
Cappella dei Principi (S. Lorenzo), 5, 14, *53*
military exploits, 5, 10, 134
Palazzo del Parione, 17
performance of *Dafne* (1611), *46*, 203, 206
role in the 1600 festivities, 4, 5, 14, 23, *61*
Medici, Isabella de' (Duchess of Bracciano), 8
Medici, Lorenzo de' ("Il Magnifico"), 192
Medici, Lorenzo de' (son of Ferdinando I), 16
Medici, Margherita de' (Duchess of Parma and Piacenza), *76*, 78, *100*, 178, 204
Medici, Maria de' (Queen of France), 1, 6–9, 52
and *Dafne*, 45, 61
and Don Antonio de' Medici, 58
and Flavia Peretti-Orsini, 48
coat of arms, 91
date of birth, 9
dedicatee, *4*, 15, 18, 38, 39, 45, 64, 135, 146
in France, 13, 45, 141
messages in 1600 entertainments, 188, 192–94, 196–97
recognized as queen, 12
religious advisers, 8, *42*
rooms in the Pitti, 48, 54, 58, *199*
wedding planning, 40–41, 49
See also wedding of Maria de' Medici and Henri IV (1600)
Medici, Maria Maddalena, 12, *16*, 49
Medici, (Don) Pietro de', *9*
Medici, Raffaello de', *12*
Medici, Vincenzo, *12*, 23, *36*, *201*
Medici, Virginia de' (Duchess of Modena), 1, *9*, *13*, 17, 52
Medici administration
Camera dell'arme granducale, *23*
Depositeria Generale, *12*, 23, *25*, *33*, *36*, *201*
Fabbrica de' Pitti, *39*, 86, 87, 99
financing, 21, 33
Galleria dei Lavori, 20
Guardaroba, *7*, *13*, *21*, 23, 24, 30, 36, 84, 86–87, 97, 99, *128*, 199
Magistrati degli Otto di Guardia e Balìa, 140
Magistrato de' Nove Conservatori del Dominio e della Giurisdizione Fiorentina, *13*, *77*
Scrittoio delle Fortezze e Fabbriche, *25*
Sopraintendenza delle Fortezze e Fabbriche, 23
Ufficio di Monte e Soprassindaci, *13*, 33, 203
Mei, Girolamo, 2
Menini, Ottavio, *42*
Michelangelo (artist), 83
Michelozzi & Ricci bank, 25
Modena, 60
Mohler, Frank, *69*, *77*
Molino, Niccolò, 60
Mon, Pier, 143
moneys of account. *See* account books
Moniglia, Giovanni Andrea, 205
Monsieur le Grand. *See* Bellegarde, Roger de
Montalto, Alessandro Damasceni Peretti di (cardinal), 4, 10, 46, 89, *126*, 143, 148, *178*, 200
Montalvo, (Don) Garzía (Grazìa), *11*, 139
Montanari, Geminiano, *123*
Monte, Francesco Maria del (cardinal), 4, 10, 46, *126*, 148, 200
Monte, Orazio del, *207*
Monterosso, Raffaello, *213*
Monteverdi, Claudio, 130, 213
Arianna (1608), *144*, 184–85, *206*
Orfeo (1607), 133, 138, 144, 145, *148*, 158, *161*, 163, *164*, *167*, 186, 196, 215
Mutii, Nicolò, 39

Neroni, Bartolomeo ("Il Riccio"), 88
Nevers, Duke of, 203

Nigetti, Matteo, 53
Nobili, Giulio de', *12*

opera, 1, *15*, 130, 148
  "invention" of, 2–4, 38–39, 46, 59, 64, 130, 164, 174
  modern-day stagings, 210–11, 213, 214
  problems of verisimilitude, 154, 164, 173, 187
  supplanted by other entertainments, 203–7
Orefice, Giacomo, 213
Orpheus, 20, 64, *131*, 133, 134, 135–36, 164, 187, 194–95, 196, 206, 207
  representations of, 115–16, 176–77, 189
Orsini, Flavia. *See* Peretti-Orsini, Flavia
Orsini, Paolo Giordano (Duke of Bracciano), 8–9
Orsini, Virginio (Duke of Bracciano), 8, 11, 12, 27, 60
  rooms in the Pitti, 48
  political position, 8–9
Ovid, 193, 195, 196

Padua, 141
Paganucci, Simone, 25
Pagnini, Jacopo, *19*
Paladini, Arcangela, 185
Palantrotti, Melchiorre
  in *Euridice*, 54, 139, 141, 143–44
  in *Il rapimento di Cefalo*, 55, 143–44
Palazzo Pitti, 11, 30, 80, 187, 210, 213
  artisans working in, 24, 36, 39, 53, *56*
  Boboli Gardens, *47*, 49, 205, 211–12
  chairs, 128
  Christine of Lorraine's rooms, 30, 87
  decorations for, 27, *28*, 36, 113
  Don Antonio de' Medici's rooms, *56*, 57–58, *199*, *200*
  Don Giovanni de' Medici's rooms, *199*
  Emilio de' Cavalieri's rooms, *48*, 57, 84, 125
  entertainments in, 17, 18, 20, 54, 79, 201, 203, 205
  Ferdinando I's rooms, 11, 83, 84, *199*
  Flavia Peretti-Orsini's rooms, 39, 40, 48, 51, *83*, 84
  guest accommodations, 53–54, 56, 113, 199
  inventories of, *48*, *85*, 128, 201
  layout, 47–48, 57–59, 84
  Loggetta dell'Allori, 113
  Maria de' Medici's rooms, 48, *199*
  multi-use spaces, 40, 48, 58, 80
  new theatre planned, 205
  Sala dei Forestieri (Sala Bianca), 49, 56, 58, 60, 128, 204, 205, 206, 210, 214
  Sala di Bona, *94*
  summer/winter quarters, 53
  temporary stages for, 40, 204
  See also Sala delle Statue; Sala delle Commedie
Panciatichi, Vincenzo
  L'amicizia costante, 18–19, *38*, *178*
Parigi, Alfonso, 178
Parigi, Giulio, 75, 102
  new comic set for the Sala delle Commedie, 200–1
  portable stage for the Pitti, 204
Paris, 9, 11, *42*, 45, 61, 141
Parma, 42, 60, *76*, 79, *100*, *102*
  See also Teatro Farnese
Pedemonte, Pompeo, 70
Peretti, Michele, *88*
Peretti-Orsini, Flavia (Duchess of Bracciano), 8, 12, 48, 60
  and Maria de' Medici, 48
  rooms in the Pitti, 39, 40, 48, 51, *83*, 84
  sister of Cardinal Montalto, 10
Peri, Jacopo
  and Jacopo Corsi, 46, 51
  argues with Rinuccini (1616), 207, 214
  Flora (1628), 178, 204, 206
  Lo sposalizio di Medoro ed Angelica (1619), 206
  not mentioned in 1600 description, 62
  on recitative, 164–66
  publishes *Euridice*, 44–45, *45*, 59, 145, 146, 207
  score known by Monteverdi, 130
  teaches Jacopo Giusti, 139, 151
  See also Dafne (Corsi and Peri); Euridice
periaktoi. *See* theatre design
Petraia (Medici villa), 50, *51*
Petrarch, 154, 164, *167*, 172
Picchena, Curzio, *15*
Piccolomini, Alessandro, *88*
Pieroni, Alessandro, *39*
Pieroni, Camillo, 39–40, 47, 49, *52*, 199–200
Pindar, 191, 192, *193*
Pirrotta, Nino, 65
Pisa, 5, 11, 31, *37*, 97
Pluto, 20, 64, 133, 135, 178, 195
Poccetti, Bernardino, *28*, *94*
Poggio Imperiale (Medici villa), 205, 207
Poli, Nives, 213
Poliziano, Angelo, 192, 194
Portelli, Alessandro, *28*
Povoledo, Elena, 65
Pratolino (Medici villa), *205*, 213
Proserpina (Persephone), *115*, 195

Radošević, Ani, 212
Ranfi, Luca, *28*
Rapp, Rolf, 213
Rasi, Francesco, 54–55, 143–44
  and Jacopo Corsi, 143
  in *Euridice*, 139, 141, 144, 145, 151, 174
Raverii, Alessandro, 207
recitative, 164–65, 170, 174, 181, 183
Regietheater, 211
Riccardi, Riccardo, *16*
Ricoveri, Francesco
  invoice for *Euridice*, 31–33, 36, 85, 198
  present at performance, 32, 36
Rigacci, Bruno, 212
Rinaldi, Ugo, 206
Rinuccini, Alessandro, 2
Rinuccini, Camillo, *128*, *202*
Rinuccini, Giovan Paolo di Niccolò, 141
Rinuccini, Ottavio
  and Angelo Grillo, 42–43, 45, 152
  and Don Giovanni de' Medici, 5, 134
  and Emilio de' Cavalieri, 37–38, 39
  and Ginevra Giannetti, 140
  and the Alterati, 2, *43*
  argues with Peri (1616), 207, 214
  Arianna (1608), *144*, 184, *206*
  balletto for the Pitti (1611), 203
  financial dealings, 11
  gentilhomme du roi, 11
  libretto known by Alessandro Striggio, 130
  Mascherata di ninfe di Senna (1613), 204
  music and language, 165–66, 170–71
  Narciso, 46, *148*, *206*
  ode for Jacopo Corsi, 38, 39
  on *Dafne* and *Euridice*, 38–39, 64, 148
  Poesie (1622), *134*, *146*, 207
  praised by Sillano Licino, 207
  sacred dialogue (1619), 185
  See also Dafne (Corsi and Peri); Euridice
Rinuccini, Pierfrancesco, *70*, 207
Rinuccini, Tommaso, *11*
Ripa, Cesare, *94*
Rivarola, Domenico (cardinal), 207
Rome, *2*, 6, 11, 13, 14, 27, *88*, 143, 206
  Cavalieri and, 20, 37, 39, 61, 81, 174
  Galleria Farnese, 189, *191*
Ronsard, Pierre de, 193
Rosenwald MS, 75
  curtain, *97*, *117*
  lighting, *124*, 125
  placing instrumentalists, 102
  set changes, 78
  stage machinery, *112*, *118*
Rossi, Bastiano de', 77
Rudolph II (emperor), 10

Sabbatini, Nicola, 72–74
  changing sets, 75, *78*, 122–23
  lighting, *124*, *125*
  noise as distraction, 122, 187
  parapet, *94*
  perspective, *81*
  placing instrumentalists, 103
  raked stage, *101*
  stage machinery, *76*, 119
  the "sky," 104–5
  Underworld sets, 121
Sabbioneta, 67
Sala delle Commedie (Palazzo Pitti), 56–59, 83–85
  associated with Don Antonio de' Medici, 57–58
  convenience, 58–59, 84
  dimensions, 58, 84–85, *205*
  location, 57–59, 84
  naming, 58
  new set (1604), 200–1
  palcaccio, 84, 96
  reconfigured, 59, 84, *85*, 210
  space for audience, 126–28
  stage machinery added, 201–2
  subsequent performances in, 122, 198–204
  windows, 58, 126
  See also Euridice (production); Euridice (stage)
Sala delle Statue (Palazzo Pitti), 40, 49, 80–83
  curtain for, 97
  Dafne performed in, 4, 131
  dimensions, 52, 82–83
  Euridice designed for, 52, 85, 110
  function, 51–52, 199, 205
  name, *51*
  original design, 81–82, 94
  other events in, 9, 12, *40*, 54, 199, 204
  repairs, 52
  reviving *Euridice* in, 210
  space for audience, 126–28
  statues, 51, 80, 83, 94
  vault, 81, 83, 91, 105
  See also Euridice (stage)
Saluzzo, 12, *41*
Salvadore di Piero (*lanternaio*), 123–24
Salvadori, Andrea, 205
  Flora (1628), 178, 204, 206
  La liberazione di Tirreno e d'Arnea (1617), 75, *119*, 204, 209

Lo sposalizio di Medoro ed Angelica (1619), 206
Salviati, Antonio, 5
Salviati, Lionardo, *88*
Salviati, Maria, *8*
Sangallo, Bastiano da, *69*
San Miniato al Tedesco, 25
Sannazaro, Jacopo, 172, *176*
Sansovino, Andrea, 83
Santi di Tito, 27
Sanudo, Leonardo, *42*
Saracinelli, Ferdinando
Ballo delle zingare (1615), 204
possible author of *Il corago*, *70*
Sauli, Antonmaria (cardinal), *141*
Seriacopi, Girolamo, 25
1589 *intermedi*, 14, 77
Serlio, Sebastiano, 68, 70, *77*, *81*, *101*, 108, 110, 201
Sesto Fiorentino, 42
Settimanni, Francesco, 61
Siena, 8, 31, 88, *91*
Signori Piacevoli (hunting society), *84*
Sillery, Nicolas Brûlart de, 11, 53, 60
Sirigatti, Lorenzo, 71
Sommi, Leone de', 71
actors, *184*
costumes, 178
lighting, 124, *126*
rustic sets, 108
Sophocles, 64, 67, 136
Sparapani, Flavia, 213
Sparti, Barbara, *213*
Stradano, Giovanni (Jan van der Streit), *116*
Striggio, Alessandro (the younger), 130, 138, *144*, *161*, 163, *164*, *167*, 196
Strozzi, Giovanni Battista *il giovane*, 2, 42, *43*
Strozzi, Piero di Matteo, 2, *5*
festa in the Riccardi gardens, *16*
Il rapimento di Cefalo, 17
Subiaco, 42
Sutherland, Joan, 212

tara, 27–28, 33
Tasso, Torquato, 172
Aminta (1573), 3, 79, 206
Teatro degli Intrepidi (Ferrara), 76, 88, 113
Teatro degli Uffizi, 13, *14*, 31, 65
capacity, 61
construction, 17, 77, 126
disuse, 205
performances in, 17, 75, 202, 204, 206
scenery etc., 77–78, *112*, *123*
statues, 80
Teatro Farnese (Parma), 67, 78
Teatro Gonzaga (Teatro all'Antica, Sabbioneta), 67
Teatro Olimpico (Vicenza), 67
theatre design
boxes, *61*, 66
construction, 64–66
curtain, *66*, *77*, *97*, *117*
flats (sliding), 74, 76, 77, 78–79
L-shaped wings, 74, 75, *78*
machinery, 67, 74, 75–77, 104, *112*, 119, 202
periaktoi, 66, 68, 69–70, 72, 74, 75, 77, 78
perspective, 68, 70, 71–74, 81, 107, 113, 126–28, 162
proscenium, 66, 88–89, 124
typical sets, 66, 68, 76, 79, 89, 107–8, 110
volumetric wings, 70, 72, 77, 78
Theodore (Duke of Braganza), 10
Thiene, Giulio, *16*, *58*, 59, 60
Tinghi, Cesare, 19–20, 58, 60, *126*, *199*, *200*, *204*
Torelli, Giacomo, 78
Tosi, Piero, 212
Trabocchi, Aldobrando, 142–43
Tucci, Nicolò, *42*, *43*

Ughi, Gabriello, *28*

Vaini, Enea, *20*
Valois, Marguerite de. *See* Marguerite de Valois
Vasari, Giorgio, 31, *53*, *69*
veglia, 58, *60*, *126*, 202, 204
Venice, 5, *41*, 60, 207, 212
Venturi del Nibbio, Stefano, 17
Vicenza, 67, *68*
Villifranchi, Giovanni, *204*
Vinta, Belisario, *4*, 11, *13*, 18, *41*
Vinta, Francesco, 18–19
Virgil, *190*, 194–95
Vitali, Filippo, 206
Vitruvius, 68

Wars of Religion (France), 9, 10
wedding of Cosimo de' Medici and Maria Magdalena of Austria (1608), 1, *141*, 199, 201–2
Il giudizio di Paride, 1, 75, *112*, 202–3
L'Argonautica, 177
Notte d'Amore, *58*, *60*, *126*, *128*, 202–3
officials compare expenses with 1600 festivities, 203
reverts to *intermedi*, 15, 202

wedding of Maria de' Medici and Henri IV (1600), 16–17
  and epithalamia, 192–95
  announcement of, 11–12, 37, 51
  appointment of deputies, 12, 22–23, 141
  banquet, 9, 14, 16, 21, 28, 31, 33–35, 86, *91*, 106, 192, 209
  Chimenti's painting, 6–9, 15, *28*
  delayed, 12–13, 41, 47
  dowry, 10, 11, 12
  giving of the ring, 6
  L'amicizia costante, 18–19
  negotiations for, 9–11, *12*
  planned comedy with *intermedi*, 13, 50
  See also Dialogo di Giunone e Minerva; Euridice; festa in the Riccardi Gardens; Il rapimento di Cefalo

Zeffirelli, Franco, 211–13, 214
Zucchi, Bartolomeo, *42*

www.ingramcontent.com/pod-product-compliance
Lightning Source LLC
LaVergne TN
LVHW080305260326
834688LV00039B/1143

* 9 7 8 1 0 0 9 0 0 5 7 1 5 *